The High Commissioners

AUSTRALIA'S REPRESENTATIVES
IN THE UNITED KINGDOM, 1910–2010

Edited by Carl Bridge,
Frank Bongiorno and David Lee

Department of Foreign Affairs and Trade

This book celebrates the centenary of the posting of the first Australian high commissioner in London. The contributions of its independent authors reflect their own views and are not the official views of the Australian Government or its employees.

National Library of Australia Cataloguing-in-Publication entry

The high commissioners: Australia's representatives in the United Kingdom, 1910–2010 / edited by Carl Bridge, Frank Bongiorno and David Lee.

ISBN: 978-1-921612-11-4 (pbk.)
978-1-921612-10-7 (hbk.)

Includes index.
Bibliography.

Diplomatic and consular service – Australia – History.
Australia – Foreign relations – Great Britain.
Great Britain – Foreign relations – Australia.
International relations.

Other authors/Contributors: Bridge, Carl, 1950–
Bongiorno, Frank, 1969–
Lee, David, 1965–
Australia. Dept. of Foreign Affairs and Trade.

327.41094

Cover design by Kylie Smith
Production, editing and artwork by WHH Publishing
Printed by Blue Star

Contents

Anzac Day march passing Australia House, the first occasion on which troops were permitted to pass through London streets with fixed bayonets, 25 April 1919. [Australian War Memorial Negative Number P00212.001]

Minister's foreword

In this centennial year of the appointment of Sir George Reid as Australia's first High Commissioner in London, I am pleased to welcome the commemorative publication compiled by the Australian Department of Foreign Affairs and Trade and the Menzies Centre for Australian Studies, King's College London, *The High Commissioners: Australia's Representatives in the United Kingdom, 1910–2010.*

In 1909 the Australian Parliament passed *An Act to provide for the Office of High Commissioner of the Commonwealth in the United Kingdom.*

The legislation, described by then Minister for External Affairs Littleton Groom as 'but the logical sequence of the bringing into being of the Federal constitution', empowered the Governor-General to appoint a High Commissioner for a term of not more than five years.

At the time, Australia was a self-governing but not yet sovereign state. It had no foreign office in the modern sense, its people were British subjects, and the United Kingdom was still making foreign policy and signing treaties for the British Empire as a whole.

Moreover, until 1926, the Australian Governor-General remained the main channel of communication between the Australian and British governments.

Yet in creating this new office Australia had established its first overseas post to represent Australia, socially, commercially and, in time, politically, in the United Kingdom. This book traces the history of the office and in doing so illuminates the larger history of Australian – United Kingdom relations in the twentieth century, the evolution of Australia from British colony to sovereign state and the gradual transition of the United Kingdom from head of an empire to member of the European Union.

As well as dealing with this important historical theme, the book is a powerful study of individuals. The holders of the office of High Commissioner in the period up to the end of World War II were remarkable men. Sir George Reid was a Federation father and former Premier of New South Wales and Commonwealth Prime Minister; Andrew Fisher, Joseph Cook and Stanley Melbourne Bruce were former Prime Ministers drawn from both sides of politics; and Sir Granville Ryrie was a former Army General and Commonwealth Minister.

From the end of World War II until 1980, former senior ministers from both sides of politics occupied the post, but after the appointment of the distinguished diplomat Sir James Plimsoll, the High Commissioners have alternated between Government Ministers and senior officials. From World War I, these High Commissioners have discharged their duties from Australia House, now the longest continuous diplomatic mission on the same site in the United Kingdom.

I hope that this book about Australia's representatives in London over the last century will stimulate further research into Australia's oldest diplomatic post. The relationship between Australia and the United Kingdom continues to be one of tremendous importance and meaning to citizens of both countries and will undoubtedly remain so as we move into the second hundred years of the office.

Stephen Smith
Minister for Foreign Affairs

High Commissioner's foreword

As the current incumbent of the office, it gives me great pleasure to join with the Minister for Foreign Affairs, Stephen Smith, in welcoming the publication of *The High Commissioners: Australia's Representatives in the United Kingdom, 1910–2010*.

It is a privilege for me to have succeeded the eminent men covered in this book as head of Australia's oldest overseas mission and one which, not just on the grounds of longevity, occupies a special place in the history of Australia's diplomatic service.

In the hundred years since 1910 our High Commissioners in the United Kingdom have helped to manage one of Australia's consistently most important relationships.

Australia and the United Kingdom have each experienced profound changes. Australia has undergone a transition from membership of a British world to part of the Asia–Pacific and from colony to independent nation, while the United Kingdom has evolved from being the centre of a global empire to a member of the European Union—while of course continuing to play a global role.

In a century of remarkable change, however, one feature of the relationship between Australia and the United Kingdom has remained constant: the extraordinary warmth of people-to-people relations and the enduring affection which the Australian and British peoples have for each other. This is the strong basis on which the modern relationship is built—a relationship between two of the most like-minded states of the world and one which is driven by a significant identity of contemporary national interest.

I have no doubt that this book will contribute to a better understanding of the work of my predecessors, their achievements and the evolution of Australia's relations with the United Kingdom over the last century.

I warmly commend this book, particularly to citizens of Australia and the United Kingdom, as we embark on the second century of the office of the Australian High Commissioner in the United Kingdom.

John Dauth
High Commissioner for Australia in the United Kingdom

Acknowledgments

The Historical Publications and Information Section of the Department of Foreign Affairs and Trade and the Menzies Centre for Australian Studies, King's College London collaborated to produce this publication as part of the commemoration of the centenary in 2010 of the posting of the first Australian high commissioner to the United Kingdom. Symposiums on the history of the high commissioners were held in London in September 2008 and in Canberra in April 2009 to assist authors commissioned by the Menzies Centre to prepare chapters for a book spanning the first century of Australian high commissioners in London.

For permission to publish the illustrations in this volume the editors wish to thank the Australian High Commission in London, the Australian War Memorial, the National Archives of Australia, the National Library of Australia, the State Library of South Australia and the State Library of Victoria; and the Hon. Richard Alston, the Hon. Neal Blewett, Lady Bunting, Mr Philip Flood, the Hon. Sir Victor Garland, the Hon. Douglas McClelland, Mr Alfred Parsons and Mr Richard Smith.

The editors wish to give special thanks to Mr John Dauth, the incumbent high commissioner for Australia to the United Kingdom, for his strong support of the project and to Vivien Allimonos and Jason Jones on his staff. We also extend our gratitude to Kathy Stapleton and Jenny Ensbey of the library of the Department of Foreign Affairs and Trade.

Special thanks are also due to Mr Michael L'Estrange, former secretary of the Department of Foreign Affairs and Trade and high commissioner in London, and the seven former high commissioners mentioned above for their help. Without their readiness to be interviewed, and, in some cases, willingness to allow access to personal papers, chapter 13 could not have been written. This book has benefited from the participation of all but one of them at the symposium in Canberra in April 2009.

At the Department of Foreign Affairs and Trade, Jeremy Hearder's guidance and astute judgment on many points have been invaluable. Dr Matthew Jordan has been a tower of strength: keeping in touch with authors, editing, and compiling the bibliography. Thanks also are due to Michelle Marginson, Ian Brown, Ian Wille and John Moore for other editorial assistance.

At Wilton Hanford Hanover, Virginia Wilton, Larissa Joseph, Les Brown, Jaana Smith and Michael Harrington have been most responsive to our need to have the book published according to a tight schedule.

Much of the work of Australian diplomats is performed discreetly and is not always celebrated or acknowledged. It is hoped that this book will stimulate further study of their activities.

Carl Bridge, Menzies Centre for Australian Studies, King's College London
Frank Bongiorno, Menzies Centre for Australian Studies, King's College London
David Lee, Historical Publications and Information Section, Department of Foreign Affairs and Trade, Canberra

Introduction

Carl Bridge, Frank Bongiorno and David Lee
with Jeremy Hearder

WHENEVER a new Australian government is elected, or even in prospect, a parlour game for the chattering classes begins. It has two aspects. Who will be appointed ambassador in Washington? And who will go to London?[1] The interest in the former is easy enough to explain, for the United States is the world's only superpower and has been Australia's most important ally for more than fifty years. But why London? The United Kingdom now plays a fairly limited role in Australia's region, and is a second-tier trading partner. And yet, alongside the twenty-two individuals who have served as high commissioners to the United Kingdom, many more have been rumoured to be packing their bags and arranging their itineraries. Australian public interest, however, tends to begin and end with the appointment itself: actual performance in the job attracts much less notice.

This speculation to some extent reflects Britain's continuing role as a major power: London is still a global city, and politics and business of great concern to Australia continue to be conducted there. Australia remains connected to contemporary British life in a variety of ways. For instance, there are more Australians living in Britain than in any other overseas country and the United Kingdom remains one of the heaviest investors in the Australian economy. But there is more to the parlour game than these material realities. Australia was a British settler society, it is an English-speaking country, and it owes many of its political, legal and cultural traditions to the United Kingdom. A powerful sense of this indebtedness has managed to outlast the British Empire itself; and it is manifest in the enduring prestige of the high commissioner's office. It is Australia's most important people-to-people post.[2]

This book marks the centenary of the posting of the first Australian high commissioner to the United Kingdom in January 1910. The occasion provides an opportunity to examine the activities of the high commissioners, who over the course of the next hundred years were responsible for representing the country in London and for managing Australia's oldest overseas relationship. The book also aims to show how the position of high commissioner has evolved in the context of Anglo-Australian relations and wider foreign policy. For Australia, there was a transition from empire to nation, from being part of a British world to part of the Asia–Pacific. For the United Kingdom, there was a fundamental shift from being the centre of a global empire to membership of the European Union.[3] These massive changes inevitably reshaped the nature of the office, but did not detract from its stature as dramatically as might have been expected. The Australian high commissioner to the United Kingdom remains the senior Australian post in Europe, not only because of the continuing importance of the bilateral relationship with Britain, but also because of its status as a diplomatic gateway to Europe and the United States.

High commissioners conduct external or diplomatic relations between Commonwealth countries. They now have a status equivalent to that of ambassador, and the same duties, which in brief are to advise their home governments on the politics of the countries of accreditation, and to interpret and project the policies of their own nations and look after the national interest.[4] But for much of the century they were engaged in 'diplomacy with a difference',[5] being insiders who felt at home in Britain and able to influence British opinion in ways no foreigner could. As Billy Hughes put it in 1909, the high commissioner would be an Australian representative in 'his own country as it were'.[6]

British–Australian relations since 1900

At the time the office was established, Australia was considered a self-governing dominion in the British Empire, taking its place alongside such other 'white' settler societies as Canada, New Zealand and South Africa. Australia's enmeshment within the imperial system was multifaceted, encompassing trade, finance, migration and defence. Indeed, Australia's sovereignty remained limited, with the British monarch as Australia's head of state, the Privy Council as the highest court of appeal, governors and governors-general appointed from Britain, and even the British parliament retaining a theoretical right to overturn Australian legislation. Britain dominated Australia's trade, all loans were raised in London, and virtually all migrants came from the United Kingdom. Australia's nascent navy was being built to operate as a fleet unit within the Royal Navy, which itself was seen as Australia's first line of defence. Australia began to develop a recognisable personality in international affairs from the time of the Treaty of Versailles, but these stirrings of dominion independence were still underwritten by British global power. The Statute of Westminster of 1931 granted the dominions legislative independence, though Australia did not ratify it until 1942.[7] London was Australia's only overseas post until Washington, Tokyo and Ottawa were opened in 1940. Except for Kuibyshev (Soviet Union) in 1943, it remained Australia's only post in Europe until after the war.[8]

World War II had exposed the fragility of the British imperial system when the Royal Navy failed to defend Australia and the United States carried the main burden of the war in the Pacific. Defence links with Britain remained strong until the 1960s: Australia was used as a testing ground for the British atomic bomb in the 1950s and it supported Britain rather than the United States during the Suez crisis of 1956. Gradually, though, the American strategic relationship became paramount. This was reflected in Britain's non-participation in the ANZUS Treaty of 1951 and Australia's and New Zealand's fighting in Vietnam for the first time in a war that did not involve the United Kingdom. The Sterling Area, too, a cooperative arrangement for trade and currency that had emerged in the 1930s depression, broke down in the 1950s. In the 1960s Britain made overtures to join the European Economic Community, succeeding finally on the third attempt in 1973. At the same time, Japan became Australia's main trading partner and trade with the United States outstripped that with Britain.[9] Today China, South Korea and New Zealand are also more significant trading partners. Sources for immigrants diversified, first to continental Europe in the 1950s and 1960s and later to Asia. Most avenues of appeal to the Privy Council were abolished by the Whitlam government and the Australian Constitution was repatriated by the Hawke government in 1986, though the Australian High Court did not define the United Kingdom as a foreign country until 1999.[10] Connections with Britain, though reduced, are still robust. Britain remains a major source of foreign investment, immigrants and tourists. Furthermore, in the current international global strategic situation, where 'coalitions of the willing' are called for, Australians and Britons have served alongside each other in East Timor and Iraq, and are still doing so in Afghanistan.

The high commissioners: a brief prosopography

Of the twenty-two Australian high commissioners to the United Kingdom—so far all men[11]—fifteen had been federal ministers. These included four who had been prime minister, and who were among the first incumbents: George Reid, Andrew Fisher, Joseph Cook and S.M. Bruce. Since Bruce there have been no other former prime ministers, nor have there been any appointments direct from the ranks of state politics.[12] The prime minister normally made the selection, but not quite in the same way as the prime minister today would be closely involved in any major diplomatic appointment. For most of the period between 1910 and 1972, the Australian High Commission in London was directly overseen by the Prime Minister's Department, not External Affairs, and the high commissioner therefore had a direct relationship with the prime minister. This arrangement reflected the particular responsibility of the Australian prime minister for managing relations with the British government, and it presented a high commissioner with both dangers and opportunities.[13] Australian prime ministers determined to bypass their high commissioner could simply deal with their British counterparts while, from the 1920s, they also had the option of communicating directly with Australian external affairs staff embedded in the Foreign Office. On the other hand, a canny high commissioner could himself bring prime ministerial authority to bear and thereby counter an external affairs minister's efforts to dominate, as J.A. Beasley did with H.V. Evatt in the late 1940s. While prime ministers since the early 1970s have continued to engage closely with the British–Australian relationship, the absorption of the high commission into Australia's diplomatic service necessarily curtailed these peculiarities of power and responsibility.

Many Australians of the early twentieth century regarded Britain as 'home', not least because so many of them were migrants. Reid, Fisher and Cook had all been born in the United Kingdom. Granville Ryrie was the first Australian-born high commissioner while Bruce, although also native-born, had spent much of his early life studying and working in the United Kingdom, and then served in the Great War in the British army. The previous occupations of the high commissioners reflect the diversity often found among parliamentarians. There were five lawyers (of whom one was also a merchant and one a farmer), two miners, a publican, an electrician, a company director, a chartered accountant, a court reporter and a university academic. Three came from the Senate (John Armstrong, Douglas McClelland and Richard Alston), and the remainder from the House of Representatives. In recent years appointees included seven who had been federal public servants, of whom five, including the present incumbent, John Dauth, had been career diplomats.

That most of those from 1919 to the 1980s were ex-servicemen was essentially a reflection of the proportion of parliamentarians and (in the case of James Plimsoll) public servants, who had served in the Australian armed forces during the two world wars. However, in Bruce's decision to choose him, Ryrie's standing as an Australian general in World War I was probably as significant as his brief time as a federal minister. Two of the high commissioners were in their late forties when they arrived in London, but the typical appointee was aged between fifty-five and sixty-five years. For fifteen it was the last public office held, while six went on to other government posts.[14]

How long each stayed in the job was affected by various considerations. Beasley died in office and John Bunting retired early owing to ill health. Plimsoll fell victim to curious manoeuvrings in Canberra and had the shortest stay of all. On the other hand, Bruce, at thirteen years, owed his longevity to competence, standing and the exigencies of war. Alexander Downer, at almost eight-and-a-half years, and Eric Harrison, seven-and-a-half years (with an earlier and separate term of a year and two months as resident minister), owed theirs primarily to the long Liberal hegemony in Canberra. Since 1972, when the post came under the aegis of the Department of Foreign Affairs, tenure has nearly always been around the more normal overseas posting of about three years.

Representing Australia in Britain

Australian representation in Great Britain did not begin in 1910. In the early nineteenth century colonial governors sent personal envoys to London to lobby on their behalf, or they drew on the services of officials who had gone 'home' for another reason. Governor Ralph Darling, for instance, sent Colonel Henry Dumaresq, while his successor, Governor Richard Bourke, benefited in the mid-1830s from the services of his own son, Dick, his private secretary in New South Wales who had returned to London to study law. The chief justice of New South Wales, Francis Forbes, a Bourke friend and ally, also lobbied on his behalf in London.[15] In the later era of responsible government, the colonies from time to time appointed agents to act on their behalf in London but, as Olwen Pryke shows in chapter 2, more formal representation emerged, especially as the colonies took over responsibility for the recruitment of migrants.[16] Beginning with South Australia and ending with Western Australia, each made provision for the appointment of its own agent-general. As both Pryke and Neville Meaney (chapter 3) indicate, the agent-general soon took on an expanded role that extended well beyond commercial and immigration matters to Pacific policy and defence. But with federation in 1901 there was recognition that the Commonwealth also needed to be able to speak with a single voice in London.

For domestic political reasons, and also because Australia had functional representation in London already in the form of the agents-general and, later, an official representative in R.H.M. Collins, it was almost a decade before legislation was passed to create the office of Australian high commissioner in the United Kingdom. In chapter 1, Kent Fedorowich explains how the office took its place within a broader network of high commissioners whose development reflected changes in the relationship of dominions to mother country in the first half of the twentieth century. The evolution of the office reflected both changing British policy and the emerging national aspirations of dominions such as Australia. Yet Meaney, and Bernard Attard in his chapters (4 and 5), suggest that the early Australian high commissioners, Reid, Fisher, Cook and Ryrie, were unable to exploit the full possibilities of the role. The most significant reason for this unfulfilled potential was the constraint imposed by the prime minister of the day—especially the domineering W.M. Hughes (1915–23)—but none of these early high commissioners seemed to possess the personal interest or qualities needed to make his mark on government policy, despite three of them being former prime ministers. Reid and, for some of his term, Fisher were not helped by the unsatisfactory nature of their premises. Until Australia House on the Strand became fit for official use in 1917 (it was formally opened in 1918), the Commonwealth Offices, as they were called, were to be found among what seemed to visiting Australian journalist C.E.W. Bean to be no more than 'an endless terrace of large, comfortable-looking residences' in Victoria Street, Westminster. These upper-storey, cramped and unsuitable premises were located alongside the offices of various other British colonies, including those of most of the Australian state agents-general. They did nothing for either the prestige of the office or the task of projecting Australia in London.[17]

Stanley Melbourne Bruce was not Australia's greatest prime minister, but no other high commissioner in London achieved as much as he did for Australia and indeed for wider humanity. It was partly a matter of his long tenure, partly that he was still relatively young and energetic when he became high commissioner, and partly his ease in settling into the job as a result of his earlier years in Britain as a private citizen and later as a minister and prime minister. His single-handed renegotiation of British loans during the depression reflected the great confidence in him of key figures in both Canberra and London, as Attard shows in chapter 5. What lay behind his impressive work at the League of Nations was his interest in Europe and his ability to speak French. His experience in World War I made him a strong believer in the importance of viable international organisations and effective cooperation, the major theme of David Lee's contribution (chapter 6). The main shortcoming in his performance was his poor relationship during World War II with Churchill. The latter was not the easiest of people, and probably was more difficult than ever during the war. But, as Carl Bridge argues in chapter 7, Bruce's errors of judgment in the way he handled Churchill made matters worse, although it is doubtful whether any of them changed history.

While Bruce managed to survive the advent of the Curtin government in 1941, with the end of the war Labor again placed one of its own in Australia House. Although he had attended international conferences as long before as 1926, Beasley lacked Bruce's diplomatic experience, previous exposure to life in Britain, and extensive network of contacts. Yet, as Frank Bongiorno shows in chapter 8, while lacking in this respect he possessed considerable political nous and sufficient seniority as a former cabinet minister to mediate, with some success, the difficult relations that developed between Australia's external affairs minister, H.V. Evatt, and British ministers and officials. Nevertheless, the sometimes stark differences between the views expressed by Beasley in London, and Evatt's vision of the postwar order, might also have compounded the bewilderment of British ministers.

The election of a conservative government late in 1949 brought a new political appointee, Eric Harrison, who was resident minister for about a year, followed by Thomas White as high commissioner from 1951 until 1956. Harrison then returned as high commissioner until 1964. David Lowe, in chapter 9, shows that Harrison benefited from his close relationship with Menzies, whereas White was hamstrung partly by the low regard in which he was held by his prime minister. Harrison's diplomacy, especially in his early period as resident minister, was also enabled by the sense of urgency provided by the cold war. Yet the efforts of both men were arguably undermined by the growing significance of Australia's relationship with the United States, and the activities of Australia's ambassador to the United States, Percy Spender, in both Washington and at the United Nations in New York.

It was Harrison who, as high commissioner, first faced the crisis in the Anglo-Australian relationship posed by Britain's attempt in the early 1960s to join the European Economic Community. By the time Downer arrived as his successor in 1964, the relationship was being rapidly transformed as the old ties of kinship were loosened. As Stuart Ward shows in chapter 10, Downer himself did not so much have difficulty adjusting to this new reality—he actively resisted it. But the transfer of the high commission from the Department of the Prime Minister and Cabinet to the Department of Foreign Affairs at the end of his tenure was indicative of a new determination among leading Australian officials and politicians to absorb the Anglo-Australian relationship into the mainstream of Australian diplomatic activity rather than set it apart as a special case. Gough Whitlam's instructions to Downer's successor, John Armstrong, that Australia House should be run as an 'embassy and not as a tourist bureau' epitomised this new approach.[18] James Curran demonstrates in chapter 11 that Armstrong himself, although as much a product of British race patriotism as every previous high commissioner going back to Reid, was the official London mouthpiece of the 'new nationalism'. Indeed, even his easy-going style seemed to signal a new way of thinking about how to project Australian identity in a post-imperial Britain.

Whereas every high commissioner up to this point had been at least a government minister if not prime minister, the greater variety in the professional backgrounds of high commissioners from the mid-1970s reflects the 'normalisation' of the post. John Bunting was a senior public servant—and the first non-politician to serve as high commissioner— Gordon Freeth a former minister, and James Plimsoll the first professional diplomat to be appointed to the post. These high commissioners were followed mainly by a mixture of diplomats and former senior ministers. The current high commissioner, John Dauth, appointed in 2008, is a career diplomat who joined the Department of External Affairs in 1969. He is a former high commissioner to Malaysia (1993–96), ambassador to the United Nations (2001–06), high commissioner to New Zealand (2006–08), and deputy secretary of the Department of Foreign Affairs and Trade (1998–2001). Although he had not previously served at Australia House, Dauth's career had already taken him to London—among his earlier appointments was a secondment to Buckingham Palace (1977–80), where he was assistant press secretary to the Queen and press secretary to the Prince of Wales.

No former prime minister has accepted the appointment since Bruce, which in itself indicates that London has become one of a handful of major Australian overseas posts rather than the only game in town. All the same, both John Nethercote (chapter 12) and Jeremy Hearder (chapter 13) show that the post has remained an important and busy one since the mid-1970s, and that Australia's high commissioner to the United Kingdom has continued to be involved in a wide and significant range of activities that reflect both the legacies of a traditional kinship and the new challenges of the modern relationship. While there was talk in Australian official circles in the late 1960s and 1970s of the United Kingdom being treated as just one among many 'foreign' countries of importance to Australia—and of 'high commissioner', if the term had to be retained at all, being regarded as a virtual synonym for 'ambassador'—something intangible has remained to complicate this expected transition. As David Malouf has suggested, the formal end of empire did not eradicate the subtle influence of a shared language, culture, history and tradition.[19]

The high commission and Australia House

This book is a study of the high commissioners, with a particular focus on their diplomatic activities. Authors have depended heavily on documents available in both Britain and Australia under the thirty-year rule. Chapter 13, covering the most recent period, from 1981 to early 2008, was the only one that could not be written with access to official documents; it owes much to the cooperation of eight former high commissioners.

The book concentrates on the period for which the archival record can be readily consulted, for much of which the Anglo-Australian connection was at the centre of Australia's relationship with the world. But these studies also trace the development of a new and valuable bilateral relationship in the era after empire.

This is not a history of Australia House, although a final chapter by Simon Sleight provides a taste of what such a study might look like. Moving away from the world of high diplomacy, Sleight provides an account of the ways in which Australia House was understood, contested and used as Australian space in London, and readers interested in this subject are also directed to Olwen Pryke's doctoral thesis, which focuses on the history of the building up to 1939.[20] Several other chapters also provide valuable details about the building, and high commission staff. Pryke has shown in her thesis that as a place of employment, its significance has fluctuated drastically across a century. By the end of 1921, once the peculiar wartime conditions had ended, there were 295 employees. Numbers climbed to 341 by 1928, but then fell back markedly during the depression, to 156 by 1933. There was then some recovery to 219 by 1935. But at its peak in 1971, there were about 1,145 staff, a veritable mini–federal public service, with most Canberra agencies represented. Apart from tending to their routine work, representatives of agencies and departments were there to respond to direction or requests from the high commissioner. They might be asked for assistance with high-level representations, or for help with important Australian visitors. There was a particularly large immigration contingent, which, along with trade representation, for a while spread to include offices in Manchester and Edinburgh. During that period the deputy high commissioner was usually a former head of a major Commonwealth department, and he handled most of the high-level management and administration of Australia House. With such numbers, the high commissioner must have seemed a remote figure to all but a few. The 'glory days' were soon over, and by 1976 the numbers had already dropped to 670.[21] Today, they have been reduced to about 200, of whom only a fifth are Australia-based.

Conclusion

The office of Australian high commissioner to the United Kingdom was founded as part of a highly unusual experiment in international organisation undertaken in the wake of eighteenth- and nineteenth-century rebellion in North America. In the twentieth century, the British Empire and then Commonwealth developed as an association of self-governing states who agreed to cooperate for certain—if never entirely agreed—purposes, and who from the mid-1920s stood in a relationship of formal equality to one another. They did not regard one another as foreign but as part of a 'Greater Britain'. These political arrangements were given meaning by complex webs of influence, interaction and identity that helped to define Britishness as a transnational phenomenon. For this reason, although between the 1910s and the 1960s the Australian high commissioner had the task of representing one state to another, he did so as a kinsman rather than a stranger. Some high commissioners were naturally more skilful than others in exploiting the full possibilities of this situation, but on the whole the experiment was a successful one. Certainly Australia, as a self-governing dominion with a high commissioner, was able to exercise much more influence with the British government than would have been the case for a truly foreign country of comparable size and power represented by an ambassador.

After the early 1960s, the end of empire rapidly brought the curtain down on these arrangements and assumptions, and there was a more significant convergence between the roles of high commissioner and ambassador than had occurred previously. Fewer Australians thought of Britain as their own country, or of British people as their kin. Yet subtle influences remain. Today, an Australian high commissioner in London might, on any working day, be dealing with investment, or defence, or climate change, or possibly hosting the latest Australian author shortlisted for the Booker Prize. But he might also find himself negotiating the repatriation of yet another set of Aboriginal remains, spotted in the catalogue of a local auction house. It is perhaps the fate of both an old empire and a former dominion, as they seek to make a 'new' future as separate but friendly countries in a globalising world, also to find themselves bending back, forever having to come to terms with a shared colonial past.

1 When is a diplomat not a diplomat? The office of high commissioner

Kent Fedorowich

A S WAR loomed in Europe during the summer of 1939, the British high commissioner in Canada, Sir Gerald Campbell (1938–41), complained to his superiors in London that he was 'getting a little bit tired of finding that Canadians outside Ottawa had no idea what a High Commissioner was or what he did; that some ranked me with the Governor-General and others with Trade Commissioners and that, when I explained, they did not seem to be very much interested'.[1] His snobbish predecessor, Sir Francis Floud, had made the same observation in 1937, adding that there had been an 'almost complete failure' on the part of British visitors to Canada to realise the existence of his office.[2] Campbell's counterpart in Canberra, Sir Geoffrey Whiskard (1936–41), the first British high commissioner appointed to Australia, provided an equally frank assessment of his duties and experiences. Whiskard admitted that most of his energies before September 1939 had been spent as a hyped-up salesman promoting British trade and migration. He claimed that, even with the outbreak of war in Europe and the worsening situation in the Far East, the demands on his time and the tasks involved had not much changed.

In April 1941, when his successor was being discussed, Whiskard was brutally frank about the kind of official needed. The volume of work did not necessitate a man of cabinet rank as there was very little for the high commissioner to do in Australia. A 'senior UK civil servant carries terrific guns here', argued Whiskard. As a result, someone from the Board of Trade or the middling ranks of the British Home Departments would be 'heavy enough' to cope with the workload, which Whiskard confessed was lucky to keep one employed for half a day each week.[3] London, however, ignored Whiskard's advice. The deepening crisis in the Far East prompted British Prime Minister Winston Churchill to send a former cabinet minister, Sir Ronald Cross, as Whiskard's replacement.[4] In December 1941, Japan's entry into the war also put paid to the Canberra office's seemingly relaxed regimen.

These experiences and reflections suggested uncertainty early in World War II about the role and status of a high commissioner. As we shall see below, the war itself would resolve some of this confusion while still leaving room for considerable ambiguity. So the question remains: What is a high commissioner? What has the office of the high commissioner entailed? What have been the high commissioner's duties and responsibilities? And how did the function of the office of the high commissioner transform itself into what is today in all but name an ambassadorial post? In other words, as Lorna Lloyd has recently asked: What was in the name?[5]

For those who study British imperial history, the term high commissioner is most closely associated with the imperial proconsuls who served in South Africa before 1910. The post, which was attached to the governorship of the Cape Colony, had been established in South Africa in the mid-nineteenth century.[6] However, these men had a much wider remit and greater power than either their dominion colleagues, when their respective governments established high commissions in London between 1880 and 1910; or, indeed, their British counterparts when high commissions were established by the British government much later in the four dominions between 1927 and 1939. For instance, after unification in 1910, British high commissioners in South Africa were also responsible for overseeing the colonial administration, especially native affairs, in the three adjoining high commission territories of Basutoland, Swaziland and the Bechuanaland Protectorate, all long coveted by South African expansionists.[7]

In the colonial setting, a motley range of regions, such as Cyprus (1898–1925), Egypt (1914–36), Iraq (1920–32), Southern and Northern Nigeria (1900–14), Palestine (1920–48) and the Western Pacific High Commission (1877–1974) also had high commissioners well before the term became commonplace with most newly emerging Commonwealth nations during decolonisation after 1945.[8] Certainly, within an imperial context, the power and authority of each office before World War II was as varied as the colonial territories themselves. So, too, were the officeholders. Look, for example, at several of the controversial politicians and military commanders who held the post of high commissioner in the colonial empire: Viscount Alfred Milner in South Africa (1897–1905); Sir Frederick Lugard in Northern Nigeria (1900–07 and 1912–14) and Southern Nigeria (1912–14) respectively; and Viscount (later Field Marshal) Edmund Allenby in Egypt (1919–25).

The aim of this chapter is to show that the evolution of the office of Australian high commissioner in London, while unquestionably influenced by Australian national aspirations and diplomatic ambitions, also needs to be understood—until the 1960s at any rate—within a wider framework of imperial relations. So far, studies of the role of dominion high commissioners in London and United Kingdom high commissioners in the four self-governing dominions have focused on the budding bilateral relations between Britain and these up-and-coming nations of Australia, Canada, New Zealand and South Africa. The setting is largely confined to the struggle for dominion autonomy in foreign affairs, with the earlier work firmly embedded in the now clichéd historiographical rubric of maturation from colony to nation. To say as much is not to dismiss previous scholarship, which has made a distinguished contribution to our understanding of the evolution of the office.[9] The task now, however, is to apply a broader, more challenging transnational and comparative approach if scholars (and practitioners) are to grasp more fully the nuances in the relationships between Britain and its dominions but also, especially during World War II, among the dominions themselves as the demands of the Commonwealth alliance thrust them into closer relations with one another.

The evolution of the high commissioner's office

Lorna Lloyd's recent book-length study of the evolution of the office of high commissioner is as welcome as it is instructive.[10] The analytical framework is divided into eight distinct but intersecting phases. The first stage, from 1880 to the outbreak of the Great War, examines the emergence of the office of high commissioner primarily in the context of Anglo-dominion relations. Between 1880 and 1910, as the four colonies of white settlement achieved dominion status, they became more conscious of their prominence and status within the British Empire. The creation of a high commission in the imperial metropolis was not simply an indication of their growing confidence as fledgling nation-states. It was also a key indicator that the dominions were eager to take increasing but varying levels of responsibility for some aspects of their external affairs.

The roles and functions of the dominion high commissioners during this foundation period reflected the nation-building exercises of each overseas territory. Of fundamental importance were the promotion of trade, the facilitation of commerce, and the supervision of financial matters between each dominion and the mother country. Closely associated with these tasks was the equally important job of upholding and defending one's own burgeoning national interests. Another vital task was the encouragement of British emigration. For instance, when the former finance minister, Sir Alexander Galt, was selected as Canada's first official high commissioner in 1879, his instructions reflected these priorities which were crucial to the future economic development of Canada. As a result, he became Canada's chief emigration agent. He was accountable to the minister of agriculture, whose portfolio, at least until 1892, undertook the promotion of migration to the senior dominion.[11] Apart from South Africa, where the official encouragement of British migration was highly politicised, the priorities surrounding emigration were similarly reflected in the duties of the New Zealand and Australian high commissioners when they were eventually ensconced in 1905 and 1910 respectively.[12]

According to Lloyd, the second phase from 1914 to the late 1930s witnessed a consolidation of the office. In London, their station was enhanced as the dominion high commissioners were granted the same privileges, but not the same exemptions, as foreign diplomats. Nevertheless, their status improved as their diplomatic functions expanded. Their influence was limited, however, by the fact that they were only one of a variety of official channels of communication between London and the dominions.[13]

The mercurial Canadian prime minister, W.L. Mackenzie King, was emphatic about what role he expected his high commissioner to play in London: he was simply an agent of the Canadian government whose primary responsibilities were to promote trade and disseminate information, particularly to would-be immigrants. The high commissioner was not to raise foreign policy issues with the British prime minister or make public statements about them. Important communications between the British and Canadian governments were to be transmitted directly between the respective prime ministers or between the secretary of state for dominion affairs and the secretary of state for external affairs, as had been standard practice since the end of the Great War.[14] The high commissioner was not to be the conduit for any of these communications. As Mackenzie King reiterated to Vincent Massey soon after his appointment to Canada House in 1935:

> This is the only way in and which we can possibly have [the] opportunity required collectively to consider and state [our] attitude and policy and which will ensure full responsibility of [the] British as well as [the] C[ana]d[ia]n Gov[ernmen]t with respect to any statements of policy or position and avoid all possibility of misunderstanding as to what has been said or meant in any verbal discussions.[15]

Privately, Massey was furious at being treated as nothing more than an errand boy.

By the late 1930s to the mid-1940s, the third phase in Lloyd's model, there is a discernible groundswell of dissatisfaction among the high commissioners because of their inferior status, whether real or imagined, to that of ambassadors. A crisis point was reached between 1946 and 1948, the fourth stage in her story, when the office might have disappeared completely had it not been for brinkmanship on the part of both some of the old dominions and newly independent South Asian states, which resulted in recognition that high commissioners were equal in status to ambassadors. At the core of this constitutional conundrum was the granting of independence to India and Pakistan in 1947, India's determination to become a republic but remain within the Commonwealth, and the desire of these newly independent nations to exchange ambassadors with other member states of what was now sometimes touted as a 'New Commonwealth'. A compromise was struck, initially brokered by New Zealand's prime minister, Peter Fraser. Dominion status was discarded, presumably because of its now mildly derogatory overtones, but the title of high commissioner remained. As a result, between 1948 and 1950, the fifth stage of Lloyd's chronology, high commissioners in most of the Commonwealth capitals were put on the same footing as foreign diplomats, with all the immunities and privileges this enhanced status commanded.[16]

According to Lloyd, until the mid-1960s the Commonwealth high commissioners had the best of both worlds. This sixth phase was a halcyon period for the high commissioners, who were 'ambassadors plus'. Not only did they benefit from the rights accorded foreign envoys, they profited from the closeness and solidarity between the Commonwealth nations at this time. However, once that cohesion began to dissipate—as it did from the mid-1960s—the office of high commissioner began to lose its lustre. The seventh stage witnessed the regularisation of diplomatic practice between affiliate states at a time of tremendous growth in Commonwealth membership brought about by decolonisation. The Commonwealth was becoming a weaker, more fractured, and increasingly insignificant international organisation.[17] This decline was best illustrated in 1968 when the Commonwealth Office was merged with the Foreign Office to form the Foreign and Commonwealth Office. Nonetheless, the high commissioner has survived, perhaps reflecting the recent resurgence in the fortunes of the Commonwealth as an organisation, but also because a posting as high commissioner in London is still highly prized.[18]

If the status of the office of high commissioner, as Lloyd has so ably shown, was problematic in the diplomatic community, there is no question that during its infancy the office enhanced the power and prestige of the dominion prime ministers. Prior to 1909, when Canada established its own Department of External Affairs, the control and conduct of external policy was firmly in the prime minister's hands.[19] Sir John Macdonald, Canada's first prime minister, left an indelible mark on the senior dominion's external relations. Even the creation of a ministerial portfolio for external affairs under the Liberal administration of Sir Wilfrid Laurier (1896–1911) failed to diminish the authority of the prime minister's office in foreign policy. In fact, it was common practice in the middle decades of the twentieth century for successive Canadian leaders simultaneously to hold both the premiership and the external affairs portfolio. Between 1920 and 1946, three Canadian prime ministers, Arthur Meighen, Mackenzie King and R.B. Bennett, fulfilled these dual roles.

Similar patterns emerged in Australia, New Zealand and South Africa at this time. In Australia no fewer than eleven prime ministers acted as their own ministers for external affairs between 1901 and 1967. Of the six South African prime ministers who held office between 1910 and 1961, only J.G. Strijdom's administration (1954–58) appointed a separate minister for external affairs, Eric Louw. It should also come as no surprise that before the establishment of separate departments of External Affairs in Australia (1935) and New Zealand (1943), such matters were managed, in Australia's case, out of the Prime Minister's Department, and in New Zealand's by an officer from the Prime Minister's Department.[20] Hence the control of the high commissioners in London was effected through prime ministerial channels. But, as ever, South Africa was the exception. Upon the creation of union in 1910, and prior to the inauguration of the South African Department of External Affairs in 1927, the office of high commissioner was attached to the Treasury because it performed a wide range of roles for a variety of government departments.[21] Nonetheless, the external affairs portfolio remained firmly under prime ministerial control.

A defining moment in the transformation of the office of high commissioner occurred in 1926. The political battles between the dominions and London over status, consultation and increased autonomy in external relations during and after the war need not long detain us here.[22] The emergence of the modern high commissioner was initiated by Canada in line with the decisions made in the aftermath of the constitutional fracas which engulfed the senior dominion in the mid-1920s. The so-called 'King–Byng affair', which pitted Mackenzie King against Governor-General Lord Byng of Vimy (1921–26), was a contest of personality and willpower as much as it was a struggle for constitutional supremacy. Again, the political intrigue and backroom manoeuvrings need not concern us here, except to say that Mackenzie King triumphed in his quest to strip the governor-general of his remaining political and constitutional powers. These were hived off into a new office, that of UK high commissioner.[23] The role of governor-general had now been reduced to that of ceremonial figurehead, a symbol of the British monarch in Canada. The high commissioner, in theory at least, was now the British government's representative in Ottawa.

These changes in representation and channels of communication between Britain and its dominions were reaffirmed at the 1926 and 1930 Imperial Conferences; and in 1931, they culminated in the enactment of the Statute of Westminster, which gave the dominions greater autonomy in the control and conduct of their external relations. Interestingly, unlike the newest and fifth dominion, the Irish Free State (which had established its high commission in London in 1923), the three southern dominions were content with the existing arrangements.[24] In fact, it was London that initiated these more far-reaching changes. It was in the fertile brain of the arch-imperialist, L.S. Amery, the secretary of state for dominion affairs and the colonies (1924–29), that the idea to extend the office of British high commissioner to the remaining dominions originated.

Amery championed the need for an independent personal channel of communication between the British and dominion governments. The role of the governor-general in this capacity was, he complained, both unsatisfactory and anomalous. Therefore, his enthusiastic endorsement of Mackenzie King's suggestion in 1926 to create a UK High Commission in Ottawa reflected his own views that the British government (as opposed to the Crown) needed its own representative in the dominions. It also dovetailed neatly with his zeal to reform the imperial bureaucracy. In 1925, a separate government department was hived off from the Colonial Office to deal specifically with dominion affairs; much to the chagrin of the mandarins at the Foreign Office who saw the creation of a Dominions Office as an unnecessary duplication of existing machinery.[25] Mackenzie King was equally dismissive, likening the Dominions Office to the fifth wheel of a coach.[26] Nevertheless, supported by Prime Minister Stanley Baldwin, Amery prevailed against sustained Foreign Office criticism that he, Amery, was poaching on their estate.

Amery argued that apart from a few trade commissioners, there was no one in the dominions who could defend British interests or expound London's points of view.[27] The office of high commissioner, he argued, would fulfil this all-important task. However, he met stiff resistance not just from the remaining dominion governments which thought the existing arrangements more than adequate, but also from the governors-general, who did not want their office and authority to be undermined and marginalised. But this rearguard action did not last long. By 1935 London had unilaterally stripped the political powers away from the offices of the South African and Australian governors-general, thus ending the dual role played by these officials as representatives of both the imperial government and the Crown.[28] New Zealand quietly submitted soon after.

The creation of this new channel of communication between London and the dominions took time to bed down. In fact, it was not until after World War II that the high commissioner became the undisputed channel of communication between the various dominion and United Kingdom governments. Until then he occupied a secondary, informal, and at times an uncomfortable, position. Prime ministers preferred to deal directly with each other, or channeled their communications through the appropriate government machinery. As we have seen, Mackenzie King conceived of the Canadian high commissioner in London as a cipher and had no more elevated an opinion of the UK high commissioner in Ottawa's role.

The outlook of Australian leaders during the interwar period was not so very different. The Australian High Commission was one of a number of channels available to Canberra. More important were the Australian representatives attached to or working in several key British government departments in London, who provided access to Whitehall. In 1924, R.G. Casey, 'the father of Australian diplomacy', was appointed as the head of the Australian Liaison Office in London.[29] Established by Stanley Melbourne Bruce when he was prime minister (1923–29) and based in the offices of the British cabinet secretary— and therefore independent of the high commission—Casey was fundamentally Bruce's personal representative. He received unprecedented access to nearly all British cabinet material supplied through the cabinet secretary's offices in Whitehall, which were overseen by the South Australian–born Sir Maurice (later Lord) Hankey.

When Bruce became high commissioner in 1933 he brought the Liaison Office under his control, once again gaining unmatched admission to the policy-making apparatus within the Foreign and Dominions offices.[30] Bruce's clever usurpation of power meant that the status of the Australian High Commission, and hence of the former prime minister himself, was greatly enhanced. He was now the gatekeeper of a vast array of information which would otherwise lie deep and hidden within Whitehall; Canada and South Africa neither sought nor gained similar access.[31] The high standing and exceptional ability of Bruce—'who is clearly unique as a Dominion representative in London', admitted Sir John Stephenson, deputy under-secretary at the Dominions Office—also contributed substantially to Canberra's preference to downplay the UK High Commission. Stephenson argued that the main reason for this was that successive Australian governments had made it crystal clear that they *preferred*, so far as it was possible, to employ the direct channel of inter-governmental communication.[32] But this habit posed major problems for Sir Ronald Cross, the UK's high commissioner in Australia during World War II. Even once Cross's own shortcomings are given due weight, the Bruce model helped ensure that the British office in Canberra did not gain the respect, prestige or influence its head felt it deserved.[33]

Who were the high commissioners?

Before 1950, there is a striking dichotomy in backgrounds between those appointed by the dominions and those selected by the British government. The dominions almost invariably selected former politicians, businessmen and occasionally military leaders who had made important contributions to the party in power or had been otherwise notable in the life of the nation. As this volume demonstrates, former prime ministers figured largely among the ranks, with Australia having the greatest number of them. Former cabinet ministers were also prominent among dominion officeholders, as were businessmen and financiers. For example, Lord Strathcona, long-involved with the Hudson's Bay Company, a former director of the Bank of Montreal, and a key architect behind the building and financing of the Canadian Pacific Railway, served as Canada's high commissioner for eighteen years (1896–1914). Appointed by Mackenzie King, Peter C. Larkin, president of the Salada Tea Company, represented the senior dominion in London between 1922 and 1930. Vincent Massey, the Liberal millionaire businessman whose family fortune was built around the Massey-Harris Company, one of the world's largest farm-implement manufacturers, held office between 1935 and 1946.[34] Other dominion notables included W.P. Schreiner, the brother of the famous author Olive Schreiner. He served as South Africa's high commissioner in London between 1914 and 1919.

It was not until after World War II that this pattern of appointing from among the party faithful was broken, albeit temporarily. Norman Robertson—who was the only man to serve twice as Canada's high commissioner in London (1946–49 and 1952–57)—was not a political partisan but a career civil servant. Oxford-educated, he joined the Department of External Affairs in 1929. In early 1941, at the tender age of thirty-seven, he was promoted to under-secretary of state for external affairs upon the death of his master, Dr O.D. Skelton. Five years later he replaced Massey in London. Dana Wilgress (1949–52) and the wonderfully witty Charles Ritchie (1967–71) are further examples of career public servants who served at Trafalgar Square.[35]

What of the appointments made to the UK high commissionerships in the dominions? During the late 1920s and 1930s these were made largely, but not exclusively, from the ranks of the Dominions Office. When the British High Commission in Ottawa was being established, Amery argued that there were 'considerable dangers' in having Britain's first representative in Canada going there straight from the diplomatic service possessing 'no training in the work of the office with which he will primarily have to deal'. Furthermore, it was essential not to give credence to the idea that intra-imperial relations were of the same character as foreign relations. Those chosen for this new posting should be 'generally versed in affairs and fit to serve as confidential representatives' of the British government, men who would learn the special aspects of their work as they grew into the position. In-depth expertise of a foreign country was, in Amery's mind, of secondary importance.[36]

Decisively, unlike the dominions, which used the high commissionership as a sinecure to reward politicians for faithful service, Britain appointed professional civil servants of long standing. Indeed, the new office was, according to Percivale Liesching, a staffer in the UK High Commission in Canberra, an important step in giving the Dominions Office the opportunity to establish its own overseas network independent of the Foreign Office. When Sir Harold Batterbee, an assistant under-secretary of state at the Dominions Office, was appointed as the first UK high commissioner in New Zealand in 1938, Liesching wrote:

> It really is good to hear that this new job is to be in your hands and the DO is going to unfurl its flag in another Dominion ... I know that you have the same views as myself about turning the DO from a Dep[artmen]t of the Home Civil Service pure and simple into a body of people with first hand experience of the other end and to that purpose it is so vital the H[igh] Com[missioner]ships should not consistently pass to persons drawn from other Departments or services.[37]

War, however, changed this situation, albeit temporarily, as circumstances overseas dictated a wholesale change in senior personnel at the UK high commissions in Australia, Canada and South Africa. In late 1940, the UK high commissioner in South Africa, Sir Edward Harding, suffered a heart attack and in February 1941 was forced to resign from office.[38] Harding's ill health and premature retirement coincided with the announcement that the former cabinet minister, Malcolm MacDonald, would succeed Sir Gerald Campbell as the UK high commissioner in Ottawa. Writing to the South African prime minister, J.C. Smuts, Churchill stated that it was now desirable at this particular stage of the war to insert political appointees with proven parliamentary skill and cabinet experience to the high commissionerships. As the parliamentary under-secretary of state for the colonies in the Conservative governments of the 1920s, and more recently as colonial secretary in the National government between 1936 and 1938, W.G.A. Ormsby-Gore, the 4th Baron Harlech, was selected to replace Harding in South Africa.[39] Harlech himself admitted to Violet Milner that he thought this was an unorthodox and 'bold idea' on Churchill's part.[40] But as one Dominions Office insider remarked, 'men of this eminence in public life elevated the status of the High Commissioner. No longer could he be treated as a mere postman or glorified sales representative'.[41] Sadly for Ronald Cross, this promising trend was not apparent, for during his entire tenure in the Australian office a diminutive wartime role was all he would be allowed. In late 1945, with hostilities over, MacDonald suggested to Viscount Addison, the secretary of state for dominion affairs, that the wartime practice of appointing politicians of ministerial rank should stop. If the Dominions Office refused to revert to the prewar habit of choosing candidates for its 'plums' from the civil service and instead continued to select professional politicians, then what incentive was there for young cadets to enter the Dominions Office or allied services?[42]

During the war Churchill had used overseas vacancies to banish those he did not like or want in his wartime administration. His motivation for MacDonald's appointment to Ottawa is a case in point: the British prime minister simply wanted to 'get rid of him'. Although he had not done badly at the Ministry of Health (1940–41), according to John Colville, Churchill's private secretary, the prime minister 'did not much care for him'. The main bone of contention was MacDonald's decision while at the Dominions Office to surrender the treaty ports of Lough Swilly, Berehaven and Queenstown to the Irish Free State in 1938. MacDonald, who lunched with Lord Reith before his 'exile' to Ottawa, confided to the former chairman of the BBC that he was quite bitter about being 'pushed off' to Canada.[43]

Churchill, however, was not alone in exploiting overseas vacancies to rid himself of politicians he did not like. Dominion leaders were equally adept at using the allure of an overseas posting, especially in London, to solve political puzzles at home. In 1951, when the replacement for New Zealand's long-serving high commissioner in London, William Jordan, was being mooted, Australian officials in Wellington were quite candid with their colleagues in Canberra:

> The appointment of the New Zealand High Commissioner in London has tended in the past to be used to assist the Government in solving Cabinet difficulties or embarrassments. W. Pember Reeves (New Zealand Agent General in London), Sir James Parr, and W.J. Jordan, are all instances of appointments being made along these lines. I see no reason why the present Government will depart from the precedence [sic] of a political appointment to London, if [W.J.] Polson refuses, which I think is most likely, then my guess would be that the appointment would be offered to either C.M. Bowden, Minister of Customs, or F.W. Doidge, Minister of External Affairs.[44]

The appointment of the General Officer Commanding, 2nd Canadian Division, Major-General Victor W. Odlum, as Canada's second high commissioner in Australia in 1941 is an excellent example of how the expansion of Canada's diplomatic network was used to remove a problematic individual from a sensitive wartime role. Ottawa, under pressure from the British to ease the World War I veteran out of his divisional command in England, persuaded Odlum to go to Canberra. Reluctantly, he went. It proved disastrous, for the independent-minded Odlum was entirely unsuited to the role. Without consulting Ottawa, he broached the prospect in Canberra of sending a Canadian force to help defend Australia if attacked by Japan.[45] He was in the post for less than a year before being replaced by a safer pair of hands, T.C. Davis, the deputy minister of national war services.

Finding a role

Although the representational function of the high commissioner was central to the office, each officeholder perceived his role differently, putting greater or lesser emphasis on specific aspects. New Zealand's Jordan, who was not particularly interested in foreign affairs, saw his function as primarily to 'sell New Zealand mutton and butter'.[46] Cross took a much more Olympian but sadly misplaced view of his role. For Paul Hasluck, then a public servant, Cross was truly one of the 'less successful occupants of that post' because of his early insistence that he was no 'ordinary diplomat'. The former merchant banker and High Tory believed that he was not in Australia simply to observe, report and represent; rather, as Hasluck remarked, Cross saw himself as a 'guide and mentor with whom the colonials should seek to have consultation'.[47] To be fair, however, although he may have lacked the earthiness necessary to establish a closer working relationship with Australian politicians, as one senior British wartime liaison officer rightly observed, the role Cross had to perform—halfway between an ambassador and a consul-general—was 'a very tricky one'.[48] Canada's Massey, however, saw the continuing ambiguity of the high commissioner's status as an opportunity. In wartime London, he said, the dominion high commissioners were in a unique position vis-à-vis the apparatus for the conduct of the war: 'not quite ministers but more than diplomats'.[49]

What Cross lacked in the common touch, MacDonald more than made up for in forging a close and intimate relationship with the prickly Mackenzie King between 1941 and 1946. Personality certainly made a difference, but also invaluable was the ability to read the people with whom one was dealing and correctly gauge the mood of the country. In April 1941, shortly after his arrival in Canada, MacDonald astutely observed that the Canadian premier was not 'endowed with the qualities of a war leader; there is in him no great dynamic energy, no genius for military affairs or statecraft of the highest order, no gift of stirring oratory. He is somewhat paedestrian[sic]'. Nevertheless, the British high commissioner knew full well the intense domestic pressures that the country was experiencing. The maintenance of national unity was paramount in Canada. This was fundamental in understanding the mechanics of the Canadian political scene. In this Herculean task, MacDonald argued that the lacklustre but 'supremely skilful' King was the only party leader of any calibre who possessed the requisite abilities to keep the senior dominion from disintegrating.[50] Acute observation of the domestic political scene was a talent that was equally pivotal to Harlech's success in a problematic South Africa. So, too, were regular and extensive trips throughout the duration of his posting—an essential and sometimes demanding part of the job in geographically extensive countries such as Canada, South Africa and Australia.

Travel was perhaps less important for the dominion high commissioners based in London. However, as M.L. Shepherd, the official secretary of the Australian High Commission (1921–27) recorded in his memoirs, travel to the continent was frequent as there were numerous administrative 'side lines' and functions to perform. These included committee work on a raft of issues based at the League of Nations or the International Labour Organization in Geneva. During the interwar period especially, one of these more sombre but fruitful duties (which is maintained with great diligence and solemnity today) was the work each high commissioner and his staff performed on the Imperial (now Commonwealth) War Graves Commission. 'As can be imagined', Shepherd noted, 'the activities were very comprehensive and far reaching'.[51]

In fact, at least during the interwar period, the Australian High Commission always included an entry in its annual report to Canberra on its War Graves Commission activities. For instance, in his 1935 summation, Bruce hinted at the breadth of the work involved. The total number of British bodies recovered from the former battlefields that year was 795, of which forty-seven were Australian. He wrote: 'Although the latter were readily identifiable as Australian soldiers from their uniforms, cap-badges, shoulder titles, etc, in most cases, it must be regretfully recorded, their names will never be known'. He also reported that the Australian memorial stone at the entrance to the Jerusalem war cemetery had been completed during the year; and that an Anglo-Iraq war graves agreement had been signed in Baghdad in mid-March.[52] The year before, which marked the twentieth anniversary of the outbreak of the war, he informed Canberra that local interest in the British war cemeteries in France and Belgium was 'unabated'. No fewer than 328 ceremonies had been conducted by local inhabitants throughout France, while twenty-six similar ceremonies were held in Belgium. 'In Egypt and Palestine, the number of people attending ceremonies in the British War Cemeteries during the year was greater than ever before, and, at Cairo, Alexandria, Jerusalem and elsewhere, impressive services were held.'[53]

For Australians, as indeed for those from the United Kingdom and the other former dominions, these pilgrimages of remembrance and commemoration remain poignant today, albeit for varying reasons.[54] Nonetheless, the Commonwealth high commissions continue to play an integral role in this remembrance process. The discovery in early 2009 of several mass burial pits containing up to 400 British and Australian World War I dead on the Arras sector near Fromelles, their exhumation by forensic archaeologists, and re-interment, is a reminder of the sensitive but ongoing work which the Commonwealth high commissioners still undertake.

Conclusion

In a landmark memorandum written in May 1928 by Sir William Clark, Britain's first high commissioner in Canada, the high commissioner's function was said to be 'an additional channel of communication between London and Ottawa, supplementary to the existing methods of communication between the two Governments'.[55] By 1947 it was clear that with the expansion of the high commissioner network during World War II, especially between the dominions themselves, the office of high commissioner was fast becoming the main conduit of communication between London and the dominions.[56] As one Dominions Office memorandum claimed in November 1944, 'it is not too much to say that the key to the successful handling of our relations with Dominion Governments is now to be found in increasing degree in our High Commissioner Service'.[57] The high commissioners were no longer glorified postmen or messenger boys. By 1950, although the Dominions and India offices had disappeared (when in July 1947 they were merged into a new Commonwealth Relations Office), the objective of making the high commissioner the pivotal channel for consultation and communication in intra-Commonwealth affairs had largely been achieved.[58]

The same processes were unfolding in the dominions. Each dominion was moving at its own pace, and each saw the high commissioner's function differently. Canada, for instance, had done more than either Australia or New Zealand in trying to define the precise role of a high commissioner. Meanwhile, in Australia, Whiskard and his controversial successor, Cross, complained bitterly that Canberra was deliberately bypassing their office, preferring to deal directly with the British prime minister or channel communications through their own very capable high commission in London, led by the urbane Bruce.[59]

Perhaps, as Hankey once observed, before 1939 it was misleading to use the word '"diplomacy" in speaking of the relations within the family circle of the British Empire'.[60] World War II changed that forever as the dominions, which contributed so much to the imperial and Allied war efforts, rose to the global challenges of total war. As the dominions' confidence and stature in the international arena grew, Britain was forced, however begrudgingly, to respond to the criticisms from these increasingly restive family members. And in this, the dominion high commissioners in London played an important role. To describe them so irreverently as 'The Children's Hour', as some junior Foreign Office officials did in 1942 when closer liaison links were being cultivated between the London-based high commissions, the Dominions Office and the Foreign Office, misses the point completely although it captures the condescension of some Whitehall officials.[61] For it was self-evident by the end of the war that the nature of foreign relations between Britain and her dominions had changed, and that the word diplomacy could indeed be used to describe this new relationship forged in war. It was, however, as Lorna Lloyd has recently argued, 'diplomacy with a difference'.[62] These same pressures also forced the dominions to take a hard look at the function and future of their own high commissions, particularly in London, although the practice of appointing politicians as high commissioners rather than professional diplomats continued.[63]

With the 'normalisation' of diplomatic relations between Britain, its dominions and the newly emerging Commonwealth after 1945, the family intimacy began to break down. Yet, surprisingly, the title of high commissioner, which is a throwback to an imperial age, has endured. What was in British eyes before 1939 simply a supplementary channel of communications between Whitehall and the dominions had by 1950 become the major diplomatic conduit in its relations with the wider Commonwealth. A similar conversion occurred in the dominions. For them, the office of high commissioner, which had hitherto been primarily responsible for the promotion of trade, commerce and migration, was the hub of a nascent diplomatic network. The title carried a certain dignity, but also ambiguity. Some of that ambiguity still remains even if the grandeur of the title has long waned. Today, high commissioners are ambassadors in all but name. Whether the title and office survive the political challenges of the next hundred years remains to be seen.

2 Foundations: Australia's early representation in Great Britain

Olwen Pryke

THIS chapter traces Australia's official representation in Great Britain before 1910 and examines the circumstances that led to the establishment of a high commission in London. From the latter half of the nineteenth century, the interests of the Australian colonies, and later the Australian states, were represented in London by agents-general. What was expected of these representatives varied as different colonial, state, national and imperial affinities dominated the debate. The ambiguity of these loyalties resulted in a series of interim measures that characterised the period from 1901 to 1910. Despite the growing urgency of the calls for a resolution to the matter, the discussion of the High Commissioner Bill was repeatedly deferred. Provisional decisions compounded the already diverse and disparate nature of the Australian representation, exposing its lack of authority and limited purview. The chapter first outlines the history of Australian representation in London before 1910, drawing on studies by Barbara Atkins, Bernard Attard and John Robert Thompson.[1] The discussion then examines what was expected of the agencies during this period, how they functioned to meet these expectations, and how an increasing dissatisfaction with their parochial and disjointed representation led to a demand for the appointment of an Australian high commissioner. The final section tracks the High Commissioner Bill from its inception in 1901 to its enactment in December 1909, exploring how Australian parliamentarians and the press envisaged the Commonwealth being represented in London.

Quasi-diplomacy? The origins and evolution of the agencies-general

Barbara Atkins, in examining the origin and development of the Australian agencies-general, warns that while the granting of responsible government gave all the Australian colonies the opportunity to appoint their own agents in Britain, they did not all do so at the same time, or for the same reasons.[2] With their new independence, and an increasingly competitive spirit, the colonies became dissatisfied with their combined representative, known as the imperial agent-general. In the light of their complaints, the Colonial Office offered to hand over his duties to any agents whom the self-governing colonies might appoint. South Australia took advantage of this offer in 1858, with the appointment of Gregory Seale Walters, who had arrived in South Australia in 1848 to organise the Patent Copper Company before returning to Britain in 1856.[3] The other colonies found it more convenient and economical to continue to use the imperial officer. A decade later, the amount of business conducted by the remaining colonies (chiefly due to the gold rushes and expansion of rail and road communications) made this arrangement impracticable. By 1892, when Western Australia finally transferred its business, all the colonies were represented by separate agents-general in London.[4]

The role and responsibilities of the agents-general were initially conceived very broadly. For example, Edward Hamilton, a pastoralist who returned to England in 1855 to become governor of the Australian Agricultural Company (1857–98) and the first agent-general for New South Wales in 1863, was ordered 'to act under such instructions as he shall from time to time receive, and to transact such business as may be entrusted to him'.[5] Almost thirty years later, the duties of the colonial agent-general remained similarly encompassing. A pamphlet published in 1899 that outlined the services provided by the various agencies contended that the main duty of an agent-general was to act for the different departments of his own colony:

> He is, therefore, called Agent-*General*—Agent to Government departments *generally*. Whatever any Government department hasn't done, he will do—buy or sell or give away, engage a policeman, or a schoolmaster, or a railway booking clerk or general-manager, or a commanding officer for Colonial forces, borrow money, pay pensions, and so forth.[6]

By the late nineteenth century, the Australian agents-general had acquired influence and some prestige in Great Britain; they were regarded as more than simply the commercial agents of their respective colonies. The various agency offices, many of which had started as a share in an 'out-of-the-way room in a by-street off Whitehall', had by this time shifted to the more salubrious Victoria Street, Westminster.[7] The agents themselves were presented at Court and travelled widely, giving lectures and attending exhibitions throughout Great Britain and the continent. They were consulted on colonial matters by the British press and access to the Colonial Office, and even the secretary of state for the colonies, was greatly improved. Indeed, Atkins has argued that the agents-general were increasingly likened to ambassadors throughout the late nineteenth century.[8] (A discussion of the men who occupied the office of agent-general in the years between 1858 and 1909 can be found in Appendix 3.)

This new grandeur, however, was not greeted with universal delight. A satirical piece published in the *Sydney Quarterly Magazine* in 1888 took up the new estimation of the role of agent-general, observing that:

> [In London] our representatives are feted, feasted, and flattered, to a degree which well-nigh turns their matured heads. They are consulted, deferred to, and invited to co-operate with all the deference due to formidable foreign potentates; and every word they utter, and every honour that is paid them, is cabled to us, so that we are led to believe that Great Britain is thinking of nothing else but Australia.[9]

Whether it was the agents-general promoting their own interests and status, or an Australian press keen to assert the importance of Australian affairs in Britain, the skewed reportage resulted in misleading indications of the influence of the agents-general. While their standing had improved, and 'a new class of business, understood to be of a semi-diplomatic nature' was assigned to the office, they were certainly not yet the equal of 'formidable foreign potentates'.[10]

By the mid-1890s, some in colonial parliaments acknowledged the desirability of 'converting the Agents-General into general agents' and again limiting their responsibilities to a purely commercial character.[11] John Robert Thompson has suggested that there was a continuous campaign of criticism directed against the retention of the Victorian agency throughout the 1890s, a period of economic depression, government retrenchment and business scandal—with one agent-general, ex-premier James Munro, being thoroughly implicated in the latter. The editor of the Melbourne Age voiced his condemnation in a series of leading articles that outlined the development of the office, praised its functioning as a practical business agency, but condemned its increasingly 'quasi-diplomatic officiousness'.[12] Clearly, the adoption of a pseudo-ambassadorial status left many Australian observers uneasy. Although the reference to quasi-diplomacy was made lightly, it implied that the agents-general might attempt to act as the official envoys of one sovereign state to another, a situation as yet anathema to the Australian press and many politicians.

It was the social role of the agents-general, however, and the officiousness with which these duties were performed, that raised most ire, both in Australia and Britain. Arthur Beavan commented briefly on this aspect of the colonial agencies-general in his *Imperial London* of 1901. Providing an English perspective, he patronisingly maintained that nowadays, 'the colonies are petted, … made much of in Downing Street, and when some Canadian or Australian comes home on an official mission, he spends his days at the Colonial Office and his nights at public dinners, to say nothing of the luncheon intervening'. Yet despite these social advantages, Beavan maintained that their position was a hollow one: 'they can initiate nothing' and any official proposition must be 'referred to headquarters'. According to Beavan, this tight control was the result of 'something approaching jealousy' with which Australasia regarded any lengthened residence of their agents-general in England, fearing that exposure to the 'fascinations of fashionable London society' would cause these officials to lose touch with colonial sentiment.[13]

By the turn of the century, the continuation of the office of agent-general was questioned more frequently by the press and in colonial parliaments. The severe depression of the 1890s deepened public concern about government expenditure for such a purpose. At this time the Age considered the sum to maintain the agencies in London a 'stiff price to pay'. Furthermore, the newspaper concluded, their work could be undertaken by 'any deputation of prominent colonists'.[14] But as the possibility of federation drew nearer, others recognised that the diplomatic activities undertaken by the agencies would be better performed by a single official representative of a united Commonwealth. When Alfred Deakin, the Victorian politician, addressed the Australasian Federal Conference in 1890, he was careful to draw the attention of the delegates to the importance of Australia being represented by a single 'Agent-General' in London who could express its views with strength and conviction.[15]

The agents' assumption of quasi-diplomatic duties reflected the evolving nature of the Australian–British relationship. Indeed, as Atkins has argued, the office of agent-general was inextricably associated with colonial status, whereas the high commissioner became the adjunct of dominion status.[16] The most significant precursor was Canada, the first of Britain's self-governing colonies to achieve dominion status and the first to appoint a high commissioner, in 1879.[17] The Australian agents-general were quick to recognise that the appointment gave the Canadian representative a higher position than their own. However, other than notifying their respective governments of the appointment, the agents-general took no action, feeling that it would be like requesting their own promotion.[18] In any event, the Australian colonial governments chose not to follow the precedent set by Canada, perhaps anticipating that Australia would soon be similarly represented in London.

The impact of federation

The assumption of quasi-diplomatic functions by the agents-general reflected a confidence in the colonial position in London—a confidence that increased when the Australian colonies federated in 1901. The leading figures of the major political parties agreed that the Commonwealth of Australia should be represented in London as soon as circumstances permitted. Indeed, '[w]hen honourable members entered the first Federal Parliament', William Morris (Billy) Hughes recalled in 1909, 'they almost expected, in the innocence of their hearts, to find the shadow of the High Commissioner rising behind the Speaker's chair, and assuming form and substance during the first session'.[19]

The possibility of more prestigious representation in the office of an Australian high commissioner unsettled the balance of representation already established in Britain, and became inextricably linked with assessments of the representation provided by the agents-general. The colonial agencies, questioned throughout the late nineteenth century for the expense of their operations and their appropriation of pseudo-ambassadorial functions, were more tangibly threatened by the establishment of a high commission. This necessarily brought to the fore state fears about the impact of the new federal government on their jurisdictions. While some commentators in the press and parliaments anticipated the eventual abolition of the agencies, most thought the offices would be maintained, if somewhat curtailed in their functions. The result was a defensive stance on the part of the state governments and their agents; an attitude which ultimately shaped understandings of the high commissioner's role, as well as the legislation that created the position.

A number of government inquiries—both state and federal—set out to define the functioning of the agencies in a bid to determine what role a potential high commissioner might play in London. In 1901, Australia's first prime minister, Edmund Barton, invited the Victorian Supreme Court Judge Henry Agincourt Hodges to inquire into the work performed by the Canadian high commissioner and the Canadian agencies-general in London. Hodges' report classified the possible functions of the high commissioner as 'diplomatique', financial, mercantile, intelligence and social. The 'diplomatique' role the high commissioner might play was necessarily restricted in Hodges' view by the governor-general, who would remain the primary channel of communication between Britain and the Commonwealth. He suggested the high commissioner could maintain a 'watching brief' to safeguard Australian interests in Britain and could be empowered to act without having first to negotiate or consult with the Commonwealth government.[20]

Not surprisingly, a state-instigated inquiry conducted almost simultaneously reiterated the stature and efficiency of the New South Wales' agency in London. Joseph Barling, chairman of the New South Wales Public Service Board, did not recommend any essential changes to the office.[21] But other commentators felt that the appointment of a high commissioner would completely alter the balance of Australian colonial representation in London. Sir John Quick and Robert Garran, the authors of *The Annotated Constitution of the Australian Commonwealth*, argued that with the appointment, the agents-general would be 'denuded of their prestige and most of their duties' and there would be no necessity for 'the continuance of the old system'. They anticipated that the agents-general, 'if not quite abolished', would revert to being 'General Agents', noting it was a title 'repugnant to the sensibilities of some of its past occupants'.[22]

Some states appeared to anticipate this diminution. In 1901 it was announced that Henry Allerdale Grainger would serve in the capacity of a general or South Australian agent, rather than an agent-general.[23] And when it was announced that John Taverner would go to London as Victoria's agent-general in 1904, it was also revealed that the annual salary for this office was to be reduced from £2,500 to £1,000.[24] This scaling back was noted by the *Australasian*, which commented that 'the State agents-general have become a neglectable quantity'.[25]

Certainly, Walter James, then agent-general for Western Australia, shared this opinion when he wrote to Deakin in 1905:

> It is a thousand pities that following upon Federation … the States' Agents should have been split up by internal differences … This condition of affairs … left Australia without a man to speak for it; each Agent thinking only of his own State and not doing that very vigorously.[26]

Clearly James's position, as an agent-general himself, was not a disinterested one. But he was not alone in his estimation of the influence of state allegiances on the image of Australia as a whole in Great Britain. In 1901, the *Sydney Morning Herald* raised concern that '[s]o long as the six colonies spoke with different voices on subjects which the mother-country could not help regarding as matters of common Australian concern, their official expressions of opinion were necessarily diverse and sometimes even contradictory'.[27] In 1905, the *British Australasian* asked why Australians persisted in representing themselves in England as a parcel of little provinces; '[p]eople are puzzled by these distinctions, and rightly so', the correspondent continued, explaining that to the average Londoner, each of the agencies-general was the agency for Australia.[28]

The division and confusion caused by this state parochialism diminished the reputation of the agents-general.[29] To shore up their increasingly insecure position in London, and to confound critics of their disunity, in 1905 the agents-general formed a committee to jointly oversee matters of general Australian interest in Great Britain. Timothy Coghlan, the agent-general for New South Wales, was elected chair.[30]

Prime Minister Alfred Deakin was careful to seek the opinion of this committee. He asked what relationship should exist between the Commonwealth and the states in Britain and how best to establish 'a live and going agency for Australia'.[31] Predictably, the subsequent report was founded on the assumption that the agents-general would continue to operate in London even after the establishment of the Commonwealth office. While the agents-general recognised in theory the possibility of the entirety of their work being transferred to a newly appointed high commissioner, in practice as long as the states controlled immigration and raised their own loans, it was necessary to maintain separate state representation in London.

The situation was further complicated by the federal government's decision to approach the agents-general to act on behalf of the Commonwealth until the high commission was established. The proposal seemed both practical and economical from the federal perspective but, in envisaging a short-term solution to the problem of Commonwealth representation in London, the federal government failed to anticipate the depth of state insecurity. Coghlan, being the representative of the preeminent state, was perhaps most pleased, the position encouraging his personal ambitions. But aside from him, it was an agreement which satisfied few. The *British Australasian* characterised it as a sort of private unofficial arrangement which carried 'nothing of the status of a High Commissioner'.[32]

The agents-general were expected to receive communications from, and act on behalf of, the Commonwealth: to pay outstanding accounts, arrange and supervise purchases, and channel inquiries. The system was informal and awkward in practice. There were often considerable delays in the execution of Commonwealth business, and there was an inevitable duplication of correspondence among the various agencies-general and the equivalent Commonwealth departments.[33]

Not only each state, but each state representative, was careful to secure their position in London. Walter James, the agent-general for Western Australia, was not averse to relaying ominous warnings; writing to Deakin of the general attitude of the agents-general, he expressed his hope that

> whoever is appointed will come with a determination to secure cooperation with the various Agents General so that we may have a chorus of six voices to his solo. If he comes with the idea of snubbing them out of existence he will make a great mistake and will find six notes of dissent almost as strong as his own voice.[34]

Suspicious about Commonwealth encroachment on their jurisdiction, the states and their agents were tenacious in their determination to maintain representation in London.

The process of negotiating the delicate relationship between the newly formed Commonwealth and the state governments was a time-consuming one. 'Procrastination is the policy of every Commonwealth government concerning the appointment of a High Commissioner', the *British Australasian* unequivocally stated in 1905.[35] Loath to offend the states, and unable to agree on the appropriate functions of the office, the Commonwealth implemented a further temporary measure.

As a result, the crucial initiative for the first *official* Commonwealth representation in London was prosaically related to the acquisition of defence force stores. Following federation, Australia began to plan the establishment of its own navy, as well as the expansion of its existing military forces. In February 1906, Prime Minister Deakin informed the governor-general of his government's intention to establish a Commonwealth office in London to deal with remittances on behalf of the Commonwealth and to supervise expenditure in connection with Australian defence stores.[36] The decision to establish a temporary Commonwealth office in London was welcomed by both the Opposition and the press. Indeed, the Melbourne *Australasian* argued that it was 'quite indefensible that the Commonwealth should have remained thus long without any direct agent of its own in London'.[37]

Deakin further advised the governor-general that Captain Robert Muirhead Collins had been selected to take charge of the new office.[38] The secretary of the Department of Defence since 1901, Captain Collins was generally considered an able bureaucrat, with 'a special aptitude for checking, criticising and organising', according to the *Australasian*.[39] Arriving in March 1906, he began establishing a centralised office for defence-related activities.[40]

The Commonwealth government soon agreed, however, that Collins's duties in London would be expanded. Federal matters previously entrusted to the agents-general were handed over to him. It proved a practical and cheap solution, if a temporary one. Thus, until the appointment of the first high commissioner, Collins handled all matters relating to the Commonwealth in London: supervising the ordering of Australian coinage, discussing the Australian coat of arms with the College of Heralds, and pursuing the details of proposed sites for Commonwealth offices.[41]

The Colonial Office recognised Collins's position, ambiguous though it was, but felt that the federal government's decision constituted 'a rather curious beginning of a Commonwealth Agency in London'.[42] By 1908, members of federal parliament were inclined to agree. Joseph Cook, the new leader of the Free Trade Party then in Opposition, found the position of Captain Collins 'a most anomalous one'. To all intents and purposes, Collins was carrying out the duties of a high commissioner, but unofficially and in miniature. Cook was not alone in urging that the Commonwealth's representation in London should be placed on a proper footing.[43]

While parliament voted in favour of the continuation of the temporary office in London, the debate made it clear that support for the appointment of a high commissioner was widespread and that there was an increasing sense of urgency in relation to establishing an office to sustain this position. 'Captain Collins has been zealous and industrious, and deserves great praise for the work done and the tact shown', observed Littleton Groom, the minister for external affairs; but, he continued, 'A High Commissioner … could better voice Australian feeling'.[44]

Making the office of high commissioner

Members of federal parliament had expected the High Commissioner Bill to take form and substance during their first session.[45] For the following seven years there were frequent statements in federal parliament and the press emphasising the urgency of the matter.[46] 'Almost every Government since the commencement of our Federal career', Senator George Henderson asserted, 'has expressed its assent to the proposition that a High Commissioner should be appointed'.[47] Although a sessional program rarely passed without foreshadowing the bill, the legislation remained unwritten at the commencement of 1909.

Why was the issue so persistently deferred? The availability of other officers able to do the work—the agents-general, the governor-general, and later Captain Collins—meant the urgency of the appointment was allayed. While the arrangement might not have been entirely satisfactory, with these practicalities attended to, the federal government was able to engage in delicate and extended negotiations with the state governments and their agents. The antagonism that characterised many of these deliberations, and the lack of consensus over the high commissioner's exact role and function, meant these issues continued to exercise federal parliament. It was both a practical and conceptual debate.

The political instability of the early parliaments also unavoidably slowed the legal establishment of the office. Both Thompson and Attard have traced the legislative history of the High Commissioner Bill in its intricate detail.[48] During the parliamentary recess of January 1909, Prime Minister Andrew Fisher and the leader of the Opposition, Alfred Deakin, were openly corresponding on the subject. They agreed on the urgency of the appointment—an exigency made more emphatic by the fact that both New Zealand and South Africa had enacted or were preparing legislation to establish the position of high commissioner for their countries.[49] But Fisher's government was abruptly replaced by Deakin's following a formal motion amounting to no-confidence in May 1909. So, the high commissionership finally came to be debated during the subsequent rancorous fusion session—the result of an uneasy union of political interests which had previously been divided on the free-trade/protection issue.

Introduced by Groom as 'but the logical sequence of the bringing into being of the Federal constitution', the High Commissioner Bill began its passage through parliament on 6 August 1909.[50] By mid-October, it had passed the Senate with just a minor amendment, but became mired in debate thereafter.[51] The Labor Opposition protested that the fusion government was stalling so as to avoid making an appointment while parliament was sitting.[52] Andrew Fisher of the Labor Party claimed the bill was 'being shuffled about'; '[t]he action of the Government is a mere device to palter with a great question', he fumed.[53] Despite these tactics, in early December the bill was returned to the upper house, and on the thirteenth of that month, parliament agreed to *An Act to provide for the Office of High Commissioner of the Commonwealth in the United Kingdom*.[54] The bill attracted bi-partisan support. According to Senator Edward Needham, it was 'received with paeans of praise—practically with a continuous song of triumph'.[55]

The legislation empowered the governor-general to appoint a high commissioner for a period of not more than five years, and to remove the appointee for misconduct or incapacity. According to clause 4, the high commissioner would 'act as a representative and resident agent of the Commonwealth in the United Kingdom, and in that capacity exercise such powers and perform such duties as are conferred upon and assigned to him by the Governor-General'. He would also 'carry out such instructions as he receives from the Minister respecting the commercial, financial and general interests of the Commonwealth and the States in the United Kingdom and elsewhere'. A salary of £3,000 was provided, plus a £2,000 expense account for maintaining the residence and entertaining. The bill outlined the intention that the high commissioner should, at the request of the state governments, perform for them similar functions to those of the agents-general, 'for the purpose of more economically and effectively advancing the material interest and welfare of every part of Australia'.[56]

Debates about the characteristics that constituted a suitable appointee were wide-ranging. Many argued that the eventual appointee would need to be well known in Australia and in Britain; his background and attainments would demand respect and an immediate hearing in London; he would support the Commonwealth of Australia and be able to speak authoritatively on its behalf; and, ideally, the candidate would not be a state politician.[57] Senator James Stewart argued that the occupant of the office should represent Australia in 'the very fullest and strongest fashion. He should be a typical Australian. He ought to be in sympathy with every Australian ideal. He ought to know Australia thoroughly, and what the people want'.[58] It is not surprising that a Labor senator was keen to appoint a 'typical Australian', one familiar with Australia and the demands of its people. Senator Higgs agreed that '[h]e will be Australia personified'; just as the high commission itself was later expected to be Australia materialised in London.[59]

Echoing anxieties expressed by earlier commentators in relation to the agents-general, some feared the high commissioner might succumb to the 'languorous influences of the social atmosphere' of London. Therefore, the Commonwealth wanted a man 'not likely to forget his duty to Australia'.[60] Indeed, Bruce Smith, sometime journalist and member of the House of Representatives, fretted 'for the digestion and the nerves' of the gentleman who accepted the post but recognised the office's social responsibilities.[61] Much of the dissent was raised by Labor members, concerned about unnecessary public expenditure and the indulgence of social privilege. 'I have heard honourable members in the lobbies suggest that the main duty of the High Commissioner will be to keep his mouth shut and gorge and guzzle as much as possible', Labor Party member James Catts informed the house in 1909.[62] Nor did Dr William Maloney condone the expenditure of 'a large amount of money in entertaining court officials with ridiculous titles'.[63] Profoundly mistrustful of the London social world, William Wilks, disillusioned Labor supporter and subsequent radical Free Trader, thought it might be difficult 'to find a representative who will remain an Australian after he has coquetted with the club life of London'.[64]

As if there were not sufficient contradiction in attempting to keep one's mouth shut while gorging and guzzling, these apprehensions also brought into relief the tensions between the desire to appear British, and the demand that an Australian high commissioner in London should remain 'Australia personified'. At a time when the typical Australian was an Anglo-Australian, it is revealing that an Australian allegiance was considered so tenuous that it might be lost in London. Long-entrenched loyalties to the British Empire, compared to the recent formation of the Commonwealth of Australia, go some way to explaining the uncertainty.

A lack of suitable and available candidates was sometimes raised as an explanation for the delay in the appointment. Even Wilks acknowledged 'the truth is that Australia is lamentably short of such men'.[65] These sentiments proved a strong rejection of earlier claims that 'any deputation of prominent colonists' could play the role of agent-general in London. A viable candidate would be educated, respectable, an astute man capable of associating comfortably with the British élite. Given that Australia was perceived to be short of suitable men, the press invented or recycled rumours that the first Australian high commissioner would in fact be an Englishman—with Lord Jersey or one of the former state governors mentioned as possible candidates.[66]

But if press conjecture was anything to go by, there were eligible men aplenty. Others rumoured to be in the running included Alfred Deakin, John Forrest, Malcolm McEachern, William McMillan, George Reid, Josiah Symon and Bernhard Wise.[67] A contemporary historian argued that the high commissionership came to be considered a valuable appointment, its political usefulness not diminished by the delay in filling the position.[68] Indeed, Senator Edward Millen referred obliquely to this lobbying in 1908 when he ventured to hope that the position 'which has been dangled before very many persons will be placed out of harm's way very shortly'.[69]

It took almost a decade before the appointment was made and, as outlined earlier, even the passage of the legislation itself was unusually protracted. As a result, cabinet had no time to appoint a high commissioner before parliament went into recess, and over the ensuing weeks the press speculated wildly about the identity of the new high commissioner. The *Bulletin* depicted Prime Minister Alfred Deakin considering 'the delicate question'—a list of potential candidates.[70] Reid's name was dramatically crossed out, while Joseph Cook earnestly attempted to persuade Deakin to accept the nomination himself.

Sir John Forrest's name was at the top of the extensive list, but in the end it came to a choice between just two men, Reid and Forrest.[71] For well over a year, even before his resignation as leader of the Free Trade Party in November 1908, Reid had been regarded as a likely candidate. Deakin had even mooted this possibility in his anonymous column for the *Morning Post* in Britain.[72] Reid's acceptance of a knighthood in November 1909 appeared to confirm the rumour. Ultimately, Forrest withdrew his name from contention and Reid was finally offered the high commissionership in December 1909. Sir George Reid was appointed Australia's first high commissioner on 22 January 1910.[73]

While the Sydney *Bulletin* could not condone Reid's appointment, the result of long-held hostility toward Reid and his Free Trade policies, and the Melbourne *Age* took the opportunity to vent its displeasure with Deakin's fusion government, the press was generally supportive. Indeed, the *Argus* commented that '[n]o act of the Federal Ministry has been received with such general public approval as that by which Sir George Reid was appointed the first High Commissioner for the Commonwealth'.[74] The *Sydney Morning Herald* regretted that the appointment had been deferred for almost a decade, as it had postponed 'recognition of the Australian Commonwealth as a national entity'.[75] Similarly, for the *Argus* the appointment supplied an 'outward and visible sign of Australia's nationhood', marking a 'new era in our relations with the empire, an era, as all expect, of infinite possibilities of mutual good'.[76] Exultant at Reid's departure for London, the *Herald* reminded its readers that they would shortly have 'an official voice at the heart of the empire—an official voice, we may say, in the world'.[77]

Conclusion

Captain Collins laid a solid foundation for Reid's subsequent appointment and the establishment of the Australian High Commission in London. Yet Collins's anomalous status constituted a rather curious beginning to the Commonwealth agency, indicative of the speculation, promises, postponements and temporary solutions which distinguished this period.

In the early years of the century, Australians found themselves negotiating a threefold allegiance to state, nation and empire. The resulting confusions in identity were played out in debates concerning the appropriate characteristics of the agents-general and the proposed high commissioner, their respective duties, and whether or not these representations should be maintained in tandem. On the whole, the state governments were loath to abolish their agencies, or abrogate any power or responsibility to the federal government. The result was an uneasy situation, where the states continued to maintain independent representation in Britain alongside, and sometimes acting against, federal representation. The agencies were criticised in the Australian press for a fractious provincialism, their representation portrayed as ineffectual and lacking authority.

This disappointment reflects not so much a diminution in the quality of the work of the agents-general as the changing demands made by Commonwealth parliamentarians and the press. This dissatisfaction is suggestive of the altered expectations that resulted from Australia's own repositioning within the empire. Significantly, the agents-general were condemned for adopting a more diplomatic role, yet this was to be an important brief for the new high commissioner.

3 The first high commissioners: George Reid and Andrew Fisher

Neville Meaney

ORNA LLOYD titled her book on the high commissioners 'diplomacy with a difference', and during the foundation years when George Houston Reid and Andrew Fisher came to occupy the position in London, this difference was most pronounced.[1] Its source lay in the fact that the office of high commissioner was intended to be a kind of diplomatic post arising out of the unique relationship of the self-governing dominions to Britain. Billy Hughes, the deputy leader of the Labor Party, unwittingly put his finger on the anomalous quality of the dominion high commissioner at that time when, in addressing the 1909 High Commissioner Bill, he said: 'I take it his [the high commissioner's] duties would be to represent Australia diplomatically. He would, in some respects, be an ambassador, residing not in a foreign country, but in a friendly one—in his own country as it were'.[2] One can see him, as he is speaking, wrestling with this problem and adding point to point as he tries to make sense of the high commissioner's ambiguous status. He would be like an ambassador, but unlike ambassadors he was not being appointed to a 'foreign' but a 'friendly' country. But 'friendly' was still not a good enough distinction, for foreign countries could also be friendly. No, the high commissioner was being appointed to 'his own country'. But this too needed to be qualified in order to justify appointing such a representative at all; and so it was 'his own country' only 'as it were'. That is, in some sense Britain was also *not* his own country. It was a conundrum, a symbolic expression of the tension between the dominion as a cultural community of identity and as a political community of interest.

The result was that the dominion high commissioners in London in this early period were in principle both less and more than a foreign envoy. On the one hand, they did not have the formal status of a representative of an internationally recognised sovereign state, nor were they members of the diplomatic corps with a right to take the business of their governments directly to the Foreign Office. But on the other, while foreign envoys in London might from time to time for expedient reasons have close relations with the British government, the dominion high commissioners had a permanent intimate connection to the government which made them more than ambassadors. The dominions were self-governing states within an imperial state. They were effectively autonomous political communities with their own distinct interests, but they were also

British communities that identified culturally with the mother country and therefore saw Britain as their 'own country as it were' in facing out to the wider world. Thus they expected that the British government would be sensitive to their distinctive concerns and would consult the dominions when making imperial policy, especially where it touched those concerns. Like ambassadors, the high commissioners could, on instructions from their governments, make representations to the British government, even if they made them generally through the Colonial Office. But, unlike foreign envoys, when frustrated they could take their case to the British public and expect a sympathetic hearing. The British government, when unhappy with a dominion's behaviour, could not as with dependent colonies impose its will on the recalcitrant dominion, or as with foreign countries break off diplomatic relations or send its representative packing. As Hughes's musings on the matter revealed, the dominion high commissioners, as representatives of effectively sovereign communities in a sovereign empire, were an odd phenomenon in the world of diplomacy.

Reid and Fisher were the pioneer Australian high commissioners, the first two representatives of the Commonwealth government in Britain, and they held this office during a decade in which there were serious conflicts of interest in Anglo-Australian relations and a world war that tested the bonds of empire. They were alike in being both Scottish Australians and former prime ministers who had played a significant part in establishing the foundations of the new federation. But as a result of their early upbringing, the part they had played in political life, the ideas they had developed about empire and nation, and their very different personalities and circumstances, they each gave to the office a distinct definition.

Pacific policy and the origins of Australian diplomacy

As Olwen Pryke showed in chapter 2 of this volume, after the grant of self-government the Australian colonies began to send representatives, called agents-general, to look after their affairs in the United Kingdom. By the 1870s, when European powers such as France and Germany began to extend their imperial tentacles into the Pacific, the role of the agents-general expanded as the colonial authorities encouraged them to take on more of a diplomatic role and to act as unofficial ambassadors to the British government in giving effect to their policies, especially in the South Pacific. In early 1883 after the premier of Queensland, endeavouring to pre-empt Germany, had sent an expedition to lay claim to West New Guinea, he instructed his agent-general in London to urge the British formally to annex the territory. When these importunities fell on deaf ears, the colonial leaders meeting in Sydney adopted a resolution aimed at excluding foreign powers from acquiring further territories in the South Pacific. And from time to time they employed their agents-general to press the British, and even on one occasion the French, in defence of this principle.

So, when the French took an interest in the New Hebrides (Vanuatu), the colonies instructed their agents-general in London to urge the colonial secretary and the foreign secretary to acquire the islands for the British Empire. As Joy Melleuish has concluded, the Australian and New Zealand representatives in London were 'very active between 1884 and 1886 in urging on the Imperial Government their view on ... the annexation issues'. These colonial agents even had direct, if informal, discussions with Félix Faure, the French under-secretary of state for colonial affairs.[3] Indeed, the London correspondent for the *Sydney Morning Herald* in August 1886 wrote a sensationalist article maintaining that after the Victorian agent-general, Sir Graham Berry, had had a fruitless interview over the New Hebrides with the colonial secretary, he had told Lord Stanhope, perhaps half in jest, that 'if France was allowed to permanently retain her position in the New Hebrides Group, it was almost certain that the Victorian government would break off diplomatic relations with this country', meaning Great Britain.[4] At the end of this diplomatic round, in which the agents-general played no small part, the colonies obtained a promise from the Colonial Office that it would not accept any French proposal without first consulting the Australasian colonies.[5] This was the high point in agents-general diplomacy.

The movement that was to bring about federation followed hard on the heels of these rather heated exchanges over New Guinea and the New Hebrides, and it was widely recognised that the Commonwealth would have to take over responsibility for defence and Pacific policy as well as trade, finance and immigration. Alfred Deakin, the Victorian politician, pointed out at the Australasian Federal Conference of 1890 that the Commonwealth would need, following the Canadian example, to have a high commissioner in London not only to look after Australia's Pacific island ambitions but also to make the British aware of Australian concerns about 'coloured' immigration and the looming power of China.[6] The authors of the Constitution specifically allocated power over 'External Affairs' to the Commonwealth, and Quick and Garran in their authoritative commentary noted that this was intended to give the federal government authority to appoint a high commissioner in London who would, while not necessarily making the states' agents-general redundant, take over many of their most important functions, such as those relating to defence and foreign relations, and also possibly trade, finance and immigration—the powers which were shared with the states.[7]

For reasons explained in Olwen Pryke's chapter, the office of high commissioner was not created during the early years of the new federation. But after the Japanese victory over Russia in 1905 and the withdrawal of British capital ships from the Pacific to meet the German challenge in the North Sea, successive Australian governments had become anxious that Japan might use its dominance in the western Pacific to press for commercial and immigration concessions and even to invade their island continent. As a result, Australia and Britain both became focused on issues of defence and foreign policy. In early 1909 Britain, fearing that as the result of Germany's new naval building program it would lose its safety margin of superiority in the most advanced battle cruisers, had appealed to the dominions to help by contributing to the cost of additional 'dreadnoughts'.[8] Likewise, the Australians had expressed their unease about being left to fend for themselves in the Pacific. In part to meet this concern, the Admiralty in August of the same year proposed at an Imperial Defence Conference the formation of a Pacific fleet made up of British and dominion squadrons. All of these developments caused the Australians to seek to obtain greater influence in the making of imperial defence and foreign policy. Indeed, while the High Commissioner Bill was proceeding through parliament, Deakin as prime minister sent to the British government 'A Proposal of the Highest Importance', which was intended to create a Pacific Pact for the purpose of containing Japan and extending the American Monroe Doctrine to the Pacific.[9]

In the debate over the bill, both the prime minister and the leader of the Labor Opposition, Andrew Fisher, linked the need for urgent action to these recent imperial problems. Deakin remarked of the appointment of a high commissioner that 'it would have been of the greatest advantage … to have had his services during the last year or two'. Fisher, who had been prime minister during the dreadnought affair, echoed these sentiments. He had suffered from not having an Australian representative in London; Captain Robert Muirhead Collins, who had been sent to London to represent Australia in defence matters but came to play a broader range of roles (see pages 30–1), did 'not occupy the standing which the direct representative of the Commonwealth should have at the centre of the Empire'.[10] Fisher promised that Labor would assist the government in hastening the bill through both houses.

There was general agreement that the appointment was important and a matter of great urgency. The minister for external affairs, Littleton Groom, in speaking to the bill, declared that the high commissioner's duties would be 'in the first place, to represent Australia diplomatically'. Deakin added that he would be 'clothed with full power and authority to speak, subject to the direction of this Parliament and the Government on any question of interest to Australia'. Billy Hughes, deputy leader of the Opposition, required an ambassador-like figure to watch over Australia's own distinctive concerns and agreed with Deakin that such a person would 'have to be able to enter into relations with the leading public men in London' and consequently that the high commissioner 'would have to be endowed with social attainments … a man who could shine [at] after-dinner speaking'.[11]

George Houston Reid

In filling the new post Deakin had little choice. Reid's claims were irresistible. Born in Scotland in 1845, the son of a Presbyterian minister, he had migrated with his family to Australia when nine years of age. After taking up a very successful and remunerative career as a barrister, he entered politics as a pragmatic liberal and had by the end of the century become premier of New South Wales. Following federation he had, as leader of the Free Trade Party, a short term as prime minister. In 1908, with his liberal beliefs on trade, defence and empire losing favour, he resigned the leadership of his party in order to facilitate the union of the Free Traders and Protectionists in an anti-Labor alliance. He was by far the most highly qualified candidate for the position of high commissioner. In addition to his long and distinguished career in public life, he had in full measure the post-prandial qualities which Hughes had described. He had an imposing head and girth and was at ease with all classes and conditions of men. During the 1897 Imperial Conference, in which he represented New South Wales, he had no difficulty in mixing with British ministers and making himself at home in London society. He was a witty and fluent, if rather facile, speaker who adapted both his language and his message to his audiences. Reid exuded a genial bonhomie and was eminently clubbable. And so, he was very quickly knighted and appointed to the post for a five-year term.

Arriving in England in early 1910, Reid saw as his first and most important task publicising Australia's potential as a destination for migrants, a good prospect for investors, and a source of primary products and minerals for the British and European markets. What was required, the inspired national spruiker told Littleton Groom, was 'Publicity–Publicity–Publicity'. It was 'the beginning and end of Australia's need in every part of the world'.[12] He knew that Australia was competing with Canada and so sought the cooperation of the states' agents-general and a liberal funding for the purpose. As a result of his importuning, expenditure on advertising rose from £8,644 in 1908–09 to £40,546 in 1913–14, and a small Publicity Department composed of Australian journalists and advertising experts was set up in the high commission. They had good contacts in the media and the imagination to try new ways of spreading the message, along with the enthusiasm to carry out an ambitious program.

Apart from making the British public more aware of Australia, these publicists' main aim was to attract migrants, especially from the countryside, who would settle the land, and to make merchants more familiar with Australian exports. For this purpose they inserted news articles and advertisements in newspapers, and distributed pamphlets, leaflets and maps widely. They also placed attractive photographs in railway carriages and put up posters and billboards on railway stations with inviting slogans such as 'Empire Land of Promise', 'Golden Australia' and 'Land of Sunshine and Success'. The Department of External Affairs even commissioned films depicting a wide range of urban and rural life under titles such as 'Glorious Adelaide', 'Marvellous Melbourne' and 'Dairying on the Darling Downs'. These films were quite popular and the Publicity Department made them available for showing at cinemas around England and Scotland. To make Australian products better known, they also did their best to ensure that samples of Australian exports were put on display at exhibitions and agricultural and cattle fairs. Reid, moreover, wanted to reach out to the European continent, and on his initiative small agencies were based in Paris, Berlin, Vienna and Geneva, and he had plans for doing something similar in North America. While keeping an oversight of the business of the high commission, he took little pleasure in detailed administration. The Publicity

Department undertook the organisation of the advertising campaign and the general management of the office was for the most part left in the hands of Collins, who had become the official secretary.

Reid made a favourable impression on London and more generally the country. His major contribution to the publicity campaign was travelling, speechmaking and networking among the great and influential figures of the day. He was a very popular performer on lecture tours and at lunches and dinners. Reid had a natural penchant for this kind of work and was a great social success. In addressing his varied audiences, his jokes, sometimes made at his own expense, would disarm those suspicious of dominion boosters and boasters, and by uniting appeals for support for Australian products with panegyrics in praise of the British Empire, he would be given a good hearing and accepted as a loyal imperialist. At Birmingham University in November 1910, he gave a glowing picture of Australia and its economic development, including its pastoral and mining resources and its wheat and frozen meat trade, and ended with an uplifting affirmation of British race solidarity: 'Although our race is spreading and striving over the face of the whole world, we always manage to stand shoulder to shoulder in the defence of our Race and Empire'.[13] His social standing in Britain was reflected in the number of invitations he received to join social clubs, most notably the Athenaeum, and to spend weekends at the country houses of the aristocracy. Whether his promotion of immigration and trade achieved its goal is, however, a moot point. In the first three years immigration did increase significantly, but the value of Australia's annual exports to Britain, after the first year, showed little improvement.

Reid travelled to the European continent and North America with ostensibly the same commercial, if not immigration, objective in mind and he managed to meet and establish a rapport with many foreign dignitaries. The German consul-general in London, who seemed interested in the possibilities of Germany importing Australia's frozen meat, escorted Reid on a trip to Berlin where he was welcomed by the under-secretary of state for foreign affairs and addressed the Berlin Chamber of Commerce in the Reichstag building on Australian trade.[14] He had an audience with Kaiser Wilhelm II, was received by the emperor of Austria, met the presidents of France and the United States, and entertained President Taft's predecessor, Theodore Roosevelt, in London. It does not seem likely that Reid's travels in foreign parts had any more effect on increasing trade with these foreign countries than had his campaign in Britain.

Reid had a quasi-ambassadorial status. On arriving in London he first had an audience with King Edward VII and then paid courtesy calls on the other dominion high commissioners and the ambassadors of the most important powers, including China and Japan. In the latter case he took some trouble to explain to Baron Kato that Australia's restrictive immigration laws were not intended to offend the Japanese, telling him that Australia was 'a small community, and felt, almost as Japan herself had always felt, a fear of losing our racial integrity, to which we, like all the peoples of the East … attached supreme importance'.[15] The British government was willing to give Reid privileged seating at important public ceremonies akin to that accorded to an ambassador, but would not grant the high commissioner a formal status equivalent to one. The Colonial Office, wishing to stress the dependent position of high commissioners, insisted that the proper channel for Whitehall's communications with the dominions should continue to be through the governors or governors-general. These were the official limits within which the British hoped to confine this new development in Anglo-Australian relations.

While the authors of the High Commissioner Act might have regarded diplomacy as the chief function of the Australian representative in London, there is no evidence that Reid was ever consulted about the major defence and foreign policy issues troubling Anglo-Australian relations or that he considered it his task to inform Melbourne about British views on these matters. There were a number of very specific diplomatic questions which were dealt with through the high commission. For example, the Admiralty had used the high commission to ask the Australian government at the time of the Agadir crisis to allow the Australian light cruiser *Melbourne*, which was being constructed in a British shipyard, to be used in the Mediterranean should war break out. The Australians, likewise, had gone through the high commission when requesting the Admiralty to consider sending out the battle cruiser *Commonwealth*, which could, after the success of the visit of America's Great White Fleet, go some way to restoring the Royal Navy's prestige in the Pacific.[16] But the high commissioner played no part in the substantive diplomacy between Melbourne and London.

For the whole period of Reid's high commissionership, Australian governments were preoccupied with achieving security against Japan in the Pacific and this led to disputes with the British government. On the eve of the departure of Prime Minister Fisher and his defence and external affairs ministers to London for the 1911 Imperial Conference, Deakin, then leader of the Opposition, offered them the fruits of his experience in dealing with the imperial authorities. The rebuff to his Pacific Pact proposal had capped a long history of British indifference to Australia's concerns. He said he hoped the Australian representatives at the conference would not forget to impress upon the British that 'Australia, in spite of herself, is being forced into a foreign policy of her own because foreign interests and risks surround us on every side'. And he concluded, 'A Pacific policy we must have'.[17]

Though Fisher was expecting great things from this conference, he did not seek any briefs from Reid about British preparations and attitudes, nor did Reid volunteer such assistance. Impressed at the conference by the willingness of the British ministers to take the dominions into their confidence, in particular to consult them on the renewal of the Anglo-Japanese alliance, Fisher urged them to give the dominions a say in the making of imperial policy. For him the conference had opened a new chapter in Anglo-Australian relations. In an interview with the *Morning Post* he waxed lyrical about what this meant. As a result of the conference:

> A community of interest of the highest immediate importance and vast possibilities has
> been formed … Hitherto the conferences have been consultative and advisory gatherings,
> and the British government has remained the sole consultative authority; today the
> Dominions are part of the Empire in all things, and no development however sudden
> should now be beyond our understanding.[18]

Fisher had expressed interest in a proposal for a standing advisory committee composed
of dominion high commissioners or resident ministers who, sitting in London, would act
for their governments between conferences. But since the Canadians thought that such
a formal body, even if consultative, might imply commitment and others felt such an
arrangement would derogate from the status of the conference, the idea was dropped.[19]
Though Reid saw much of Fisher during his visit to London and accompanied him on a
visit to his birthplace at Crosshouse in Ayrshire, it is not known whether Fisher discussed
these matters with the high commissioner. If he did, there is no evidence that it affected
the way Reid performed his role.

Australian optimism about a new consultative empire sharing in the making of a
common defence and foreign policy did not last. To meet a new German and Austro-
Hungarian battleship building program, the first lord of the Admiralty, Winston Churchill,
without a word to the Australians, scrapped plans for contributing two *Dreadnought* battle
cruisers to the combined Pacific Fleet, appropriated the New Zealand *Dreadnought* which
had been intended for the same fleet, and induced the Canadians to contribute to a new
squadron of the Royal Navy to be stationed at Gibraltar. For the Australian government
this was the 'greatest blow yet dealt to Imperial co-operation'. Fisher and then the Liberal
Party leader, Joseph Cook, Fisher's successor as prime minister, pressed the British to hold
a conference to seek a new agreement on imperial defence cooperation in the Pacific.[20]
The high commission had not given the Australian government any advance warning of
Britain's abandonment of the Pacific Fleet plan upon which the Australians had placed
their hopes for security. The Australian ministers learned about this betrayal from the
British and Australian press.

Reid did not have much sympathy for the Deakin–Fisher view of Greater Britain.
He was an heir to a liberal triumphalist vision of the British Empire in which Australia
had its self-governing but dependent position. In his speeches eulogising Britain and
the empire, he told the story of progress towards freedom. Though the empire had
been born out of violence and tyranny, yet with the democratising of parliament, the
abolition of protectionism, the grant of self-government to the British-settled dominions,
and the extension of justice and civilisation to the colonies of Asia and Africa, it had
been transformed during the later years of Queen Victoria's reign into the greatest
empire the world had ever seen. The empire's navy could be relied on to safeguard all
its peoples and possessions and give peace and order to the wider world. The freedom
granted the self-governing dominions and the loyalty that came from belonging to a
common race and sharing a common culture was a much stronger basis for union than

any scheme for political integration which, Reid claimed, 'some Dominion statesmen mean when they speak of "having a voice in the counsel of the Empire"'. In addressing the Royal Colonial Institute in March 1913, he took issue with the Round Table movement and pointed out what he conceived to be the impracticality, if not indeed danger, of imperial federation.[21]

By this time, because the Australian protests about the British failure to honour their commitment to a Pacific Fleet had become public knowledge, Reid could not ignore the topic altogether and in the same speech he slipped into his orthodox praise of the empire some commendation of Australian defence policy. Australians, he said, valued their liberty and were willing to pay a heavy price for their defence and 'the Empire's too, if need be', and he mentioned Australia's compulsory military training and fledgling navy. Britain could no longer afford to maintain a fleet which could give security for all parts of the empire, and thus Canada should help with the patrolling of the North Pacific and Australia and New Zealand assume responsibility for the South Pacific. While confessing that he was no expert on naval strategy, he suggested that 'you can never reduce this great Empire to the condition of having all its big ships in one or even in two narrow seas'.[22] This was the closest he came to giving some support to his government's position.

During his visit to Australia in late 1913 and early 1914, Reid gave many talks and lectures around the country on the grandeur of the empire on which the sun never set. Though he alluded to Anglo-Australian differences over defence, the main object of these speeches was to make the parochial Australians appreciate the debt they owed the mother country for safeguarding their trade and territory. Returning to London, he confided to the colonial secretary that while in Australia he had taken as his task, 'to impress on the public mind of the Commonwealth a more powerful impression of the greatness of the Empire, and of other nations, and a more avid sense of all that they owe out there to the power and protection and the generous spirit of imperial statesmanship'.[23] Reid was not the sort of high commissioner whom the Australian ministers could rely on to press their grievances over Pacific naval defence in Whitehall.

Just a few months after Reid's return to Britain, the empire was at war with Germany and its allies. The outbreak of hostilities put an end to the campaign to attract migrants, find new markets and encourage investment. The resources of the high commission were turned over to helping Australians in London, especially sick and wounded soldiers. Reid's only interventions with the British authorities were for the purpose of ensuring that the first Australian Imperial Force contingent undertook its final training in Egypt rather than on the dreary Salisbury Plains, and of persuading Britain to repay Australia's loyalty by giving preference to its exports such as frozen meats and metals.[24] There were no more overseas trips, except briefly to British General Headquarters in France and a leisurely trip to Egypt to address the Australian Imperial Force, which was encamped just outside Cairo and training in preparation for active service. In the latter case, after greeting the soldiers with 'You Australians are the b——y limit'[25] and then exhorting them to have 'hearts of solid oak, nerves of flawless steel', he recorded in his autobiography that he 'had the honour of an audience with the new Sultan' and had taken a luxury government boat trip down the Nile to see Luxor.[26] During the first year of the war he was not asked to make inquiries about Britain's attitude to Japan and Japan's intentions about the future of the German North Pacific islands, and he did not of his own volition offer any comments on what had become Australia's major strategic preoccupation. Reid sat on many committees and attended many conferences on war questions, but he later admitted that he was 'never really behind the scenes'.[27]

The problem which exercised Reid most keenly throughout 1915 was whether the Fisher government would allow him a further term as high commissioner. He claimed that while he was in Australia, the minister for external affairs in the Cook Liberal administration had agreed orally to such an extension. Fisher denied that such an agreement existed and informed Reid that he would be given a further year in office and then replaced.[28] The Labor prime minister explained to parliament that 'no-one who has been living out of Australia for five years can be thoroughly in touch with and properly and effectively represent it'.[29] In January 1916 Reid, after protesting his treatment at the hands of the Fisher government, retired from the office and was almost immediately offered a safe Conservative seat in the House of Commons. He campaigned as an 'independent Imperialist' and was elected unopposed. He died in London on 13 September 1918 of cerebral thrombosis.

Andrew Fisher

Reid's successor in the London post had a very different early life from his fellow Presbyterian Scot. Born in Crosshouse, Ayrshire in 1862, the son of a coalminer, Andrew Fisher had at a very early age, probably under the legal age, followed his father down the pits and into the miners' union. Seeing no prospects for advancement in Scotland he migrated to Queensland in 1885 and after settling in Gympie became the president of the local branch of the Australian Miners' Association. He supported federation and in 1907 was elected leader of the Parliamentary Labor Party. Three years later he won a clear majority in both houses and presided over a reform-minded administration. Shortly after the outbreak of the European war he had an even more substantial victory at the polls. Fisher was prime minister for the greater part of Reid's term as high commissioner.

Fisher did not look forward to taking up the reins of government in wartime. He was a pragmatic utopian socialist inspired by the poetry of Robbie Burns, the bard of Ayrshire. He owned a number of copies of Burns's works, and throughout them verse expressing Burns's vision of the equality of all people, such as 'Man to Man the world o'er shall brithers be', was underlined. He was repelled by the brutality and carnage of war. He could only reconcile himself to accepting the leadership of the country with the thought that 'just as poets had dreamed of it he believed that in the future they would see developed a mighty power (a spiritual power) for organisation and law wherein there would be an international creed for the welfare of the people of the earth'.[30]

In the midst of the federal election, Fisher's first reaction to the prospect of Britain being drawn into the war was to promise that Australia would give 'its last man and last shilling' to help the mother country. Yet, a few days later when the empire's involvement seemed certain, he set out the doctrine he had been developing since the *Dreadnought* affair, namely that his idea of patriotism was 'to first provide for our own defence and if there was anything to spare to offer it as a tribute to the Mother Country'.[31]

As the pressures of the war began to tell, Fisher found himself faced by complex and bewildering problems arising out of these two responses. Japan, on entering the war on Britain's side, seized the German North Pacific islands and so brought Australia's putative enemy to its equatorial frontier. Recognising that Japan might, if it suited its purpose, switch sides in the global conflict, Fisher requested the British government to summon an Imperial Conference to discuss Pacific naval defence and peace terms. When the Colonial Office rejected the proposal, Fisher outwardly acquiesced for the greater good of the empire but inwardly seethed. As evidence mounted to show that Japan intended to take advantage of the European conflict, he began to express his frustration and to urge that such a conference should be held without delay.[32]

British war policy was also suspect. The Allied assault on Gallipoli, in which the first contingent of the Australian Imperial Force was involved, cost many Australian lives without achieving any progress. Fisher was so concerned that he commissioned a parliamentary journalist, Keith Murdoch, to visit the troops and report on their welfare. At the end of the year just before the British government evacuated the peninsula and gave up the attempt to force the Dardanelles, Fisher received a damning letter from Murdoch which lambasted both the original strategy and its execution. At the same time in Britain the press was demanding an inquiry into this humiliating reversal and the exposure of those responsible. Fisher was not happy that the Australian troops should have suffered from such poor leadership.[33]

When it became clear that the European war was not going to be won easily or quickly, Fisher was faced with growing agitation to bring in conscription for overseas service. Even though voluntary recruits had enlisted in great numbers, a Universal Service League, backed in New South Wales by a wide range of community leaders, issued a manifesto calling on Australia to adopt the principle of compulsion in order to give maximum aid to the mother country. Fisher was greatly troubled. He did not think that conscription was warranted and understood the divisive potential of such a proposal. This controversy added further to the wartime pressures which taxed his physical and mental resources. By the end of the first year since taking office, Fisher was in a 'high state of nervous tension aggravated by a chill, which he was unable to throw off', and on 26 October he resigned the premiership and took up the position of high commissioner in London.[34]

Fisher, still thinking of himself in some ways as prime minister, brought this baggage with him to London. The press welcomed him very enthusiastically as the leader of a dominion which had offered the mother country 'the last man and the last shilling' and had sent the Australian Imperial Force to accomplish such heroic feats at Gallipoli. In his early interviews and speeches he seemed to confirm this image and gave the loyal imperial answers. He repeated his promise of aid and illustrated it by telling his listeners: 'We have sent you 200,000 men and we are preparing to send you 100,000 more'. But the earlier assurance was now qualified in every restatement by 'if need be'. Moreover, speaking just after Asquith's Coalition government had brought in conscription of single men, he asserted that Australia's further assistance would be under the voluntary system. As he put it, 'there has never been any question of conscription'. Under Australian defence policy, he added, conscription was only for home defence, and Australians could only serve overseas with their consent.[35]

Similarly, addressing the question of consultation, notably on Pacific defence and the Dardanelles military fiasco, he gave at first the loyal answer and assured the British: 'We are not going to criticise. The Imperial Government is in charge'. But Fisher did wish to criticise, and this was made evident when a *Times* reporter pushed him to be more frank and he revealed how frustrated he had felt when the British government had failed to consult him about imperial policy affecting Australian interests. 'If I stayed in Scotland,' he said,

> I should have been able to heckle my member on questions of Imperial policy and vote for
> or against him on that ground. I went to Australia. I have been Prime Minister. But all the
> time I have had no say whatever. Now that can't go on. There must be some change.[36]

A little later he was even blunter in expressing his resentment about the treatment he had received from the British authorities, asserting that he had 'not come to London to be invited to the counsels. I intend to walk in'.[37] But Fisher was not going to be able to walk in. As he recounted to his former close colleague and minister for defence, George Pearce: 'I have had a skirmish here and there since I took up duty. The old boys are unchanged by war conditions. Some of them are unchangeable'.[38]

Though Fisher had described the post of high commissioner as a 'sort of ambassadorship', he was never able to play this role.[39] Unlike Reid he did not mix easily with the British government élite. He was not made for the niceties of diplomacy. He never sought a knighthood and would not have accepted one even if it had been offered. He declined an honorary degree at Oxford and a French *Légion d'honneur*. He disliked court dress and the other accoutrements of the privileged world of high society. Unlike Reid, he did not enjoy the lecture circuit or clubland. His speeches were often awkwardly expressed and sometimes almost querulous, and this did little to help give him easy access to British officials.

It was, however, Hughes, Fisher's successor as prime minister, who did the most to prevent him from taking part in the processes of making high policy. Hughes was in

London or in Paris—which amounted to the same thing—for nearly a third of Fisher's term as high commissioner. Arriving in England hard on his former leader's heels, Hughes made a great impact on both the British leaders and the British public. While at this time their personal relations would seem to have been quite amicable as they took trips together to Scotland and the Western Front, the dynamic Hughes still made it plain that Fisher would not represent him in his dealing with the British government and he excluded his high commissioner from all his discussions with British officials. Above all else, he was unwilling to confide in Fisher because he was determined to keep all power in his own hands and so escape the scrutiny of his predecessor under whom he had served and who had so often in the past curbed his impulsive actions. Moreover, Hughes knew at the time of this first visit that Fisher disagreed with him over the proposed treatment of Germany in the peacemaking. Whereas Hughes saw war as a continuing struggle between nations for survival and supremacy and called for the British to take revenge on Germany, Fisher held the Kaiser and the militarists alone responsible for the war and wished to have the German people join with the Allies at the end of the war in an international union for a permanent peace. Hughes might well have seen Fisher as leaning towards those he despised as 'Babble[rs] of peace and the Brotherhood of man'.[40] So, after returning to Australia, Hughes turned to Keith Murdoch, who had ingratiated himself with British ministers and press magnates, to act as his agent in dealing with the imperial government on matters of high policy. As a result Fisher had to content himself almost totally with the formal and administrative functions of his office.

The only exception, and that an indirect one, was his membership of the Dardanelles Commission, which the British prime minister established in mid-1916 to investigate that strategic blunder. As a gesture to the part played by the dominions in the assault on the Gallipoli peninsula, the Australian and New Zealand high commissioners were made members of this body. The Australian cabinet would only allow him to accept the invitation on the understanding that he sat as an individual and not a representative of the government. He attended less than half the commission's meetings, but when he did he asked searching questions. He also did his best to protect Murdoch from being attacked for his criticism of the British plan and its execution. In the end Fisher did not quarrel with the commission's conclusions, but he did submit a minority report which took issue with the logic of its method of setting out the conclusions and its claim that senior naval officers who might have differed from their minister should have been willing to give evidence. The latter, he believed, undermined the principle of responsible government that required ministers to be accountable to parliament and people for the conduct of their departments. He held that officials should only speak about internal departmental arguments and advice with the permission of their minister.[41]

After the British introduced full conscription in May, Hughes determined that Australia should follow the mother country's example, and this produced a decided coolness in the relationship between the prime minister and the high commissioner.

While not necessarily opposed in principle to conscription for the defence of the empire, Fisher knew from his own experience that any attempt to impose it would divide the Labor Party and the country. He was the only former prime minister who refused to sign an appeal to the people to vote 'yes' in the referendum on the subject. In the end his judgment was vindicated. Though conscription was defeated, albeit by a narrow margin, the campaign left a legacy of bitter recrimination and personal antagonism. A number of Fisher's former colleagues from both sides of the question wrote to him suggesting that if he had remained their leader, he would have prevented the great disaster which had befallen the party and the country.[42] For many reasons, not least of which was Fisher's stance on conscription, Hughes rejected every suggestion that Fisher, in the enforced absence of the prime minister, should represent Australia at the 1917 Imperial War Cabinet and Imperial War Conference.

Although restricted to a narrow administrative role, Fisher in his first years in office set himself to the task and did much to advance Australian interests. He hastened on the completion of Australia House. By 1917 he and his staff were able to move into this grand stone edifice, which stood on the Strand as a symbol of the permanence of the British Empire and Australia's proud place in it. As the numbers of the Australian Imperial Force in England, France and Palestine grew, the work of the high commission expanded greatly. It had to deal with such matters as the payment of pensions to servicemen and their dependants and export controls of war materials. By the end of the war, the high commission was directly responsible for more than 200 employees, many of them incapacitated servicemen who were unable to return to the front line.

Fisher took a special interest in the welfare of the Australian soldiers and in making sure that their military deeds would be properly recognised and recorded. He spent much time visiting troops, especially those who were sick and wounded and in hospital. He complained to the military authorities about excessively harsh punishments, visited the troops in France, and even travelled to neutral Switzerland to inspect the conditions of the Australian prisoners of war who had escaped from Germany and were being held in internment camps. Social activities and entertainments for the troops were organised and he made the basement of Australia House into a social club for soldiers on leave in London. He was assiduous in seeing that Australian servicemen's valour and achievements were properly publicised. On 25 April 1916, the anniversary of the landing of the Australian and New Zealand troops on Gallipoli, and on all subsequent Anzac Days during his term of office, he took trouble to ensure that the occasion was properly celebrated. A service attended by King George and Queen Mary was held in Westminster Abbey, Australian units marched through thronged streets, and afterwards diverse entertainments were organised for the troops. On his initiative a War Records Section was also established. An official photographer was appointed and sent to Belgium and France to take pictures of the Australian Imperial Force. Artists were commissioned to go to the Western Front and Palestine to make paintings and sketches of the Australian military forces. Captured enemy armaments and other war memorabilia were collected. All of these mementoes were intended to form the basis for a permanent war museum.[43] The results of this comprehensive program now form an important part of the Australian War Memorial's holdings.

The deterioration of Fisher's physical and mental health, which had caused him to resign as prime minister, continued in London and he was forced to rest for ever longer periods at home. He restricted his public speaking to ceremonial occasions, such as the formal opening of Australia House in August 1918, and then only spoke briefly. His condition gave Hughes a further reason for not inviting him to participate in any way in the Imperial War Cabinet and conference meetings of that year or the Paris Peace Conference of 1919. After Hughes's return home, Fisher was authorised to sign the peace treaties with Bulgaria and Turkey on behalf of the Australian government, but that was all. He was aware that he was no longer able to perform his duties as he would have wished. His absence from Australia House was noted and he was subject to attacks in the Australian press and parliament.

As the end of his term as high commissioner approached, rumours began to circulate that he might seek to re-enter politics and help to resuscitate the anti-conscription Labor Party. It was even suggested that he might stand for a Labour constituency in Scotland and thus follow Reid into the House of Commons.[44] It is not known whether Fisher was the source of these speculations or if he gave them any encouragement. While he seemed at some points willing to play with such possibilities, at bottom he knew that he was no longer fit to undertake these tasks. In replying to a letter from an old colleague urging him to consider taking up again the Labor Party's cause, he admitted that he was 'more run down in health when I left the C[ommon]wealth than my friends knew and it would be folly to try to tour for some years to come'.[45] Fisher, after his term as high commissioner had expired, returned to Australia for a brief visit and, though flattered by the many appeals to stay and help restore the Labor Party to its former glory, he rejected these overtures and sailed back to Britain where he died in 1928.

Conclusion

It is clear that the ambitions of those who had been instrumental in establishing the high commission in London were not fulfilled during the tenure in that office of Reid and Fisher. The founders' aim that the high commissioners would have essentially a diplomatic role was not achieved. Successive Australian governments were not willing to employ them as their representatives in handling negotiations with the British government on high policy matters, or to treat them as sources of information and advice in dealing with Whitehall. Indeed, when Fisher had been in London at the 1911 Imperial Conference he, as far as we know, did not consult Reid on any of the important questions being discussed at its meetings. Likewise Hughes, when he succeeded Fisher as prime minister and was in London and Paris in 1916, 1918 and 1919, did not consult his erstwhile leader on any of the major problems of war and peace which were debated at the imperial cabinet and the peace conference. It may be that in negating the original purpose of the office, Fisher, Cook and Hughes believed their respective high commissioners were out of sympathy with their policies and therefore untrustworthy. More probably it was simply that the prime ministers were jealous about maintaining complete control over the relationship with the imperial government and so preferred to handle the great issues of state by communicating with London either through the governor-general or through private discussions with British ministers when they visited the United Kingdom. At no stage did any of the three prime ministers show a disposition to look upon the high commissioner as a 'diplomat' who could properly serve the Australian government in its dealings at the highest level with its British counterpart.

Cartoon from the *Bulletin,* 11 November 1909.

THE DELICATE QUESTION
"Now, dear Alfred, will you let me put YOUR name in the hat and make the draw myself?"
(Joseph Cook is standing and Alfred Deakin seated.)

Sir George Reid, 1909. [State Library of South Australia Image Number PRG 280/1/3/203]

Photo of Australia House construction site, c. 1910 [Australian High Commission, London, Department of Foreign Affairs and Trade]

Sir George Reid (left) addresses King George V and Queen Mary (centre) in the pavilion at the laying of the foundation stone of Australia House, 24 July 1913. [Australian High Commission, London, Department of Foreign Affairs and Trade]

Sir George Reid addressing the 1st Australian Division, Ammunition Column, c. 1915. [Australian War Memorial Negative Number H18821]

King George V (centre) shaking hands with Andrew Fisher on arrival at the main entrance to the Australian Imperial Force and War Chest Club. With Queen Mary, the King had come to inspect Australian troops newly arrived on leave from the trenches in France, October 1917. [Australian War Memorial Negative Number CO1849A]

On a visit to inspect Australian soldiers who had just arrived on leave from the trenches, King George V, Queen Mary and party cross the street from Australian Imperial Force headquarters to the Australian Imperial Force and War Chest Club. From left to right, Andrew Fisher; His Majesty King George V; Colonel Thomas Griffiths, CMG, DSO, Commandant of Australian Imperial Force Headquarters 1917–1918 and 1919; Her Majesty Queen Mary (holding bouquet); Mrs Fisher; Mrs A. Samuels, Commandant of the Club, October 1917. [Australian War Memorial Negative Number CO1849]

King George V and Queen Mary arrive at the opening of Australia House, 1918 [Australian High Commission, London, Department of Foreign Affairs and Trade]

4 Diplomacy by default: empire foreign policy and the high commissioners during the 1920s

Bernard Attard

Empire foreign policy and Australia

THE participation of the British dominions in World War I transformed their relationship with Great Britain and changed their standing in the world. It led to their separate representation at the Paris Peace Conference, separate signatures on the peace treaties, and separate founding membership of the League of Nations (and, in Australia's case, holding a permanent mandate over the former German New Guinea). In 1917 and 1918, the dominions also shared in the formulation of British war policy at the meetings of the Imperial War Cabinet and subsequently continued to help frame imperial policies as members of the British Empire delegation at Versailles and at the conference of prime ministers in London in 1921. But this common purpose was soon undermined by the demands of some dominions for the formal recognition of their equality and the removal of the remaining elements of constitutional subordination to the United Kingdom. Canada in particular asserted its right to determine its own foreign policies separately and thus dissociate itself from a single imperial approach.[1]

The Commonwealth government welcomed the consultative arrangements that originated during the war and accepted with some scepticism Australia's membership of the League, but lacked enthusiasm for the constitutional innovations of the 1920s.[2] To varying degrees, however, each affected the development of Australia's representation in London during the postwar decade. The prime minister, S.M. Bruce, was a member of the committee on inter-imperial relations of the 1926 Imperial Conference whose report famously defined the position and mutual relations of Britain and the dominions as 'autonomous communities … equal in status, in no way subordinate one to another'.[3] Yet, despite this emphasis on dominion autonomy and equality with the United Kingdom, the Australian approach to questions of security and external relations throughout the 1920s was based on two inter-connected assumptions.[4] The first, as Bruce explained in parliament shortly before the 1926 conference, was that 'when war has been declared by the Imperial Government, all parts of the Empire are at war', even though it was still 'open for the Dominions to determine what, if any, active participation, they will take in the conduct of hostilities'.[5] The second was that Australia was incapable of defending itself, and thus preserving itself as a 'white man's country', without 'the protection afforded … by Great Britain'.[6] It followed that the Commonwealth's involvement in peace or war depended on British policy, and its security still rested largely upon the strength of the empire's defences. Australia's external relations and safety, therefore, could not be separated from those of Britain and the rest of the empire.[7]

Certainly, this commitment to imperial unity was subject to important qualifications. It did not mean that Australia was bound inevitably to follow Britain's lead without consent or discussion. As Bruce observed in an exchange with the British Labour prime minister, Ramsay MacDonald, in 1924, any common policy would still have to be 'submitted by the respective [dominion] Prime Ministers to their individual Parliaments for their ratification and assent'.[8] Furthermore, Australia was prepared to act separately if there was any 'danger that Empire defence may … be relegated to the second place'.[9] Bruce himself announced a five-year defence program when MacDonald's government decided to halt the construction of the British naval base at Singapore.[10] Yet, even qualified in these ways, the underlying orientation of Australian policy was the same. As the prime minister affirmed after the 1926 conference: 'Our first obligation is to play a part, by consultation, in the foreign policy of the British Empire. Our second obligation is to cooperate in the defence of the Empire as a whole'.[11] Consultation, then, was the great desideratum. Hughes loudly asserted the Commonwealth's right to have its views heard during and after the war. His successor was no less insistent that Australia was entitled to 'have a voice in the determination of the foreign policy of the British Empire'.[12] The particular challenge was to find ways of institutionalising this at a time when the centrifugal forces in Anglo-dominion relations appeared to be uppermost.

In practice, as Peter Edwards has shown, the empire's consultative arrangements gave particular prominence to the prime minister at the expense of other ministers or official representatives.[13] It was he who attended the Imperial Conferences in London and his department that was the main point of contact with Whitehall. Before the war, communications had passed exclusively through the governor-general. In 1918, a right of direct telegraphic correspondence with the British prime minister was introduced in certain circumstances, and in 1928 the governor-general was displaced altogether as the channel of communication. Contacts between governments now occurred without the mediation of Australian or British representatives based in London and Canberra.[14]

But meaningful consultation also depended on a constant supply of information, as well as the capacity to assimilate it, particularly when the international conditions that underpinned discussions at imperial conferences might quickly change. For these reasons, by the 1920s the prime minister also needed greater organisational support for the conduct of external relations. Neither Hughes, Bruce nor the Nationalist party room was prepared to delegate wide discretionary powers to a resident minister or other representative in London who might 'bind Australia to a participation in an unsought for degree in foreign affairs'.[15] But the problems of information and consultation remained. For Bruce, the longest-serving prime minister during the 1920s, they boiled down characteristically to a question of creating 'the machinery that will enable us to have a real voice in the foreign policy of the Empire'.[16] It was largely due to his efforts that such machinery existed in London by the end of the decade.

Cook, the League and the liaison officer

Although some of the implications of these postwar developments for the office of the high commissioner were anticipated as early as 1919, Fisher's apparent inactivity on the Strand and the question of who would replace him were of far more immediate concern in Australia after the peace conference. The succession, at least, was soon beyond doubt. One correspondent assured Fisher in June 1920: 'Sir Joseph Cook is marked and labelled for London this year'.[17] Fisher himself retired the following April after a three-month extension to allow for paid leave and there was no obvious opposition to Cook. But Hughes could not spare his treasurer until late in the session and did not finally offer him the job until November 1921.[18]

By any measure, it was a remarkable personal achievement for a man who had started his working life down a coal pit in Staffordshire, although no more so than Fisher's. Sydney's *Daily Telegraph* observed: 'The new High Commissioner will go to London, illustrating in his own person the Dick Whittington things that may happen to a man in Australia'.[19] His career had, in fact, been a testament to the Smilesian virtues of self-help. Born in England in 1860, he emigrated in 1885—soon followed by his bride, Mary Turner—to Lithgow in New South Wales, where Mary's brother was already settled and Cook became active in the local labour movement.[20] Personally ambitious, largely self-taught and, for the time being at least, a devout nonconformist, Cook was essentially individualistic and conservative in temperament: Methodism, trade unionism and political activism were the paths to self-improvement. In 1894, as leader of the New South Wales Parliamentary Labor Party, he rejected a conference decision that bound parliamentarians to obey caucus decisions, split the party and soon joined the ministry of George Reid, who became his political mentor. He entered the first federal parliament a Free Trader and eventually succeeded Deakin as the leader of the Liberal Party, winning an election in May 1913 with a single-seat majority. Twelve months later, he secured the first dissolution of both houses, having achieved virtually nothing as prime minister, and lost the subsequent poll. Labor's disintegration over the conscription issue gave him the opportunity to return to office as Hughes's deputy in a coalition 'Nationalist' ministry in early 1917. A year later, the working-class colonist from the West Midlands who had effaced the more obvious traces of his origins was moving in the highest imperial circles. With Hughes, he attended the Imperial War Conference (and, for a time, the Imperial War Cabinet, before apparently falling out with him), then crowned his *annus mirabilis* as a member of the British Empire delegation at Versailles, where he was the senior British delegate on the commission—'an angel of obedience', according to his British colleague[21]—that drew up the boundaries of Czechoslovakia. In 'the lottery of party play', he had indeed drawn a winning ticket.[22]

Appropriately, the announcement of Cook's appointment as a Knight Grand Cross of the Order of St Michael and St George on 3 August 1918 coincided with the formal opening of Australia House by George V.[23] The possibility of taking Fisher's place had probably suggested itself while he was still in London; certainly, by the time he returned to Australia he was ready to escape from Hughes's domineering leadership.[24] Soon after accepting the high commissionership, he confided to John Latham, who had been his adviser in London and at Versailles: 'How I wish you were going with me. There will really be more scope this time'.[25] The news of his appointment was hardly a surprise, but it provided a further opportunity for the press to bemoan the state of Australia's representation in London. The *Brisbane Courier* concluded that 'the office of High Commissioner becomes very largely an expensive sinecure to be filled by an elderly and trusted politician, according to the party making the selection, as a reward for services rendered'. The *Daily Telegraph* was equally trenchant: 'If Sir Joseph Cook does not redeem its reputation he is likely to be the last of the High Commissioners'.[26]

Cook at least possessed some of the necessary qualifications. Despite his humourlessness and occasional irascibility, he was self-assured, socially at ease, and a competent public speaker. The governor-general, Munro-Ferguson, had commended him to the King's private secretary during the war as 'worth some attention. He is not a good administrator but he is a leader of experience, able and capable of giving a sound opinion on Australian affairs. He is a Methodist from the Midlands, of the type of your Northumberland and Durham Miner leader, less strong in character but without that Quaker like attitude to the war'.[27] Latham complained about his 'mediocrity, self-satisfaction, idleness & discourtesy',[28] but he had been a success with English politicians. In December, the secretary of state for the colonies, Walter Long, wrote to the governor-general, Munro Ferguson: 'the more I see of him the more I like him personally, and the more I admire his unquestioned gifts. He takes broad and statesmanlike views on questions: he is very moderate in the expression of his opinions and is a charming man to work with'.[29]

It is unlikely Hughes himself regarded Cook as an ideal appointment. After his involuntary retirement to the backbenches, he told Shepherd, the official secretary at Australia House: 'I know the gentleman very well. He has most excellent qualities. But he is not an efficient administrator. He knows nothing at all about business. It is really a very great pity. But there it is and must remain for another four years at least'.[30] Despite this, Hughes asked the Colonial Office to show the high commissioner all the official cables between London and Melbourne, except prime ministerial communications. He also established an effective working relationship with him.[31] It was, however, to be short-lived. After the federal election of December 1922, Hughes was forced to resign so that Bruce could form a coalition with the Country Party. Unlike his two predecessors, Cook had not been caught out by a complete change of government. All the same, Bruce was a man of a different generation and stamp. He already believed that there was 'only one factor that counts in the least, and that is the personality of the High Commissioner' and in this respect he found Cook wanting.[32] He soon told the British Conservative politician Leo Amery, when considering Australia's need for an 'informal Ambassador' in London: 'Pending the finding of the right man, the High Commissioner can be used to a certain point, but … I do not think that Sir Joseph Cook—notwithstanding the fact that he has many excellent qualities—is quite the suitable person for the position which I have in mind'.[33]

Bruce's lack of faith in Cook limited the extent to which the high commissioner could become part of the machinery of consultation in Anglo-Australian relations while the older man remained in London. Still, the frequency with which Cook was asked to lead the Australian delegation at the League's annual Assembly in Geneva and other international meetings meant that he was soon acting anyway as a diplomat by default.[34] As early as 1919, an official in the Prime Minister's Department observed in a memorandum about the high commissioner's duties: 'The diplomatic functions have hitherto been small, but with the advent of a permanent League of Nations, in which the Australian Government will be directly represented, the diplomatic duties will increase and possibly become continuous', although they would still essentially 'necessitate action through or in consultation with the British Government'.[35] The consequences of this would only be clear when Bruce himself was high commissioner. But even during the 1920s the sudden flaring of an international crisis while the League was in session—or the reference of a dispute to it—might cast the Australian representative into the diplomatic arena, however briefly and whatever his aptitude for the task. This was no clearer than during the Chanak crisis in September 1922, when advancing Turkish troops confronted British forces on the eastern side of the Dardanelles, just opposite the Gallipoli peninsula.[36]

The closeness of the consultations at the London conference of prime ministers in 1921 had been, as Hughes had feared, 'a last magnificent flare of a dying illumination'.[37] The Chanak crisis caught Australia and the other dominions entirely by surprise. Cook was attending the League's third session when Hughes received a cable from the British prime minister, Lloyd George, asking for an offer of troops as a demonstration to the Turks of the empire's resolve to stand its ground.[38] News of the request had already appeared in the British press and been transmitted to Australia. In public, Hughes felt bound to respond positively; privately, he demanded to know why the dominions had not been forewarned of the approaching crisis. He also wanted the League to mediate between the Turks and Greeks, whose fighting had caused the stand-off in the first place, and instructed Cook to act accordingly.[39] The high commissioner rose to the occasion. He told the leader of the British delegation, Lord Balfour, that his government 'felt they were entitled to [a] fuller explanation than had been hitherto given to them of all elements in [the] situation',[40] and at the League's Political Commission produced a cameo worthy of Hughes himself. As one British diplomat put it:

> Sir Joseph Cook … proceeded to show himself more Cecilian than [Lord Robert] Cecil in his demand for intervention by the League. He appeared to have no notion that Australia should adapt her utterances on foreign policy to a form which should at least not embarrass the Foreign Office of the British Empire. Nor did he seem capable of discussing and reasoning in private a common line of British policy.[41]

Despite this performance, Cook was not being wilfully obtuse. He reported to Hughes that both Balfour and Cecil believed the League would not intervene while Britain and the other major powers were already negotiating and finally assured him: '[I] [h]ave impressed Balfour with [the] strength of feeling in Australia and he asks me to tell you he is doing his best in [a] very difficult and delicate situation'.[42] That, however, was the end of the matter as far as he was concerned. Back in London, he continued to receive confidential summaries of events from the Colonial Office, but Hughes did not involve him in his dispute with Lloyd George over Australia's right of attendance at the Lausanne conference, which finally renegotiated the Allied peace treaty with Turkey.[43]

The lesson Hughes's successor drew from the episode was that the Australian government should never again be left in the dark about British policy. He thus aligned himself with British public figures like Amery and the cabinet secretary, Sir Maurice Hankey, who believed that the United Kingdom should maintain itself as a global imperial power free of European commitments. [44] In attaining this objective, the dominions appeared to be their natural allies. After the 1923 Imperial Conference, Bruce arranged for the secondment of Allen Leeper, the son of the Warden of Trinity College at Melbourne University, who was then a first secretary in the Foreign Office, to conduct a review of the foreign section in the Prime Minister's Department.[45] Leeper saw immediately that the 'crux of the whole problem' in London was 'the political status of the High Commissioner'.[46] This officer should become 'the authoritative spokesman of the Australian Government to the British Government on all political matters—in fact an accredited Ambassador in everything but name'. But difficulties 'largely of a personal nature', as well as British objections, ruled this out.[47] Instead, he proposed the creation of a political section in Australia House, staffed in the first instance by a single officer, who would maintain contact with the Foreign Office. Together with other organisational reforms in Melbourne, this involved nothing less than 'the establishment of a special *Australian Foreign Service*'.[48]

Bruce wanted the liaison officer to be a person 'of such standing and character as to enjoy the confidence of the Foreign Office'.[49] The selection to fill the post of Richard Casey showed precisely the qualities he had in mind. The wealthy son of a prominent Melbourne businessman, Casey had been a staff officer with the Australian Imperial Force and was known personally to the prime minister. Like Bruce himself and the expatriate Leeper, Casey was a member of the Oxbridge-educated, second generation of a British–Australian social élite, 'by any standard an officer and a gentleman', and, as far as Amery could tell, 'a very good type of young fellow' to boot.[50] He was also the high commissioner's junior by thirty years: the contrast could not have been greater. If the colonist Cook represented one kind of Australian, the native-born Casey most certainly represented another.

The new liaison officer later recalled that Cook had been 'highly indignant' about the freedom he was allowed in London.[51] Casey would communicate directly with Melbourne and be entirely independent of any official in Australia House, including Cook, whom he was only required to advise of his official correspondence. He was also found accommodation away from the Strand under Hankey's supervision in the Cabinet Office.[52] Bruce explained: 'he will supervise and accelerate the flow of information … and, it is hoped, will be the means of keeping the Commonwealth in closer touch with the information which is normally available, but the importance of which a British officer might not appreciate'.[53] Despite the hurt to his dignity, Cook put on a brave face. Casey reported: 'Sir J.C. has been most helpful from the start—and is making the way easy as far as he can … Once Sir J.C. became seized of your intentions with regard to direct communications with me—he set about having the matter put down in black & white'.[54] Yet Cook was almost certainly unaware that the prime minister also wanted Casey 'to be considered as his mouthpiece and representative on all matters of foreign policy'.[55] Soon Bruce was using the liaison officer as his personal representative inside Whitehall and beyond.[56] This much he acknowledged to him with reference to the Foreign Office and the Dominions Office: 'During Sir Joseph's regime you have been the connecting link … and Sir Joseph Cook has not appeared in the picture to any extent'.[57]

But despite his value to Bruce, the liaison officer was still a junior official. Amery reminded him: 'Casey after all is hardly of the standing to be able to discuss with the Foreign Secretary the Australian point of view about any projected departure in foreign policy, or to convey your instructions with sufficient authority'.[58] For these purposes, 'someone of really high standing' was required. Whether or not the Commonwealth's representative was the high commissioner, Amery was

> sure that it would make a great deal of difference to the real control by the Dominions over foreign policy and to the real understanding of the dominion point of view here, if it were possible to have someone here to whom the Foreign Minister or myself could talk about the situation as it developed and who could communicate to you in their own language and get your views.

In the meantime, he had to make do with Cook and the other high commissioners *faute de mieux*. On becoming secretary of state for the colonies in a new Conservative administration in November 1924, Amery arranged a meeting for the dominion representatives at Downing Street with Stanley Baldwin, the prime minister, and Austen Chamberlain, the foreign secretary. The 'High Commissioners' Tea Party at No. 10' was 'an unqualified success', he told Chamberlain, and confided to his diary: 'Austen gave a short survey of the world situation, laying special stress on Egypt … The High

Commissioners were all very pleased and no doubt communicated very fully with their Governments'.[59] Cook, for his part, used the opportunity to explain Bruce's intentions for Casey.[60]

Amery felt that he had gone 'as far as we could without forcing the hands of the Dominion Governments by treating the dominion High Commissioners as their diplomatic representatives'.[61] Even so, he continued to meet them regularly. In March 1925 they had a general discussion about dominion representation and the creation of a separate dominions office (which happened later that year, with Amery as the minister in charge). Amery also arranged a further meeting with Baldwin and Chamberlain, who explained British policy towards the negotiation of a European security pact at Locarno in the autumn.[62] In July, he started to see them weekly, raising the Locarno negotiations again in October.[63] Amery's attentions presumably smoothed some of Sir Joseph's ruffled feathers. Cook observed in his annual report that the Locarno pact had been the most important political event of the year, 'and it will be noted that the discussions which have taken place upon it have incidentally brought to the front once again the question of the status of the Dominion High Commissioners'.[64]

The meetings were eventually stopped because of the objections of the Canadian prime minister, Mackenzie King, who 'thought that they amounted to an assumption that the High Commissioners were the channel of communication with their Dominions'.[65] In Geneva, however, Cook's diplomatic duties continued come what may. Although Casey occasionally deputised for him, the high commissioner still led the delegation at the annual Assembly if no minister was sent out from Australia, and represented the Commonwealth at other international gatherings, including the Special Assembly in 1926 which considered Germany's admission to the League Council, and the three-power naval disarmament conference the following year.[66] He had made a poor start in diplomacy, complaining intemperately about his treatment by the Permanent Mandates Commission in 1922, but eventually picked up some sense of diplomatic proprieties.[67] At a session of the International Labour Conference in June 1926, the president of the New South Wales Trades and Labor Council, Jack Beasley, accused the Italian fascist government of being hostile to workers. Cook apologised to the Italians in private and dissociated the Commonwealth from Beasley's remarks. 'I have had to correct him in committee several times', he reported. 'He "cuts little ice" and is not in harmony even with his own group.'[68] It could scarcely be imagined that Beasley would one day occupy his own office overlooking the Strand.

Completing the 'Casey experiment': Ryrie and the birth of a modern mission

In August 1926 Cook accepted a six-month extension of his term. Bruce told the press that it was 'most desirable that Sir Joseph Cook should be available for consultation during the course of the Imperial Conference'.[69] In fact, he had already been thinking about his successor for some time. The choice was complicated by the likelihood that the Imperial

Conference would probably be discussing the status of the dominion representatives and his own sense—nudged along by Amery—that further changes were due in London. He wrote to Casey in January:

> At the moment I have no clear views on this subject, as far as the individual is concerned, but I feel very strongly that the position of High Commissioner is one of such importance that the occupant of it should be a man of outstanding ability. Could one find the ideal occupant of the position it would unquestionably mean that his relations to the Foreign Office, and to the Dominion Office would be very much closer than those of Sir Joseph Cook have been.[70]

During the conference itself Bruce floated the suggestion that the high commissioners might act as the 'unofficial channel' between the dominions and Britain, with access to British ministers and confidential papers on foreign affairs. There was also general agreement among the dominion prime ministers about 'the desirability of developing a system of personal contact, both in London and the Dominion capitals'.[71] What this meant in practice, however, was left to each government. Amery arranged for Cook to receive copies of secret government papers and the material on foreign affairs circulated to the dominion capitals.[72] Bruce also welcomed Baldwin's offer to invite dominion representatives to the Committee of Imperial Defence—the defence committee of the British government chaired by the prime minister—when it considered matters affecting individual dominions 'or the general defence of the Empire'.[73] The idea had actually originated with Hankey, the committee's secretary. After further discussions with Amery in Canberra in November 1927 during his tour of the dominions, arrangements were made for the high commissioner to be informed of the agenda and nominate any meeting he wished to attend.[74]

The results of his visit to England must have confirmed Bruce's views about the kind of man he wanted in Australia House. Before his departure, he cabled his deputy, the leader of the Country Party, Earle Page, nominating Sir Brudenell White, the former chief-of-staff of the Australian Imperial Force and currently the chairman of the Commonwealth Public Service Board, possibly for a shortened term of three years.[75] The proposal clearly surprised Page, who thought White's qualifications were 'admirable', but replied that the cabinet felt 'considerable hesitancy about his political sense'.[76] He also thought that the matter could wait until Bruce's return. In the event, a senior military officer was chosen, but not the prime minister's candidate. In March 1927, the cabinet agreed unanimously to offer the high commissionership to the chairman of the Public Accounts Committee, Major-General Sir Granville de Laune Ryrie KCMG: 'A darker horse', the South Australian *Register* observed wryly, 'has never won an important official event!'[77]

Quite how Ryrie had displaced White can only be guessed, but the member for Warringah had never expected to be considered or even been mentioned in the press.[78] A grazier who had combined soldiering with a career in state and federal politics, the highest office to which he had risen was assistant minister in Hughes's last government before being dropped when Bruce formed his coalition with the Country Party. Born at Micalago station in the Monaro in 1865, he was a bluff, good-humoured man who had a reputation for 'expressive and lurid' Australian vernacular and had been known in parliament 'to grow exceedingly boisterous, and almost brutally candid'.[79] Hughes thought that the government was 'sending a man to represent Australia in London … who with all his excellent qualities as a soldier, is quite unfit for the job'.[80] Stonehaven, the governor-general, a former diplomat and British Conservative minister, took another view:

> Ryrie is quite a different type from previous High Commissioners: a typical Australian country gentleman, the 3rd generation of a family of squatters. He has been a Member of the Lower House of the Federal Parliament for many years, & has held office as Assistant Minister for Defence. But in choosing him Bruce was not influenced, I fancy, by his Parliamentary record, so much as by his personal qualifications. He wanted to have a man representing Australia in London who could possibly become persona grata not only in official circles but in others not much frequented by High Commissioners hitherto, possibly through lack of opportunity or inclination.[81]

Still, doubts lingered.[82] Bruce had clearly wanted someone who would be socially acceptable in England as well as competent to handle the new duties he envisaged for the high commissioner. His ministers were probably more concerned with the politics of the appointment and the opportunity to reward one of the party faithful. There was a chance that Ryrie was suitable in all these ways, but it remained to be seen.

Bruce himself pressed on with the changes he had started in London. He extended the Leeper reforms by creating the new post of League of Nations officer in Australia House, to which he transferred Cook's private secretary, Osmond Fuhrman, as a member of the Department of External Affairs under Casey's supervision. Fuhrman had served with distinction in the Australian Imperial Force and for a time been Hughes's private secretary.[83] Thomas Trumble, formerly the secretary of the Department of Defence, travelled out to London with Ryrie and the high commissioner's wife Mary (née McFarland) to replace Shepherd as official secretary.[84] Finally Casey, who was in Australia for much of 1927, was instructed to meet the high commissioner weekly and give him access to his communications with Canberra.[85] Although still based in the Cabinet Office, Casey felt that he would have 'no difficulty in working harmoniously with Australia House'.[86] But he soon discovered that Ryrie required only the shortest of briefings, reporting in March 1928:

> Since I have been back in London I have, by arrangement, seen the High Commissioner each week at a stated time, and have kept him verbally and briefly informed. I am on good terms with him and with them all at Australia House. My weekly period with him, however, is only about a quarter of an hour. He does not want anything except headlines, and it has rather come down to an understanding that I do not fail to inform him of anything of outstanding importance to Australia.[87]

He did just that, noting in August, for example: 'I have kept the High Commissioner fully informed of the [Anglo-Australian] Antarctic negotiations, by word of mouth and by submitting a complete file of correspondence to Trumble at regular intervals. They seem quite content to leave it to me. In fact I very much doubt if they have read the material I have bombarded them with'.[88]

Ryrie attended the Committee of Imperial Defence for the first time in May 1928 and soon distinguished himself by his plain speaking and failure to sing from the hymn sheet assigned to the dominion representatives by Amery and Hankey. At a meeting in July he endorsed the ten-year rule (the inter-war British defence planning assumption that there would be no war within the next decade) for Australia, adding with reference to the Singapore base:

> He did not consider Japan was really a potential enemy at the present time, and it was, therefore, a most inopportune time to start the construction of coast defences, which might well be obsolete before the danger from Japan justified their construction. In view of the large amount of money that America had invested in Australia, it was hardly likely that the United States would countenance an aggressive policy on the part of Japan against Australia.[89]

Amery thought this 'a very silly little speech' and Hankey was soon having second thoughts about the value of inviting the high commissioners; according to Casey: 'from what he had seen of the scheme in practice, he did not feel confident that anything very constructive would result and he did not propose to endanger the principle by putting it very freely into practice'.[90]

Criticism of Ryrie's performance at the League was more public. In July 1929 the *Manchester Guardian* created 'a slight storm at Geneva' when it reported that the Australian high commissioner appeared to know less about New Guinea than the members of the Permanent Mandates Commission to whom he was reporting. Casey explained again: 'This came about by reason of there having been a lot of questions put to Sir Granville to which he could not reply and on which he asked leave for Fuhrman to reply for him— which arises out of the fact that he won't read the papers with which he is supplied'.[91]

At first, Bruce had been hopeful. He told Casey in March 1928: 'As far as I can make out from letters I have received from Britain, Ryrie has done extraordinarily well, and he has been very acceptable to everyone in London'.[92] But it was early days yet and obvious soon enough that the high commissioner was failing to meet the expectations Bruce himself had raised. Ryrie, however, could hardly be blamed. He was doing a job for which he was unprepared by training or experience, and was overstretched considerably by the increasing demands on his time. The number of international meetings he was required to attend was growing 'much beyond the power of the High Commissioner to cope with them'; on average, four months each year were being spent abroad.[93] During 1929 he represented the Commonwealth at the International Labour Conference, the Permanent Mandates Commission, the League Assembly, and conferences on the

Geneva Convention and the treatment of foreigners; all this while carrying out his social, diplomatic and other duties in London and touring war graves in the Middle East with Rudyard Kipling.[94] Despite Hankey's reservations, in 1929 he also attended five of the seven meetings of the Committee of Imperial Defence, which Bruce continued to use as a forum for raising Australian concerns about British defence policy, particularly after a new Labour government announced a review of naval expenditure which would doubtless affect work on the Singapore base.[95]

Conclusion: 'the house is wired'

The fact that a high commissioner was discussing imperial defence in a committee chaired by the British prime minister was evidence enough of the changes that had occurred since the war in the functions of Australia's representatives in Britain. They affected access to information as well as individuals and had begun at a relatively junior level with Casey's appointment as liaison officer in 1924. At first, as far as the high commissioner was concerned, the changes had been ad hoc and were mostly a consequence of Australia's membership of the League of Nations. As a result, however, both Cook and Ryrie represented the Commonwealth in Geneva in times of crisis as well as at diplomatic meetings that dealt with the more routine business of international relations during the 1920s. In the second half of the decade, Bruce extended the 'Casey experiment' by giving the high commissioner access to the most sensitive information on British foreign relations, bringing the senior representative directly into Anglo-Australian political discussions, and formalising the arrangements in Australia House for dealing with League-related matters.[96] Although largely due to the efforts of the other dominions, the high commissioner's standing in London now also fell just short of diplomatic status. By the end of Ryrie's term, seats were reserved for the high commissioners in both houses of parliament; they were entitled to the same tax exemptions and Court privileges as foreign representatives; and on ceremonial occasions they ranked immediately behind a secretary of state, unless a minister from the dominion was present, but (in Australia's case) ahead of a state premier. Finally, one of Ryrie's conditions for accepting office was that he be provided with an official residence, the lease being taken on number 18 Ennismore Gardens in South Kensington for this purpose.[97] Almost all these changes were unnoticed in Australia, but that did not mean they were any less significant.

In important respects, then, by the end of the 1920s Australia House had started to function as a recognisably modern overseas mission, albeit in a geopolitical context in which Australia was still deeply embedded in imperial institutions and its representatives were allowed privileged access to the British state. Bruce's difficulty in finding a suitable representative meant that he had been unable to realise the opportunities created by his own reforms, but Amery's enthusiasm for involving the dominion representatives in the machinery of imperial consultation was undiminished. He recorded in his diary in November 1928: 'Armistice Service in the morning. We adjourned for hot soup to the

Cabinet Room afterwards. I suggested to the PM he might ask in the High Commissioners but he doubted whether there was enough soup suggesting that I should remind him about it for next year'.[98] On this occasion, Ryrie and his colleagues were literally out in the cold. Still, at about the same time Amery was telling South Africa's high commissioner with reference to the union government's proposals to accredit the latter as an envoy extraordinary and minister plenipotentiary in Britain: 'The house is wired and the lights are in. All General Hertzog need do is to turn the switch'.[99] Appropriately enough, it was Bruce himself who turned the switch for Australia when he took up the high commissioner's duties in September 1932.

5 The high commissioners, empire development and economic diplomacy between the wars

Bernard Attard

ALTHOUGH the high commissioner's diplomatic duties grew during the 1920s, the federal government's pursuit of economic development after the war did much to reinforce the traditional orientation of Australia's representatives in Britain towards the promotion of trade, migration and investment. The Great Depression during the 1930s shifted the emphasis from the projection of Australia's apparently endless possibilities to the protection of farm incomes and the renegotiation of debt. One way or another, however, economic issues continued to dominate Anglo-Australian relations and it was still largely in relation to them that the high commissioner was judged. This was equally, if not more, true of Australia House. Two developments were particularly striking over the entire period. The first was the growth and contraction of a substantial Australian administrative centre on the Strand; the second, the change in priorities from the expansive promotion of 'Australia unlimited' to a much narrower concentration on trade diplomacy and hard bargaining in the City of London. These two themes in the history of the high commission between the wars are the main subjects of this chapter.

'Men, money and markets': the high commission during the 1920s

The essential elements of Australia's development strategy during the 1920s need only be summarised here.[1] With the restoration of peace, state and federal governments set out again to promote growth in the customary manner, through assistance to migrants, public investment, and the encouragement of closer settlement. What was new were the Commonwealth's efforts to coordinate the process and the insistence of both prime ministers during the 1920s—Billy Hughes and S.M. Bruce—on the connections between economic development, national security, and the preservation of a white Australia. All three would be served by the dominion's closest possible integration into an imperial economic system that revolved around Britain. The complementary relationship with the mother country had been the basis of economic development since the colonial era, but integration was now an explicit objective of public policy. As a corollary, Australia's leaders urged Britain to adopt an imperial economic policy that would serve the same end by granting preference to empire producers in its market and providing empire governments with access to cheap capital in the City. Australian development was therefore viewed in a wider imperial context. In October 1923, Bruce put the matter as clearly as he could in his opening statement to the Imperial Economic Conference: 'There is no question but that the solution of the problem of Empire development is dependent upon three things, men, money and markets'.[2] In truth, this was empire development seen through the prism of Australia's interests as evolved over a century of colonising experience.

The consequences of this approach were soon felt in London. In 1920, Hughes persuaded the states to hand to the Commonwealth responsibility for the overseas recruitment of migrants and their transport to Australia. Two years later, the British agreed to share the costs of assisted passages; in 1924 migration was linked to public borrowing by the '£34 Million Agreement', which committed the United Kingdom to share the interest charges on development loans in proportion to the number of assisted migrants settled in Australia. The ambitious target was 450,000 over ten years. The postwar migration program was thus the first reason for a major administrative expansion on the Strand which counterbalanced the winding back of war-related activities.[3] In March 1921, the minister for immigration and repatriation, Senator Edward Millen, opened the Migration and Settlement Office at Australia House. Very soon it was the largest department in the building, employing eighty-nine staff by June 1925.[4] But the Migration Office was only the most conspicuous example. In 1914 Reid's office on Victoria Street had employed fewer than seventy people, excluding cleaners.[5] When Scullin asked Senator Coleman to find economies in July 1930, 240 were employed by the high commissioner's office and Commonwealth departments with personnel in London, including what remained of the Migration Office, which had already suffered heavy redundancies, and 65 staff engaged in a range of domestic services from cleaning to the operation of lifts and portering. Apart from the high commissioner's staff, Australia House also accommodated representatives of the three services; the Council for Scientific and Industrial Research; the Development and Migration Commission; the departments of Trade and Customs, Markets, and Health and Repatriation; the External Affairs Branch; the Auditor-General; the Public Trustee; and the semi-independent Australian Trade Publicity Office.[6]

If nothing else then, the high commissioner was the head of a virtual branch office of the Commonwealth public service on the Strand. Soon after taking charge in 1927, Sir Granville Ryrie observed: 'Australia House, as an organ of administration, is surely unique. Gathered under one roof and owing allegiance to the High Commissioner are a number of officers representing statutory bodies in Australia, which are not only separately housed but are independently controlled'.[7] The administrative challenges were, therefore, also unique:

Officers in charge of these offices, in the sense that they represent their respective Departments in Australia, derive authority from, and must observe, the rulings of those Departments, but in another and larger sense their offices are simply integral parts of a single Commonwealth representation in London and as such they are guided by the High Commissioner on matters of policy and principle. In the nature of the case this peculiar condition of affairs seems unalterable, but it makes the problem of administering Australia House a much more complicated one than that of administering a Department in Australia.[8]

Bruce had also been mindful of the diverse nature of Australian activities in London. He told Sir Joseph Cook in January 1924:

[T]he analogy to be kept in mind is the relation of a Cabinet Minister to his Department, with such modifications as are necessitated by the distance from the seat of Government, and the peculiar character of some of the duties to be performed. The fundamental things to be aimed at are, unity of control, with definitely allocated responsibility, and the cordial co-operation of the staff.[9]

The high commissioner would be the final authority in all matters affecting administration, staff, appointments and 'the control and discipline of Australia House'.[10] But in practice much of this was delegated to senior officials who also carried out representative duties of a more specialist kind. The most important of these, the official secretary, was described in 1920 as 'not only a permanent Under-Secretary, but from the financial and trade point of view [he] may be compared with the General Manager of a large banking institution or business concern … He is effectually a Deputy High Commissioner, and is required to deal with issues, the magnitude of which is not realized in Australia outside ministerial circles'.[11] Both Malcolm Shepherd, the official secretary from March 1921, and his successor, Thomas Trumble, had been in charge of Commonwealth departments—Prime Minister's and Defence respectively—before coming to London, and Shepherd himself went to Defence when Trumble replaced him in 1927.[12] In 1926 the increasing complexity of the federal government's financial operations in the City had led to the appointment of another senior public servant, James Collins, as financial adviser.[13] Collins had been secretary to the Treasury and was largely responsible for the negotiation of the war debt funding agreement with Britain in 1921.[14] He later explained his duties in London:

as business required, I interviewed the Governor of the Bank of England and other leading bankers in London, and … terms for long loans, short loans and Treasury Bills were negotiated by me with underwriters and bankers. The High Commissioner … sometimes took part in work of that kind but invariably much weight and responsibility fell upon me.[15]

Shepherd, Trumble and Collins had started their careers in the colonial establishments and transferred to the Commonwealth service at federation. They were part of a distinct administrative cohort prominent during the 1920s that served the generation of politicians from which Cook and Ryrie were drawn. By contrast, the three other notable senior figures in London beneath the rank of the high commissioner during the 1920s were all outsiders to different degrees and had a much looser relationship to the Australia House bureaucracy. The external affairs liaison officer, Richard Casey, worked from the Cabinet Office in Whitehall Gardens.[16] The director of the Migration and Settlement Office was also virtually autonomous and had direct access to the prime minister on policy matters.[17] The first director, Percy Hunter, was an old New South Wales associate of Hughes and did little in London to enhance his reputation.[18] His replacement after a lapse of almost two years was the Perth businessman Lieutenant-Colonel C.M.E. Manning, whose wife also had considerable experience as a former chairwoman of the Women's Migration Council in Western Australia.[19] Finally, the status of the most talented individual based in Australia House, Frank Lidgett McDougall, was almost impossible to define. McDougall had originally migrated from England to South Australia before the war to take up fruit growing at Renmark. He first came to Bruce's attention in 1922 as a member of a delegation sent to England by the Australian Dried Fruits Association. McDougall returned to London permanently in 1925 and was soon drawing his income as the part-time secretary of the Dried Fruits Control Board and the local liaison officer of both the Development and Migration Commission and the Council for Scientific and Industrial Research.[20] He was also the Australian representative on the Imperial Economic Committee and the Empire Marketing Board, assisted the high commissioner with his letters to the press, and did his best to ginger up Trumble, Collins, Manning and the other 'Commonwealth Government instrumentalists' in Australia House.[21] But his first and greatest value to Bruce—who described him in a lighter moment as 'a secret service agent'—was as a lobbyist in the cause of empire preference and a kind of economic counterpart to Casey.[22]

Thus Australia's high commissioners during the 1920s presided over a growing and somewhat unwieldy office and senior functionaries who were not always accountable to them. They were acquiring more obviously diplomatic duties and becoming increasingly involved in the mechanisms of imperial consultation. But the promotion of Australia as a producer and destination for British migrants and capital was still their most important task. With the Commonwealth's entry into overseas capital markets, they also were responsible for the supervision of a heavy borrowing program.[23] In 1925 Cook negotiated the federal government's first loan on Wall Street, an issue of $75 million by J.P. Morgan & Co., and Collins later told Lyons when trying to impress him with his own importance: 'work in finance had been regarded in departmental circles as the most important function of the High Commissioner himself'.[24] Finally, they carried out the social and ceremonial duties of dominion representatives in the imperial capital, participating in increasingly elaborate rituals designed to display to the rest of the world the unity and coherence of an empire bound together by a monarchical and hierarchical order.[25]

When Sir Joseph Cook took up his duties in January 1922, the London office's reputation in Australia had sunk to its lowest point. Australia House had suffered from the long delay in appointing a replacement for the official secretary, Edward Box—who had resigned in 1919 to join a Scottish distiller—the absence of any clear policy direction from Australia, and the further decline of Fisher's health during a particularly difficult period in Anglo-Australian relations.[26] Shepherd had already started an administrative reorganisation while he was the acting high commissioner.[27] Cook's arrival came as a considerable relief, the official secretary having found it 'too strenuous to work at the office all day and attend social functions until midnight almost every night'.[28] Otherwise, there was little sympathy between the two men, who had first worked unhappily with each other when Cook had been the New South Wales postmaster general in the 1890s.[29]

Cook himself was in his element. He soon told Hughes:

> Suffice to say that I have been living more or less in a swirl since my arrival here. I have been made most welcome & am beginning to settle into a steady swing. I find the work interesting & also find plenty of it to do *every day*. I am treating the office as I did every other office I have ever had to administer. I have people here in shoals anxious to know things about Australia.[30]

His highest priority was the promotion of Australia as 'the Land of the Better Chance'.[31] In July 1922, the government whip, Reginald Burchell, who had just returned from England, reported: 'There is no gainsaying the fact that at present the High Commissioner is doing his utmost to place at the disposal of the commercial world the facilities which Australia House undoubtedly possesses. He is aiming at creating a distinct commercial atmosphere at Australia House'.[32]

By far the most important promotional event for Australia in England during Cook's term, the Great Empire Exhibition staged at Wembley in 1924 and 1925, was imperial as well as national. More than seventeen million attended during the first year, including an 'unusual influx' of Australians (14,000 of whom signed the visitors book at Australia House).[33] The high commissioner was a member of the exhibition's executive council and management committee as well as responsible with the agents-general for the London organisation of the Australian contribution, which covered over five acres.[34] With the British government still unwilling to discriminate in favour of empire producers, the dominions had to make do with the goodwill generated by events like the Wembley exhibition and the propaganda directed towards British consumers by bodies like the Empire Marketing Board. Cook had these efforts in mind when he observed with obvious delight in his report for 1926: 'Even more successful was the King's Christmas pudding, in which all the Dominions were represented'.[35] His representational and social duties could also be viewed in the same light:

> It is not generally appreciated in Australia that this exchange of social courtesies has often an incidental but very important business side ... I have considered it not the least important part of my duty as High Commissioner, and in the advancement of Australian interests, to attend many of the official functions to which I have been invited, and I am convinced that much advantage to the Commonwealth has resulted therefrom.[36]

In March 1925 alone he attended eighteen official functions, luncheons and dinners, including two Court receptions at which he presented Australian visitors, and a private dinner given by Leo Amery, the secretary of state for the colonies.[37]

Cook made it 'his business to be the chief permanent link' between Australia and Great Britain.[38] Under his stewardship, the high commissioner's office reverted to the traditions established by Reid, his mentor and patron. According to Shepherd: 'Sir Joseph had had a wonderful time in office'; when both left London in 1927, 'Australia's stock stood higher than that of any other Dominion' and Australia House was 'one of the busiest spots in London'.[39] The *Times* paid Cook a personal tribute in a lead article: his term of office had been 'years of steady work for the increase of our Imperial estate'.[40] He was the first high commissioner to return permanently to Australia and, after chairing a federal Royal Commission which investigated the finances of the South Australian state government, lived quietly in retirement until his death in 1947.

His replacement, Granville Ryrie, immediately sounded the familiar Australian themes. As a pastoralist and the first native-born high commissioner, he emphasised his qualifications to serve the Australian producer and British consumer and migrant. Migration was still 'of the greatest importance not only to Australia, but to the whole Empire'; Australians wanted British investment and goods, despite the recent inroads into the Australian market made by foreign manufactures; the problems of migration and markets were, as always, linked, for 'any increase in the prosperity of the Dominions must lead to an immediate increase in the business that the Dominions are able to do with this country'.[41] But Ryrie's candour, especially about the shortcomings of the British motor industry, was not always welcome and made him an easy target for an Australian press that could be relied on to make copy at his expense. In March 1929, the *Bulletin* observed: '"The Old Brig" bears the reputation in London of being the Empire's champion brick-dropper'.[42] Yet despite the occasional fuss, his career in England was set fair to follow a familiar course.

The crash

In October 1929 two events changed things completely. The first was Labor's return to federal government for the first time in thirteen years. Lacking a majority in the Senate, however, it also lacked real power. The second, the Wall Street crash, heralded the onset of a worldwide depression and marked a watershed in the history of the high commission.

Ryrie himself was unfazed by Labor's success. Casey duly reported:

Sir Granville is not feeling very disturbed about the change of Government in Australia—as far as his personal position is concerned. His contract gives him something over two years still to run, and he has told me that he will not allow himself to be displaced unless they are willing to pay him his salary for the unexpired portion of his appointment— which I imagine they will find it very difficult in the present financial state of things in Australia.[43]

But whatever the high commissioner's personal feelings, the effects of the economic crisis could not be avoided. Labor immediately raised the tariff and took steps to end assisted immigration, measures that were both deeply resented in Britain.[44] The Migration Office—which had been shrinking since 1928—was closed, the handful of remaining officers absorbed into the high commissioner's staff and the post of director abolished at the end of Manning's contract.[45] The chairman of the Public Accounts Committee, Senator Percy Coleman, who was in Geneva to attend a meeting of the International Labour Conference, was asked to find further savings at Australia House.[46] Some posts were abolished, other staff reassigned and various economies made, including a substantial cut to McDougall's remuneration, the sale of one of the two official cars, and the end of regular cinema showings. Trumble attempted to protect the interests of the locally engaged staff, reminding James Scullin, the prime minister: 'In this category are many officers who have rendered long and excellent service and possess claims to a better status than is at present accorded'.[47] It was to little avail because Trumble himself was out of favour. When the posts of financial adviser and official secretary were amalgamated to save more money, Collins displaced him and, with two years of his contract to run, Trumble was controversially given the job of defence liaison officer with only junior officers to support him after the naval branch and military and air staffs were also dispensed with.

The financial crisis that had made the redundancies in London necessary finally overwhelmed the Scullin government.[48] With the collapse of export earnings and loan markets closed to Australia, it struggled to meet the country's overseas commitments and soon approached the British authorities for assistance. The crisis was deepened by the Commonwealth Bank's reluctance to cooperate, the withdrawal of support by two factions within the Labor Party, and the default of interest payments in London by the New South Wales Labor government led by Jack Lang in March 1931. Ironically, Lang had walked out of the Loan Council during the 1920s to preserve the state's 'absolute freedom in raising loans'.[49]

Since October 1929 Ryrie had represented a government with which he had no political sympathy and which could now be best described as 'a lifeless shell awaiting inevitable extinction'.[50] One obituarist recalled: 'What duties the curtailed activities of Australia House left him he discharged loyally and thoroughly'.[51] But he could only do so if he was called upon, and it soon became clear that ministers preferred dealing with Collins directly.[52] Moreover, while Casey stayed in London, he remained the confidential channel between London and Canberra.[53] Even so, as the senior Australian representative, Ryrie still had important duties.[54] He was required at the Bank of England when Collins' financial negotiations extended to the governor and otherwise did his best to calm investors, observing in his 1931 report: 'Never before in our history was it necessary so constantly and particularly to explain the position of our country'.[55] After Lang's default, he refused to allow the British authorities to put pressure on Scullin to make an immediate statement that the Commonwealth would pay the interest owing to New South Wales's bondholders. With the assistance of Casey and Trumble, he continued to attend the Committee of Imperial Defence and dealt with the Admiralty over Labor's defence cuts. Finally, although the reasons can only be guessed at, he was summoned to the palace several times during the difficult negotiations over Isaac Isaacs' appointment as the first native-born governor-general.[56]

The latter was in fact one of Scullin's few achievements in government. Labor finally lost office at the end of 1931 and was replaced by the United Australia Party under the leadership of a former Labor minister, Joseph Lyons. By now Ryrie only had a short time left in London. After a four-month extension to allow his successor to attend the Ottawa conference, he sailed for Australia in July and retired to his pastoral property, Micalago, where he died in 1937.[57] In England he was remembered as a soldier, squatter and expounder of 'the Imperial outlook': 'Among the qualities which commended him to Australians as a representative and gave him a distinctive position in London were his attachment to the land, his special solicitude for the primary producer, and his capabilities as a "bushman".[58]

Bruce, the United Australia Party and the politics of economic diplomacy

The new government decided almost immediately to send the former prime minister, Stanley Melbourne Bruce, back to England as resident minister after he had completed the negotiation of an Anglo-Australian trade treaty at Ottawa in the middle of 1932.[59] In England he would also carry out the duties of the high commissioner. There were several reasons for his mission. The most obvious was a large New South Wales loan maturity which would have to be refinanced in October, despite the weakness of Australian credit in London. A greater prize, however, lay beyond this—the possibility of lowering the interest charges on a much larger proportion of the overseas debt.

The political pressures to succeed and the risks of failure were both enormous. The United Australia Party's appeal to the electorate had been to 'tune-in with Britain' and put its trust in 'sound, honest finance and government'.[60] This meant rejecting unorthodox monetary policies and Lang-inspired demands to suspend overseas payments. Scullin had already carried out a successful voluntary conversion of the domestic debt. One of Lyons's first tasks was to implement the compulsory exchange of the unconverted balance. With Australian bonds overseas bearing much higher rates of interest, Lang announced that New South Wales would default in London for a second time.[61] In such a charged political atmosphere, the party's survival appeared to depend more than ever on the rewards to be gained from the grim struggle to keep faith with the country's overseas creditors. Only a cabinet minister in England—and one of Bruce's standing—would be sufficient 'as a pledge of Australia's full realization of her financial responsibilities and as a corrective to the unfavourable impression created by Mr. Lang's default'.[62]

Bruce's qualifications were indeed outstanding, but it was also obvious that he would never fit comfortably into any government in Canberra again. He had returned to Australia barely a month before and was regarded with Latham as one of the two 'strong men' most likely to succeed Lyons if his health broke down. Yet, with the prime minister holding the Treasury portfolio, he would have to be content with the post of his assistant.[63] He did not himself believe, however, that he would be acceptable once more as a national leader and was still bitter about the treatment he had received from senior party figures after the 1929 election defeat.[64] Finally, he knew that he was a potentially divisive figure in the United Australia Party, particularly given the intrigues of would-be king-makers like his former coalition partner, the leader of the Country Party, Earle Page.[65] Lyons himself was accused of wanting to get him out of the country when he first offered him the high commissionership in February 1933 and, again, when Bruce finally accepted it in September.[66] But Bruce himself did not believe this and already had good reasons for wanting to leave politics.[67] His overseas mission simply reinforced the sense that he had run his course in Australia. As a relatively young man—younger, in fact, than any previous high commissioner—he was still drawn to public life. The particular combination of duty, self-importance, vanity and desire for status or influence that motivated him can never be fully known. He confided simply to Casey: 'for some unknown reason I have a desire to do some sort of job of work for Australia and probably misguidedly I imagine I can be of some service'.[68] His diffidence was probably no more than skin deep.

From September 1932, Bruce exercised the powers of high commissioner as a resident minister in England; after his resignation from the government in October 1933, he held the post as a public official. The financial and trade-related issues he dealt with provided continuity between the two phases of his career. During the Depression, Australia's economic objectives overseas had changed fundamentally. Britain's commitment to *laissez-faire* in economic policy had steadily ebbed away. This was already evident during the 1920s when the Bank of England attempted to use moral suasion to regulate capital exports to the empire.[69] But the imperial government's abandonment of the gold standard and free trade during 1931–32 was the point of no return. It altered irreversibly the United Kingdom's relationship to the dominions and created scope for an economic diplomacy in Whitehall and the City in which Australia was soon heavily involved.[70]

As early as June 1932, Casey—now a member of federal parliament—explained to a senior British official that Bruce's task in London was 'more important in the near view at least than Ottawa. His real mission … is to get by hook or by crook (the latter not in the Lang sense) a reduction in our overseas interest burden'.[71] The sum due annually in England was just over £26 million, equal to three-quarters of the trade surplus that year.[72] The option now existed to redeem £84 million of the most expensive loans. But this could only be exercised successfully if holders were willing to exchange their maturing bonds for new securities that offered less interest or the government was able to sell enough fresh debt to pay them off. The steady fall in the cost of money in the first half of the year and subsequent refinancing of the British War Loan to a 3.5 per cent nominal rate created the opportunity to do so. But they also increased enormously the domestic pressures on Lyons to achieve immediate results.[73]

The Commonwealth's underwriter, the senior partner of the broking firm R. Nivison & Co., Lord Glendyne, did not believe it would be possible to float a loan large enough to retire all or even most of the optional maturities in a single operation. In Australia, the Loan Council and the press remained impatient for a substantial drop in London charges. Some were even prepared to consider a partial default if necessary.[74] By April 1933, Bruce had concluded that a £43 million operation was the least the government could get away with, even though it would be impossible to underwrite and success depended on the moral support of Britain's financial authorities.[75] Unfortunately for him, neither the chancellor of the exchequer nor the governor of the Bank of England was prepared to help in forcing a loan onto the market. They were also unimpressed by Bruce's conjuring of an Australian default in the event of failure. In May they surprised him completely by suggesting that the current official restrictions on capital issues in London might not be lifted to allow the loan to proceed.[76] For all his brinkmanship, Bruce was unwilling to contemplate repudiation of interest payments in any form. He had no alternative but to finesse. Bond prices had recently been weakening in response to anxieties about the Geneva Disarmament Conference, as well as the World Economic Conference due to meet in the summer. The market's nerves offered a way out.[77] Without telling Lyons about the British threat to block an Australian loan, he convinced the Loan Council that a major financial operation was now out of the question and obtained its authority for a much smaller conversion of the most expensive loans instead.[78] Subsequently, although still trying to enlist British support to force the pace, he got through the balance of the £84 million more or less as Glendyne had originally envisaged in a series of separate operations which he completed in February 1934.

While still working through the first round of conversions, his attention turned to a 'new danger'.[79] During 1933, the British government took steps to raise domestic farm incomes by restricting the quantity of food imported into the United Kingdom.[80] The measures it proposed would affect commodities like meat and dairy products for which Britain was the only significant market and Bruce had bargained hardest to obtain concessions at Ottawa. The Anglo-Australian agreement already capped some Australian meat exports for twelve months and allowed the British to impose quotas on all meat from July 1934. Purchases of other commodities could be restricted a year later.[81] None of this made the new British policy any more acceptable. At the World Economic Conference in June, Bruce described the general climate that had developed in favour of restriction as 'an attitude of intolerable pessimism'.[82] But it could not be ignored and he concluded that voluntary cooperation was the only way to moderate its impact on Australia.

The government had agreed when Bruce was appointed high commissioner that he could return briefly to Australia for consultations and to bring himself in touch with public opinion. In fact, he used his visit from late March to the beginning of May 1934 to try to persuade the federal and state governments, commodity marketing boards, and farmer organisations that the Commonwealth was best served by offering to negotiate with the British. As one Labor senator later pointed out, it was an unprecedented campaign by a public official.[83] He had an early success with Lyons, who called a Premiers' Conference in April to consider the proposal. But the combined opposition of the states, the Country Party and producer bodies was enough to kill it off, particularly with a federal election approaching in which the United Australia Party was likely to lose its majority and become dependent on Country Party support. After Bruce's return to London, the government stumbled from one crisis to another as the British authorities started to allocate half-yearly meat quotas to the dominions and, in January 1935, finally threatened to impose the Australian quota by order-in-council.

The experience was a turning point for Bruce. 'My efforts were, I fear, not very successful,' he confided to Casey, 'and the position was further complicated by what I suggest was a considerable lack of guts shown by the Government and its present bedfellows the Country Party to face up to the problem and recognise the issues involved'.[84] He never again attempted to influence economic policy in a similar way. Yet, despite a succession of international crises that increasingly absorbed his time and attention, trade diplomacy and debt renegotiation continued to occupy him in London. Between November 1934 and the middle of 1936, he completed a second round of conversions covering a further £89 million of debt. Altogether over £4 million sterling had been saved in annual interest and exchange charges since his arrival in England.[85] Bruce also participated in the Anglo-Australian trade negotiations in London in 1935 and 1936 as well as the failed attempt to renegotiate the Ottawa agreement in 1938.[86] But he recognised the limits of his influence and believed that ministers should take the lead in trade talks because, as he advised Menzies, only they could hope to hold the government to the terms of any agreement.[87] Finally, as David Lee shows in chapter 6 of this volume, he renewed his close association with McDougall, who convinced him early in the decade that only a general increase in world consumption could raise agricultural incomes and create the economic conditions for international stability.[88] Action on the economic front would also provide the League of Nations with a useful role to counterbalance its obvious political failure. With no other delegates prepared to give a lead at the 1935 Assembly, Bruce himself called for national action to improve dietary standards which would ultimately allow the reform of domestic agriculture and the elimination of trade barriers. For the rest of the decade, he and McDougall advocated the nutrition approach in Geneva and encouraged the League to take practical action to promote it.[89]

Conclusion

As both resident minister and high commissioner during the 1930s, Bruce sought to avoid an Anglo-Australian breakdown over debt and quantitative restriction, to ease the burden of overseas interest payments, and to promote international policies conducive to the growth of Australia's national income. He displayed a characteristic mixture of pragmatism and impatience with political constraints, and an equally characteristic propensity to lead, act independently, and sometimes overreach himself. He did not achieve the spectacular conversion the Lyons government had hoped for, nor did he persuade it of the desirability of voluntary restriction of food exports. In both instances, he was frustrated by the scale of his ambition and the political and practical obstacles in London and Canberra. He was finally left to manage the conversion operations as he saw fit but, in contrast to his influence over Australia's responses to the international crises of the period, he was detached from the formulation of commercial policy. There is no evidence that the government consulted him about the trade diversion measures imposed simultaneously on Japan and the United States in 1936.[90] What is clear enough, however, is that he no longer believed that reliance on empire development could provide a secure foundation for Australia's future prosperity. Not long after the beginning of the trade diversion episode, he told the Tasmanian economist L.F. Giblin: 'the solution of Australia's problem of increased exports cannot be found in the British market ... but must be based on an improvement in world trade and the finding of means to bring about increased consumption'.[91] Neither this change of heart nor his early failures diminished his effectiveness as the Commonwealth's representative in London. Menzies later recalled that he was 'an unsurpassed High Commissioner, who gave prestige to Australia, who was profoundly respected in both the City and in Whitehall ... and whose skill in close negotiation I have never seen excelled, or, for that matter, equalled'.[92]

Australia House itself continued to be administered by the most senior officials the Commonwealth service could offer. After Collins's retirement in 1933, the combined post of financial adviser and official secretary was abolished.[93] The new official secretary, John McLaren, had been in charge of the Prime Minister's Department and was knighted in 1935.[94] His successor in 1936, Stuart McFarlane, returned to Australia to take charge of the Treasury.[95] John Duncan, who followed McFarlane in 1938, was appointed deputy high commissioner in 1942 to relieve Bruce of routine duties. After the war, he became Australia's first minister in Chile.[96]

As for domestic matters, Bruce soon assured Lyons that he was making special efforts 'to ensure that the best possible use is made of Australia House and particularly of the Exhibition Hall'.[97] The London office still had its critics. In 1938 a visiting minister alleged that it was 'not the credit, or the asset, which it should be in Australia'. Even the building resembled 'a morgue'.[98] But after the smooth visit of one large ministerial delegation, the efficiency of the staff was praised by McLaren as 'not least of the factors contributing to this happy state of affairs'.[99] With the resumption of assisted migration in 1938, activity on the Strand started to recover.[100] Sadly, it was soon overshadowed by the deteriorating political conditions across the channel. In December the government followed Bruce's advice and decided to admit 15,000 refugees over the next three years. Almost as soon as the news broke, Australia House was receiving hundreds of inquiries by mail and from personal callers each day.[101] Like Bruce's conversion to economic internationalism, it was another example of the ways in which Australians were becoming involved in a more complex pattern of external relations. The era of reliance on men, money and markets in a sheltered British world was passing.

6 'Ambassador-at-large par excellence': S.M. Bruce and the League of Nations

David Lee

THE Australian journalist Trevor Smith aptly described the influence of Stanley Melbourne Bruce on the evolution of the office of Australian high commissioner in London in the period from 1933 to 1939. Smith observed that Bruce, a few years into his term, enjoyed

> a status which knows no precedent and one which is not likely to be followed. For Mr Bruce has created for himself the unique status and prestige of an ambassador-at-large par excellence. He has risen (and remains) far above his official post.[1]

One reason Bruce achieved such 'unique status' as high commissioner in London in the 1930s was that he was then combining the role of Australian envoy with that of principal representative at the League of Nations, the global organisation of nation-states which Australia had joined in 1919 after Prime Minister W.M. Hughes signed the Treaty of Versailles (including the Covenant of the League of Nations) for Australia in its own right. This was at a time when the only other Australian overseas post was the quasi-diplomatic, but mainly commercial position of commissioner in New York. As a consequence of his dual roles as high commissioner and chief representative at the League, and of the way in which they reinforced each other, Bruce became not only a diplomat of international renown but also one of the most consequential Australian diplomats of the century.

Australian high commissioners in London and the League of Nations

As both Neville Meaney and Bernard Attard showed in earlier chapters, before Bruce became high commissioner in 1933, the ambassadorial status conferred on his predecessors had not made of the office a real diplomatic position. The main functions of the office were representational and commercial.[2] Its diplomatic role was limited by the fact that communication within the British Empire was handled, until 1926, through the governor-general and the British secretary of state for the colonies. By the time that Bruce succeeded to the office in 1933, however, the Balfour Report of 1926 had defined the British dominions as of theoretically equal status with the United Kingdom. Dominion governors-general had evolved from representatives of the British government to representatives of the Crown acting on the advice of responsible dominion ministers; and the 1931 Statute of Westminster had removed the ability of the Westminster parliament to legislate for the dominions, although Australia itself refrained from adopting it until 1942.[3]

These developments enhanced the role of high commissioners in London as political representatives of dominion governments. As Bernard Attard has shown in chapter 4, Bruce's predecessors as high commissioner, Cook and Ryrie, had represented Australia at the League of Nations Assembly. But, usually, ministers led the delegations. In 1921 Bruce himself had done so as a government backbencher before becoming a minister. In 1924, as prime minister, he sent his first attorney-general, Sir Littleton Groom, to the important assembly meeting which debated the Geneva Protocol; two years later, in 1926, he arranged for Groom's successor, John Latham, to lead the Australian delegation to Geneva; and in 1927, 1928 and 1929 the ministers Senator George Pearce, Senator A.J. McLachlan and C.W.C Marr led the delegation. After Bruce himself was appointed high commissioner in 1933, because of his prestige as a long-serving former prime minister and his acknowledged diplomatic skills, he quickly established himself as the de facto permanent Australian representative at the League. Bruce in effect became Australia's ambassador-at-large based in London.

Joseph Lyons, Australia's prime minister from 1931 to 1939, sent Bruce to London as resident minister not long after the United Australia Party won its landslide victory over the Labor Party late in 1931. Lyons did not immediately replace Sir Granville Ryrie with a new high commissioner when the latter returned to Australia in 1932, probably because he had always hoped that Bruce, a potential rival for the prime ministership, would succeed to the post. From as early as March 1933, Lyons sought to persuade Bruce to consider accepting the position through the mediation of R.G. Casey, Bruce's former liaison officer in London.[4] Casey was by that time a United Australia Party backbencher and soon to become Lyons's treasurer.[5] In 1933 Bruce was still comparatively young at fifty, in good health, and had many years ahead of him if he chose to return to Australian politics, a course which, at the conclusion of the Ottawa conference, he appeared to be contemplating. This is evidenced by a letter he wrote to Lyons on 23 August 1932, commending the work of his colleague Henry Gullett, the ex–Australian Imperial Force war correspondent serving as Lyons's trade minister, and adding 'that if you are looking to a successor to myself as resident Minister in London, there is no doubt that Gullett could do most excellent work'.[6]

In September 1933, however, Bruce decided to resign his ministry and his seat in the House of Representatives and to accept the post of high commissioner. In doing so he exchanged the role of politician for diplomat and assumed the duties of representing the Australian government to the British government in London and at the League of Nations in Geneva.[7] From mid-1932 to his assumption of the high commissionership in London in October 1933, Bruce had already begun to make his mark on the international stage. He had successfully negotiated a bilateral trade agreement with the

United Kingdom at Ottawa. Then, at the World Monetary and Economic Conference in London in June 1933, he had spoken out against the dominant mood of insularity and economic nationalism by recommending a coordinated effort to stimulate consumption internationally.

After his appointment as high commissioner, Bruce led Australian delegations at annual sessions of the General Assembly for the rest of the decade, occasionally reinforced by ministerial co-delegates, except only for the meeting in 1939 when his economic adviser in London, F.L. McDougall, deputised for him.[8] During this period Australia adopted a higher profile in League matters than in the 1920s; indeed, it was primarily through the League that Australia began for the first time to express its international personality.[9] This was largely due to Bruce's having become principal Australian delegate in Geneva. A former prime minister, conscientious in his duties, meticulous, thorough and respected by the British government, he quickly gained the high regard of officials and representatives in Geneva. At a time when instructions from Canberra were irregular, Bruce was left with considerable autonomy to shape Australia's embryonic foreign policy.

Australia's reputation, and Bruce's with it, were further enhanced when Australia was elected as a temporary member of the League Council for 1933–36.[10] When Australia joined the League of Nations, the Council, its executive organ, consisted of three permanent members, Great Britain, France and Italy. By 1933 Japan had recently left it over the Manchurian crisis, followed by Germany on 19 October of that year.[11] The Soviet Union would join the League and take a permanent position on the Council from 18 September 1934; but at the time that Australia joined it, its members were Great Britain, France, Italy, China, Czechoslovakia, Denmark, Germany, Mexico, Panama, Poland and Spain.[12] The Council's appointment of Bruce as rapporteur on financial questions at his first meeting set him on a path to becoming an acknowledged authority not only on strictly financial matters but also on social, economic and technical aspects that he would come to see as the areas in which the world organisation could make its strongest contribution to welfare and peace.[13] In the Assembly's Economic Committee, Bruce quickly tried to focus the League's attention on economic matters, such as the protectionist measures adopted by developed, manufacturing countries in agriculture and the effects of these restrictions on countries such as Australia whose exports were largely in this area.[14]

The Italo-Abyssinian war

By 1934 it was becoming apparent that the fascist dictator of Italy, Benito Mussolini, was preparing to annex Abyssinia, a sovereign state and member of the League of Nations since 1923, but also an African country surrounded by European dependencies. Internationalists and proponents of collective security disapproved of the prospect of a European colonial power and League member annexing the small African kingdom.

Others regarded it as a backward country—where government writ did not run very far—that might benefit from Italian tutelage. The British government was torn between British public opinion, which favoured the League of Nations system, and the government's desire to conciliate France and Italy, fellow League members and bulwarks against the rising power of Germany. By May 1935, the British government feared that if the League did not become more active before the meeting of its Council in Geneva in September 1935, then Mussolini would soon invade Abyssinia, triggering pressure in the League to take action against Italy. Consequently, the British government worked energetically to prevent a conflict. In June 1935 it proposed ceding Abyssinia the small port of Zeila in British Somaliland, and a corridor to it, to compensate its emperor, Haile Selassie, for those parts of his land that he could be persuaded to cede to Italy.[15] The plan was premised on the consideration that Abyssinia's sovereignty as a fully fledged state and League member could not be compromised and that any settlement had to be acceptable to both Italy and Abyssinia. Nevertheless, Mussolini rebuffed an overture along these lines from Anthony Eden, the British minister for League of Nations affairs. He wanted complete political, economic and military control of Abyssinia.

When Italian and Abyssinian troops clashed on the disputed border between Abyssinia and Italian Somaliland, Selassie appealed to the League Council, on which Bruce was now sitting as a representative, to safeguard peace.[16] The reference of the Abyssinian issue to the League posed an acute dilemma for Britain and its dominions, and for Bruce. Italy had been an ally of Britain and France during the war, and the coming to power in 1922 of Mussolini had not significantly affected Britain's relations with her.[17] British and French inclinations towards the conciliation of Italy were strengthened by the common anxiety of all three countries about the threat now posed by Nazi Germany. This had prompted them to form a front against German expansionism at the Italian town of Stresa in April 1935, and to declare that there should be no unilateral repudiation of European treaties.

In the period from June to September 1935, attempts both inside and outside the League to keep the peace between Italy and Abyssinia failed; on 2 October 1935 Italian troops violated the Abyssinian frontier; and in the following days Italian aeroplanes bombed Abyssinian towns and a state of open warfare ensued between Italy and Ethiopia.[18] The historian David Carlton has observed that British ministers made no attempt to seek advice from the dominion governments per se in the making of its policy before and during the Italo-Abyssinian war. But when British ministers did later consult the dominions, they would meet with the five high commissioners in London or Geneva, where the latter frequently represented their governments. Moreover, it was during the Abyssinian and later Rhineland crises in 1935–36 that the British government revived the practice of convening regular meetings with the dominion high commissioners in London.[19] This process had two advantages for British ministers. One was that face-to-face approaches were more likely to be successful for British ministers than cabled communications with distant governments. A second was that the oral advice of dominion high commissioners was more malleable than the written instructions of dominion governments. This informal process gave Bruce considerable scope to shape the policy of his own government, as well as to influence that of Great Britain.[20] The Italo-Abyssinian crisis provides a good example of how Bruce's role as dominion high commissioner combined with that of principal Australian representative in Geneva and how he used his dual diplomatic functions to influence the policy of both the British and Australian governments.

In meetings on this question between the dominions secretary, Malcolm MacDonald, and the dominion high commissioners, Bruce was the most critical of the application of sanctions against Italy. In his view, the choice for the League was either to impose all the sanctions available, including the most effective one—an oil embargo—or not to apply them at all given that the imposition of partial sanctions would not stop the invasion of Abyssinia but merely alienate Italy from the Stresa front. Bruce was mindful that the situation was complicated by serious differences between Britain and France over how to deal with Italy. Fearful of war with Germany, France was most anxious to keep Italy on side.[21] In these circumstances, Bruce preferred that the League should confine itself merely to voting for a resolution condemning Italian aggression against Abyssinia while separately Britain, the dominions and France would pledge themselves to rearm so they would be better able to resist future fascist aggression. As Bruce explained it to Lyons in a cablegram:

> If action taken in way of economic sanctions, I am of opinion such action must be effective. Intention of sanctions was to limit immediately the war area and put an end to the war, and not designed as a means whereby, by some limited action embarrassing to the Covenant-breaking nation, other members of the League could reinforce and make clear their moral detestation of the course adopted. It is difficult to visualise economic sanctions being made effective to the point of preventing a war in view of U.S.A., Germany and Japan being outside League.[22]

Bruce informed Lyons that he had put this position to Eden and the foreign secretary, Sir Samuel Hoare, 'not as views of the Australian Government but as points requiring consideration by the British Government when considering their action'.[23] Without the official sanction of his government, Bruce relied on the reputation he had gained in Geneva and his authority as a former Australian prime minister to influence the British government against sanctions.

In retrospect, Bruce's suggested course of action had much to commend it when judged against the contradictory policy that Britain eventually adopted. On the one hand, the British government was publicly urging the application of limited sanctions in Geneva. Indeed, Samuel Hoare astonished the world by the forcefulness of his speech in Geneva at the beginning of September, when he announced that 'Britain would back the League in steady and collective resistance to all acts of unprovoked aggression'.[24]

Hoare's speech was interpreted as meaning that Britain was prepared to stop Mussolini, if necessary by force of arms, from annexing Abyssinia. Under British leadership, the League (including Australia) then voted for partial sanctions to be implemented against Italy.[25]

The British government's policy remained ambiguous and unsettled. On the one hand, Eden, lord privy seal and minister for the League of Nations, supported making collective security work even at the risk of provoking hostilities with Italy. He preferred extending sanctions as a means of forcing Mussolini to the peace table. On the other hand, the Foreign Office and the foreign secretary, Hoare, were not confident that the League could or should play such a role. They were more concerned with salvaging the Stresa front. In contrast to Eden, Hoare favoured using a promise to lift the partial sanctions to persuade Mussolini to accept a settlement that gave him most of what he wanted without involving the complete destruction of Abyssinia.[26] Bruce supported Hoare's position over Eden's and used the regular meetings of dominion high commissioners which were then taking place to influence the British government accordingly.

At the same time as he was encouraging the League to apply sanctions against Italy, Hoare was concluding with France and Italy a secret agreement that involved pressing Abyssinia to cede a large portion of its territory to Italy and to hand over an even larger part as a 'zone of economic expansion and settlement', receiving in return a corridor to the sea.[27] When the news of the secret deal was leaked to the press, the public outcry in Britain forced Hoare to resign as foreign secretary in favour of Bruce's close collaborator in Geneva, Anthony Eden. From that time on there would be no possibility of effective League action on Abyssinia—the Italian victory was proclaimed in May 1936 and sanctions were withdrawn in June. In contrast to the British policy of publicly supporting collective security, while privately trying to conclude a secret deal with Mussolini, Bruce openly admitted the powerlessness of the League to act in this case.[28]

The British government, and particularly Eden, valued the prestige that Bruce had gained for himself in Geneva and the two worked closely together. Indeed, Eden recalled later that other members of the League of Nations were envious of the close relationship between himself and the pre-eminent dominion high commissioner, Bruce. On one occasion, Romania's delegate to the League, Nicolae Titulescu, saw Bruce and Eden deep in conversation. At the time dissatisfied with his relationship with the foreign minister of Romania's ally, France, Titulescu galvanised the company with an exclamation: '*Moi, je veux être Dominion!*'[29]

The measure of the influence which Bruce had attained with the British government was well illustrated in the abdication crisis of 1936. The crisis had arisen when British public opinion started to focus on the association of King Edward VIII with Wallis Simpson, an American woman who had divorced a US naval officer and then remarried an American businessman. In June 1936, Simpson commenced divorce proceedings against her second husband, bringing about the possibility that she would then be able to marry the King before his coronation.[30] The possible marriage, against which many of the King's subjects had strong religious, legal, political and moral objections, precipitated a constitutional crisis in the British Empire.

Bruce, like all members of the Lyons government in Canberra, had strong objections to the marriage, and played a key role in representing Australian and wider dominion opinion on the marriage to British Prime Minister Stanley Baldwin. After learning from Baldwin of his lack of success in persuading the King not to marry Simpson, Bruce gave him a detailed memorandum on the subject in November. It illustrated the degree to which Bruce had been accepted not only as the pre-eminent dominion high commissioner but as a valued adviser to British prime ministers. He was emphatic that if the King persisted in his intention to marry Simpson, 'In these circumstances you would have to tell him that unless he was prepared to abandon any idea of marriage with the woman you would be compelled to advise him to abdicate and unless he accepted such advice you would be unable to continue as his Adviser and would tender the resignation of the Government'.[31] Bruce was a strong voice among the many that stiffened Baldwin's resolve against the marriage. On 10 December 1936, the King's written abdication notice was witnessed by his three younger brothers including Prince Albert, Duke of York and later King George VI, whom Bruce as prime minister had arranged to open the parliament buildings in Canberra in 1927. Because the Statute of Westminster of 1931 had replaced a single Crown for the entire empire with multiple crowns for each dominion, Edward VIII's abdication required the consent of each dominion; Bruce helped to facilitate Australia's assent to the abdication. He was the most vocal and influential of the dominion high commissioners in favour of the abdication and he was motivated by the sense that it was necessary, because of the moral and political significance of the Crown in the dominions, to help preserve and unite the British Empire in perilous times.

The nutrition initiative

While Bruce was sceptical of the League's capacity to enforce collective security, he was one of the foremost advocates of expanded efforts in economic and social affairs. Bruce shared with the South African statesman Jan Smuts the view that the Covenant of the League provided the members of the British Empire with a common code of practice in the absence of which their foreign policies might follow divergent paths.[32] Bruce was keen to widen the League's membership and promote its unity at a time of increasing international tension by concentrating on economic and social issues. As prime minister, Bruce had taken a keen interest in the application of science to the improvement of industry and had established a national research body, the Council for Scientific and Industrial Research.[33] In Geneva and London, he remained enthusiastic about the capacity of science to improve humanity's condition and his main source of inspiration on the question of nutrition was the fertile mind of Frank McDougall.

In the 1920s, McDougall had persuaded Bruce to bring the Scottish scientist John Boyd Orr, then head of the Rowett Institute near Aberdeen, to Australia. Boyd Orr retained his connections with both McDougall and with Bruce when the latter moved to London in 1932.[34] Boyd Orr was much impressed by a 1935 League of Nations report on nutrition and public health that publicised the extent of international malnutrition: the diets of two-thirds of the world's peoples were inadequate. He and McDougall persuaded Bruce to bring the League's attention to the link between agriculture and nutrition with the aim of inducing its members to increase consumption and thereby improve world nutritional standards.[35] Bruce and the visiting Australian attorney-general, Robert Menzies, tried to induce Britain to take the lead, but neither it, nor France nor Italy, was prepared to do so. Bruce therefore took the initiative himself, speaking in the plenary session of the League and its Second Committee. On 19 September 1935, he declared:

> An increased demand in the countries of western civilization for the health promoting foods would be followed inevitably by an increased world demand for all agricultural products. Thus, in addition to humanitarian reasons which I have already put before you, I should, from the standpoint of enlightened self-interest of Australia, rejoice to see growing public and governmental interest in increased consumption.[36]

The Assembly passed a resolution authorising its technical bodies to undertake further work on the connections between nutrition and health. This led to appointment of a scientific committee that drew up dietary standards later applied in Allied rationing systems during World War II.[37] One historian has argued that if the League had done nothing else than initiate the study of nutrition and 'provide for continuous international cooperation for the solution of the health, economic, and social problems bound up with it, it would have justified its existence'.[38]

Bruce's role earned him plaudits throughout the world, and in December 1936 the Lyons government even nominated him for the Nobel Peace Prize, partly on the basis of his work on nutrition. But Bruce's nutrition campaign was overshadowed by the gathering European storm: he launched his nutrition initiative at the same time that Hoare made his galvanizing speech on Abyssinia; and the assessor of Bruce's nomination for the prize was at the time unclear about the far-reaching significance of his achievements. Although Viscount Cecil won the prize in 1937, Bruce was later proud when Lord Boyd Orr (as he now was) took out an individual prize in 1949 for what had in fact been an endeavour pursued collectively by Boyd Orr, Bruce, McDougall and others since 1935: to help maintain world peace by improving nutritional standards.[39]

The Rhineland crisis

While Bruce was applying himself to the problem of nutrition, another crisis was developing in Europe. France had supported the admission of the Soviet Union to the League of Nations and signed with that country in May 1935 a treaty of mutual assistance which Hitler used as a pretext for Germany to break both the Versailles and Locarno treaties by occupying the Rhineland on 7 March 1936. This was an area which had been demilitarised under the Versailles treaty. The German dictator followed up with a speech in the Reichstag declaring his willingness to atone for the fracturing of Locarno by entering into new pacts of guarantee in the west and of non-aggression in the east, by undertaking to return to the League of Nations, and promising to conclude an air pact with his western neighbours. From Canberra, Lyons tried to influence the British government and the League, via Bruce's presidency of the League Council in 1936, to accept the German occupation of the Rhineland and negotiate with Hitler. On this occasion, however, Lyons was at odds with his high commissioner, who had already indicated that he personally supported the harder line proposed by Foreign Secretary Eden for consultative military talks with the French.[40] The French were furious at the German behaviour, but after at first contemplating unilateral military action, decided to follow the procedures of the Treaty of Locarno that required, in the first instance, the League Council to decide on whether the German occupation of the Rhineland involved a breach of its obligations.

The Council convened in the Court of St James in London on 14 March under the presidency of Bruce, whom F.P. Walters, a senior official and later a historian of the League, described as 'the best, perhaps of the many first-rate chairmen who presided over the Council, Conferences, or Committees of the League'.[41] The secretary-general of the League at the time, Joseph Avenol, agreed with Walters, telling the Australian diplomat Alfred Stirling that 'Bruce was one of the two best "*ou peut-être un des trois*"—among the many Chairmen the Council had had in its fifteen years'.[42] Bruce, however, was presiding over a Council that was fatally divided.[43] The Soviet foreign minister, Maxim Litvinov, criticised the trend of German foreign policy and offered Russian support to any action that the Locarno powers took. He was supported by the French foreign minister, Pierre-Etienne Flandin, who indicated that France was prepared to act but wished to do so in concert with its allies.[44] Britain and the dominions, on the other hand, reached the consensus that Germany's occupation of an area which was patently German territory was a lesser violation than Italy's blatant aggression in Abyssinia, and was not a subject over which to go to war.[45]

With France ultimately unwilling to act against Germany without British support, and Britain unwilling to give France the necessary guarantees, the League and the Locarno powers did nothing. Bruce took the view that, as with the Abyssinian and Manchurian crises, it was beyond the capacity of the League to oppose Germany's occupation. In a meeting of dominion high commissioners during the Rhineland crisis, he drew the conclusion that '[t]here was general agreement that the responsibilities of the League in its present form were too wide, and it was only in the development of regional pacts that a measure of collective security could be obtained in the future'.[46] He developed this thesis later by proposing to modify the Covenant of the League of Nations to preserve the rule of law in international affairs—this could be achieved, he thought, if economic sanctions were not automatically applied by nations, which was practically the case anyway, and if military sanctions 'should be limited to obligations undertaken in regional pacts of mutual support against aggression duly recorded with the League of Nations'. Most importantly, Bruce considered that the League should make it an urgent priority to encourage economic growth and restore world trade, a task to which he turned his hand in 1939 as chairman of the Bruce committee on the reform of the League of Nations.[47]

The Montreux conference

The Abyssinian and Rhineland crises, and the trend towards re-armament, prompted the Turkish president, Kemal Atatürk, to seek to remilitarise the Turkish Straits, which comprised the Dardanelles, the Sea of Marmara and the Bosphorus. Under the Treaty of Lausanne of 1923 following the Chanak crisis of 1922, the straits had been demilitarised and placed under the control of an international commission. The 1923 Straits Convention gave full freedom of passage through the straits, except that no power would be permitted to send through them a force greater than the Black Sea's most powerful fleet, Russia's.[48] Great Britain, France, Germany and Italy also pledged themselves to act together if they were called on to defend freedom of passage. In April 1936, after the Rhineland crisis, the Turkish foreign minister, Rüstü Aras, circulated a note to all the signatories to the Treaty of Lausanne inviting them to take part in a conference to revise the Lausanne Convention. While Turkey could have proceeded to remilitarise the straits through a *coup de main*, Atatürk decided that, by proceeding legally, he could achieve his objective without undermining the League of Nations system or the sanctity of international law.[49]

On 29 May 1936, the dominions secretary, Malcolm MacDonald, cabled the Australian government advising that the British government favoured renegotiation of the Straits Convention. Turkey's friendship, he advised, 'was likely to prove of much greater value than the retention of purely theoretical rights in regard to a somewhat illusory demilitarisation and an already limited freedom of passage through the Straits'.[50] Because the empire had ratified the Lausanne treaty, including the Straits Convention, on behalf of the dominions, MacDonald wanted to know whether Australia wished simply to indicate that it was prepared to accept adjustments negotiated by Britain, or whether it actually wanted to participate in the conference separately. Senator George Pearce, now the minister for external affairs, was inclined to adopt the former course. Before making the decision, however, he directed the secretary of his department to ask for Bruce's opinion.[51] Bruce disagreed with Pearce. 'Such an action', he cabled his old friend in terms reminiscent of Hughes's insistence on the necessity of Australian representation at Versailles in 1919, 'is hardly in accord with our status and would give colour to suggestion that Dominions claim to be independent members of League of Nations is scarcely in accordance with fact'.[52] Pearce heeded the advice and commissioned Bruce to represent

Australia at the international conference that opened in the Swiss city of Montreux on 22 June 1936.

Bruce was selected to preside largely because, by his own account, none of the big powers wished to take the chair.[53] While this might have been a contributing factor, the Turks probably wanted Bruce in the role because of the good relationship that Aras had developed with him on the Council, and because of Bruce's success when he presided over that body during the Rhineland crisis.[54] When the delegates began discussions in Montreux, the Soviet commissar for foreign affairs, Maxim Litvinov, proposed to close the straits to the warships of non–Black Sea states while maintaining full liberty of passage for Black Sea states. This received support from Jean Paul-Boncour, the delegate of Russia's ally, France. It did not, however, suit the interests of the British government.[55] After negotiation in and outside the conference, the British agreed to a compromise in which the number, size and armaments of non–Black Sea states' warships were limited, both in passage through the straits and in the Black Sea, while those of Black Sea states were accorded significantly greater freedom than before.

Bruce's task of helping the parties reach a comprehensive agreement given the gulf between the British and Soviet–French positions was difficult: the biggest obstacle to surmount was the question of the rights of belligerents in a war in which Turkey was neutral. Essentially, the British wanted to preserve full belligerent rights in this situation, while the Russians produced a formula whereby the straits would remain closed to the warships of all belligerent states except in cases involving Turkey's own rights and obligations as a League member. On 9 July, the Soviets made their amendment even more invidious to the British by proposing that in a war, Turkey being neutral, states could render aid to one another through the straits according to the arrangements set forth in regional and mutual assistance pacts.[56] This formula would have meant that Turkey, though neutral, might be obliged to render assistance in war to France and the Soviet Union by virtue of the security pact which those two countries, but not Turkey, had signed in 1935. It raised the danger for Britain that Germany might react against the Montreux Convention by denouncing a naval limitations accord which it had reached with Britain in 1935. In the end, a crisis meeting of the British cabinet, over Admiralty objections, agreed to the compromise position of closing the straits in time of war, 'subject only to the obligations of the Covenant and obligations to which Turkey may be a party'.[57] The British compromise allowed agreement to be reached.

In his closing remarks to the conference, Bruce declared that Turkey in 1936 had provided a 'magnificent example' to the whole world in trying to reach a solution to international problems through legal methods and expressed the hope that the Montreux conference would pave the way for easier and better regulation of international conflicts.[58] The agreement gave practical expression to Bruce's thesis that international collaboration on the basis of peaceful negotiation, especially between erstwhile enemies, offered the most efficacious means of preserving world order. Shortly afterwards, the Melbourne *Herald* noted:

> He seems to have a particular flair for presiding at momentous international conferences. His personal dignity, measured speech, quickness and tact are invaluable assets on these occasions and his aptitude and capacity for these events are reinforced by his undoubted passion for world affairs.[59]

George Rendel, a British diplomat and member of the delegation to Montreux, was similarly complimentary about Bruce's presidency of the conference:

> Bruce was at the height of his powers, active, clear-headed, objective, courteous, conciliatory and fair. If the Conference succeeded and a reasonable new Convention was produced he must bear a major share of the credit. There was hardly a day when he did not save the conference from a conflict which must have led to a complete breakdown, when he did not bring it back to sanity and good humour, and when he did not firmly and wisely steer it back towards the real goal.[60]

Lord Stanley, the head of the British delegation, agreed that 'we have had the best President we could possibly have found', and Litvinov commented: 'This is not the first time it has been my privilege to take part in conferences presided over by the Rt. Hon. S.M. Bruce, and I can only say that my admiration for his talents as a President has increased on each occasion'. For Turkey, Aras remarked that 'we should rejoice that those tragic happenings which marked one of the most heroic episodes of the Great War spared [Bruce, a British Army Gallipoli veteran] so that one day he might come and preside here over the peaceful solution of the question of the Straits'.[61] Of immense personal significance was a gold cigarette case which Atatürk himself sent to Bruce and which the latter was to use for the rest of his life.[62] Bruce himself jocularly remarked to Casey that, after Montreux

> I have some apprehensions … as I have by some evil chance, established a reputation as the Professional Chairman for International Conferences and I may find myself in some embarrassment in dodging the unpleasant and sticky jobs they will try to land me with.[63]

Even Bruce's old rival Billy Hughes had nice things to say: 'Your activities on behalf of the Commonwealth have won you the golden opinions from all sorts & conditions of men & I am sure have kept you pretty busy.'[64]

The Bruce report

Between 1937 and 1939, Bruce devoted much attention to how Australia and the British Empire could recover from a depression that had almost reduced Australia to insolvency. These ideas helped influence his prescriptions for reforming the League of Nations and indeed the whole international economic system. In early 1937 Bruce produced a paper, developed originally by his economic adviser, McDougall, and a circle of academics and policymakers with whom he associated in London, titled 'Economic Appeasement'.[65] Smuts had contributed the word 'appeasement' to political debate in 1919. For him at the time it meant a policy of magnanimity and prudent restraint exercised by a stronger party against a weaker. The term later came to have a derogatory connotation, namely as a policy of propitiation followed by weaker powers against stronger ones.[66] Bruce used the term not in the sense of appeasing Germany but partly in Smuts's original sense. Its main thrust, building on the nutrition campaign of 1935–36, was to revive world trade by improving living standards. This aim would be achieved by increasing purchasing power via lower food prices, and bettering working conditions through the auspices of the International Labour Organization, a specialised agency of the League. Specifically, Bruce recommended replacing quotas on food imports with subsidies for growers; he also advocated raising the living standards of peasant farmers in Europe through rural credits and assistance for housing. Barriers to trade, he envisaged, would generally be lowered and this would entail reducing the British tariff and surrendering some of the preferences won by the dominions at Ottawa.[67]

The plan was radical and unorthodox; almost certainly—in view of the implication that Australia would need to surrender some of its preferential access in British markets—it would have been unpalatable to the Australian government had he shared with Canberra the full text. A key selling point was its potential appeal to the Roosevelt administration in the United States, which favoured plans to reduce political tension in Europe through economic means. Roosevelt's secretary of state, Cordell Hull, had already announced on 10 February 1937 that an international economic settlement would pave the way for a political settlement.[68] Bruce agreed with Hull, arguing that 'I do not accept the view that political appeasement must be achieved before any progress can be made towards economic co-operation'.[69] When Bruce submitted the paper to the secretary-general of the League of Nations, Avenol, he wrote that:

> I am convinced that in this direction there is an opportunity for the League to play an invaluable part and at the same time to restore its prestige which has been so badly shaken by recent happenings in the political sphere … I am certain that quite apart from the good work that would be done in connection with the problem, it is vital for the prestige and future wellbeing of the League that it should afford active leadership towards bringing about economic appeasement.[70]

Bruce returned to England from a visit to Australia and the United States in the middle of 1939 at a time of increasing international tension to which Avenol responded by pressing for the reorganisation of the League. On 27 May 1939, the League Council, at Avenol's request, appointed Bruce to chair a committee of five to seven to advise on the matter. In addition to its role on matters of sovereignty and peacekeeping, the League had played an expanding role in fostering international cooperation to address transnational socioeconomic problems that could not be overcome solely by national action, for example on narcotics, refugees, health and finance. Indeed, in retrospect, its functional agencies redeemed the dismal political record of the League: in demonstrating the potentialities of international cooperation in social and economic areas, they may be regarded 'as the League's most enduring contribution to the modern world'.[71] Bruce had been instrumental in promoting both these programs and the inclusion of a social welfare ethic in them since 1935. Following the Council's action, Avenol impressed on Bruce the importance of the task and hoped that Bruce's committee would prepare a report 'of a very wide nature', permitting the League to escape the 'impasse' confronting it.[72]

The Bruce committee, which met in Paris from 7 to 12 August 1939 and issued its report on 22 August, had four main recommendations: to unite all social and economic activities of the League under a single effective and representative agency; to recognise the increasing interconnectedness among these activities and provide for their better coordination; to increase their efficiency and vigour through greater publicity; and to give non-members of the League, particularly the United States, the opportunity to participate as equals. The report pointed out:

> The League is not and never has been an institution concerned solely with the prevention of war. Its economic and humanitarian work, which is now an essential element in the promotion of peaceful civilisation, has always constituted a large part of its activities, as is witnessed by the fact that more than 60% of the budget is now devoted to it.[73]

The resulting 'Bruce report' accordingly recommended the establishment of a central committee for economic and social questions to direct the work of all the relevant League committees: it would consist initially of 24 members chosen by the Assembly, meet at least once a year and consider a budget presented by the secretary-general.[74]

Although overtaken by the outbreak of war, the report was a landmark in the history of international organisation that subsequently paved the way for the establishment of the Economic and Social Council of the United Nations and its coordination of the work of the United Nations' manifold specialised agencies. It was the culmination of a movement to transform the League into an organisation to promote the idea that international economic policies should promote the wellbeing of the masses. The report was underwritten by an approach to international organisation, later described as 'functionalist', which asserted that the development of international and social cooperation is a fundamental prerequisite for the preservation of peace and the elimination of war. As espoused by one of its leading exponents and a contemporary of Bruce's, David Mitrany, functionalism asserted that peace could be preserved less by organising around points of national conflict, like the Italo-Abyssinian war, than by seeking out areas of mutuality, elevating living standards in undeveloped areas, reducing the impact of national borders on the working of the global economy, and promoting higher standards of health, culture and social justice.[75] Bruce's disposition was to look to issues such as nutrition and health that united the peoples of the world, rather than trying ineffectively to mobilise force to resolve the political issues that were dividing them. The Bruce report, influenced as it was by such ideas, helped to persuade the then isolationist United States administration of the importance of international collaboration at a time when the League as a political body was thoroughly discredited.[76]

Conclusion

The period from 1933 to 1939 was a high point for the office of the Australian high commissioner in London. This chapter has argued that an essential reason for this was that the incumbent, Stanley Melbourne Bruce, combined two roles—envoy in London and principal representative in Geneva—and so became a diplomat of considerable importance. At a time when international tension was rising and the League of Nations failing as a political organisation, Bruce marked out a path by which the organisation could be refashioned. Throughout the Italo-Abyssinian and Rhineland disputes and the lead-up to war with Germany, he argued a case for the League not to try to perform a function for which it was not equipped—namely that of enforcer of collective security. Instead he sought to develop the League's effort in social and economic areas as a goal worthy of pursuing in its own right and as a way of easing political tension.

He scored a marked success in 1935 in launching the nutrition initiative, which many years later was to bear fruit in the establishment of the United Nations Food and Agriculture Organization, and his 1939 report laid out the blueprint for the United Nations Economic and Social Council as central coordinator of the UN's manifold specialised agencies. Moreover, his experience as both a dominion prime minister and a dominion high commissioner in the conferences and councils of one international 'organisation', the British Empire, helped equip him to become one of the best chairmen that another international organisation, the League of Nations, ever produced. His skill in presiding over the League of Nations Council in 1936 led to his chairing the Montreux conference, which, in a dismal period for resolving international disputes by multilateral negotiation, achieved the extraordinary feat of fashioning an international regime for the Turkish Straits that has lasted to this day.

The Australian High Commission in London in the 1930s under Bruce reached a status which had known no precedent and which was not to be followed. After 1939 the League of Nations lapsed into desuetude and the Australian government established direct diplomatic representation in other places than London, meaning that Bruce's role in the 1930s as Australia's sole 'ambassador-at-large par excellence' would not be repeated.

Sir Joseph Cook (centre, holding paper), then minister for the navy, in a crowd of men entering the first meeting of the Paris Peace Conference, which established the League of Nations, 7 May 1919. [National Archives of Australia Image Number M3609:4]

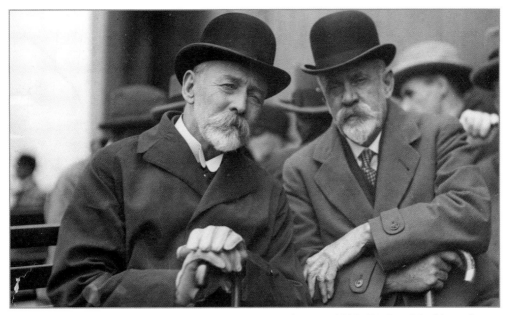

Sir Joseph Cook (left), with A.E. Hunt, public service arbitrator, 1925. [National Archives of Australia Image Number M3582:3]

From left: Sir Joseph Cook, Lady Cook, Lady Novar and the Bishop of Rockhampton on the tenth anniversary of Anzac Day. [National Archives of Australia Image Number CP374/21:30]

Sir Joseph Cook delivering a speech in front of the memorial to the 2nd Australian Division at Mont-Saint-Quentin, 30 August 1925. [National Archives of Australia Image Number M3623:3]

Sir Joseph Cook (left) in the uniform of a Knight Grand Cross of the Order of St Michael and St George at St James's Palace, London, with the Canadian high commissioner, 1925.
[National Archives of Australia Image Number M3614:9]

Sir Joseph Cook opening the apple exhibit in Exhibition Hall, Australia House, 1 April 1925.
[National Archives of Australia Image Number CP374/21:30]

Sir Joseph Cook and Lady Cook, 1927. [National Archives of Australia Image Number
A3560: 3668]

Sir Granville Ryrie in full military ceremonial uniform in 1928. [Australian War Memorial Negative Number PO1778.010]

Sir Granville Ryrie (left) with artist Will Longstaff in front of the latter's painting *Menin Gate at Midnight.* [Australian War Memorial Negative Number PO1778.008]

The Montreux conference in session with S.M. Bruce (centre) presiding, Montreux, 1936. [National Archives of Australia Image Number M112:1/1]

S.M. Bruce (left) formally opening (or closing) the Montreux conference, 1936. [National Archives of Australia Image Number M112:1/16]

7 'Undependable busybody'? S.M. Bruce and World War II

Carl Bridge

I THINK the High Commissioners are the most undependable busybodies. Bruce is bad': so wrote Sir Alexander Cadogan, permanent head of the British Foreign Office, in his diary on 13 September 1939, soon after the outbreak of World War II.[1] It was hardly a flattering assessment of the members of what the high commissioners liked to think of as the 'junior war cabinet'.[2] Stanley Melbourne Bruce, a former Australian prime minister, privy counsellor, sometime chairman of the League of Nations Council, and Australian high commissioner in the United Kingdom from 1933 to 1945, was universally acknowledged as doyen of the British Commonwealth's diplomats in London, yet here is Cadogan describing him at a critical time as an 'undependable busybody'. British prime ministers Stanley Baldwin and Neville Chamberlain sought and valued his counsel, but Winston Churchill hardly ever did. Anthony Eden, the British dominions secretary and later foreign secretary, thought Bruce full of 'almost inexhaustible good sense and patience'. One of Australia's official war historians, Paul Hasluck, wrote enigmatically that 'in an unusual way, [Bruce was] an influential participant in the conduct of [the] war', while other historians have their reservations. Peter Edwards detected a long-term waning of Bruce's influence after Churchill came to power in May 1940, and Mary Cumpston found Bruce in wartime to be 'an increasingly lonely and frustrated figure whose counsel was unsought'. The ever-suspicious Australian Labor external affairs minister, Dr Herbert Vere Evatt, tried to have him removed, but Prime Minister John Curtin, Evatt's rival, praised Bruce's work and kept him in office, despite, or perhaps even because of, the hoary old taunts from the Labor left that he had been 'duchessed' and was an 'English gentleman, born in Australia'.[3]

How did this arch-appeaser of the prewar years manage to remain in post when virtually all the other so-called 'guilty men' of Munich were swept away by the war? How well did he serve Australia as high commissioner and, after June 1942, accredited representative in the British war cabinet? Was he 'undependable'? And, if so, from whose point of view? It seems that, from a British, or rather Churchillian perspective, he was a constant annoyance, engaged in special pleading for Australia and refusing to see things globally. Judged from Canberra, he was doing a good job, though he might have managed a little better.

The arch-appeaser

The roots of Bruce's appeasement were threefold: ethical, economic and strategic. Ethically, he was deeply opposed to war. Severely wounded on Gallipoli, he had returned to Australia and entered federal politics as a Nationalist while also continuing to chair the board of the family import firm, Paterson, Laing and Bruce. It was while on one of his regular extended visits to the firm's London offices that he was first called upon in 1921 to represent Australia at the League of Nations. There, as the only delegate to have seen active service in World War I, he spoke movingly of the League's great anti-war purpose:

> If you had seen men mutilated and dying, without possibility of being helped; if you had ever heard the cry of a wounded man out between the lines, with no possibility of assistance being given to him, and with the likelihood that he may be there dying for days; if you had seen hundreds of men gasping their lives out, their faces discoloured because of some hideous and frightful gas—then I venture to say that you would look on this question with a different eye.[4]

We should be in no doubt that he took his responsibility to keep humanity out of war, if he possibly could, very seriously.

Economically, Bruce saw appeasement as a means of promoting multilateral trade liberalisation. He saw eye to eye with Cordell Hull, the US secretary of state, and with his under-secretary Sumner Welles, who wanted to lower the world's trade barriers as a means of both combating the Depression and removing the grievances of nations such as Japan, Italy and Germany. Such moves would also, incidentally, make the most of Australia's and the United States' natural advantages as efficient producers of primary products.

Strategically, Bruce, in common with all British planners, was anxious to avoid a situation in which the British Empire was embroiled in wars simultaneously in Europe against Germany and in the Pacific against Japan. However, as a thinking Australian, he understood well that Australia was the most exposed of the British dominions to Japanese aggression, and, when push came to shove, Britain with its limited resources had to favour home defence over Asian ventures. For Bruce, then, appeasement of Japan was an urgent priority, by means of economic and territorial concessions in China and Southeast Asia. Moreover, appeasement of Germany in the Sudetenland and the Polish Corridor, and Italy in Abyssinia, would strengthen the ability of British forces to curb Japan. Appeasement in both Europe and Asia was far preferable to facing the hard military fact that the British Empire did not possess the wherewithal to police the world single-handedly. Bruce was an early advocate of rearmament, especially in the air, and in September 1939 was one of the originators of the Empire Air Training Scheme. He was also keen as early as November 1938 to earmark a powerful King George V class battleship for the Far East.[5]

As David Lee has shown in chapter 6 of this volume, in his capacity as chairman of the League of Nations Council during the critical phase of the Abyssinian crisis in early 1936, Bruce advocated recognition of the Italian *fait accompli* and the ending of the incomplete and ineffective sanctions.[6] A confidant of Chamberlain during the Munich crisis, Bruce was close to the epicentre of decision-making. He represented all the high commissioners and put their anti-war position at a crucial inner cabinet meeting on 27 September 1938, and he encouraged his prime minister, Joseph Lyons, by cable and telephone, to ring Chamberlain, a move which helped prompt Chamberlain to contact Mussolini and trigger the meeting that averted war.[7] A few months later in a speech in Sydney, he said that Munich had been brought about because the Czechs had treated the Sudeten Germans badly and had foolishly allied themselves with France.[8] When Germany brazenly invaded Poland a year later, Bruce coolly advised Lyons' successor, Robert Menzies, that Poland needed to take a 'reasonable and restrained attitude', abandon its 'false notions of extreme prestige', and cede to Germany Danzig and the Polish Corridor.[9] 'Polish unreasonableness may land us all in war', he cabled on 30 August 1939.[10] And he and Te Water, the South African high commissioner, argued strongly against the Poles and in favour of appeasing Germany.[11] This time, however, it was a bridge too far for Chamberlain and his cabinet.[12]

War and peace aims

Not surprisingly Sir Maurice Hankey, the British cabinet secretary, was unsuccessful when he tried to persuade Chamberlain to include Bruce as a dominions representative in his new war cabinet.[13] From his position outside the inner circle, Bruce now attempted to influence affairs by advocating a set of very liberal war and peace aims (among other things, suggesting the granting of territorial concessions and freeing up world trade) in the hope of influencing the German population and United States and other neutral opinion to push for a negotiated peace. He enlisted Menzies in this bid, despite the better judgment of the majority of the Australian cabinet, and in Britain had the first of many spats with Winston Churchill, who rightly distrusted Hitler and wanted to win the war convincingly first. The initiative foundered on the rocks of French realism but, through Sumner Welles, perhaps had an indirect influence on Roosevelt's Atlantic Charter a year later.[14]

Bruce also incurred Churchill's ire when he described the prime minister's plan to strike at Germany's Swedish iron ore supplies through Narvik as a 'nebulous thought' and proceeded to kill the scheme by mobilising the opposition of Lord Halifax, the foreign secretary, Smuts, the South African prime minister, and Menzies.[15] This did not, however, avert the disaster of the wider Norwegian campaign which, to Bruce's surprise, finally destroyed the Chamberlain government in May 1940 and brought his *bête noire*, Churchill, to the premiership. Hard on the heels of Norway came the fall of France and the beginning of the Battle of Britain, which prompted a depressed and pessimistic

Bruce to encourage Menzies to appeal to the United States to offer a safe home for the British fleet should one be needed.[16]

Appeasing Japan

Bruce's and Menzies' fears of a potential Japanese invasion of Australia were a principal cause of these desperate calls for appeasement. Their worries were not alleviated when Bruce learned of a paper, prepared by Churchill soon after he took up the reins as first lord of the Admiralty in 1939, which advocated letting the Far East go until after the subjection of Germany.[17] The fall of France and loss of the bulk of the French fleet meant that there would probably now be no British fleet to steam to Singapore to take on the Japanese, and the British chiefs of staff recommended Australia station an army division in Malaya instead. In due course the 8th Division was sent.

Emboldened by Britain's weakness, in July 1940 Japan pressed for the closure of the vital Burma Road supply route to China, and Britain, with Australian agreement and to the chagrin of the Americans, acquiesced for a three-month period. Bruce and Menzies, however, were not satisfied with this temporising pseudo-solution and pushed, again without success, for a 'wide settlement' involving the full territorial and trade appeasement of Japan.[18] Nevertheless, Australia showed its intentions by appointing a minister, Sir John Latham, to Tokyo and none to Chungking. In order to reassure the Australians, Churchill sent what became a famous cable to Menzies on 11 August, which read in part:

> If ... Japan set about invading Australia or New Zealand on a large scale I have explicit authority of Cabinet to assure you that we should then cut our losses in the Mediterranean and proceed to your aid sacrificing every interest except defence position of this island on which all depends.[19]

Just over a month later Japan made its intentions clear by joining the Axis.

In the meantime, Churchill continued to fail to consult the Australian government adequately about the use of its forces. In September, Australia's flagship, HMAS *Australia*, took part in the aborted assault on Dakar in West Africa. The ship was used without Menzies' knowledge or consent, which elicited a stern protest through Bruce.[20] Then Menzies himself visited London in early 1941 to appraise the situation, only to be hoodwinked into the disasters in Greece and Crete and to get precious little reassurance about strengthening the Far East ('What irresponsible rubbish these Antipodeans talk!', was Cadogan's comment on hearing Menzies).[21] Bruce was so dissatisfied with Crete that he forecast a parliamentary revolt should Churchill not mend his dictatorial ways, remove the 'yes men' from cabinet, and listen to their replacements. He implored Menzies to return to London, as only a serving prime minister could stand up to Churchill, but Menzies' own party had overthrown him before he could do anything about it.[22] Instead, the short-lived Fadden government sent cabinet minister and former Country Party leader Sir Earle Page to London as special envoy and a 'continuous cabinet voice' to liaise with Churchill's cabinet. When Curtin became prime minister after Fadden's demise he confirmed Page in post.[23] Still on the periphery, but informed by some well-placed Australians in the Cabinet Secretariat, in whose rooms he had based himself from the start of the war, Bruce was delighted to report to Curtin that a King George V class battleship, HMS *Prince of Wales*, which like Germany's *Bismarck* could 'catch and kill anything', was finally steaming to Singapore.[24] And, when Page arrived, Bruce was at once pleased and annoyed to find that Page expected him to dictate his first cabinet speech to him word for word, which Bruce duly did.[25]

'Beat Hitler First' and Evatt second, though not Churchill third

The advent of the Curtin Labor government, with its ambitious and paranoid minister for external affairs, Dr Herbert Vere Evatt, coincided with the Japanese attack on Pearl Harbor and the United States' entry into the war. Suspicious of the previous government's political appointees, whom he regarded as imperialist stooges, Evatt set about trying to replace Bruce and Page in London and Casey in Washington with his own men. Casey, who saw the writing on the wall, accepted a position as British minister resident in Cairo in February, and Page, who fell ill, returned home in March.[26] Bruce, however, remained in post, despite occasional challenges, until the end of the war. How he did so is an intriguing story with many twists and turns, and only the main features can be sketched here.

As one of the appeasement generation, Bruce had remained a strong critic of Churchill and when Singapore fell and Churchill's leadership was again in question, Bruce spared nothing in telling Curtin and Evatt what he thought. On 22 February 1942, for example, Bruce told Curtin that while he understood why Churchill had diverted the Australian 7th Division to Rangoon on its way back to Australia from the Middle East, he thought Churchill's way of doing it 'arrogant and offensive' and contradictory to a guarantee that had been given to Page to consult Australia first. Nevertheless, he urged 'restraint' on Curtin, as did the British Labour politician and Evatt confidant, Sir Stafford Cripps, who said that Churchill was 'near the end of his tether' in reconstructing his cabinet.[27] Thus did Bruce manoeuvre his way out of a difficult situation.

That Bruce had a long-established reputation for standing up to Churchill did him no harm with Curtin and Evatt, both of whom were making their political reputations by doing the same thing. Thus, when Evatt claimed to 'discover' the 'Beat Hitler First' Anglo-American grand strategy for the first time in May 1942, Bruce (who could hardly not have known something of it) was quick to side with Evatt and berate Churchill and his colleagues for keeping the Australians in the dark. So noisily did he do so that even Evatt pleaded with him to take it easy. Evatt told him that it would be a 'bad thing … to quarrel' with Churchill, and Bruce noted: 'It is clear that Winston has exercised his charm and unquestionable astuteness upon Evatt'. Thus was Bruce more nationalist than the arch-nationalist Evatt himself, *plus royal que le roi.*[28]

At the height of Curtin's famous 'cable fight' with Churchill over the return of the 6th and 7th Divisions in March 1942, Curtin extracted a promise from Churchill that Australia could have a permanent accredited representative in the British war cabinet. It was decided that after Evatt left for Australia, Bruce would take up the post. On the surface this looked as though Bruce had finally got what he had wanted for years: a seat at the innermost council table. But things were not as they seemed. It was constitutionally impossible to give him a vote-—he only had a say—and furthermore, he was only sent papers and attended when Churchill, or his deputy Attlee, chose to invite him, which was not often. ('HMG [in the UK] must have the right to sit alone', Churchill informed Bruce tartly on one occasion; and on another: 'Don't scold me. I won't be scolded'.)[29]

Thus, paradoxically, Bruce had to keep alive his informal conduits which were tried and tested. His formal power amounted to very little at all. He complained on several occasions that his situation was a 'farce', and he might have resigned had Curtin not instructed him to stay on.[30] Curtin, it seems, beat off two attempts by Evatt to have Bruce replaced, in early 1942, perhaps by Evatt's New South Wales Labor colleague, Jack Beasley, and in mid-1943 by Evatt's Baillieu Group business adviser, W.S. Robinson. During Evatt's second visit to London, in 1943, Bruce had a showdown with him when Evatt rudely hung up his phone on Bruce mid-conversation. Bruce's account of the 1942 visit mentions Evatt's 'prickly temper' (which Bruce later put down to Evatt's 'inferiority complex') and that Bruce always met this with 'courteous firmness'.[31] Bruce was also aware that Evatt had shown some of Bruce's most confidential and critical cables to Robinson, who had forwarded them in code to Brendan Bracken (Britain's minister for information) and thence to Churchill, and that Evatt had tried unsuccessfully to use one of them to have Bruce recalled. Evatt, however, was unaware that Bruce knew of this under-handedness. Curtin, who was anxious to keep Evatt where he could see him, was happy to thwart his foreign minister by means of the simple expedient of renewing Bruce's contract. Though frustrated over Churchill's obduracy, Bruce did his duty, reporting efficiently and accurately on the situation until after the war ended.[32]

As Bruce noted over not having seen the key cabinet document (coded 'WW1') that enshrined the 'Beat Hitler First' strategy:

> That this should have happened I do not believe was due to any deliberate intention not to honour the undertaking arrived at [to keep Australia informed], but to the personality of the Prime Minister and the defects of his great qualities. The treatment accorded to Australia was similar to that meted out to his own colleagues in the War Cabinet … My task as I understand it is, quietly and if possible without friction, to ensure that we will be fully informed … and have the opportunity to express our views before decisions are taken. I believe I should be able to ensure this, but I have no illusions that the task will be an easy one.[33]

And so it proved to be, though not 'without friction'. When a frustrated Bruce had the temerity to present Churchill with a nine-page memorandum on how he should reconstruct his cabinet now that the 'emotional period' of the war was over and a 'central thinking machine' was called for, Churchill prepared a 'fairly acid' reply but did not bother to send it.[34] Attlee, as dominions secretary, acted, as Peter Edwards has observed, more as a 'buffer' than a 'conduit';[35] so bland was Attlee that Bruce found it difficult to complain, as it was 'rather like beating a child'.[36] In 1944, just before the Prime Ministers' Conference, Churchill minuted: 'I regard Mr Bruce's presence [in the war cabinet] as an inconvenient survival of the emergency period, and I hope it will be brought to an end after the conference of Dominion Premiers'.[37] Indeed, this happened and Churchill agreed instead to see all of the high commissioners at a regular monthly meeting.

Bruce's assessment of 'WW1' is a fitting epitaph to his whole achievement after Churchill's arrival as prime minister. His 'glory days' as high commissioner were definitely in the 1930s over loan conversion, the abdication crisis and Munich. After that, though he did as much of his job as he was permitted to do, his main boast should have been that, like Saint Simon, he survived.

Out and about

Something of the flavour of the Bruces' daily lives in this period comes through in the sources. In peacetime they lived in a large, government-rented house in Ennismore Gardens, in fashionable South Kensington. Each working day morning Ethel Bruce put a fresh carnation in Bruce's buttonhole and he set off with his car and driver to Australia House, arriving punctually at 9.30. They were keen bridge players and attended the theatre once a week. On weekends they played golf or took some of the high commission staff's children on picnics in the countryside. The war broke up this routine. Possibly worried about bombing, they first moved out to a flat in rural Cranleigh, but then returned to another apartment in Prince's Gate, Kensington, where they remained for the duration. At some point Bruce adopted the boiler suit style favoured by Churchill at home and he often worked straight through weekends. Ethel Bruce was active in the services canteen at Australia House and the high commissioner would sometimes sleep on a camp stretcher in his room in the building. He had his hair cut in the BBC World Service building next door (the shop is still there) and the barber recalled that he was always too preoccupied to chat.[38]

Bruce spent most of his time in the Whitehall rooms of Alfred Stirling, the external affairs liaison officer, and from the end of 1940 in a suite of rooms in the Cabinet Secretariat in Storey's Gate near St James' Park. He came to resent the time he spent on ordinary high commission business at Australia House, telling one of his staff in mid-1942: 'If I don't get out of this place I'll go daft'.[39] J.S. Duncan, the official secretary at the high commission, and later deputy high commissioner, did most of the routine administration, thus leaving Bruce to be an ambassador-at-large, ranging around Whitehall gleaning information for his government. He knew much but influenced little. He was also careful about what he passed on to Canberra. As he wrote to his fellow Australian diplomat Keith Officer in 1943: 'I need hardly say that I use a very great discretion as to how much of what I know I pass on to Australia in view of the confidential manner in which the information has been obtained'.[40] Australia House was lucky to avoid any bomb damage until 1944, but the London offices of Paterson, Laing and Bruce were destroyed in 1940 and one of the junior staff at the high commission was killed at home in that year.[41]

Conclusion

Bruce's wartime years were not his best. He held on when his fellow appeasers retired or went to other posts. His being caught in the crossfire between Evatt and Curtin and between them and Churchill proved a sort of blessing as each 'problem' cancelled the other out. But, though he was a reliable source of detailed information and cogent analysis for his government, and though he confronted Churchill courageously—that is, from an Australian point of view he was a *dependable* busybody—one has to wonder whether Australia might have been better served by someone who believed in Churchill's judgment and who sought to get on the right side of him and his ministers the better to influence their policies. The war's grand strategy would not have been changed, nor should it have been, but Australia might have been somewhat better supplied and unnecessary disputes avoided. Who that person might have been, it is hard to say. Certainly Robinson and Beasley would not have done better. Maybe Casey or Menzies would have done, but then Bruce would not have been at their sides to advise them.

8 John Beasley and the postwar world

Frank Bongiorno

ON 9 JULY 1948 the Australian prime minister, then visiting London, received an unusual letter. A Mr Fowler had noticed in the press that Mr Chifley had been inconvenienced in having to use a transformer to get his electric razor to work in Britain. The observant and helpful Wembley Park resident had glad tidings: there was a Swiss razor that could be adjusted to take any electrical current so that 'shaving time is greatly reduced'. Fowler offered to bring the shaver along for Chifley to see. Three days later, Chifley's private secretary replied. The prime minister, he said, was very interested indeed, but due to the shortness of his visit to London would be unable to see Fowler. Chifley added, however, that he would be very pleased if he would call into Australia House to see Mr Beasley, the Australian high commissioner, who would examine the razor on Chifley's behalf. 'Mr. Beasley has some knowledge of electrical matters', it was explained.[1]

John Albert Beasley (1895–1949), better known as 'Jack' or, less affectionately, 'Stabber', did indeed have 'some knowledge of electrical matters', for he was an electrician. The son of a blacksmith-turned-farmer from Werribee near Melbourne, one of Beasley's earliest jobs was digging electricity poles. He rose quickly to become supervisor of appliance sales in the electricity department of Sydney Municipal Council, president of the Electrical Trades Union from 1924 until 1930, and the union's delegate to the Labor Council of NSW. As youthful president of the latter organisation in the 1920s, a period of great turbulence in the labour movement, Beasley was well prepared for the pressures of public life.[2]

Beasley was Australian high commissioner in the United Kingdom from 15 August 1946 until his death, while visiting Australia, on 2 September 1949.[3] He was the only high commissioner to die in office. Beasley also served as resident minister in London, with all of the powers and duties of high commissioner, from January 1946.[4] Although he was destined only for a relatively short term, his time in London coincided with a significant era in world affairs and Anglo-Australian relations. These were the early years of the United Nations, of the attempts to found a postwar order that would avoid the errors of 1919, rebuild the shattered economies of Europe and Asia, and redesign an international economic order left in disarray by depression and war. In the European colonial empires, there were powerful stirrings of nationalism and, in the British case, the foundation of a new multiracial Commonwealth. Overshadowing the whole was the emerging cold war between the United States and the Soviet Union. Meanwhile, for Australia, there was the foundation of the postwar mass migration program, the attempt to form closer connections with London in defence, trade and finance, and an unprecedented activism in international affairs, when Australia tried to use the opportunities provided by peace negotiations and membership of the British Commonwealth and the United Nations to play a more influential global role. The period is especially associated with the vigorous if erratic diplomacy of Herbert Vere Evatt, Australia's external affairs minister, and for some historians the 1940s represent a heroic era when the British Empire fractured, paving the way for a new, more independent foreign policy.[5]

Background and appointment

Beasley has not been much noticed in Australia's response to a postwar world that seemed to create opportunity and danger in equal measure. At first glance, the omission seems odd because his appointment was widely recognised at the time as significant, and by no means the case of a party hack being rewarded with a plum post at the end of a political career.[6] Historians have long recognised a swing to empire in Australian diplomacy in the period following the controversies of 1942, while cooperation with the United Kingdom was integral to so many facets of Australian policy in the final years of the war and its aftermath that an appointment to London in 1945 was both prestigious and significant.[7] Beasley, moreover, had just turned fifty when he became resident minister, and although he was in poor health nobody appears to have believed he was being put out to pasture. He had been a politician of the front rank in the Labor governments of the war years, serving as minister for supply and development and later supply and shipping. In these and other key roles, he was instrumental in the organisation of Australia's war effort and proved himself a capable administrator. After his health broke down in 1944, he resigned to become vice-president of the Executive Council, a less arduous role, but after recovering became acting minister for defence and then minister when John Curtin died.[8]

Australian press commentary at the time of Beasley's appointment emphasised the significance of a serving minister of his calibre being appointed to London. For the *Sydney Morning Herald*, it was well that Bruce was being 'followed by a man of Mr. Beasley's standing and experience, in view of the legacy of vast and complex problems left by the war, problems which we have little hope of solving successfully save by close Imperial co-operation'.[9] A similar theme was also the keynote of the assessment of the British High Commission in Canberra. Beasley, they said, was 'a man of great ability with a pleasing manner' and 'one of the outstanding figures in the Labour Party of Australia today ... [H]ad his health not broken down last year he might well have been in the running for the leadership of the Party on Mr. Curtin's death'.[10] In this case, the acting high commissioner had erred—there was no serious prospect of Beasley becoming prime minister—but one can sympathise with the diplomat's lack of understanding of the nuances of Australian Labor political culture.

Beasley had not acquired the sobriquet 'Stabber' at Sunday school. It was a reference to his central role, in 1931, in destroying the Scullin Labor government. Beasley was effectively federal leader of a group of New South Wales Labor parliamentarians who were loyal to the demagogic Labor premier, Jack Lang, and the proposal for dealing with Australia's overseas debts called the Lang Plan. It involved the temporary repudiation of interest payments and was anathema to moderate members of the federal Labor Party, including James Scullin, the prime minister; Ted Theodore, who as treasurer advanced an inflationary plan for dealing with the economic crisis; and a former Tasmanian premier, Joseph Lyons. In November 1931, the Langites introduced a motion into the House of Representatives that Scullin treated as a matter of confidence. When the critical division was called, Beasley and his followers voted with the Opposition to defeat the government. Labor was now hopelessly divided and, in the subsequent election, swept from office by the conservative United Australia Party, led by Lyons, who had switched sides. Lang also lost office in 1932 after being dismissed by the governor and then trounced in an election. Eventually, after protracted negotiations and a political journey along a most circuitous route, Beasley broke with Lang and rejoined the Labor Party in early 1941, just in time to become a member of the Curtin government. He served it loyally, although some observers wondered just what he and Bert Evatt were plotting when one disappeared into the office of the other. Conveniently, they had adjoining rooms in Parliament House.[11]

We can be fairly sure that one thing they plotted carefully was Beasley's elevation to high commissioner. The Australian diplomat Alan Watt, speaking to a British diplomat in Washington at the time of Beasley's appointment to London, attributed the move to the government's desire to have someone in London 'who could represent them politically in a way in which only a Cabinet Minister could do, and to the confidence which Dr. Evatt had personally in Mr. Beasley'. 'They had worked together', said Watt, 'in much the fashion in which Mr. Curtin had worked with Mr. Chifley. Conversely, what Mr. Beasley might recommend would carry greater weight with both Dr. Evatt and the Government as a whole than any advice from Mr. Bruce'. Watt also correctly pointed out that Beasley had never 'commanded the full confidence' of Labor members after the Scullin government's downfall, and that the overwhelming support for Chifley as Curtin's successor had only underlined this lack of trust.[12]

The Australian labour movement has an extremely powerful culture of loyalty, based on working-class solidarity and mateship. As the veteran Laborite W.G. Spence remarked in 1909, 'The man who fell once may be forgiven, but he is not fully trusted'.[13] Beasley was forgiven by many, but certainly never regained the full trust of those who recalled the bitterness of 1931 and the decade in the political wilderness it inaugurated. The epithet 'Stabber' clung to him like a limpet to a rock.

Beasley, then, would have realised that further progress within the party was barred, but also that his health was unlikely again to stand up to the rigours of ministerial office. The quieter life of a post in London would have been attractive in the circumstances. He might, however, have preferred Washington if it had been available. There had been discussions within the government during 1945 that suggested Beasley would go there, and Frank Forde to London. According to Watt, Beasley 'had been brought into close touch with many influential Americans with whom he had got on well', and he had also enjoyed good relations with them when attending the International Labour Conference in the United States in 1944. Nevertheless, the government appears to have decided to leave F.W. Eggleston in Washington for the time being, despite his having become a virtual invalid. Perhaps Beasley's particular skills were seen as better suited to London.[14] Some commentators suggested that his appointment as resident minister while still retaining the defence portfolio was a signal that he would be especially active in the field of Anglo-Australian defence planning, a major priority for the Chifley government.[15] Beasley certainly got on well with Sir Frederick Shedden, the secretary of the Defence Department in Australia, and he maintained a warm and regular correspondence with him during his time in London. He was also on good terms with British Defence Minister A.V. (Bert) Alexander, with whom he associated during the Paris Peace Conference of 1946 and socially in London.[16]

While it is possible that Beasley's interest in defence was a factor in his appointment, the government would also have been aware of the massive logistical problems involved in dealing with the movement of people and goods in view of postwar shipping shortages. It was in the fields of shipping and supply that Beasley had especially distinguished himself during the war, and the government had initiated a mass migration program. Certainly, Beasley found himself heavily involved in such matters early in his period as resident minister, and Australia House had been the subject of anguished complaints from Australian servicemen seeking to take British brides back to Australia. There was also insufficient shipping for displaced persons whom Australia had undertaken to accept.[17] Beasley's expertise in shipping, moreover, came in handy in 1948 when, as leader of the Australian delegation to the Geneva Maritime Conference, he played an active role in drafting of the resulting convention.[18] None of this demonstrates that the government had these duties in mind when it appointed Beasley, but it is hard to miss that his skills and experience were nicely calibrated with them.

Early performance

The British were unsure of what to make of Beasley, not least because of a remarkably checkered political career even by the turbulent standards of interwar Labor politics in New South Wales. The British High Commission in Canberra tried to clarify the situation by explaining that 'it used to be said that there were two Mr. Beasleys'. There was one 'whose knowledge of his subject was complete, his style and especially his ease admirable, one who pleaded his case rather than argued it'. But there was also another, rather more militant and 'highly impassioned' Mr. Beasley who brought the techniques of the socialist stump orator into the parliamentary chamber. 'Even before the war', the acting high commissioner added drily, 'this second Mr. Beasley was appearing less and less and now he seems to have vanished altogether'.[19] Watt nevertheless believed that Beasley had a prejudice against the British, which he shared with Evatt, and was 'suspicious that the U.K. is not always whole-hearted in pressing Australia's interests, or what the present Australian Government allege are their interests'. Here, Watt considered Beasley's Roman Catholicism influential which, in combination with his 'being one of the more extreme members of his party', disposed him to associate the United Kingdom 'with both capitalism and imperialism'.[20] Nevertheless, on the basis of what he had been told by British officials in Canberra, Sir John Stephenson, deputy under-secretary in the Dominions Office, told his secretary of state that it looked as if Beasley 'would be an acquisition and those members of this office who have met him confirm this view'.[21]

Beasley was a soft-spoken teetotaller and non-smoker who arrived in London with his wife and four children. There were later descriptions of him as a shy and unassuming man.[22] An early source of bad publicity was the news that a substantial consignment of food and wine had been shipped to London with the family. 'Having been spared the perils and privations which Mr. Bruce shared with Londoners during six years of war, Mr. Beasley might surely submit to England's peacetime regimen', commented one Australian newspaper.[23] Chifley was able to explain in reply to parliamentary questioning that the food was required by Beasley to entertain guests; that it would reduce pressure on scarce British food supplies; and that Beasley knew nothing of the consignment of wine which was a gift from the industry and a response to its complaints that Australian toasts had been ignominiously drunk with the South African and French product because the Australian drop was unavailable. So it was really a thoroughly patriotic consignment but Beasley was wounded by 'unfounded criticism', and later insisted on the correction of an erroneous report that he had also taken family furniture to London and then charged the shipping costs to the government.[24]

Some Australian press coverage of Beasley and his family was deeply malicious. The Melbourne *Herald* reported that, on arrival in London, Beasley was 'wearing an "Anthony Eden" hat and twirling a silver-crested umbrella'. The reporter also couldn't help noticing wharfies unloading 'mountains of luggage prominently marked "The Right Hon J. A. Beasley," including special cases containing a shiny silk "topper" and a cutaway morning suit'.[25] An article in *Smith's Weekly*, after a wide-ranging survey of the Beasleys' London experience that made it fairly plain that they were living a 'not unluxurious life'— its subjects included the expensive private schooling of his children and a 150 guinea gown bought for his daughter to attend a royal garden party—went on to describe his wife Alma as dressing 'quite well—quiet clothes suitable for her tubby figure ... She is often at a loss to know why people laugh so heartily at things she says, but has come to regard herself as an accepted comedienne'. Beasley's regular 10.15 morning arrival at Australia House in his black Humber was also described in comic vein as 'quite a show': 'Doormen and porters panic. They open doors, clear a path, stand to attention, and keep both lifts held in readiness. The fever in the foyer rises as Beasley strolls in, usually with chauffeur hovering behind'.[26] In conditions of postwar austerity in both Australia and, to a much greater degree, in the United Kingdom, these reports were intended to be damaging, and seemed specifically designed for maximum effect on the reputation of a left-wing Labor man.

The Beasleys did lead an interesting and comfortable existence, but the years immediately after the war were hardly an ideal time to make a new life in London. They arrived in winter, despite the Australian industrialist W.S. Robinson's stern warning that it would be in their interests to delay coming until spring. Both goods and labour were in short supply, with rationing in full swing.[27] The Beasleys had just one hard-pressed maid, which for a household of their size in London was inadequate.[28] They initially lived in the official high commissioner's residence at Ennismore Gardens, acquired for Bruce in the early 1930s, but when its lease came up for renewal in 1948 it was exchanged for a smaller but still substantial property in Kensington.

The Beasleys grew accustomed to their new lives and, especially for the children, there were some exciting and unforgettable experiences, such as daughter June's audience with Princess Elizabeth.[29] In March 1948, Jack reported to Shedden:

> We are all well and after two years have grown accustomed to the way of life in London. Strange how you learn to go without and to wait a long time to get even what you actually need. We are still a long way off normal times so I suppose the best policy is to 'keep the chins up' hoping each day will bring better things.[30]

There was also early praise for Beasley. One matter requiring his urgent attention was the state of Australia House itself, which had suffered during wartime austerity. Bruce spent little time during the war there and, with the end of hostilities, the building seemed shabby and neglected.[31] According to Beasley himself, the conditions were 'unattractive. The appearance of the whole place was drab ... As I felt the conditions were quite unworthy of our country, I immediately arranged for a general clean-up'. The air raid walls needed to be dismantled but Beasley was especially struck by the lack of a decent room for receiving distinguished visitors. He persuaded the Australian Wool Board to provide an almond pink carpet, red coverings for the furniture and woollen curtains; all a fine advertisement for Australia's most famous export—so long as you ignored the hideous clash between the pink and red. The room was facetiously, but perhaps accurately, known as 'Mrs. Beasley's Drawing Room'. Mrs Attlee performed the official opening, and the room was used on one occasion to receive Queen Elizabeth, whose image alongside her husband George VI graced one wall, directly opposite a photo of a merino ram—a neat summary of what continued to make British Australia great.[32] By way of contrast, the unfortunate library staff along with their books were banished to 'cold makeshift quarters' so that their room could be used for the high commission's New Year party. In May 1948 they were still there.[33] On a more positive note, a canteen was established in Australia House, with fresh foodstuffs imported directly from Australia.[34]

There were also evidently problems of administration, and Beasley called together his staff to let them know that 'much as their wartime endurance was appreciated and understood, peacetime had brought new responsibilities. He wanted a new era of courtesy, promptness, and efficiency'.[35] Keith Officer, the Australian diplomat who passed through London during 1946, expressed an avuncular concern about how the high commission itself was operating:

> I fear that the whole office in London rather suffer from the irresponsibility complex
> and the lack of any definitely defined duties. I view it all rather sadly, because I fear that
> as a result some good chaps may be spoilt.[36]

By 1949, the high commission had over 830 staff, 250 of them involved in immigration. The office was spread across three London buildings: Australia House itself, Canberra House near Piccadilly Circus—used mainly by services staff—and even a part of Africa House in Kingsway, where the Australian Scientific Research Liaison Office was located. The high commission ran fifteen official cars.[37] In order to help oversee such a huge concern, Beasley chose as his deputy Norman Mighell, an experienced and effective administrator. Mighell, a Gallipoli veteran and lawyer, had been appointed chairman of the Repatriation Commission in 1935, and between 1941 and 1946 held the critically important wartime posts of either Commonwealth coal commissioner or head of the Coal Commission. Beasley and Mighell got on well.[38] On the other hand, the new high commissioner's relationship with Australia's liaison officer in the Foreign Office, John Hood, was somewhat difficult, and at least in the early months Beasley 'seemed a little concerned that he [Beasley] might be out of touch with things'. But the problem was initially beyond the control of either Beasley or Hood. Quite apart from Hood's being short-staffed and overworked in view of the growing scale and complexity of Australian diplomatic activities, there was also now recognition in the higher ranks of the Department of External Affairs that the physical separation of the external affairs officer from Australia House was a redundant arrangement. Still, better staffing arrangements did lead to improvements during Hood's tenure, and Beasley also later worked closely with another external affairs officer, Peter Heydon.[39] The continuing shortage of shipping, however, remained possibly the most daunting challenge the office faced in the year or so after the war's end. It was a source of many complaints about the performance of the high commission itself, from servicemen, war brides, intending migrants and others. The Melbourne *Argus* correspondent Paul McGuire reported in March 1946 that Beasley was 'displaying great energy' in an effort to deal with the problem, such as by bringing together the state agents-general to make 'the strongest representations at the highest levels'.[40]

Beasley also won early praise for his role as Evatt's successor in leading the Australian delegation to the Paris Peace Conference of 1946. Officer described 'a very happy team under Beasley's leadership. He has shown both tact and ability and made an excellent leader'.[41] The meeting provided the only moment when Beasley found himself in the international spotlight, when he clashed spectacularly with the Soviet representative, Andrey Vyshinsky, after the Russian accused Australia of engaging in delaying tactics by introducing so many amendments. 'I refuse to be bounced and bullied by anyone', replied Beasley, who spoke with what was described as 'extreme agitation'. 'We are not going to be timid because one big Power feels it is able at this moment to thrust itself upon us.' As the Soviet delegation gathered around Vyshinsky and roared with laughter, Beasley said there had 'been a lot of blind stabbing in this conference': it is not known whether the Russian delegates had heard of Beasley's famous nickname. This 'extraordinary scene' was reported in the international press, and won Beasley praise for his strong, if not terribly 'diplomatic' stand. And although the Melbourne *Age* criticised Beasley for his loss of temper, and for having '"dressed down"' Vyshinsky and the Soviets 'in a style more suitable to a Trades and Labor Council than a peace conference of 21 nations', McGuire thought Australia had taken 'a long stride forward in responsibility and nationhood when she stood boldly for great principles ... it was time someone said it, and I personally am proud that it was an Australian'.[42] The incident certainly revealed that Beasley was unafraid of taking on those in high places and, where necessary, in the style with which he was familiar from his years in the maelstrom of New South Wales Labor politics. As he once declared in a letter to Chifley from London, 'It is not good to run away at any time'; it might have been Beasley's motto.[43] And, like Evatt, he was insistent that an Australian voice should be heard in international affairs.

Communism, liberal internationalism and Anglo-Australian relations

The episode also hinted at another aspect of Beasley's emerging diplomatic persona that set him apart from Evatt and perhaps even Chifley: his aggressive anti-communism. Here, Beasley was closer to the position that British Foreign Secretary Ernest Bevin came to occupy than to Evatt's; and nearer the views of Shedden, Australian military planners and the Australian Department of Defence, than External Affairs.[44] The high commissioner was in the Commons in January 1948 when Bevin made a landmark foreign policy statement that, in Beasley's words, 'put the blame for the international uncertainties fairly and squarely upon Russia' while announcing British support for union among the free nations of Western Europe in the face of the communist threat (he called it 'Western Union'). Beasley described the speech in a letter to Chifley as 'certainly one of the gravest utterances since the war', and Bevin's attitude as 'the unavoidable conclusion' which had 'the support of all sections of the people here'.[45] That Bevin and Beasley were in broad agreement with one another but not with Australia's external affairs minister was made clear in April 1948 when Beasley informed the foreign secretary that Evatt was accusing the British government 'of "stoking up for war" and behaving in a most fascist way'. Beasley, by his own account, told Evatt that he 'seemed to have forgotten that such a thing as communism existed'.[46] When Beasley again met with Bevin a fortnight later, the foreign secretary painted a grim picture of the communist threat in Western Europe and insisted on the need to encourage unity there, a situation that sometimes seemed to Bevin 'not fully recognised in Australia'. There is no indication that Beasley disagreed with any aspect of this analysis.[47] That Beasley was indeed impressed with Bevin's views is revealed in his report to Shedden of these conversations with the foreign secretary:

> The Chiefs of Staff Appreciation is a very interesting document and bears out much of what Mr. Bevin has had to say to me on a number of occasions lately. He said quite recently 'Keep an eye on the Far East' and it may well be that your boys will have their troubles as we are having them in Europe today.[48]

Bevin was sowing this seed in fertile soil because Beasley had plenty of hard experience fighting communist infiltration of the New South Wales Labor Party in the 1930s.[49]

Beasley's anti-communism frequently found expression, both publicly and behind closed doors. Speaking in Belfast late in 1946, he was perhaps inspired by the Ulster setting to an especially combative rhetoric, declaring that '[w]e must let the other fellow know that we are not going to be subdued ... I hope that those who sponsor our cause know who is right, and will not surrender our rightful position'.[50] At Newcastle-on-Tyne for the launch of a new liner, he had in his sights '[s]inister and ulterior forces [which] cause industrial unrest for the same purpose as influences in the higher field of international diplomacy, namely, to prevent the British Commonwealth getting back to its former place and to allow some other power to supersede us'.[51] Here, we have all the hallmarks of a full-blown theory of communist conspiracy and Beasley was increasingly pessimistic about the prospects of international agreement. As early as April 1947, he wrote to Shedden that the 'uneasiness' surrounding the United Nations 'causes doubts as to the extent either Regional planning or collective security can be relied upon for our security'. The main problem, he thought, was 'owing to Russia's refusal to, as Bevin says, put her cards "face up" on the table'.[52] At the regular dominion high commissioners' meeting held in December of the same year, after learning that Bevin was trying to broker a compromise between the superpowers over the future of Germany, he opined that

> it was all very well to let M. Molotov talk, but what he and M. Vyshinsky said was not without effect, not even in this country. It could be discounted by intelligent people, but it was apt to deceive the less intelligent, both here and in Germany. Would it not be good tactics to corner M. Molotov on such subjects as German frontiers and reparations?[53]

It would be hard to imagine a statement more at odds with the policies of Evatt or the secretary of the Department of External Affairs, John Burton, whose view was that ganging up on the Soviets, or even appearing to do so, risked dividing the globe into hostile power blocs.[54] Burton, moreover, was so incensed by what he saw as the failure of both the high commissioner and the External Affairs Office in London to recognise the course of British foreign policy, comprehend its implications for their own country, and then state Australia's viewpoint, that he advised Evatt either to replace Beasley and Norman Makin in Washington, or send over new officers with 'the right to be associated with all the political activities of the Australian representatives'.[55] But the issue here was really a sharp difference of perspective between Burton and Evatt on the one hand, and Beasley on the other. For whereas Evatt, Burton and perhaps Chifley still held out hope of agreement between the western powers and the Soviet Union, Beasley 'did not consider that the Soviet Government would be likely to make any concessions in the interests of agreement with the other Powers'.[56]

Indeed, at times Beasley gave the impression that he felt the British government was too soft in its dealings with the Soviet Union. In April 1948, he 'urged that a policy of toughness ... should be applied against Russians in the British sector of Berlin'.[57] When the dominion high commissioners met in May 1948, it was Beasley's view that 'international discussions ... under United Nations auspices, had ceased to have any substantial value. The United Nations had lost most of its prestige'.[58] But it was not long before Beasley was inquiring gently at a high commissioners' meeting about whether the British government had a candidate for president of the UN General Assembly, a query obviously inspired by Evatt who wanted the job for himself.[59] Although by this time relations between Beasley and Evatt were in a bad state of disrepair (see pages 124–5), they would presumably have been worse still if Evatt had known of the things Beasley was saying in high commissioners' meetings; or if he had been aware of the high commissioner's role in advising British ministers on how to move Chifley towards a more explicitly anti-Soviet public posture.[60] Yet, even as Chifley's administration seemed to shift closer to a 'realist' position on the cold war, Beasley's anti-communism remained raw.[61] It was a sufficiently powerful impulse in March 1949 to overwhelm momentarily his not inconsiderable hostility to the Dutch, for he felt that disapproval of their Indonesian policy did not warrant Holland's exclusion from NATO and 'the Pact must be viewed in its wider aspects'.[62] Back in Australia a few months later, he remarked: 'Russia is still the problem, although I think the Western Powers are becoming more aware of her ruses. They know Russia is still the most heavily armed country in the world, and that she is bluffing about cutting her forces'.[63]

Beasley's failure to articulate official Australian government policy—indeed, his habit of expressing views diametrically opposed to those of the foreign minister and perhaps also the prime minister—necessarily calls into question his effectiveness. But, in line with government policy, Beasley was tenacious in claiming for Australia a right to consultation on matters of direct interest to her people and vigorous in opposing the idea that key decisions should be made by the great powers alone. For instance, on the question of the disposal of the former Italian colonies, he insisted that Australia had a right to be involved, using the same kinds of arguments that Hughes had deployed at Versailles in 1919; the shedding of Australian blood in the struggle over these very colonies in the recent war entitled her to a say.[64] Yet, as leader of the Australian delegation in Paris,

Beasley had been more willing than Evatt to compromise with allies in reaching a solution on this question. Whereas, in a cable to Beasley, Evatt criticised the Foreign Office and some of the other dominions for their 'lack of support', forgetfulness of Australian wartime sacrifice, and 'appeasement' of the Soviets, the new high commissioner sought closer cooperation with the 'British Group'. It is hard to imagine anyone other than a former minister of his seniority being able to stand up to Evatt, via phone and cablegram, in the way that Beasley did during the Paris negotiations.[65]

In London high commissioners' discussions over a peace treaty with Japan, or Dutch actions in Indonesia, Beasley asserted for Australia a special role based on geography, on Australia's part in the defeat of the Japanese and, implicitly, on Australia's claim to the status of a leading Pacific power.[66] But these ambitions invariably came up against power politics. Why, asked Beasley in one dominion high commissioners' meeting in 1947, had the British government entered into talks with the United States about the Indonesian crisis, without any prior discussion with Australia? Hector McNeil, a junior Foreign Office minister, replied that the meetings had occurred at the suggestion of the Dutch, 'who were desperate about their reconstruction. The United States could supply dollars and pressure by them would have an effect which advice from other quarters would not'. But, for Beasley, it 'was another instance of the total disregard of Australian interests in a territory on her door-step. The Foreign Office always failed to recognize Australian interests'. This claim produced a sharp exchange. McNeil conceded that the UK government 'might have been impolite' but 'emphatically repudiated the allegation that they had disregarded Australian interests'. The meeting then developed into a discussion of Commonwealth consultation that served only to underline the impossibility of Beasley's, and Australia's, ambitions. The South African representative rejected any idea of 'arriving at a common policy by an exchange of arguments', and the Canadians had said similar things previously. Beasley was well aware of these views, but argued that this 'did not affect the duty of the United Kingdom Government to take the Australian Government into their confidence on a matter vitally affecting Australia'. The Canadians, after all, had the United States at their side to protect them; Australia and New Zealand did not.[67]

During 1948 and 1949, as Beasley became increasingly preoccupied in high commissioners' meetings with economic affairs, he continued to complain about the 'inadequacy of the machinery for Commonwealth liaison'.[68] He was especially worried that, in the effort to assist European recovery and establish closer connections between the United Kingdom and the nations of Western Europe, dominions such as Australia would find themselves isolated and disadvantaged. He had no difficulty with the anti-communist aspect of Western Union, but he was concerned with its potentially injurious impact on Australia's economy.[69] At a meeting in April 1948, for instance, he asked whether Western Union would weaken the sterling bloc, if Marshall Aid would undermine dominion efforts to procure goods from the dollar area, how the imperial tariff system was likely to fare under new arrangements, and about the likely effects on the dominions of the diversion of capital equipment to Europe. These questions implied that Britain was neglecting Australian interests, and there was a threat in his questioning whether the dominions might for 'their own protection' need 'to make arrangements for direct financial balancing with the dollar area'.[70] In other words, Beasley was hinting that Australia might be forced to leave the cooperative sterling system and deal directly with the United States.

Yet, notwithstanding his good relations with many Americans, Beasley was also touchy about US influence, and especially any suggestion that the United Kingdom attached a greater value to her relationship with the superpower than that with Australia. Late in 1948 at a high commissioners' meeting he 'expressed concern lest the United Kingdom Government should give way too much in the face of United States pressure'.[71] The United States' desire to dismantle imperial tariff preference was one of Beasley's worries, but at a November 1948 Paris meeting of Commonwealth delegations to the UN General Assembly, he also protested against the UK delegation for negotiating amendments of their own draft resolution on Palestine with the US rather than the Commonwealth delegations, thereby 'giving ground for the charge that [the] United Kingdom were being dragged along at the coat-tails of the United States'.[72] Nevertheless, the absence of Commonwealth unity underlined the unrealistic character of Beasley's expectation that Britain should consult with the dominions in the process of formulating foreign policy. The realities of power politics, moreover, dictated that American views on the future of Palestine should be taken more seriously than antipodean demands for consultation.

Commonwealth Relations Office official Sir Saville ('Joe') Garner recalled that high commissioners' meetings 'changed their character and lost much of their usefulness owing to the behaviour of some of the High Commissioners at the time'. He singled out Beasley's 'new note of aggressiveness' for particular censure, while conceding that the 'bitter tirades of personal abuse' indulged in by India's Krishna Menon were worse.[73] Garner might have had in mind the Indonesian issue, over which the Australian and Indian representatives were very critical of British policy during a couple of tense meetings on 7 and 8 January 1949. Beasley made it clear on both occasions that he felt the United Kingdom had been too soft with the Dutch and, in the presence of the foreign secretary on 8 January, went so far as to suggest that 'the level of United Kingdom representation at the [UN Security] Council's meetings on Indonesia had given the impression that the United Kingdom did not take the Council seriously'. For Bevin, this reflection on the internal affairs of the Foreign Office was evidently too much, and what followed can only be described as a dressing down of the high commissioners, and especially Beasley and the Australian government: 'He could not allow to continue the misrepresentations of United Kingdom officials which had been heard at these meetings. These officials, when they spoke at the Security Council, spoke under his instructions and criticism must be directed at him'.[74] On this occasion, Australia's interests might have been better served if its high commissioner had held his tongue, or at least better judged what should be left unsaid; just as the British, in the interests of Commonwealth harmony, had refrained from saying openly what everyone knew: that the 'paramount' importance of Western Union necessarily limited their own willingness to provoke the Dutch over Indonesia.[75] Again, Beasley showed scant regard for such niceties, declaring openly in a high commissioners' meeting that 'the Dutch might use Western Union for blackmail'.[76] On another occasion, too, Beasley made himself look silly when, prompted by the Queensland agent-general, he lodged a formal protest with the director-general of the BBC after an academic said on air that the British had much more in common with western Europeans 'in art and culture, than ... let us say, the farmers, bushrangers, and so on of Australia and Canada'. Beasley was apparently so dissatisfied with the BBC's response that he unsuccessfully sought an interview with the prime minister. As the Melbourne *Herald* remarked, it was 'a fussy little protest', a 'humourless and touchy' reaction that made Australia appear immature and Beasley ridiculous.[77]

While they were capable of aggression on occasions, an incident in November 1947 reveals the trust that could still be relied on among the statesmen of the old dominions when required. Both Australia and New Zealand wanted to discuss the British government's policy on Germany's future at a forthcoming high commissioners' meeting, at which Bevin would be present. Alarm bells began ringing for Commonwealth Relations Office officials when Peter Heydon reported that Beasley hoped to conduct a 'cross-examination'. Officials were worried that Bevin would not wish to commit himself in front of 'the two Indian High Commissioners', so they explained the difficulties to Heydon, suggesting 'that it would be most unfortunate if Mr. Beasley were to leave the Friday's meeting feeling that we had withheld information from him, and that, if he was not satisfied with the range of information provided, the best thing would be for him to take it up personally, after the meeting, with Mr. Bevin'. Heydon replied that Beasley would not place the British government in difficulty: '[I]t would be easy for Mr. Beasley to see Mr. Bevin subsequently, as apparently, they already have a mutual arrangement that Mr. Beasley may visit Mr. Bevin whenever he should wish to do so'. The meeting record indicates that Beasley did indeed behave impeccably, while the episode reveals the continuing significance of the bonds of trust between Britain and 'the four White dominions', who could be relied on 'not to steer the conversation on to ground on which we cannot tread'.[78] There was, naturally, a powerful self-interest operating, for the old dominions' privileged access to information was threatened by the emergence of India, Pakistan and Ceylon. The Australians' British race patriotism was also perhaps flattered by being taken into the foreign secretary's confidence in a way that excluded these nations.

Yet there were occasions when Australia somewhat perversely flouted the rules of this white men's 'club'. As Commonwealth Relations Office official Francis Cumming-Bruce explained to the secretary of state for Commonwealth relations, Philip Noel-Baker, late in 1948, Evatt's behaviour was such that Foreign Office officials were now 'inclined to impute to the Australians all kinds of sinister motives which might, for all I know, be justified in comparable circumstances in the case of foreigners, but are really nonsensical in the case of Australia'.[79] In other words, the Australians were seen to have behaved in a manner distinguishable from the usual quarrels that might break out within any large and lively family. And although their main difficulty was with Evatt, Beasley himself was also sometimes seen as a culprit. Patrick Gordon Walker, the parliamentary under-secretary of state for Commonwealth relations, recorded in his diary that at the 1948 Prime Ministers' Conference, Evatt wanted a reference to methods of Commonwealth consultation included in the final statement, despite prior agreement that it should not be published. He left Beasley to deal with the final meeting. According to Gordon Walker, the Australian high commissioner 'made an extraordinary personal attack on Attlee' and also told Lief Egeland of South Africa 'that Evatt had told him to insist to the point of busting the meetings'. 'Australia', reflected Gordon Walker, 'succeeded in justifying & deepening the dislike everyone seems to feel for her'.[80]

Yet, if viewed in the context of the relationship between the two Australians, the incident appears in a different light. Instead of doing as Evatt ordered, Beasley had revealed his instructions to the representative of a dominion likely to be especially hostile to publicity being given to Commonwealth consultation. In fact, it looks rather like a case of Beasley managing Evatt as best he could. British officials came to appreciate the high commissioner's efforts in this challenging field of endeavour. In November 1948 Cumming-Bruce, disturbed by the 'malady' in Anglo-Australian relations that had developed in the wake of Evatt's initiatives as president of the UN General Assembly in Paris, asked Gordon Walker 'if he would have a frank talk with Mr. Beasley, rubbing in that the Australian approach to almost all questions of tactics in relation to Russia is at present fundamentally different from that of the United Kingdom and that this is responsible for much of our current difficulties'. Gordon Walker arranged to have lunch with the high commissioner and 'as usual found Mr. Beasley anxious to help after a few preliminary skirmishes'. A further meeting was organised; it 'developed into a dialogue' between Foreign Office official Frank Roberts and the Australian high commissioner about Berlin. 'It was clear', said Cumming-Bruce, 'that this greatly illuminated our position for Mr. Beasley and I am hopeful that we may have a clearer understanding on the Australian side on this issue in future'. Sure enough, Cumming-Bruce soon learned that Evatt said he 'now for the first time sees what's in our mind'.[81]

It is advantageous, if one wishes to be thought helpful, to associate with unhelpful people. Not only will their actions generate demand for your powers of conciliation, but you are also likely to compare favourably. In these respects, Beasley was well served by Evatt's regular appearances in London, but in most other ways he made Beasley's job very difficult indeed. In April 1948 Beasley called on Bevin to tell him about 'a very bitter correspondence' he had been carrying on with Evatt, who believed that the high commissioner 'was wasting his time in London and ... had no influence'. Beasley added that there were occasions when the British government had asked him to assist it in its dealings with Canberra, but that Evatt took no notice of him and simply went 'ahead with his policy'. Bevin confirmed in his reply both his desire to work closely with Beasley and the Australian government, and that there were indeed 'certain difficulties' that prevented him from speaking frankly and openly with him. Chifley, however, had been made aware of the problems, and Bevin said that he was doing his best to remove them.[82] Beasley had also written to Chifley complaining of Evatt and in July 1948, while in London, the Australian prime minister asked Bevin for 'a frank statement of his attitude to Evatt'. Bevin replied 'that the real trouble was lack of confidence in Dr. Evatt ... we never knew where we were with him. At one time he was anti-Soviet, at another anti-American and at others anti-UK. It was very hard to define exactly our complaints, but he would sum it up in the phrase that there was no sense of being pals with Dr. Evatt'. Bevin went on to explain that this problem did not apply to the other three old dominions, with whose high commissioners 'he could work on terms of absolute confidence'. And although he also 'had complete confidence' in Beasley, there was the problem that everything he told Beasley was necessarily reported back to Evatt 'and at that stage the difficulties began'. Chifley confirmed Beasley's testimony 'that he had no personal complaint' concerning Bevin, but that the high commissioner had indeed gained the impression that the foreign secretary 'had to hold things back from him'.[83] Even so, Beasley had not given up on the task of trying to reduce the amount of daylight between the attitudes of Bevin and Evatt, and in the very month of Chifley's visit, the Foreign Office learned through a BBC informant that he 'had been hammering Dr. Evatt in the hope of persuading him to depart from the equivocal attitude he has hitherto adopted about Western Union'.[84]

Death and assessment

Beasley returned with his wife to Australia on a visit in mid-1949, officially for consultation with Chifley, but there were also rumours that he might seek to re-enter federal politics at the next election, or that he would be discussing the establishment of a Commonwealth shipping line of which he would be chairman on a £5,000 a year salary. Beasley denied that he intended leaving his post early; his term would not expire until August 1951. While he had continued in poor health during his time in London, there is no suggestion that his years there had produced any marked deterioration. So the end came unexpectedly. On 18 August Beasley was taken to Sydney's St Vincent's Hospital with high blood pressure. Although he initially seemed in no danger, a stroke followed a fortnight later. Beasley went into a coma and, after briefly regaining consciousness, died at the age of just fifty-three.[85]

A product of the winner-takes-all culture of Labor politics in New South Wales, he had done much to transform that culture into one based on compromise and power-sharing. In this respect, he gave every sign of possessing the combination of forcefulness and tact required of a high commissioner in a difficult era. He was assertive in arguing for Australia's right to participate fully in decision-making on a range of international issues—perhaps too assertive—but it was hardly his fault if the consultation that Australia desired was no longer feasible. Moreover, although there were occasions when it might have been better if Beasley had said nothing, it was his highly developed Australian nationalism rather than loquaciousness or egotism that was at fault. Beasley also faced the problem of having to deal with Evatt, as well as the traditional confusion caused by the special role accorded to prime ministers in Anglo-Australian matters.[86] On the other hand, his status as a senior minister effectively representing the prime minister allowed him to offset some of the more controversial policies generated by External Affairs under Evatt. Moreover, Watt's fears concerning Beasley's alleged anti-Britishness proved unfounded. He looked sympathetically on Britain's manifold problems, and, as a Labor man, with some pride on a fraternal party's efforts to deal with them.[87]

Beasley's greatest failure was probably his inability or unwillingness to convey to the British government Australia's particular views on liberal internationalism and the role of the United Nations, a problem derived from his own limited faith in such multilateralism and his strong anti-communism. Whereas Beasley might have been able to clear up some of the misunderstanding that developed between the governments, it is arguable that the gulf between his own perspective and that of Evatt and, to a some extent, Chifley, might actually have magnified it. Yet the lack of consistency in Australia's own policies, to say nothing of Evatt's singular diplomatic style, would have made life difficult for any high commissioner and impossible for a weaker man than Beasley.

In the difficult circumstances of postwar austerity, Beasley also helped place Australia House on a footing to cope effectively with the challenges faced by its staff. In sum, he can be seen as a sensible choice for high commissioner, although one who left a mixed rather than an outstanding record of achievement. If he was sometimes left stabbing in the dark by the disagreement between governments, he at least did it with the vigour one would expect of a hard man from the Australian Labor Party's turbulent years.

9 Cold war London: Harrison and White

David Lowe

NEITHER Sir Eric Harrison nor Sir Thomas White features prominently in studies of Australian foreign policy or Anglo-Australian relations, yet both served for significant periods and at significant times in the Australian High Commission in London—especially if we include, as I do here, Harrison's year as resident minister, April 1950 to March 1951. In brief, when Harrison returned to Australia in 1951 he was succeeded by White, who was high commissioner from the middle of 1951 to 1956; and then Harrison returned for an extended term as high commissioner (1956–64).

Both were, of course, Menzies appointees. They continued a postwar trend away from former prime ministers as high commissioners, with Bruce the last, to senior ministers, the first of which was former Labor minister Jack Beasley in 1946. Harrison entered parliament in 1931, serving first as a United Australia and then a Liberal Party member for the Sydney seat of Wentworth until 1956. Harrison remained a member of the Menzies ministry while in London, initially as minister for defence, then as minister for the interior. (It was quite a novelty that his change of ministry was conferred in London by the lord high chancellor, Lord Jowitt.) White served as a National/United Australia/Liberal Party representative from 1929 to 1951 as the member for Balaclava in his hometown of Melbourne.

The two men had other characteristics in common. Both were war veterans, but their experiences had very different implications for their respective standings with Menzies, as is explored further below. Harrison and White were both empire revivalists. Harrison lamented the tendency to replace 'Empire' with 'Commonwealth', or any other changes in nomenclature that suggested a watering down of a vital concept.[1] In London, he occasionally annoyed the British with suggestions that they were not doing enough in the way of revival by committing to the great battle against communism. In his second period at the high commission he enjoyed shocking his hosts by declaring that the empire was coming to an end, and daring them to maintain an inner core of like-minded members.[2] In fact, he even earned a mild rebuke from Menzies in February 1957 for his public suggestion that the British Commonwealth be divided into two groups (suggestively, along lines that were either racial—British and non-British—or those who recognised the

Queen as sovereign as against those who only recognised her as head of the Commonwealth). Menzies' response was the softest of wrist-slappings, especially when read with his accompanying comment that the Commonwealth structure had become 'anomalous', and that he was 'not unduly oppressed by the alleged or real sensitivities of our Asian colleagues'; and it also speaks to the closeness of the two men that Harrison was able to respond in jovial chastened tone and with 'LONG LIVE THE COLOMBO PLAN' in capital letters.[3] We might also note that Harrison was the minister for the 1954 Royal Tour of Australia, about which so many superlatives hang and historians continue to wonder (and in fact, when he arrived in London in 1951 he was immersed in preparing for the intended, but never undertaken, tour of Australia in 1952 by King George VI).

White was equally as proud of his British race identity, and concerned to bolster the racial basis of Anglo-Australian relations after the war. He was a classic exponent of both strong ties with Britain and greater spending on Australia's defences because, as he challenged the House of Representatives in 1947, 'As a white man's outpost on the fringe of teeming millions of Asiatics, can we defend this country at such low cost?'[4] In speeches he gave in the United Kingdom in the mid-1950s, he told of Australian nationhood and development through Australia's involvement in two world wars, and Korea, 'alongside the Mother Country'.[5]

To borrow Menzies' phrase, Australian historians have not been 'unduly oppressed' by the performances of Australian high commissioners abroad, especially less well-known ones such as Harrison and White. One way to explore their respective terms in London is to ask how they fit the thesis proposed by Peter Edwards that prime ministers have dominated the making of Australian foreign policy-making.[6] Up to 1945 the thesis holds good in the eyes of most commentators, sustained partly by the umbilical cord of communication from the high commission in London to the prime minister in Canberra. Only a few—and especially Christopher Waters—have interpreted the adventurous Evatt period as constituting an interregnum or ushering in a major directional shift in Anglo-Australian relations;[7] but it is widely agreed that Evatt at least tested the prime ministerial dominance of Australian foreign policy-making more than any other to that time. What then, of the immediate post-Evatt years, in which Menzies slipped back into a prime ministerial role of apparent pre-eminence in the conduct of overseas relations—albeit with Percy Spender posing as big a test to him as Evatt had to Chifley—and with two Menzies appointees, not former prime ministers but senior politicians, taking up office in London?[8]

A further consideration in any exploration of the performance of high commissioners in the period under consideration in this chapter—especially early in the decade—is the common belief that another world war was in prospect. The Menzies governments, while wary of unconditional commitments and mindful of radicalism accompanying rapid postwar change in Southeast Asia, gradually accepted during 1950–51 the British plan to send the first expeditionary force raised upon the outbreak of another world war to the Middle East. From 1952 the Australians were less inclined, and less encouraged, to think in these terms, and they began to draw stronger distinctions between the threat of world war and the prospect of longer-term cold war—but even then, in the context of universal conscription for eighteen-year-olds, a significant spike in defence spending coordinated by a National Security Resources Board, and real military commitments to Malaya, Korea and even, via the air force, to the Middle East, the sense of a semi-war footing remained strong through to the mid-1950s.[9] Did this climate offer Harrison and White additional scope and authority as high commissioners in London?[10]

This chapter will explore these themes while following a mostly chronological structure, moving from Harrison's first period in London, as resident minister, then to White's term as high commissioner, followed by Harrison's return for what was the longest of the terms examined here, seven and a half years as high commissioner. In the course of examining White's and Harrison's work and achievements, we need to consider some distinctive characteristics of the two men, as well as something of their respective relationships with Menzies.

Eric Harrison, part 1

Several commentators, and also his colleague Paul Hasluck, likened Harrison to a storm-trooper during the 1949 election campaign. His two main speeches were on defence and the dangers of communism, and he reveled in the contest of the campaign. As Hasluck put it, 'He enjoyed politics like a rugby match. When you see a head kick it'.[11] As leader of the House after the 1949 election he performed his duties like a garrison commander. Otherwise, Harrison is best known for his loyalty to Menzies. Descriptions such as 'staunch lieutenant', 'constant, admiring and vigorous ally' and 'staunchest supporter' feature in the few short analyses of the Harrison–Menzies relationship.[12] These descriptions speak logically to his military experience: he enlisted in the Australian Imperial Force in 1916 and served on the Western Front in the 5th Field Artillery Brigade from December 1917; and during World War II he was a captain in the militia, serving as liaison officer for the US military forces in Australia during 1942–43. But the above descriptions also help us bridge his military experience with his sense of his own role as a senior member of a unit led by Menzies. On two occasions in the turbulent 1939–40 period he willingly surrendered portfolios so that Menzies could form coalition governments with the Country Party. In short, Harrison made a good, party-disciplined cold-war warrior. As resident minister during 1950–51, he was quickly plunged into the diplomacy and strategy of Anglo-Australian discussions on the fight against communism.

In general terms, he was deeply involved but not deeply embedded with Whitehall and the Attlee ministry in cold war conversations. There was respect but little in the way of special concession granted to him. He was, for example, invited to attend a meeting of the UK Defence Committee in May 1950 that considered the situation in Malaya. This move was prompted by the minister of defence, Emanuel Shinwell, and it triggered some reflection in Whitehall and Downing Street about the desirability of high commissioners attending such meetings on occasions where their own interests were clearly at stake. The means for implementing this practice were clear. In 1947 the Chifley government had successfully proposed that the UK and New Zealand high commissioners in Canberra attend meetings of the Australian Council of Defence when matters affecting these parts of the Commonwealth were discussed. But the arrangements had been a dead letter since then—and in Harrison's case, his attendance was to be considered an exceptional circumstance rather than setting a precedent. It was explicable in terms of his unique status as Australian defence minister in London. (In fact, some bristling at Harrison's public remarks about the need for the United Kingdom to do more in the cold war contest probably helped to ensure that it was a one-off.)[13] Harrison also represented his prime minister at three sessions (out of twelve) at the Commonwealth Prime Ministers' Conference held in January 1951, when Menzies was laid low with influenza. Consciously or not, his main contribution sounded like an echo from the days of Bruce. In discussion about the nexus between Australia, New Zealand and Malaya (ANZAM)[14] command and the North Atlantic Treaty Organization (NATO), in the event of global war he argued for a Washington-based strategic council composed of representatives of all allied powers, and the right of Australia to be represented in the UK war cabinet when matters affecting her interests were discussed.[15]

Conclusions about Harrison's impact in just over one year spent in London can only be tentative. As a senior minister in the Menzies government, and resident minister rather than high commissioner, Harrison's status was somewhat ambiguous but not insignificant in the eyes of Whitehall. He enjoyed good standing partly on account of his well-known closeness to Menzies, and partly also because of Whitehall's enduring lack of confidence in Australia's burgeoning Department of External Affairs. This aspect of Anglo-Australian relations may seem a back-handed way of exploring the work of the high commissioners, but it is very important. The Australian high commissioner, as a direct channel to the prime minister, was likely to remain more influential if Australian policy-making outside of cabinet and the Prime Minister's Department was not regarded so highly. The view from London, and from the UK High Commission in Canberra, was that External Affairs changed little in the transition from Evatt to Percy Spender, and the efforts of both ministers and senior members of the department were likely to remain, at best, maladroit. The Foreign Office's Far Eastern expert, Sir Esler Dening, noted in May 1950 that '[t]he Australians behave like a bull in a China shop'.[16] And from Canberra, the British High Commission would argue much the same until the middle of the decade. In August 1951, Acting High Commissioner Garnett reeled off a list of poor performances—Spender over the negotiation of the Colombo Plan; John Burton, the former departmental secretary who abandoned his new post at Colombo to contest elections in Australia; W.R. Hodgson, who did not impress the British as the Commonwealth representative on the Allied Council for Japan; and the inclination of Australia's new external affairs minister,

Richard Casey, to drop in casually on Chiang Kai-Shek in Formosa, without heed for the diplomatic implications.[17] In particular, Spender's aggressive diplomacy during the formation of the Colombo Plan for aid to South and Southeast Asia during the first half of 1950 raised British hackles; and his visit to London soon afterwards in August and September confirmed the civil servants' impression of an over-ambitious external affairs minister straining at the long leash that he had been allowed by his prime minister.[18]

Harrison himself felt these strained Anglo-Australian relations most keenly in the early months of 1951 when the drafting of the ANZUS Treaty took place in Canberra. As has been outlined in several accounts, the Attlee government was worried about the scope of what security agreement might be offered to the Australians and New Zealanders by United States Special Envoy John Foster Dulles. Sparks flew when the Australians, especially Spender, concluded that the British were set on spoiling chances of a security treaty and for their part, the British deduced that the Australians were prepared to sign a treaty that would deal a huge blow to British prestige in the region. Harrison delivered some of the tersest messages from Spender to Patrick Gordon Walker, secretary of state for Commonwealth relations; and he also added asides passed on from Menzies about how difficult it was to control Spender.[19] Caught in a complex web of diplomatic communication and political rivalry, he passed on personally notes sent by Spender, as well as notes from Menzies, all the while managing the difficult act of representing both prime minister and external affairs minister faithfully, with interpretative additions when prompted.

In fact, a month after the angriest exchanges, as parties in both countries were trying to repair the damage, Harrison volunteered to Gordon Walker that he, Harrison, was returning to Australia soon because there had been a fight between Spender and Harold Holt for the deputy leadership of the Liberal Party, and Menzies wanted Harrison back to take up this role (and, the implication was, to watch his back). So, the British were treated to another update on the ministerial restlessness around Menzies, learning that the trigger for Harrison's return was less the publicly arguable double dissolution of 1951 than internal party turmoil.[20]

By the time he returned, Harrison had played mildly pro-active roles (though never running far ahead of his government's thinking) in other cold war developments, including Australian military assistance for Malaya and Australian involvement in the Korean War. In November 1950, for example, the British informed Harrison of their deliberations with French and US allies, on the question of whether United Nations Command aircraft should be given the right to pursue Chinese military aircraft across the Yalu River. Harrison quickly passed the news that the three powers had decided against this course to Spender, who endorsed the related proposal to establish a demilitarised zone along the river. Although this idea was overtaken by events, Canberra had had a chance to express a view at an apposite time. Similarly, after the British prime minister, Clement Attlee, had called the Commonwealth high commissioners together in December to explain the purpose of his emergency visit to Washington, Harrison was able to take the lead in expressing the Australian hope that the Korean conflict could be kept a limited one and that President Truman be encouraged to rein in the adventurous General MacArthur. In the wake of Harrison's report of this meeting, Spender was able to shape a public statement that reiterated the Australian desire that the conflict be limited and capable of resolution without further escalation. It was helpful that he could include mention of Harrison's having conveyed the Australian government's position to Attlee prior to Attlee's departure for Washington. [21]

Tommy White

Sir Thomas White was widely known as 'Tommy' White, and was well decorated, with not only a knighthood but also a Distinguished Flying Cross. He was, in fact, the first officer of the Australian Flying Corps to be awarded 'wings'—in World War I—before serving also in World War II (in Brighton, UK overseeing Australian aircrew serving with the Royal Air Force). He was then involved in a minor way in the formation of the Liberal Party at the end of World War II, and in a more significant way in the founding of Legacy, an organisation caring for the dependants of servicemen.

White's experiences in World War I read like a tale from a *Boy's Own Annual*. In November 1915 he was captured while on a mission near Baghdad, and imprisoned by the Turks. But they could not hold him for the war's duration. In July 1918 he escaped from a train in Constantinople and stowed away on a ship to Odessa—from where he made his way to London. White's published account of his time in captivity, *Guests of the Unspeakable* (1928), is well known as an early classic in the genre of Australian prisoner of war tales. (And he remains an iconic figure. Today, the T.W. White Society is a group of Royal Australian Air Force and Australian Army officers and civilians with a mutual interest in enhancing military–civilian community relationships.)

White was a particularly strong public advocate for ex-servicemen, and devoted his first parliamentary speech to the significance of building an Australian War Memorial. Soon after this, in Opposition, he dwelt on the unique quality of the Scullin Labor government—it was a one hundred per cent non-soldier ministry.[22] Not surprisingly, then, unlike Harrison, White resented Menzies' lack of military experience. The year in which this surfaced most strongly was 1938 when he traveled with Menzies and Earle Page to London for negotiations on trade preferences. The three Australians went to France for the unveiling of the Villers-Bretonneux memorial to Australians killed in World War I. In the wake of the ceremony, White noted in his diary his contempt for those attending who had not fought in the war; and later, back in Australia, took a dim view of the Lyons cabinet's support for appeasing Hitler, and an equally dim view of ambitious cabinet members such as Menzies and Casey who circled Lyons. In April 1939 White stood for leadership of the United Australia Party and did not come close in a vote won by Menzies; and the same happened in September 1943 when the party tried to rebuild itself in opposition. As Allan Martin writes, when Menzies regained power at the end of 1949, White's detestation of Menzies, mixed with jealousy of his superior gifts, was only barely concealed.[23]

As White was high commissioner for five years, some of his contemporaries were able to observe him in a considered manner. The external affairs officer, Colin Moodie, recalls arriving in London to take up a post at the high commission in February 1953 to find a rabbit warren of branch heads, expatriates and frustrated Englishmen. 'The High Commissioner,' he recalled, 'Sir Thomas White, was a nice man ... but drawn towards the representational and social side of his duties, unlike Beasley and Bruce before him. Some things interested him, like immigration, but not on the whole foreign affairs'.[24] Moodie was frustrated that White did not spend more time with British ministers (and claimed that he never visited the British prime minister or foreign secretary officially); but added that this was partly also the product of Menzies' poor regard for him. The latter point is borne out by both anecdote and the nature of correspondence between the two men. For example, at the end of Menzies' visit in 1953, for the coronation, he met with White. Moodie recalls the tale relayed to him by the secretary of the Prime Minister's Department, Allen Brown:

> White would go on about his social activities, attendance at Garden Parties and the like, while Menzies, accompanied by Brown, just sat. During the next visit, Menzies announced that he wouldn't take Brown; he had looked too lugubrious [at the previous meeting]. On Menzies' return, Brown enquired how the talk went. Menzies replied, 'It was no good, I could still see you sitting there.'[25]

There is some evidence to suggest that White was third on Menzies' list of possible high commisioners, after fellow cabinet members Philip McBride and Athol Townley, both of whom continued in cabinet.

White, however, took very seriously the opportunities for representation of Australia's social and cultural interests afforded by his London posting; and a ceremonial dimension may have been enhanced by his becoming the most senior high commissioner in London from June 1954. He is well remembered as high commissioner for his promotion of Australian artists and select Australian produce, including wine. White was founder-patron of the Society of Australian Writers, formed in London in 1952, and he was inaugural president of the Australian Musical Association, established in 1955 and which had its headquarters at Australia House (see page 229).[26] He and his wife, Lady Vera White, were at the centre of multiple engagements and planned entertainments for the thousands of Australians in London for the coronation in 1953;[27] and they proved excellent hosts for the increasing number of Australians passing through London at the start of the new 'Elizabethan' era.

White retired from his post as international tension over the Suez Canal was nearing a climax (just after nationalisation), and so his diplomatic skills were not tested in the same way that Harrison's had been. The only statements he made, in August 1956, were declarations that Australia should back Britain in whatever course London decided on, and that Nasser was the Mussolini of the Middle East.[28] Otherwise, the silences in Australian and British documentary records are instructive. White, it is clear, was a very minor presence in the diplomatic activity surrounding the French defeat in Indochina in 1954 and the subsequent US proposal for allied intervention or 'united action', as it was called.[29] In fairness to him, however, some of the explanation for this lies in the changed dynamics of Australian foreign policy-making. By 1954 meetings of the ANZUS Council and five power military planning group worked through the strategic implications of unfolding events in Indochina in ways that shifted the centre of gravity away from London; and White was overshadowed by Spender's efforts, as ambassador in Washington, to encourage the Menzies government to support the Americans in a stronger stance against communist-led forces in Vietnam. It was telling that Canberra sent to Washington one of Australia's most senior professional diplomats, Arthur Tange, to try to curb Spender's activism; and equally telling that Tange failed.[30]

When London learned of Australian activities and policy positions relating to Indochina, either from Washington or Canberra, they learned mostly via one of three sources: from their own representatives overseas; from Casey directly; or via Laurence McIntyre, successor to Keith Waller as senior external affairs representative in London, or Moodie or Gordon Jockel, his juniors.[31] White, under instruction, passed on Canberra's views and met with Lord Reading, the minister of state for foreign affairs, early in the escalation of diplomacy, at the time of the Americans' 'united action' proposal. Beyond reminding Reading of the Australians' need to tread warily with Washington in order to maintain the ANZUS alliance, he appears to have added little.[32] Similarly, there is not much sense of White's 'value-adding', as we might say today, to Menzies' several visits to London. Before and during Menzies' visit of May 1952, for example, when the prime minister met with the heads of many departments, and endured some tough questioning from Churchill and Eden on Britain's exclusion from ANZUS, there is no evidence that White assisted.[33]

When, having returned to Australia, White was interviewed on a Melbourne radio station about his time in London, he prepared notes for the encounter, emphasising immigration, 'diplomatic activity', trade and cultural societies, in that order.[34] It was a picture broadly consistent with how he was remembered. In public representations of Australian interests, White drew on his experience as minister for trade and customs during the 1930s, and his preoccupation with populating Australia rapidly with British stock. His speeches have strong echoes of the 'men, money and markets' priorities by which Prime Minister Bruce had characterised Anglo-Australian relations in the 1920s. In fact, he used this phrase or a variation—'men, money and machinery'—to describe Australia's needs.[35]

Probably the most distinctive of his 'diplomatic activities' was White's strong interest in the British creation of the Central African Federation, comprising the self-governing

Southern Rhodesia and crown colonies of Northern Rhodesia and Nyasaland. There was a strong family interest. The Whites' oldest daughter settled in Southern Rhodesia with her husband, and their two young boys holidayed with their grandparents in the official residence, Stoke Lodge. When White wrote to Casey in 1954 recommending that Australia consider sending a high commissioner to the new federation, he sparked a brief flurry of interest: the lessons of colonial experience in Africa, including constitution-making and the handling of the Mau Mau rebellion in Kenya, might have relevance to Australian colonial administration in Papua New Guinea. Ultimately, a combination of British discouragement and the pre-emptive action by Australia's Department of Commerce and Agriculture in appointing a trade commissioner nipped this initiative in the bud.[36]

Even had White been more disposed to greater adventurousness in foreign policy, two important and related developments challenged the influence of Australia's high commissioner in London during the mid-1950s: the growing importance of the American alliance; and the rapid growth and activism of Spender and his staff in Washington and at the UN General Assembly in New York.[37] It is instructive that when Harrison took over from White in 1956, he campaigned for terms that made for parity with the standard that Spender had set in his appointment to Washington, rather than any previous standard used for London.[38]

Waller, the most senior external affairs officer in London at this time, worked mostly without reference to White, and seemed to pick up from the Casey–Bruce legacy. He spent part of every day in the Foreign Office, was on the distribution list for a wide range of British telegrams, and relished the challenge of trying to smuggle Australian interests into policy formulations in the Foreign Office and Commonwealth Relations Office, while keeping Canberra up to date. Waller served with both Harrison and White. He admired Harrison's capacity to take in a brief and his determination to represent Australian positions effectively; and by contrast, he had less faith in White, who, according to Waller, never sought advice, and rode his luck, with those around him fearing disaster. Waller concluded quickly that White's wife, Vera, a daughter of Alfred Deakin, was 'the brains in that combination', and he told Casey that in the event of a crisis, he had resolved that he would seek Vera's help in steering the high commissioner in the right direction.[39]

Eric Harrison, part 2

While rumours again suggested that White's successor, Harrison, might not have been Menzies' first choice (one newspaper report had cabinet members Philip McBride and Arthur Fadden turning the post down),[40] the former resident minister returned to Australia House with enthusiasm. A feature of Harrison's second, and much longer, term in London was his settling into the role of the political commentator who could keep 'the boss' (that is, Menzies) informed and entertained. While many Australian ambassadors and high commissioners drew on their senior staff members to draft most of the monthly 'political appreciations', Harrison took on this task with the relish of one who prided himself on knowing how to be heard. Harrison adopted the voice of an old campaigner, the insider/outsider whose wry observations might appeal to the veteran, Menzies. In August 1960, following a recent reshuffle in the Macmillan ministry, he rode his luck (too far) with playful metaphor: 'I would agree that there does seem to have been a distinct element of grooming in the changes, and further that the late Foreign Secretary had most of the groom's attentions. However, it seems to me rather that a substantial part of the stable was being groomed and not just one animal'.[41] A month later, he was even more the confidant, informing Menzies of the British Labour Party's woes:

> Gaitskell has not been any great shakes as a leader, though perhaps the circumstances of the time rather than deficiencies of character account for this. When everybody is indulging in doubt and criticism, a leader needs, I think, to be less self-questioning, less honest even and certainly more resolute than he …

> What has all this motley crew been doing to bring Labour to such a state that people are actively wondering whether the party has any future at all?[42]

That Menzies read at least a good number of Harrison's appreciations is clear. Occasionally, he highlighted Harrison's phrases and judgments (such as Harrison's memorable, 'Traditions do not merely die hard here. They simply do not die'[43]) or added marginal notes.

The future of the Commonwealth and the implications of Britain's application to join the European Economic Community (EEC) dominated the middle and latter part of Harrison's tenure in London. It was a testing time for one such as Harrison who, like his prime minister, found it hard to see how the widening membership of the Commonwealth as more African and Asian nations gained their independence could be harnessed to common goals, and who worried about the new, post-imperial role that the British were imagining for themselves. As David Goldsworthy has written, the task for Australians such as Harrison and Menzies was not easy; 'coping with Britain's retreat from empire necessarily meant trying to cope with the post-imperial order that Britain was simultaneously seeking to fashion for itself'.[44]

Harrison struggled to relinquish his preference for two classes of Commonwealth membership, an option that had not quite been ruled out but was rapidly being seen as unworkable by British policy-makers in 1960–61 (largely on the grounds that UN membership seemed inevitable for most newly independent nations, and it would be counter-productive to set up a stricter set of rules for a higher class of Commonwealth membership). Race clearly played a role in Harrison's thinking. In November 1957 he mischievously invited Menzies to ponder the impact of newly independent member of the Commonwealth, Ghana, attending a forthcoming Commonwealth Prime Ministers' Conference. Ghana's prime minister, Kwame Nkrumah, wrote Harrison, had made a point of visiting a witch-doctor before leaving for the conference.[45]

Menzies relied on Harrison for insights into Macmillan's cabinet dynamics and issues of timing surrounding his planned trips to London. For his part, Harrison absorbed personally the blows dealt to Menzies in the early 1960s: the affront of being left out on a limb over his four-power summit meeting suggestion in the United Nations in October 1960 (which was overwhelmingly defeated when voted on, as the United Kingdom and United States had scarcely mobilised votes, and Nehru poured salt on the wound by scorning the idea); being overlooked in favour of Nehru for the acting chair at the 1961 meeting of Commonwealth prime ministers; South Africa's quitting the Commonwealth at this conference, under pressure from newer members; and the apparent disregard for the long-held preferential trade relationship implied in the British application to join the EEC. In the wake of the 1961 Prime Ministers' Meeting, Harrison told Macmillan of Menzies' hurt, and then suggested to his prime minister that he maintain pressure on Macmillan ('I don't think that he should get away with things too easily'). Harrison even checked records of attendance at previous Commonwealth/Imperial Conferences, to establish that Menzies was more senior than Nehru by virtue of his 1930s appearances at two Imperial Conferences.[46] The high commissioner was more blunt again with Duncan Sandys, secretary of state for Commonwealth relations, referring to Macmillan's 'apparent preference for a brown face'.[47]

Knowing Menzies' key ministers well was also clearly an advantage during the tense discussions about British intent to join the EEC. When the minister for trade, John McEwen, visited London in the early months of 1962, he tied up senior UK cabinet ministers and put his case for Australian trade interests bluntly and effectively. Harrison was able to part-sympathise with the British, reminding them of McEwen's role as head of the Country Party, but he also saw the advantage in tough talking; and he provided astute commentary to Menzies both about McEwen's impact and the timing of Menzies' own visit soon afterwards.[48] The story of Menzies' visit and of the profound shock he and others endured at the significance of the (unsuccessful) British application to join the EEC is told in detail elsewhere.[49] When combined with Menzies' dismay at British condemnation, in the United Nations, of South African apartheid, and British legislation at the end of 1961 to restrict Commonwealth immigrants (aimed chiefly at the West Indies and South Asia, but with consequences for all Commonwealth members), the sense of a sea change in Anglo-Australian relations was unmistakable. While Harrison was actively engaged in providing astute insights about British cabinet dynamics and policy positions, it is hard not to conclude that he struggled to absorb the full consequences of these rapid changes for the British Empire/Commonwealth. Instead, he readily agreed with Menzies' mournful reflections, such as: 'I sometimes doubt whether the Government of the United Kingdom appreciates that old friends are best'.[50]

Harrison's final years in London brought into sharp relief the mixed fate of a successful politician and prime ministerial confidant turned diplomat. On the one hand, he was, by dint of his seniority and adroit handling of his responsibilities, feted in London. By 1964 he was dean of the high commissioners, number four on the hierarchical London Diplomatic List, and overseeing a staff of 900. He enjoyed the rare privilege of being a member of more than one livery company, something that was highly prized (the forerunners to guilds in the City of London, by the 1960s liveries' activities were primarily charitable and social). Harrison was made a member of both the Tallow Chandlers and the Butchers liveries; and his prime minister was only a member of one, the Clothmakers.

Yet, Harrison's tenure ended awkwardly in the context of Australian politics and his proud relationship with Menzies. Health might have been a factor—he had a hip replacement operation that was not immediately successful and left him in some pain. At the beginning of 1962, when he was due to return, Menzies successfully persuaded Harrison to stay on a little longer. At that stage, Menzies enjoyed the slenderest of majorities, and a by-election following the movement of a successor to Harrison was out of the question.[51] One-and-a-half years later, with Menzies' majority improved, he requested that Harrison return soon, but was met with an aggrieved response from Harrison who complained about it looking like he had 'just been holding the fort and would be yanked home by PM at first opportunity'. Nor did Harrison think this appearance would help his chances of 'a Board or two'.[52] It was an exchange that briefly soured the relationship and one that Harrison later regretted, but it was perhaps indicative of the status paradox of a former senior politician occupying the London post.

Conclusion

The themes of prime ministerial dominance in Australian foreign policy-making and the enabling effect of war for a high commissioner provide some guidance to an understanding of the London careers of Harrison and White. During his first year in London, Harrison benefited from his involvement in cold war crises and also from the closeness of his relationship with Menzies; yet his modest success was also the product of some diplomatic dexterity and his knowledge of power struggles within the Menzies cabinet. White, on the other hand, was content to concentrate on issues other than cold war crises, and he was undermined in his role by the low regard in which Menzies held him. In other words, the sense of connectedness to the prime minister could be important, and the cold war emergency could assist the high commissioner, especially early in the decade, as it did for Harrison, but neither theme guaranteed prominence or success. The significant qualification is that I am still measuring success chiefly in terms of diplomatic/government representation: White was arguably very successful as a cultural ambassador, and his support for Australian artists in the United Kingdom laid a strong foundation on which his successors built. Making Australia House a focal point for social occasions and Australian literary, theatrical and musical talent was an achievement that should not be underestimated. More than 1,000 people attended an Australia Day reception at Australia House in 1954. In some ways, White paved the way for a later period when cheaper air travel and 'new nationalism' made for frequent traffic—tourist and cultural—through the high commission.

When Harrison returned, for eight years from 1956 to 1964, he continued to enjoy a special status as loyal lieutenant to Menzies. The veteran prime minister seemed to enjoy Harrison's wry style of political analysis, punctuated by witticisms and suggestions. But some of the main forces shaping Anglo-Australian relations lay outside the cold war, with the pace of decolonisation, a growing United Nations, British relations with Europe, and a rekindled special relationship between the United Kingdom and United States bringing changes which made Harrison and many other Australians begin to feel uncomfortably marginal.

Consistent with this conclusion, and perhaps an appropriate note on which to conclude here, is an occasional echo, in assessments of how the Australian high commissioner should function, of earlier glory days under Bruce and some of his predecessors. Australia's external affairs minister from mid-1951, Richard Casey, could not help himself. Occasionally, he harked back to the time when, as liaison officer in London from 1924 to 1931, he had access to secret papers at the same time as many British policy-makers; and he wondered if something might be replicated by way of a secret cipher section in Waller's office in the early 1950s. Casey was musing aloud in London when he ventured this idea, and, as was the case with many of his musings, his Foreign Office audience was politely non-committal.[53]

Heading for Australia House: a British cartoonist depicts the Australian arrival. [*British Australian and New Zealander*, 27 June 1940, p.2, State Library of Victoria, courtesy of Newspapers Collection]

Outside the Boomerang Club, a social hub for Australian troops on leave in London. [State Library of Victoria, Argus Newspaper Collection of Photographs, Pictorial Press (London), Image Number H99.205/804]

S.M. Bruce and Ethel Bruce with Second Australian Imperial Force troops in London, c. 1940. [State Library of Victoria, Argus Newspaper Collection of Photographs, Image Number H99.201/238]

Australian Prime Minister John Curtin (left) welcomed on his arrival in England in 1944 by S.M. Bruce. [Australian War Memorial Negative Number SUK12096]

J.A. Beasley and members of the Australian Navy staff in London walking up the gangplank of HMAS *Shropshire* to greet the Victory Contingent Unit from Australia in June 1946. [Australian War Memorial Negative Number 130215]

J.A. Beasley meeting the English rugby team before they leave for Australia at Australia House, London, 1946. [National Archives of Australia Image Number M1409:38]

J.A. Beasley speaking at a ceremony after he had been presented with the Hurlingham Club Flag, 1947. [National Archives of Australia Image Number M1409:48]

J.A. Beasley (left) with John Masefield, the poet laureate (right), at the opening of an exhibition of paintings by the Australian artist Norman Bull. [National Archives of Australia Image Number M1409:48]

Field Marshal Viscount Montgomery of Alamein (left) and J.A. Beasley as they leave the Anzac Day Memorial Service at the Church of St Martin-in-the-Fields, London, 25 April 1948. [Australian War Memorial Negative Number 134750]

Sir Thomas White (left) talks with the former commanding officer of the Overseas Air Headquarters, Royal Australian Air Force, Air Commodore Bill Garing, CBE, DFC, 1953–54. [Australian War Memorial Negative Number MALTA0410A]

E.J. Harrison, minister for defence 1949–50, then resident minister for Australia in the United Kingdom. [Photograph courtesy of Dwyer Collection, National Library of Australia]

Sir Eric and Lady Harrison on the deck of the P&O liner SS *Canberra*, 10 October 1963. [John Mulligan Photograph Collection, National Library of Australia Image Number nla.pic-an24492847]

10 Sir Alexander Downer and the embers of British Australia

Stuart Ward

ON 3 NOVEMBER 1967, Peter Grose made the following wry observation in the *Australian*:

> One of the quirkier acts of history gave us Sir Robert Menzies as Prime Minister to preside over the decline in Anglo-Australian relations. But history must still be congratulating itself on the irony of appointing Sir Alexander Downer to oversee the latest and most serious slide of all.[1]

Grose was referring to the dual shocks of the Wilson Labour government's plan to withdraw Britain's military capability from 'east of Suez' and its determination to secure British membership of the European Economic Community. Neither of these issues was particularly new, but they came together in 1967 to underline that Australia and Britain were drifting apart, both economically and strategically. Moreover, profound changes in trade, finance, migration patterns and the deployment of military hardware were having a dramatic effect on the sentimental and cultural ties between the two countries. Long-cherished ideas about an underlying Anglo-Australian community of culture—commonly expressed in the language and ritual of Australian 'Britishness'—were subjected to an inevitable reappraisal. That the task of steering Australia House through these shoals fell to Alexander Robert Downer would indeed produce many ironies.

Many of Downer's closest friends and colleagues in the United Kingdom regarded him as the exemplar of the Australian Briton. A Whitehall character appraisal described him as 'violently Anglophile, and this takes the form of wanting to see as many Englishmen emigrating to Australia as possible'. With the exception of Prime Minister Menzies, he was undoubtedly 'our best friend in the Government'.[2] Downer's father was a colonial premier of South Australia, an influential federationist, and an early senator. The son's background and upbringing enabled him to move freely in influential circles in London and studies at Brasenose College, Oxford, and the Inner Temple saw the forging of many personal and political links that he would later develop during his time as minister for immigration in the Menzies government (1958–63) and high commissioner (1964–72).

Perhaps the most vivid indication of his extensive social network was an invitation, on the eve of succeeding Eric Harrison at Australia House, to be godfather of Charles, 9th Earl of Spencer (brother of Princess Diana). The Earl's godmother was no less than Queen Elizabeth II.

The description 'violently Anglophile' neatly captures the turmoil and drama of Downer's eight-year tenure at Australia House. The 'violence' referred not to an uneven temperament or combative nature, but to the passion and determination that he poured into his struggle to preserve the world view of his generation. Downer was, first and foremost, an Australian, but one whose conception of Australian nationalism was inseparable from his wider dedication to the 'Greater British' family. And it was this vision of Australians as 'one people' with their British counterparts that came under heavy siege in the 1960s. By the completion of his term as high commissioner in October 1972, which left him second only to Bruce in longevity in the office, the Australian high commissionership had become a vastly different post from the one he had assumed in 1964. Yet in almost every respect, these changes occurred despite his best endeavours and were to cause him considerable personal distress.

The early years

Not unusually for a new high commissioner, one of Downer's early initiatives was to seek improvements to the high commissioner's official residence, Stoke Lodge. Soon after his arrival he wrote to Canberra requesting an eightfold increase in the maintenance budget from £500 to £4,000. His letter to the cabinet secretary, Sir John Bunting, is revealing, not only of the material state of Stoke Lodge, but also the new high commissioner's understanding of his role and its relationship to his past experience of British life:

> The upstairs sitting room, which is the private sitting room for the High Commissioner and his family, has been furnished in a style which is quite unbecoming to any person occupying this position in such an elegant and sophisticated society as London … In case you should think [the figure of £4,000] rather high, may I ask you to be guided by my own judgement in this, as well as my long, albeit intermittent, experience of life in England … I think it is fair to ask the Government to make an effective contribution towards my own efforts of trying to elevate the general standard of our representation in the United Kingdom.[3]

Having attended to the London residence, he then moved to buy a private country estate in Wiltshire, Oare House, consisting of an early eighteenth-century house, six cottages and one hundred acres of fields and woods. Although an entirely private matter, this unconventional behaviour (for an Australian high commissioner) inevitably attracted attention. In April 1966, an article in the left-leaning Australian journal *Nation* brought down a scathing assessment:

Sir Alexander is entitled to those eccentricities he pays for from his own purse. If he chooses to exhibit the bustling downunder spirit by advertising for a butler in 'The Times', to buy his own country mansion, and to make sentimental speeches ... about the Queen, surely Cabinet knew of his propensities when it despatched him ... In this age of experts, Australia could get itself respected by the intelligence of its representatives. If we are stuck for some foreseeable time with a gentleman who takes London for an enlarged version of the Adelaide Club, we must look to a powerful second line to do the work.[4]

In the eyes of some critics, Downer's personal style compromised his capacity to represent Australian interests abroad. Yet, this impression, initially at least, was unfair and said as much about the unexamined assumptions of Downer's detractors as it did about the abilities or beliefs of the high commissioner himself. As the divergence of interest between Australia and Britain widened, however, Downer's 'British' sensibilities would become increasingly problematic.

Early signs of this appeared in 1965, with Downer's first public pronouncements about the prospect of British entry into the European Economic Community (or Common Market as it was then known). At that time, Britain's membership application was in abeyance, having been formally vetoed by French President Charles de Gaulle in January 1963. The Macmillan government's recasting of Britain's economic future in European terms, at a substantial cost to the preferential trade advantages for Commonwealth countries in the UK market, had initially caused great consternation in Australia. Indeed, it was widely assumed that Macmillan was breaching some sacred British covenant, a perception that shaped the response of the Menzies government at all levels. But the drawn-out experience of Britain's membership negotiations in 1962 had the effect of absorbing most of the shock. Indeed, by the time Downer took up his appointment at Australia House, there were clear indications that Australian political and business leaders had begun to adjust their horizons.[5] Yet Downer was seemingly unaware of this new mood and in his first public speech on the EEC in March 1965, he offered a distinct flavour of things to come:

Most of us, you know, prefer to call it the British Commonwealth, because though we are primarily Australians we are also British ... Despite the revolutionary changes in the world in the last 20 years, there is still a tremendous reservoir of goodwill and affection for Britain in my country. You know of our loyalty to the Queen, our enthusiasm for the Royal Family. You may not be so keenly aware of the essentially British flavour of our communities. But there are now danger signs. Events of the past few years have created an uneasy feeling, only recently assuaged, amongst all sections of opinion that Britain is no longer as interested in the Commonwealth as formerly. May I give you an example? Whatever the merits of the economic argument for entry into the Common Market, this policy has left a deep bruise on Anglo-Australian relations ... I believe it would be one of the greatest tragedies in history if Britain were to become a European power at the sacrifice of four centuries of achievement of our ancestors.

He went on to plead with his audience: 'We are your own people, your own kinsmen, who have a deep feeling for you, who ever have been first at your side in your hour of direst need, and who in the past have been accustomed to look to you for leadership'.[6] The message was plain and widely publicised: Australia had not yet reconciled itself to the inevitability of Britain's turn to Europe, and continued to view the problem in terms of the abandonment of fellow Britons abroad for the sake of material gain.

The speech was reported back in Australia where the Opposition leader, Arthur Calwell, inquired in parliament whether the high commissioner's views were those of the government. Menzies found a way of avoiding the issue.[7] From his perspective in London, however, Downer was puzzled by Calwell's remarks and wrote to John Bunting asking for clarification of the government's 'present day thinking' on the EEC.[8] It was immediately clear to officials in Canberra that 'what Mr Downer really wants is some assurance' that his speech 'was in line with the Government's attitude'.[9] But ascertaining the government's exact position at this time proved a difficult exercise. As Bunting explained, 'Ministers have been silent on the subject lately, both in cabinet and publicly', largely due to the uncertainty that surrounded Britain's future prospects in Europe. The government was anxious to avoid stating any firm position that it might later have to retract, and to that extent it was clear that Downer's statement had caused some mild embarrassment. Menzies' advice to Downer was that 'the Common Market is a good subject to keep off … Our best course, publicly and privately, is to be on the sidelines for the time being'.[10]

Yet these words of restraint could not withstand the pressure of time and events. Into 1966, with mounting rumours about an impending change in British policy towards Europe, Downer publicly reiterated his anxieties in similar terms—only this time adding a thinly veiled threat that Australia might retaliate by substituting Japanese imports for British. This sparked an internal scuffle in the government, with Trade Department officials leaking to the press that Downer had 'usurped the prerogatives' of Trade Minister (and Deputy Prime Minister) John McEwen in communicating the government's position on the EEC. According to senior Liberals, McEwen was the source of a report that the new prime minister, Harold Holt, would 'give Sir Alexander one of the sternest rebukes ever administered to an Australian representative overseas'. Holt denied that he had made any such commitment, but was only lukewarm in his support of Downer, informing parliament that 'anything he would say on a matter of such importance to our two countries would be said in a helpful spirit and as a statement of the effects as they appear to him'.[11]

The new foreigners: Australians at the gates

Further strains in the relationship emerged over the question of Australians' rights of entry into the United Kingdom. This had been a minor sore point ever since the introduction of the UK Commonwealth Immigrants Act in 1962. The new legislation represented the first attempt by a British government to distinguish between its own nationals and other 'British subjects' abroad for the purposes of immigration. The immediate context was the increase in arrivals from the West Indies and South Asia from 1948. By the end of the 1950s, pressure had begun to mount on the government to curtail the inward flow of Commonwealth migrants. And in order that these measures should not be deemed racially discriminatory, they had to be seen to apply equally to immigrants from the 'white' Commonwealth. The 1962 act thus operated, on the face of it, to restrict the unfettered rights of Australians to travel and work in Britain, and complaints were raised at the time on these grounds. But the act also provided for far more liberal rights of entry for migrants deemed to have skills useful to Britain, which in practice meant that Australians continued to enjoy unrestricted access to the 'mother country', even if the mere fact of applying for an entry voucher still rankled with some.

By the mid-1960s, however, difficulties at the entry gates began to appear, partly due to an increasing number of Australians who had failed to familiarise themselves with the rules, and partly due to the introduction of a new time limit on the entry vouchers. Typically, problems arose when Australians whose entry vouchers had expired attempted to re-enter Britain after a short stay 'on the continent'. The Australian High Commission was often the first port of call for these stranded Australians, and Alexander Downer intervened personally and constructively in a number of cases.

Towards the end of 1966, however, these incidents were beginning to try the high commissioner's patience. An open quarrel with the Commonwealth Office was triggered by an article in *The Times* in November titled 'Cool Greeting for New "Foreigners"', which documented some recent examples of Australians being turned back at passport control because of irregularities in their vouchers. One hapless young Australian woman attracted a wave of sympathy for her treatment at the hands of a UK customs officer, who allegedly told her: 'I am sick to death of you foreigners coming here, earning money and spending it abroad'. Downer himself was quoted prominently in the press as saying that 'ham-fisted attitudes' by British immigration authorities were alienating many young Australians in ways that could seriously damage Anglo-Australian relations.[12] The story soon found its way to Australia and drew the ire of several newspapers, including the *Sydney Morning Herald*: 'To be treated like this in a country where we have so many historical and cultural roots is, we feel, almost beyond belief'. The *Canberra Times* felt that 'close relatives should not be made to feel like aliens in what they used to think of not long ago as their own land'. Meanwhile, the *Australian* voiced cynicism over the whole purpose of the vouchers: 'That this should happen because of a bureaucratic muddle—so useful in disguising a colour bar—is ridiculous.'[13]

Downer's indignation was shared in influential quarters in Australia and, for that matter, among senior figures in the British policy establishment. The permanent secretary of the Commonwealth Office, Sir Saville 'Joe' Garner, minuted frankly in the aftermath of the *Times* furore:

> There are two incontrovertible facts:
> i) Most Canadians, Australians and New Zealanders are in fact the same people as
>   ourselves
> ii) They blend into the landscape here and adjust without creating any problems
>   whatsoever.
>
> Neither proposition is true of most citizens from non-British countries … In other words,
> is it not time for us to be honest and to state frankly that there will be discrimination?

He noted the 'immense reservoir of good will' that Britain could turn to in the 'old' Commonwealth which was not, he argued, mirrored among the countries of the 'new' Commonwealth in Asia and Africa 'who take every opportunity of calumniating us'. That being so, it was surely 'idiotically against our own interests to undermine this' and he predicted 'that a bold statement by the British Government would be thunderingly popular in this country'.[14] The bonds of Britishness, then, were not an entirely one-sided affair. Garner's minute was warmly applauded by British High Commission staff in Canberra.[15] Moreover, Australian concerns received a sympathetic response in the British press, with one *Times* editorial lamenting the 'succession of events that are widening the gap between Britain and lands largely settled by British stock'.[16]

By the same token, Australian objections could also have the effect of wearing away at this goodwill. In November 1966, Downer called on Garner personally to press his concerns. Garner's record of the conversation hints at a changed man:

> I listened to a very involved, emotional, repetitive harangue. The general gist was that we
> were running a grave danger of alienating Australia, that there were already a number
> of influences affecting the warm relations between our two countries … that many
> Australians still regarded Britain as home and expected to receive a friendly welcome
> and that, if present causes for complaint continued, we should reach 'the open sea' and
> even the position of the Queen would be gravely affected.

Garner 'was not given very long to reply to this tirade', but made it clear that he himself had been pressing views sympathetic to Australia's cause. But he nevertheless recited the established UK policy line—that immigration procedures 'had to look non-discriminatory for political reasons'; that there was no discourtesy in the practice of questioning visitors on arrival; and that the publicity (which he implied Downer had helped to generate) 'was making it worse not better'. Finally, he noted pointedly that 'it seemed strange to me that all the complaints came from Australia and that I had never heard of any from either Canada or New Zealand'. Downer concluded this heated exchange by handing Garner an Australian passport, drawing attention to 'the emotive significance of the crown appearing on the front page … and to the wording "Australia, British Passport"'.[17] But the intractable political reality was that, regardless of the level of sympathy within the civil service, no British government was prepared to part with the principle of a non-discriminatory policy. Therefore, no concrete solutions to the problem were ever devised.

'Humiliation, deceit, shame, and national disgrace': perfidious Albion

A far more serious set of problems emerged in the spring of 1967. It was at this time that the Wilson government announced a renewed EEC membership bid, while almost simultaneously signalling its intention to withdraw Britain's entire military capability from east of Suez. That the two issues were linked in this way was no accident. The poor performance of the British economy in the postwar era, mounting pressure on sterling as a reserve currency, and Britain's diminished standing and influence in an increasingly bipolar world, had prompted the need for drastic measures to stem outward exchange flows, and to secure new markets to boost Britain's foreign exchange earnings. To that end, the EEC and east of Suez represented two sides of the same coin. Moreover, they both seemed, to the Australians at least, to imply a downgrading of their status in the British order of priorities. The chancellor of the exchequer, James Callaghan, informed Downer with brutal frankness that the new economies in defence in Australia's region were 'the price of entering the Common Market'.[18] Downer regarded this as an unforgivable act of betrayal on the part of British ministers who had personally and repeatedly guaranteed Britain's commitment to Southeast Asian defence throughout his tenure. Only four months earlier, Defence Secretary Denis Healey had 'unhesitatingly' assured him of the government's adherence to the status quo. On that occasion, Downer had noted that as someone who had spent 'nearly 4½ years' in Southeast Asia in World War II (for the most part as a prisoner of war), he 'knew well the value of the military presence in those countries'.[19]

In Canberra, the Holt government objected vehemently to Britain's proposed troop withdrawals for two reasons. First, it would inevitably involve massive additional costs in maintaining Australia's 'forward defence' posture in the region in Britain's absence, requiring 'the recasting of Australian external policy in fundamental terms'.[20] Second, the British presence was an important counterweight to the ongoing (and far more crucial) presence of the United States in the region. In early 1966, the Foreign Affairs and Defence Committee had stressed:

> The vital thing for Australia was to have the United States remain in the area and everything else must be measured against this. Any prospect that the British would abandon their presence in South East Asia must tend to embarrass and undermine present United States policy.[21]

The government was somewhat less agitated about the EEC problem. McEwen made it clear that he would not resume the same hardline stance he had adopted during the first British application five years earlier. In an interview in June 1966, it was clear that he had learned the lessons of the 1962 negotiations: 'I don't imagine that they can secure terms that absolutely safeguard the Commonwealth and if Britain feels it is imperative for her to go in on terms that are less than perfect, then I accept that situation'.[22] He made similar remarks to the cabinet a year later in October 1967, emphasising that Britain was 'so determined to maintain a position of willingness, even anxiety, to join the EEC that she will take no action … that might appear as the slightest contradiction of that position'.[23] It was not that McEwen no longer feared for the prospects of Australian exporters, many of whom still stood to be grievously injured. But as he explained to Holt, he simply did not 'believe that it would be possible for the British to achieve entry under conditions which would avoid damage to us', and this inevitably meant there was 'very little scope for us, or other Commonwealth countries, to influence the terms upon which Britain might enter the EEC'. Therefore, he advised the prime minister to adopt a posture 'which is determined primarily by domestic political and economic considerations' and would give the Government the 'best presentational position with the Australian public … if and when market damage occurs'.[24]

When Holt visited London in June 1967, ministers were surprised to find that he preferred to steer away from the detail of the EEC. Holt was far more exercised by the east of Suez dilemma, which raised more immediate questions about Australia's future defence policy in the region, and he pleaded with Wilson not to make any far-reaching announcement on the issue. On both EEC and defence matters, he sought as little publicity as possible. With remarkable candour, he informed Wilson that for domestic political reasons he could not allow himself to be drawn on the question of which Australian industries were 'essential' and which might be 'expendable' in an enlarged Common Market. That being so, he suggested that they might simply leave discussions on EEC matters to one side. Holt would tell the Australian press that he had 'had a discussion with Mr Wilson in general terms and that he had pointed out to Mr Wilson the problems of each and all Australian industries'. Wilson agreed to this subterfuge, provided that Holt did not later take the attitude that 'it had been Britain which was to blame' for any hardship to Australia resulting from British entry.[25] Thus, the prime minister's public utterances on these unprecedented challenges were rare, and restrained. The contrast with the approach of the Menzies government only six years earlier could not have been more stark.[26]

This left only Downer to air publicly his understanding of Australia's reservations about the direction of British policy. In the course of a series of speeches in 1967 (branded by Whitehall as a 'mini-campaign' against British membership of the EEC),[27] Downer raised many of the very emotional and sentimental issues that his government had evidently forsworn. During one well-publicised address in Bath, he declared that 'if the ultimate destination of Britain is merely to become one of a group of European states', then Australia must inevitably 'proceed in some directions quite independently of what most Australians regard as the Mother Country'. He asked his audience whether it was 'really wise policy for Britain to draw apart relentlessly from this dynamic, vibrant, thriving, progressing continent in the South Pacific—a continent peopled, in the main, by your own stock adapting your own institutions, living substantially the same way of life as you do here—a people who, by any standards of private or international conduct, must be regarded as your best friend?' He concluded with an impassioned appeal for a 'recrudescence' of the Commonwealth ideal, intoning: 'This is a cynical and materialist age. Historic ties, emotion, sentiment, are at a discount: they are said to be old-fashioned and have no place in contemporary politics. I disagree'.[28]

A *Times* editorial of the following day was given over entirely to refuting Downer's message, declaring with a tone of finality: 'The clock cannot be put back ... Australia cannot escape its Asian destiny'.[29] Although Downer did receive warm congratulations from various quarters in London—from expatriate Australians to 'anti-Common Marketeers'—his words found very little echo in Australia. Whitehall officials, while closely monitoring his activities, reached the conclusion that Downer's public criticisms had been made on 'his own initiative', and did not accurately convey the position of the Australian government.[30] Downer himself conceded, in private correspondence with his former chief, Robert Menzies, that in 'speaking up' for Australian interests he had 'perhaps at times [gone] beyond the bounds of conventional diplomacy. I do so only because I am convinced that the present British Government does not represent British public opinion on these great matters'.[31] Ironically, British ministers had formed exactly the same opinion of Downer as a conduit of Australian opinion. During a meeting in early 1967, Callaghan told Downer that 'you might be surprised yourself when you return to find that Australian thinking may be in advance of your own'. Downer replied that this might be the case with regard to 'Sydney opinion', but he 'doubted whether people in Melbourne and Adelaide held those views'.[32]

Callaghan's suspicions were not wide of the mark. As Downer's comments filtered back to Australia, several commentators queried the efficacy of his approach. The *Australian Financial Review* ran an editorial with the headline 'A Case for Dr Freud?', arguing that Downer's attempts to denigrate Britain's EEC aspirations were 'at best neurotic and at worst cynically self-seeking'. The *Age* described Downer as 'a true-blue politician of the old school whose British admirers, even the warmest, could offer him no hope'. Moreover, questions were raised about 'the practice of appointing former politicians to Australia House', with the attendant risk of 'confident ramblings about private convictions'.[33] The *Australian* voiced incredulity that 'even in his well-publicised speech deploring the growing rift between the two countries, he still managed to refer to Britain as "this remarkable land of our ancestors"'.[34]

Judging from Downer's private correspondence, it seems that the matter was, for him, deeply personal. He gave full voice to his despair in a note to his old friend and colleague, Lord Casey, now the governor-general:

> I need not tell you of my own reactions to this episode of humiliation, deceit, shame, and national disgrace. I am so disgusted by the double talk of Ministers, of their unending brazen breaking of promises to me personally as High Commissioner, and to our Government in Canberra, that I wonder whether I can usefully continue here in my present position.[35]

Downer experienced the breach of the British covenant as a personal betrayal at the hands of people with whom he had forged deep and treasured links reaching back to his Oxford days. What made the situation all the more unpalatable was that the Conservative Party seemed even more intent on selling out the Commonwealth than Wilson and Labour. As Downer explained the situation to the treasurer, William McMahon: 'Heath is a complete European, people such as Enoch Powell are just plain little Englanders. Neither of them has any real inkling of what Australia and New Zealand are doing, or of our basic pro-British feeling and attachments'. He recounted one particularly galling episode when the shadow Commonwealth relations secretary, Selwyn Lloyd, called on the Australian High Commission for some advice on an impending visit to Australia: '[He] asked me whether in summer in Australia it was safe to eat ordinary food, such as salads! For a man who has been Foreign Minister and Chancellor of the Exchequer … and is well into his sixties, such ignorance about Britain's best friend is disturbing'.[36]

By this stage, it was becoming clear that Downer's personal difficulties in comprehending the new outlook, attitudes and motivations of his British counterparts were beginning to interfere with his political judgement. The problem was succinctly conveyed by Denis Healey, the defence secretary, in an indiscreet moment with Australia's high commissioner in Singapore, Alf Parsons: 'Poor old Alex … really doesn't understand us and we find there is not much point in talking to him … how much longer does he have to serve?'[37]

Downer was to find the changing views of the government he represented equally difficult to comprehend. When John Gorton secured the prime ministership in 1968, he embarked on a distinct change of tone and rhetoric to bring Australia's relationship with Britain into line with the new material realities. Downer interpreted this as a 'lukewarm attitude to things British', and his impression was confirmed when Gorton arrived in London in January 1969 to inform him (en route to London from Heathrow) that Britain 'had become for Australians a foreign country … sentiment alone could not sustain our association'. Downer recalled in his memoirs that it had been 'too early in the morning to argue with the Prime Minister', and he instead sought solace in the world beyond the car window: 'Though the light was grey, the trees bare, Kensington Road and Hyde Park did not look like a foreign country to me'.[38]

'Thank God Alick Downer is here': Downer's London constituency

Downer had been appointed in the twilight years of the Menzies government, at a time when the views and sentiments he nurtured were still a part of Australian, and to a lesser extent, British political culture. But with each change of government, and more importantly, the ever-tightening tensions in the relationship, these attitudes and priorities became subject to a process of revision in Australia to which Downer was not party. Callaghan's suggestion that the climate of opinion in Australia had simply passed Downer by was an astute assessment, although the process in Australia was more complex and ambivalent than he seemed to have grasped.

There were, however, also 'local' reasons for the problem. In his official capacity in London, Downer came into daily contact with a vast constituency—Australians and Britons alike—who fundamentally shared his dismay over the new trends in British policy. His public speeches in defence of the old Commonwealth ideal were invariably greeted by rapturous applause among those who identified with his outlook. Downer was also in the company of six state agents-general, many of whom like the former Liberal Party federal president, John Pagan, actively promoted the cause of restoring British–Australian unity. Downer's private papers are full of letters of congratulation from a wide variety of admirers, many of whom occupied influential positions in British politics, media, business and elsewhere. To make the point, it will suffice to quote from one, penned by Conservative backbencher Sir David Renton:[39]

> It would be interesting to you to hear the remark so often made among our Conservative colleagues: 'Thank God Alick Downer is here! He may be able to save something for the future'.[40]

The irony of this unbridled vote of confidence is that Renton not only supported British entry into the EEC, but was one of the junior Home Office ministers in 1961–62 who helped draft the Commonwealth Immigrants Act—one of Downer's perennial bugbears. Many Conservatives were torn between the practical measures necessary to restore Britain's flagging fortunes, and the emotional and cultural consequences these measures entailed.

Towards the end of Downer's tenure, the senior Department of Foreign Affairs representative at Australia House, Bill Pritchett, described the 'expatriate establishment in London' in which Downer freely moved:

> What distinguishes this group from other groups and the general run of Britons and Australians having similar connections, is social standing, in the British class sense, and, more often than not, money. This group is a natural point of gravitation for many visitors from Australia, providing them not only an agreeable, and for some flattering, social milieu but useful contact with British people of substance ... By and large, its sentiments and attitudes in the Anglo-Australian context are traditional, sometimes still even 'colonial', and its politics are generally 'Tory', certainly as regards relations with Britain.[41]

In other words, Downer was not alone in his views. His outlook and attitudes were encouraged and indeed reinforced by an extensive network of people whose sheer numbers and entrenched status enabled them to form their own distinctive view of the Anglo-Australian relationship irrespective of the tenor of opinion in Australia. Downer was very much in tune with many of his contemporaries, and saw his role as fundamentally representative of that constituency. As he recorded in his private correspondence: 'Wherever I go I find deep anger, and shame'.[42] For Downer, it would have been a derogation of his moral duty not to speak out as he did.

These convictions were reinforced by Downer's belief that members of the royal family, with whom he had close links, shared his misgivings about the parlous attenuation of the Australian–British nexus. In one of his periodic meetings with the Queen's private secretary, Sir Michael Adeane, Downer noted the following exchange:

> I took the opportunity, once again, of reminding Adeane that recent policy decisions of the British Government concerning Defence and Trade were not helpful to the causes which he and myself are dedicated. I observed that the Defence [east of Suez] White Paper would aggravate any tendencies in Australia—and elsewhere—which were inimical to the Queen's position. He wholeheartedly agreed with this. I asked him whether the Queen understood the possible consequences, and how worried we were. He said that she realised these things only too well, and shared our anxiety.[43]

Downer received further encouragement in February 1968 when in his keynote address at a New Zealand Society dinner at the Savoy, the Duke of Edinburgh surveyed the course of Commonwealth affairs since the mid-1950s. Prince Philip noted in particular the acute difficulties over the Common Market and east of Suez. In the presence of the Commonwealth secretary, George Thomson, he made an unusually pointed remark:

> It is never a pleasant task to admit to over spending, or to make difficult decisions about cutting commitments and expenditure, as I gather Mr Thomson has discovered … Well Gentlemen, I can tell you this: If ever our friends in New Zealand or Australia find themselves in difficulties, there is a goodly number of people in this country who will overcome any obstacle to go to their assistance—bases or no bases, carriers or no carriers, F111s or no F111s.

According to Downer, the room erupted spontaneously into rapturous, sustained applause, while Thomson sat immobile: 'He did not clap. I made sure he noticed my own applauding noises, and loud Hear Hears as close to his ear as I could reach across our mutual neighbour'.[44]

These convictions also underpinned Downer's behind-the-scenes efforts to secure an official residence for the royal family in Australia—an Australian Balmoral, which would be occupied by the royals during their periodic visits. Downer explained the simple logic behind the scheme to his friend, Sir Mark Oliphant (then governor of South Australia): 'In the present climate of opinion in Australia, and with what is likely to happen in the next few years, nothing could reinforce the position of the Monarchy better in our own country than a voluntary action on the part of the Queen and Prince Philip of this nature'.[45] Towards the end of 1968, a particular property caught Prince Philip's eye—'Bolaro' in the Southern Highlands of New South Wales—and the possibility of acquiring it was carefully examined and ultimately rejected as not feasible.[46] Nonetheless, Downer was overjoyed by the positive reports that flowed back from Australia during the Queen's 1970 visit to attend the Cook bicentennial celebrations:

It delights me to tell a lot of our British brethren, sometimes in speeches, that there is more overt enthusiasm for the Royal Family in Australia than here. And I relish the sight of the journalist enemies of all that I hold most dear, as a public man, being routed by the spontaneous accord given to the Queen. What price now professional liars such as Don Whittington, that decadent creature Max Harris (alas! from my own state), the twisted Republican Horne of the Bulletin, and others of that ilk? ... I have not been so happy for years, and if some of the foes of Menzies and myself walked into the room it would give me the greatest delight to plug them and flatten their false teeth and their false ideas.[47]

The Tories return: Britain into Europe

Downer was further heartened by the surprise Conservative election victory in June 1970. He had expressed his hopes at the outset of the campaign in a personal message to Edward Heath: 'I do hope the Election will be fought from Conservative platforms not merely on domestic issues ... the present British Government is particularly vulnerable on its Commonwealth, foreign and above all defence policies—so much so that to me, and many of my friends here, the issue before the people today is Little England or Great Britain'. Although the opinion polls did not augur well for the Conservatives, Downer noted that 'it would be pusillanimous for any patriotic member of the British race to be dismayed'.[48] This kind of language and sentiment was ill-attuned to Heath's well-known European sensibilities, and no sooner was the new government in harness than the EEC came back with a vengeance. Heath appointed the bullish Geoffrey Rippon to oversee Britain's renewed negotiations for entry, which seemed more promising with de Gaulle's recent retirement.[49]

By this time, the Australian government's attitude had been transformed beyond recognition. McEwen informed cabinet that 'no amount of representations, personal or otherwise, are going to achieve a special position for Australia' in the negotiations.[50] Instead, he promptly turned his energies towards establishing a stronger framework for economic relations with East Asia, particularly Japan.[51] In his first encounter with Britain's negotiating team in London in July 1970, McEwen's only request was that Britain should attempt to secure the 'longest possible transitional period' to allow Australian suppliers to adjust to the new conditions. This, the British found both realistic and acceptable.[52] When Rippon visited Australia two months later, the British High Commission could happily report that 'most of the emotion has gone out of the issue'.[53] It seemed, then, that Britain's final passage into Europe would be relatively free of controversy in Australia.

But the protracted saga of Britain's turn to Europe had one final act in store—one in which Downer was to play a central role. Less than a month before the conclusion of the negotiations in June 1971, a row broke out between Rippon and Doug Anthony, who had succeeded McEwen as minister for trade and industry and deputy prime minister. During a tour of the EEC capitals, Anthony discovered that the three-year transitional period that Britain had secured in the negotiations would not apply to Australia's crucial agricultural sector—that while the British had obtained breathing room to allow their own industries to adjust, Australian primary producers would be subjected to the full blast of internal EEC preference from the very day of Britain's accession. Anthony was beside himself, not only because this flew in the face of Britain's modest assurances, but also because their abandonment had never been communicated to his government. It was perfidious Albion all over again.

Anthony arrived in London in early June armed with a potent press statement, in which he effectively accused the British of gross duplicity. The primary casualty of Britain's double-dealing would be the Australian butter industry, dependent on the British market for more than half its livelihood in conditions of global overproduction, and which would soon face a wall of protectionism in favour of inefficient European producers.[54] Britain, he reiterated some weeks later, had 'washed its hands' of responsibility for Australia's problems. 'We did not come here as a bleating child holding on to a mother's apron string', he protested. 'We can stand up for ourselves, but a promise was given to us and it has not been fulfilled. I am wondering what we can trust in what is said to us.'[55]

The British, in turn, were livid. Rippon delivered his most withering counterassault during a chance meeting with Downer at a diplomatic banquet at Hampton Court. In response to a quip from Downer ('you look like the cat who swallowed the canary'), Rippon let fly. 'Australians', he said, were 'noted for their plain speaking', and he was 'going to speak plainly in return'. Downer recorded Rippon's litany of complaints:

> We were, he said, a selfish country. We contributed little to international aid. We cared nothing for Britain. 'It would matter nothing to you if this country sank under the North Sea'. We thought of our own interests, and nothing else ... 'You cannot', he proceeded, 'continue to live on England's back'.

Needless to say, Downer was affronted by all this, and challenged Rippon to make these views public so that he might rebut them—at which point Rippon changed tack and offered some dubious words of assurance: whatever happened, Australia and Britain 'would always be close together'. There were 'no countries with firmer bonds than ours'. Otherwise he could never have addressed Downer in such an insulting way. 'If you had been a foreign Ambassador, then you would have every justification in walking away from me, and elevating this into a major diplomatic incident. But because you are an Australian I can talk to you thus.' Remarkably, even amid this wrangling, the tone and substance of the relationship could still be comprehended in terms of kinship. Downer himself chose to put Rippon's rude behaviour down to the fact that he was a 'fellow Brasenose man', and 'so we can always talk on that sort of basis'.[56]

Having received reports from Downer and Anthony, Prime Minister William McMahon (who had recently deposed Gorton) sent Heath a strongly worded letter virtually demanding that Britain go back to Brussels and secure the transitional period for Australia they had promised, but Heath simply waved this away: 'I really must urge you that it is not to anyone's advantage to belittle what has been undertaken'.[57] Within a matter of days, Heath communicated to all Commonwealth prime ministers that the negotiations were complete and that the government had decided to accept the terms that had been agreed. Britain would sign the Treaty of Rome and enter the EEC on 1 January 1973.

'Just another post'? The transfer of Australia House to Foreign Affairs

It was against this backdrop that a decision was taken to transfer responsibility for the administration of Australia House from the Department of the Prime Minister and Cabinet to the Department of Foreign Affairs (which External Affairs became in 1970). Although Britain's impending entry into Europe was not the fundamental rationale behind this decision, it certainly provided an appropriate occasion to make the symbolic switch. In a future where Britain would increasingly identify its role in a European orbit, it made sense to place Anglo-Australian relations on a 'foreign' footing. In August 1971, the secretary of the Department of Foreign Affairs, Sir Keith Waller, began to press the case for the transfer: 'A factor in the past was that Australians thought of themselves primarily as British', he maintained. 'Most now think of themselves as "Australians".' That being so, the underlying logic that had dictated 'the need to mark our relations with Britain as something special … no longer exists'. No other Commonwealth country had a separate department of state to deal with Britain, and with the merger of the Commonwealth and Foreign offices in Britain in 1968, it seemed both natural and normal that Australia should adjust its own administrative practices accordingly. Moreover, Britain's entry into the EEC, its future approach to the Commonwealth, and its diminishing defence role in Southeast Asia, created a whole new set of issues that were 'essentially of a foreign policy nature'.[58]

Waller's argument was also heavily buttressed by criticism of the existing arrangements. He complained that his department was not 'receiving reporting on some of these matters of the depth and thoughtfulness which we need to make with confidence soundly based policy recommendations to the government'. In sheer practical terms—day-to-day reporting, evaluation and policy analysis—'the time has probably come when we need to deal with the United Kingdom in much the same way as we deal with other countries of real importance to us like the United States and Japan'.[59] He was supported by his minister, Nigel Bowen, who pointed out to McMahon that 'as Foreign Minister of Australia one has less information as to what is the thinking of the United Kingdom Government on various issues than from the other capitals in which we have the higher representation from Foreign Affairs'.[60] This was interpreted by one senior official in the Prime Minister's Department as 'a vote of total no confidence in the present High Commissioner'.[61]

Downer, for his part, was completely left out of these deliberations for nearly ten months, until he was advised formally of the impending change in May 1972. He promptly complained to Bunting in unusually bitter terms:

> I think you know my views, but for the official record I wish to state that I disagree with what the Government is doing, and I desire to point out that although I have been the Head of this Mission for a period now approaching eight years, my views have not been solicited on this matter either by the Prime Minister or any member of the Administration at any time, nor have I been consulted.[62]

The reasons for Downer's exclusion from the decision were never made explicit, but his attitude was well known and probably unwelcome. Downer enlisted the support of his deputy high commissioner, Robert Boswell, to counter Foreign Affairs' arguments. Boswell bristled at the suggestion that Australia House could ever be regarded as 'just another post'. For him, the possibility that Foreign Affairs might assume responsibility was taken as a threat to the unique way that officers of Australia House were able to go beyond normal protocol to 'stimulate extra mural links'. Boswell defended the lack of reporting coming out of Australia House by arguing that 'quite authoritative newspapers' gave 'a broad survey of the English scene' and that 'these were available in Australia'.[63] But this only underlined the vastly different perspectives and practices of the two departments. Moreover, he sought to depict the role of high commissioner as far more valuable than that of a mere overseas diplomat: 'Although the professional diplomatic outreach of the Office of a High Commissioner may be criticised he performs and is chosen for his role as the man who moves into the inner circles of political London'.[64]

By this stage, both the Prime Minister's Department and the prime minister himself were becoming increasingly unnerved by the rhetoric and sense of urgency emanating from Foreign Affairs. It is possible that Downer's misgivings were having some effect in this regard, although the record is inconclusive. By August 1972, McMahon was of the view that Foreign Affairs was 'too anxious' about acquiring Australia House, and he instructed Bunting that the department was 'not to have carte blanche'.[65] Specifically, he sought to preserve prime ministerial authority over three key spheres: ties to the palace, relations with the Commonwealth Secretariat, and the appointment of the high commissioner and deputy high commissioner (both of whom should continue to report directly to the prime minister). These requirements were communicated to Bowen in a letter that effectively undermined the entire rationale behind the transfer. McMahon emphasised the 'unique importance of the British relationship', embodying a complex network of ties that 'are so much deeper over a broad area than those with other countries'. Over sixty years, he contended, Australia House had developed a range of features which 'distinguish it from other overseas posts'—features that he was anxious to preserve in order to maintain 'the broader and deeper links between the two countries'. The entire thrust of his message was that Britain remained much more than just another country, and Australia House more than just another post. He went so far as to remind Bowen that 'nearly half our population are either themselves migrants from Britain or are the children of migrants. For them, Britain has a special place not occupied by any other country in the world'.[66] Clearly, the prospect of relegating Britain to the ranks of other 'foreign' countries stirred deep reservations about the disappearance of a sense of shared culture and heritage.

Downer was sent a copy of McMahon's letter and he responded with delight: 'I thought his letter was excellent—but having read it, I could not help but think why is it necessary to make any alteration at all … merely, I suspect, to satisfy the ambitions of our Foreign Affairs Department'.[67] Foreign Affairs, for its part, was incensed by what it saw as blatant backsliding. When Bunting advised Waller of the prime minister's reservations, the latter reared up and stormed out of the meeting—despite repeated entreaties to stay and talk through their differences. Bowen, too, expressed his 'puzzlement' and 'apprehension' about the entire 'philosophy behind the Prime Minister's letter'.[68] In his reply, Bowen freely conceded the continuance of prime ministerial authority over ties to the palace, but rejected outright the rest of McMahon's demands. He reiterated the arguments for the inherently 'foreign' nature of diplomatic relations between Australia and Britain 'as two independent countries', and flatly refused to accept the transfer of Australia House to his department on any other basis.[69]

There then ensued a delicate negotiation between the two departments, resulting in a compromise whereby McMahon retained responsibility for ties to the Crown, Commonwealth Prime Ministers' Conferences (but not general matters pertaining to the Commonwealth Secretariat), and the right to appoint the high commissioner (in consultation with the minister for foreign affairs). Foreign Affairs acquired the right to appoint its own career officers to the crucial deputy high commissioner post, thereby securing effective control of the mission. Bowen conceded the principle of direct lines of communication between the prime minister and Australia House, on the condition that this should be understood as no different from a 'similar right' that the prime minister might exercise 'where appropriate, with all Australian Heads of Mission'.[70] In other words, the principle of regarding Australia House on the same footing as other posts was maintained to the end. McMahon announced the decision in October 1972, noting that it took place 'against the background of Britain's entry into Europe'. Far from representing a simple and straightforward bureaucratic switch, the decision symbolised a significant change in the role and function of Australia House, and the nature of Anglo-Australian relations more generally. But it was a decision attended by doubt and internal discord.

A parting gesture?

Before the transfer was implemented, Downer completed his term at Australia House at the end of October 1972, and retired initially to his country estate in Wiltshire.[71] To the last, he remained an unrepentant critic of what he termed Britain's 'Europhoria'. Asked in his final interview in the London office whether his departure, only weeks before Britain's accession to the EEC, was a 'final symbolic protest', Downer replied that he was 'not saying'.[72]

His last despatch to McMahon, reporting on a farewell visit to the British home secretary, Robert Carr, traversed many of the major themes that had dominated his eight years in London: the importance of 'sentiment in statecraft'; the 'damage that is occurring to pro-British sentiment amongst Australians'; how recent events 'did not provide much hope for a meaningful Commonwealth in the future'; and his long-held belief that 'member nations of the Crown Commonwealth should receive preferential treatment over those other Commonwealth nations who were Republics', especially when it came to the ongoing problems for Australians at British entry ports. Particular problems occurred when the Commonwealth gate was not manned and Australians were ushered to the 'Aliens' queue. Downer took exception to the fact that 'sometimes officials not of British origin, such as Pakistanis and Indians', were employed at the customs barriers, and that this 'inevitably aroused resentment amongst our own people'. The meeting concluded like so many previous encounters—with the minister voicing his broad sympathy with the problem, and promising to look into the matter more closely, but without offering any concrete solution. The high commissioner concluded his final missive with an expression of faint hope that this time, finally, he had got through.[73]

As it happened, Downer was to be permitted one final, albeit pyrrhic victory in his campaign for recognition of the unfair treatment of Australians at UK entry gates. Less than a month into his retirement, the Heath government suffered the ignominy of defeat in the House of Commons on a motion to bring UK immigration practices into line with the Treaty of Rome. The legislation in question made no changes to Commonwealth entry procedures per se, but enhanced the entry rights of EEC citizens to place them on a more favourable footing. These measures sparked a rearguard action in the *Daily Express* to have the measures revised, with particular—indeed overwhelming—emphasis on the rights of Australians and New Zealanders. The *Daily Express* campaign was launched on 16 November, with a leader by proprietor Max Aitken headlined 'Make Way for Our Friends Mr Heath or Reap the Whirlwind'. It quickly gathered momentum, garnering the support of a substantial rump of Conservative backbenchers.

The spectacle of the Heath government in disarray in the Commons over the very issue that had so marked his tenure at Australia House gratified Downer. He recorded his heartfelt gratitude in a private letter to Aitken:

> Your immediate contribution is immensely valuable in that you have shown Australians that a large section of British public opinion does care for the British nations overseas, and that the all-too-large element in the House of Commons which is Euro-obsessed does not represent the sentiments of the average Englishman. For all this, as an Australian public man, and also as one who loves England and intends to act in future as an unofficial ambassador between the two countries, I am tremendously grateful to you and your virile, patriotic, John Bull newspapers.[74]

There was some suggestion, however, that Downer was not merely cheering from the sidelines. He explained his position to Aitkin: 'Having relinquished my post as High

Commissioner only 4 weeks ago I would find it impossible to enter this controversy publicly, although I have been engaged in some activities behind the scenes'. These activities came to the attention of W.B. Pritchett, who served as acting high commissioner for several months while Downer's replacement was selected. Pritchett was dismayed by the *Daily Express* campaign and the outcome of the Commons vote, both of which only served to reinforce an outdated perception of

> … Australian resentment about the new rules, of Australian dependence on Britain, of the rights to work and settle in Britain still being regarded as a necessary part of our national life, and so on, that is not consistent with our status and dignity as an independent nation. Australians are being presented as a people concerned about betrayal and desertion, deeply concerned about Britain and the EEC, anxious to hang on to the old Commonwealth relationship in all its traditional features.[75]

According to Pritchett, this gross misrepresentation of the Australian position had been positively encouraged by key figures among 'the expatriate establishment in London'—in 'one or two cases that we know, quite violently so'. Foremost on his list of 'violently' pro-British expatriates was the former high commissioner: 'Sir Alexander Downer is living in Wiltshire … but visits London. Given his wide connections in the establishment I have sketched, and beyond, it is reasonable to expect that he has been expressing his strong personal views forcibly'.[76]

Pritchett's testimony, however speculative, marks an extraordinary denouement in Downer's tenure at Australia House. The 'violently Anglophile' description that was once a term of endearment bestowed by a British admirer had come to signal a liability in the eyes of the Department of Foreign Affairs. Downer's term thus represents a watershed in many respects—a transformation, not only in the role and administrative status of Australia's largest overseas mission, but also in the underlying terms and tenets of the Anglo-Australian relationship. Never again would Anglophilia—violent or otherwise—be deemed a particularly useful quality in an Australian high commissioner. Downer's successors would continue to use and even nurture the many cultural and sentimental links that inevitably remained. But they would henceforth approach their dealings with Britain within the wider prism of Australia's 'foreign' affairs.

11 The 'new line in the Strand': John Armstrong and the 'new nationalism'

James Curran

WHEN John Armstrong arrived in London in late January 1973 to take up the post of high commissioner, he came armed with a ready-made rhetoric announcing the nation's coming of age. Speaking to the *Daily Mail*'s diplomatic correspondent, he observed that

> Britain is finished East of Suez from what we gather. America is withdrawing from Vietnam. So the day has come when we can stand alone ... You don't attack America—it's too large, too amorphous. You attack England because it's easy to attack your brother ... I want to achieve a new warmth in the family again. My monument will be in an attitude of mind which brings more understanding between two peoples.[1]

These were not controversial statements for an Australian diplomat in the early 1970s. But they did show that the collapse of Australia's cold war policy—the determination to keep the British and the Americans engaged in Southeast Asia—remained the backdrop against which Australian policies and priorities were being reconsidered. The need to redefine relationships with 'great and powerful' friends had become the testing ground for Australia's 'new nationalism', in a period when the nation sought to assert its individuality in world affairs. Yet despite this somewhat combative stance, Armstrong's desire to rekindle a sense of 'family' showed that despite the vast changes in the Australia–Britain relationship that preceded his appointment, there remained a tendency to slip into the easy comfort and familiarity of the past. After all, Armstrong had himself come to political maturity steeped in the sentiments and symbols of Australia's membership of the British Empire. Here, as the nation's chief representative in the old imperial metropole, the recipe for replenishing the relationship was a tried and tested one: keep the disagreements in the family. But when he was asked a few months later to reflect on the Whitlam government's early foreign policy achievements, Armstrong dispensed with the cautious clichés of diplomacy and showed his true colours. He had been most pleased, he said, with 'the independence at last shown by a country with every reason to show independence but with a tradition of slavishly following other nations'.[2]

Armstrong's tenure at Australia House came at a critical time for Anglo-Australian relations. Building on the work of its predecessors, the Whitlam government sought to put the relationship with Britain on a new and 'foreign' footing. This idea of treating Britain as a 'foreign' country had been first conceptualised at the prime ministerial level by John Gorton[3] (see page 154), but it was Gough Whitlam who formalised it in both symbolism and practice. In the wake of Britain's changing defence and economic priorities, Australian politicians and policy-makers from the late 1960s embarked on a course of bringing the relationship into line with its material realities. As Whitlam himself put it only days after his election win, Australia needed 'to move away from the father and son relationship of the past to a more normal bilateral relationship in which we should regard Britain as we would regard any other country with which we have especially important relations, such as Japan, the United States, Indonesia and New Zealand'.[4] The Labor prime minister was determined to rid the relationship of what he called 'the relics of colonialism'. This desire translated into a program of updating the formal trappings of Australian nationhood— including the ending of appeals from the state supreme courts to the Privy Council, the adoption of a new national anthem, the abandonment of imperial honours in favour of a new Australian honours system, and amendments to the Royal Style and Titles Act and the oath of allegiance.

Like William McMahon, Whitlam also wanted to abolish the very title of 'high commissioner' itself, seeing it too as a remnant of the old imperial relationship. The turning of high commissioners into 'ambassadors' was held up as an appropriate reflection of the 'changing relationship between Commonwealth countries', but Whitlam did not push the issue once it was made clear that the Queen and the Commonwealth Secretariat were not in favour of the change.[5] Moreover, it was pointed out to him that many of the African, Asian and Caribbean states 'quite liked the title and wanted to retain it'.[6]

In addition to these symbolic moves, the changes that Whitlam made to Australia's defence policy in Southeast Asia and its voting patterns at the United Nations unnerved British officials. In February 1973 Whitlam had announced his intention to withdraw the Australian infantry battalion and artillery battery stationed in Singapore under the Australia, New Zealand and United Kingdom (ANZUK) agreement. This was part of the Five Power Defence Arrangements through which Australia, Britain and New Zealand had committed to immediate consultation in the event of an armed attack on Malaysia and Singapore. Britain and New Zealand feared not only a reduced operational strength in the event of Australia's departure, but that it would lead to greater pressure on their own units to be withdrawn.[7] In the face of this reaction, Whitlam had agreed to leave a logistical support element within the ANZUK force. The British defence secretary, Lord Carrington, had warned the new Labor government that if Australia pulled out, the British would have to reconsider their own commitments in the area. British officials thought that the ANZUK commitment was being 'thrown to the Left-Wing wolves' in the Labor Party as a means of preserving ANZUS. The British found Whitlam constantly unhelpful and evasive on these matters.

Alarm was also registered at Whitlam's instructions to Australia's mission at the United Nations to reverse its traditional stance and vote with the Afro-Asian group in favour of resolutions that were critical of British policy on Rhodesia. It was a decision that Whitlam apparently described to Lord Carrington as one which saw Australia "'rejoin the rest of the world" and leave an old fashioned minority (which includes us)'. Serious reservations were also being expressed about Australia's reliability on intelligence issues. Whitlam's decision to reveal to the media the purpose of an Australian signals unit in Singapore and Lionel Murphy's raid on the offices of the Australian Security Intelligence Organisation in March 1973 led to 'serious doubts … about Australian security in the minds of the country's intelligence partners'.[8]

All this pointed to a fairly downbeat assessment of the relationship in the government's first year. The British high commissioner in Canberra, Sir Morrice James, suspected that Whitlam and his colleagues 'regard Britain as some sort of elderly omni-tolerant aunt', a tempting target to score cheap political points at home. But his bottom line was that the Australian stance on ANZUK and its 'irresponsibility' in intelligence matters had 'directly affected British interests'. The question was how to deal with this new assertiveness in Australia's international relations. James also reported that the secretary of the Department of Foreign Affairs, Keith Waller, had counselled British diplomats in Canberra to have patience with Whitlam. But Waller had also told them that 'if and when the time came … [they] should not flinch from making it clear that [they] considered a given course of action by Australia to be an unfriendly act'.[9] At face value this might seem extraordinarily candid, coming from the same senior official who had lobbied hard to place relations with Britain on a foreign footing. An 'unfriendly act' is normally the diplomatic prelude to war. But this was precisely Waller's point: since Australia and Britain were treating each other as 'foreign' countries, they could more easily use this sort of direct and blunt language.

Throughout this period John Armstrong, unpractised in the formal art of diplomacy but well known for his bonhomie and business acumen, was the face of Australia's 'new nationalism' in London.

A culture of Labor loyalty

John Ignatius Armstrong was only the third Labor appointee to Australia House—the others being Fisher and Beasley. Armstrong had long coveted the post; indeed, he seemed to have extracted the promise of it from both Arthur Calwell and Gough Whitlam.[10] But he also ascribed this ambition to the friendship he enjoyed with Beasley, a close family friend and mentor when he entered parliament in the late 1930s. At the time of his appointment in December 1972, Armstrong revealed that 'it was only because [Beasley] was High Commissioner that I felt maybe I'd do it one day'.[11]

The culture of Labor loyalty ran deep in Armstrong's family. He was the epitome of the affable, if affluent, party man. Born on 10 July 1908 to Irish parents, he spent his early life in the family-run hotel in the inner-Sydney suburb of Pyrmont. Schooled at Marist Brothers Darlinghurst, he was a keen athlete and developed a particular talent for boxing. Joining the Labor Party at the age of twenty-one, he quickly rose to prominence within local ranks. Showing some sensitivity to how his wealthy background might affect his political rise, he listed his occupation as 'barman' to avoid being labeled a liquor tycoon by Labor supporters. Service as an alderman on the Sydney Municipal Council was quickly followed by preselection for the state seat of Glebe at the 1935 election—but he withdrew after pressure from Jack Lang, the former New South Wales premier, who in return provided appropriate assurances that Armstrong would be given preference for a forthcoming Senate vacancy. This connection with Lang was to become a minor talking point for British officials in Canberra when Armstrong's diplomatic posting was announced, with one noting that although Lang's proposals during the Depression 'involved battles with the British Government, the Bank of England and British finance houses', there was 'no reason to believe that there is any residual antipathy towards us' borne by the new high commissioner.[12]

Armstrong entered parliament at the 1937 election, becoming at that time Australia's youngest ever senator. He served a standard senatorial apprenticeship, filling positions on the standing committees on Regulations and Ordinances, and Disputed Returns and Qualifications. But his progression was temporarily halted when he opted to go with Lang's breakaway Labor Party (Non-Communist) in April 1940. Armstrong rejoined the caucus following the restoration of unity and was selected by John Curtin in 1942 to serve on the Commonwealth Rationing Commission.

Like most Australians at the time, Armstrong was steeped in British race patriotism. His first taste of official London came in 1943 when he visited as a delegate of the British Empire Parliamentary Association. Speaking in Canberra upon his return, he said that he had come back to Australia 'strengthened in … feeling that the maintenance of peace in the world will lie fundamentally in the British-speaking peoples coming to know each other better and having more confidence in each other'. Armstrong was using the Curtin—and later Chifley—formulation of 'British speaking'—a strange phrase that signified the way in which Australians had supposedly welded the various English, Irish, Scots and Welsh components of the United Kingdom into an indissoluble whole.[13] In 1953 he likened the Queen's role in keeping the British Commonwealth together to Tennyson's words on the power of prayer—that 'the world was held by golden chains around the feet of God'.[14]

Armstrong, however, always looked for opportunities to trumpet his nationalist credentials, particularly in advocating the appointment of Australians—not 'imported articles'—to senior positions in the military hierarchy, and in his unapologetic defence of the nation's convict heritage.[15] Likewise, he was quick to cite the recommendation he claimed to have presented to the last cabinet meeting of the Chifley government for the introduction of an Australian honours system, later disclosing that among the 'corny' titles he had suggested were the 'Order of the Waratah, the Wattle and the Southern Cross'.[16] A strong supporter of the American connection, he nevertheless maintained—in words reminiscent of the Empire Day speeches of Curtin and Chifley: 'We shall develop in the Pacific, under the Southern Cross, a great land, and it is our duty to ensure that this land is kept for the British and white races for ever'.[17]

In April 1948, after two years heading the munitions portfolio, Armstrong was appointed by Chifley as minister for supply and development. According to Ken Turner, in both positions he displayed a strong administrative capacity and a passionate interest in the development of Australian industries.[18] In October 1948 he was also appointed by Chifley as minister in charge of preparations for the royal tour to Australia by King George VI, but the monarch's ill health prevented the visit from taking place.[19] Armstrong attracted minor controversy in this position, telling an Australian-American Association dinner that Australia needed 'the type of men who built New York' to safeguard the nation's future because they possessed the characteristics that 'unfortunately we do not see in the Englishman'. These rather benign comments were taken by the Opposition as proof that he was not fit to be minister for the royal tour. Chifley leapt to Armstrong's defence, praising 'his many contacts that will help him to make the tour run smoothly and harmoniously'.[20] In his own self-deprecating style, Armstrong remembered the reason for Chifley's support rather more humorously. He recalled the prime minister telling him that 'you have more suits than anyone in the Cabinet, which means that you will not need any clothing coupons to enable you to do the job'.[21]

Armstrong did not bring to the position of high commissioner a deep or sophisticated understanding of international relations. His parliamentary speeches on this subject in the 1950s and early 1960s were predictable and workmanlike. He told the parliament in November 1954 that he liked to 'keep [his] approach to international problems as simple as possible'. The 'fundamental approach of Australians to foreign policy', he noted, 'is dictated first by love of country and secondly by a natural desire to preserve Australia'.[22] He was a vocal critic of the ANZUS Treaty, saying it 'had no teeth' and lamenting that Washington did not go further in declaring its commitment to Australia's defence. But he was no kneejerk critic of the American alliance. In the tradition of Curtin's 'looking to America' declaration of December 1941, from which he explicitly quoted, Armstrong in August 1954 declared: 'to reduce the matter to absolute simplicity, that is where our future and our safety lies'.[23]

There was nothing remarkable about Armstrong's oft-expressed support for 'great and powerful friends' as a bulwark against a threatening Asia during the cold war. He thought that Australia's 'tremendous area' with 'only 9,000,000 people must be an affront to the people of Asia. They must consider … that this part of the world belongs to them. If they could conquer this part of the world, with its great wool production and secondary industries, in a very short time the European populace of this land would disappear'.[24] He nevertheless registered an awareness that the rise of Asian nationalism presented Australia with new challenges and that great-power protection alone would be insufficient in meeting them.

Armstrong rose to deputy leader of the Opposition in the Senate in 1951 and held that position until 1956. But his parliamentary career was cut short when he lost party endorsement in 1960. His term ended in 1962, but in 1965 he was elected lord mayor of Sydney, serving two years before Liberal Premier Robert Askin re-adjusted the boundaries of the city in such a way as to throw out the council on which Labor had a majority.[25]

'Setting up a new mission'

Armstrong arrived in London at a critical time both in the history of Anglo-Australian relations and for the running of the high commission itself. He told one journalist just two months into his term that there was 'no post in the world which is the same as London'. Yet this sort of statement was at odds with the desire of both Labor and Coalition governments to normalise the relationship, and to make formal what had once been so informal.[26] In his first meeting with the British high commissioner in Canberra, Morrice James, Whitlam had indicated his intention to 'cut down on a lot of monarchical paraphernalia', adding that though many of these actions might be regarded by some as 'anti-British', he himself 'did not intend to publicise them this way'. In a sign that he meant business, Whitlam rebuffed the British desire to survey Christmas Island as a possible site for a new BBC relay station, telling James that he 'did not like the idea of hosting propaganda from Britain on Australian territory'.[27] The British had sensed correctly that the new government was 'anxious not to seem dependent on old friends such as the US and the UK'.[28]

But Whitlam—and Armstrong—were also the beneficiaries of a long period of reassessment and reflection on the Anglo-Australian relationship that had been taking place in the Canberra bureaucracy since the early 1970s. It had been precipitated not only by the external shocks of Britain's turn to Europe and her military withdrawal from Southeast Asia, but also by the discussions concerning the transfer of responsibility for Australia House from the Department of the Prime Minister and Cabinet to Foreign Affairs (see pp. 159–161). Thus, for example, a departmental policy planning paper on the Anglo-Australian relationship in 1971 argued that 'in recent years a certain abrasiveness has emerged in our dealings with Britain … mutual trust has given way to an element of secretiveness; the old informal channels in London seem to have dried up'. But the policy planners found it difficult to pinpoint when and how the change had taken place: 'It is difficult to characterize these changes, they have been gradual and almost intangible, and there is little one can actually point to'. The paper settled on a few reasons for the 'decline in this "special relationship"—a natural divergence of interests, with Australia turning to South East Asia and the Pacific, and the United Kingdom turning inward and to Europe'; the 'strains imposed by successive British approaches to Europe'; the diminished significance of the Commonwealth; and lastly, what it called the 'death-pangs of Britain's imperial heyday'.[29]

The timing and tenor of this assessment is a reminder that the reappraisal of the relationship predated the Whitlam government and, further, that it did not necessarily portend an entirely new world. Indeed, officials in Canberra expected 'in time, the pendulum may swing back'—Britain was 'in the process of learning to regard Australia as a grown-up', and they presumed Australia for its part would 'refrain from asserting her new found sense of sovereign equality, and from taking such pleasure in twisting the lion's tail'. But it showed that the process of finding a new framework in which to understand relations, of making what once was so familiar, 'foreign', to be inherently problematic— even for the diplomatic service, which had advocated the change so vehemently.[30]

The change of government in December 1972 only served to further emphasise the need for any new high commissioner to draw a 'new line in the Strand'.[31] In response to a request from Canberra for what should be included in the ministerial directive for the new appointee, W.B. Pritchett—who had been acting high commissioner following Downer's retirement—lamented that Australia House and the relationship with Britain were in a state of 'neglect'. He complained that 'we do not even know what sort of nation we are dealing with in Britain today and what is its situation'. In line with the emphasis on the need to treat Britain as a 'foreign country', Pritchett maintained that the new high commissioner would require a 'well informed, up to date account and evaluation of our relations with Britain and "feel" of the total relationship, just as with Indonesia or Japan or India'. The presentation of Australia's image in Britain was equally out of date, and had been allowed for too long to continue 'in essentially traditional terms ("We are British")'. Casting judgment on the former high commissioner, Pritchett felt that 'too much importance can be given to socialising and semi-ceremonial' duties. Only if the new appointment could carry all of this off would the mission 'become a ship under way instead of a haystack floating in the flood'. For Pritchett, all of this pointed to the urgent necessity for an entirely new departure:

> In certain respects we are really setting up a new mission, or introducing a new concept of the Mission and its work. We are also for the first time in our modern history coming to grips with our relationship with Britain and the large changes that have taken place in it.[32]

The 'very different High Commissioner'

Whitlam told Armstrong that he wanted Australia House run as an 'embassy and not as a tourist bureau'.[33] But Armstrong's appointment on 12 December 1972 was seen immediately as a sign that political nepotism was alive and well, and 'a deliberate downgrading of the status of Britain in Australia's foreign policy'.[34] Some commentators asked why Whitlam had moved so quickly to fill the vacancy when there had been an acting high commissioner in place for some time. Whitlam replied that he had been urged by Foreign Affairs to make the appointment 'promptly because there [had been] an embarrassing hiatus' at Australia House, and he cited his government's different stance from Britain on Rhodesia at the United Nations as a compelling reason for the change. 'Clearly', he added, it was damaging to Australia's international reputation to have 'this post, the first diplomatic post that Australia ever set up—vacant any longer'.[35] At the same time, however, both Armstrong and Whitlam went to great lengths to emphasise that the fundamental changes in the relationship were about putting it on a pro-Australian, not anti-British, foundation. Indeed, when Whitlam told Morrice James of his intention to appoint Armstrong, he stressed that it was intended to show that the government had 'no (repeat no) intention of "cutting the painter" with Britain'.[36]

But the press was equally quick to note the change of style and tone that Armstrong would bring to the position. In early reports, he was referred to variously as the 'envoy in shirt sleeves', 'a relative of Barry McKenzie',[37] a 'character', 'our blunt man in London' and the 'very different High Commissioner'. His arrival was interpreted in the *Sydney Morning Herald* as a 'jarring symbolic change—the infusion of an Australian in the Gorton–Whitlam mould rather than one in the Menzies–Downer tradition'.[38]

Armstrong told the British High Commission in Canberra that he was 'treading on air' in the days after his appointment was made public. If so, he soon came down to earth with a thud. Armstrong created a small tempest in political and diplomatic circles with comments just before his departure that it was 'inevitable that Australia will become a republic … I think the Commonwealth is breaking up … there is a slow erosion of ties between Britain and Australia'. An editorial in *The Times* assured readers that the words were 'carefully pitched so far into the future that it will probably not offend the Queen to whom he will shortly present his credentials'. But Armstrong also pointed to the 'bad friends and the bad feelings' that Britain's decision to enter the EEC had caused, and the turmoil greeting Australians at Heathrow's immigration gates where they were now 'aliens'. It was 'something Australians could never wear with dignity', he remarked bitterly of this situation, adding that 'my Irish father and mother would turn in their grave'.[39] In what had become a standard refrain for disgruntled Australians on this question, Armstrong complained: 'They have put Europeans in a position where Britain's former rivals are now in a better position than their friends who fought with them'.[40]

The former British high commissioner in Canberra, Sir Charles Johnston, told officials in the Foreign Office that Armstrong's position on the question of a republic had been misrepresented by the Australian press—he was 'no more of a Republican than Prime Minister Whitlam himself'. Johnston even sought the advice of the governor of New South Wales, Roden Cutler, as to the seriousness of the republican or quasi-republican comments recently ascribed to leading Labor figures. Cutler apparently replied: 'Ah, you know, when you put a beetle in a bottle, it makes a lot of noise'.[41]

In the first character assessment of Armstrong sent back to London, Morrice James depicted him as the 'archetypal Sydneysider', noting that he was

> very much a Whitlam nominee and a Whitlam man. Armstrong is pre-eminently a good mixer and a man's man in the classical Australian mould: as befits an Irish-Catholic ex politician (and noted business tycoon) he is affable, outgoing, down to earth and direct, with no social pretensions.

James felt Armstrong was a 'deeper, and probably abler' thinker than given credit for: both Waller and the secretary of the Defence Department, Sir Arthur Tange, had told the British diplomat they were impressed with Armstrong's questions during his briefings in Canberra before leaving for London. James, however, interpreted this as evidence not of untapped diplomatic expertise but rather of Armstrong's consciousness of 'how much he has to learn about Anglo-Australian relations (and other aspects of international affairs) in this day and age'. He added that Armstrong would be ably assisted by a career diplomat, David McNicol, as his deputy. It was a measure of the department's 'awareness of Armstrong's shortcomings that they should have appointed someone so senior and experienced to support him'. As a 'non-intellectual', Armstrong, according to James, would 'always have some difficulty in coping with the more sophisticated aspects of his job, but will try to make up for this by friendliness and approachability'. He concluded that although Armstrong clearly had Whitlam's confidence, he was not to be given any sort of access to the 'more delicate business' that passed between Whitlam's office and that of the British high commissioner.[42] The omission of Armstrong from these channels was tantamount to dismissing him as any sort of serious player in the relationship during this period.

In accounting for Armstrong's appointment, several factors are worth noting. It was certainly the fulfilment of a political promise—one which not even the entreaties of a powerful newspaper and business tycoon could split asunder. According to Whitlam's former private secretary, John Menadue, the prime minister had emphatically rejected an approach made after the 1972 election by Rupert Murdoch to be appointed to the London job—Murdoch apparently considering he was entitled to 'something' given his belief that he had played a major role in the election result. When Menadue raised the idea with Whitlam, the response was a blunt 'No way'.[43]

Armstrong recalled an earlier rocky relationship with Whitlam. The latter had initially seen Armstrong, as he did anyone who did not live and breathe politics, as lazy. As Armstrong recalled, 'If you didn't work on the job or at the job every hour of the waking day ... Gough thought you were loafing'.[44] But they patched things up when Whitlam ran for Opposition leader; Armstrong's residual power in Labor's New South Wales branch was clearly valuable. His selection for London might have been a simple case of gratitude for loyal party service mixed with appreciation of his fund-raising and status in the business world. On this point, the *National Times* noted that Armstrong's only similarity with the outgoing Downer was that he had the financial resources to tackle the job 'without being nervous about running over the budget for home entertaining'. Armstrong's personal shareholding wealth was estimated at around $400,000—big money in the early 1970s.[45]

But it might also be seen as a reflection of Whitlam's preference for keeping the post and the relationship with Britain under a close watch. Whitlam, who also held the foreign affairs portfolio until November 1973, clearly relished the prospect of being in charge of the relationship. Armstrong said that he received the 'shortest briefing' from the prime minister before leaving Australia, which was essentially to 'maintain and strengthen the relationship'. The *Sydney Morning Herald* argued that 'the test of [Armstrong's] effectiveness will depend partly on one's view of what High Commissioners should be doing these days. With modern communications and increased availability of travel (and so many new ministers about to make use of it), serious Government contact is above ambassadorial level. Prime Ministers—and Mr Whitlam is no exception—prefer these days to do their own lobbying'.[46] Armstrong himself characterised the position as being Whitlam's 'mouthpiece in London ... a voice for his government', and he committed to doing just that—'straightforward and without any trimmings'. It was probably just the style Whitlam wanted at a time when he was looking to strip the relationship of 'constitutional relics'.[47] Armstrong was to be the kind and affable face of the 'new nationalism'.

At his first press conference in late January 1973, Armstrong moved quickly to put his own stamp on the job. Referring to the British decision to enter the EEC, he remarked that it was a 'shame that the things which divide us should be put out of proportion', but with a little bit of effort 'by everyone we can hold this tremendous link forever *almost*'. This slip of the tongue showed that beneath the brash confidence of the 'new nationalism' there remained an uncomfortable truth—that Australian and British interests were ultimately and irrevocably diverging. The 'bonds' of emotion and sentiment were not as secure as they had once been. When asked about what 'relics' were left on *him*, Armstrong responded by reaching for his favourite convict analogy: 'You mean are there any ankle or wrist marks left? No, I don't think there are any left. I don't think we suffer from much really'. Nevertheless, he maintained his view that the Commonwealth was splitting up: 'there is nothing in common with so many of the countries in the Commonwealth that I don't know what can hold it together'. Here he was siding with Rupert Murdoch's views at the time that the future lay in the cultivation of deeper bilateral relations between Australia and Britain rather than the Commonwealth. He defended political appointments to the role of high commissioner and added that 'it is so important that the man here has a close connection with the Cabinet rather than with the Department. It is important that the man here represents the Prime Minister, knows the thoughts of the Prime Minister and the background of the decisions which the government at home makes'.[48]

But on one early occasion Armstrong showed himself to be embarrassingly out of touch with 'the thoughts of the Prime Minister'. On Australia Day 1973, Whitlam had announced a nationwide competition to find a new national anthem, proclaiming that it would 'be a symbolic expression of our national pride and dignity'.[49] Only days later in London, Armstrong's anthem 'tip' to the British press was that *God Save the Queen* 'won't be ditched ... when you see these suggested national anthems put into the papers here you wouldn't take them rather than *God Save the Queen* would you?' Armstrong may well have been unimpressed by some of the doggerel making its way into the public eye but, wanting a bet each way, admitted that *God Save the Queen* was not 'completely appropriate for the new Australia'. As a compromise he proposed that a 'couple of bars of *God Save the Queen* should be put into whatever anthem which comes along that is acceptable to the people of Australia, because there is something stirring about one or two bars of the "Queen" being added to any new anthem'. To another audience, he suggested with 'an enormous guffaw' that the *Ballad of Barry McKenzie* be the nation's chosen tune.[50]

At other times Armstrong could play the consummate diplomat. He hastened to tell the press that he did not have a 'special programme of his own' to implement as high commissioner, merely that his instructions were to 'maintain and develop the strongest possible ties with Britain and that was it'. The relationship's future, as he saw it, lay in the 50,000 British migrants who came annually to Australia—what he called the 'continuing blood stream' into the country.[51] When Armstrong gave speeches about the 'new nationalism' he would in the same breath as trumpeting Australia's new-found self-confidence continue to emphasise these people-to-people links, drawing on the very same language he had used in the 1950s. Speaking to the Victoria League in July 1974, Armstrong again remembered

> Tennyson who said 'And so the whole wide world is bound by golden chains around the feet of god'. But in this instance may I say the Commonwealth is bound together by the golden threads that have been spun and woven by the countless men and women, not only of today, but those of yesterday … Every Englishman, or Englishwoman, who goes to Australia as a migrant, and takes with him the traditions of this country, to implant in other Commonwealth countries, does his part in maintaining these golden threads, and every Australian young man and woman who crowd your streets in London, who come in great numbers … go back to Australia dedicated even more strongly to forge the bonds that bind us.[52]

In his first cable back to Whitlam after four weeks in the job, Armstrong trod a careful path in detailing the reaction of British officialdom to the new Australian Labor government. In essence, he noted, it was one of 'approval … the Prime Minister's personal reputation as an activist, as a man seeking to change Australia's image in the world, is approved'. But it was not all about stroking the Whitlam ego. Armstrong had already sensed the unease in some Whitehall corridors at the pace of change in the relationship: 'in certain quarters the feeling is he [Whitlam] might be going too quickly without consolidating decisions already made'.[53] Armstrong was reflecting a widespread perception in both Britain and Australia that Whitlam's zeal on constitutional 'relics' and his rush to stake out new policy positions on key international issues was making heads spin. As the London *Daily Express* put it more flippantly: 'The speed of Australian Prime Minister Gough Whitlam's political changes is only matched by his quick change of nicknames. From "Goffles" he has become 'Instant Coffee"'.[54] This sense of the world being turned upside down can be seen in the comments made to Armstrong by Don Willesee, then special minister of state, who told him in April 1973 that 'Gough is still keeping up the amazing pace, pulling new ideas out of that computer he has in his mind', before adding: 'Our new stance in foreign policy has gone down tremendously well with the Africans, has worried the ASEAN countries, has abrased the Americans and the British may be a little worried that we are putting emphasis on the Commonwealth—probably a little more than our bilateral relationship with Britain'.[55] Armstrong's concern was much less with the issues of symbolic change; these he dismissed as 'matters for discussion' that were not 'important'. It was the businessman in him that was much more alarmed at the 'atmosphere of uncertainty in government and business circles as to our general policy towards British investment in Australia'. And it was on this question that he strongly urged Whitlam to 'correct these erroneous impressions'.[56]

'Differences and irritants'

Armstrong could only maintain the line that Whitlam had given him the 'shortest briefing in the history of diplomacy' for a limited time because it was not long before he received more definitive instructions.[57] In April 1973, Whitlam sent Armstrong a long and comprehensive ministerial directive setting out the nature of the Anglo-Australian relationship, his plans for how it would change under the new government, and what the prime minister expected of his high commissioner. Drawing on Pritchett's prescription for a renovation of both the relationship and the mission, the letter covered the subjects of foreign, trade, defence, immigration and cultural policy, and the role and position of the monarchy in national life—and as such can be seen as perhaps the most important policy document reflecting the new government's approach to Britain.

Whitlam stressed first and foremost the need to escape old definitions. He opened his philippic by telling Armstrong that 'Australia's relations with Britain are undergoing important changes and it is appropriate that the appointment of a new Australian High Commissioner in London, who will not be circumscribed by judgments or attitudes deriving from the past, should coincide with these changes'. Armstrong was then provided with a short history lesson. What Whitlam called the 'phase ... of change' in Anglo-Australian relations had three main causes; the first political, the second bureaucratic, the third a matter of diverging interests. First, the government had been elected on the basis that 'it would initiate a programme of change for Australia', and this involved taking a 'fresh look at even our closest relationships in the light of what we believe to be Australia's best interests in the world as it now exists and as it is likely to develop in the future'. Political and constitutional links with Britain were already being considered in this context. Secondly, the transfer of responsibility for Australia House to the Department of Foreign Affairs meant that the relationship with Britain was to become an 'integral and important part of our general foreign relations and not something apart, as they have been in the past'. Thirdly, diverging interests had made a 'change of relationship' inevitable. There was a new and pressing need, Whitlam added, to be 'clear in our own minds' about the type of relationship that Australia wanted with Britain.[58]

The first task for Armstrong was the need to assist in helping overcome the 'negative' attitudes that had come to dominate the way in which both sides understood the relationship. Such attitudes had arisen primarily because the relationship did not carry the same weight that it had formerly. In 'nearly all fields—and often by deliberate choice on our part or on the part of the British—the relationship between us has become markedly less important than it was 30 or 35 years ago'. Australia, once 'entirely of British stock', now had a population with more 'diverse' origins; Britain ranked only third in trading importance after the United States and Japan; and the British maintained only a modest defence presence in Southeast Asia. Where once Australia had 'tailored [its] defence effort so that it locked into the British system, that shield failed'. Britain was now dealing with its 'imperial aftermath'. Nevertheless, before moving on to the substantive issues that he wanted Armstrong to address, Whitlam catalogued the enduring links with Britain, including the 'ties of blood', trade and commercial investment, and its sophisticated defence and intelligence apparatus.[59]

But the essence was that Whitlam wanted a 'new relationship'. While its elements were 'not new', he added that 'we shall be approaching them in a new way'. Ease of access to the highest levels of the British government and civil service had to be maintained despite diverging paths. Continuing British interests in Southeast Asia, though diminished, were to be cultivated. Australia should not lose sight of the possibility that Britain 'may be able to influence their partners in the European communities on attitudes towards developments in East and South East Asia'. Britain should also be regarded as 'an especially valuable window' on the European Community itself. Whitlam was quick to add, however, that there was to be no suggestion that Britain would represent Australia to Europe. Lastly, there was the matter of the monarchy, a factor which along with membership of the Commonwealth gave Australia 'a certain position in British political life, and certain assured places in Britain which, apart from Canada and NZ, others do not have'. But Whitlam wanted to break the old patterns of association and embrace the multi-racial Commonwealth:

> I wish to make the connexion with Britain through the monarchy a less exclusive one than it has been in the past ... I attach importance to Australian membership of the Commonwealth as a valuable framework for cooperation and for keeping in touch with a wide range of African, Caribbean and Asian countries; and I wish to avoid any suggestion that the Commonwealth connexion between Australia, Britain, Canada and New Zealand is exclusive.

There were already moments of tension in the relationship and Whitlam did not shy away from these differences. Whitlam reminded Armstrong of Australia's refusal to grant a British request for a joint survey of a BBC relay station on Christmas Island and its cautious reaction to proposals for a British nuclear-powered submarine to enter Australian ports. Most importantly, there was a divergence of approach on South Africa and Rhodesia, where Whitlam stressed that Australia needed to 'allay suspicions that it is a racialist and colonialist power'. On constitutional matters, Whitlam reinforced the message that such changes were 'not aimed at Britain: they are designed to reflect the development of a more independent Australia'.[60]

It was therefore critical that Armstrong seek to update the Australian national image and ensure that previously informal links were formalised. Here was the essence of the Whitlam prescription for Australia House needing to be run more like an embassy than a tourist bureau. Contacts had to be maintained within and beyond the corridors of Whitehall—in industry, the professions and academia, and Armstrong was asked to 'make a special effort to build up personal relations with influential figures in the information media in Britain'. This was primarily because Whitlam had seen that 'in recent years Australia has had a bad press in Britain' and had attracted criticism for its policies on Vietnam, the treatment of Aborigines and migration. The new government's positions on these questions presented an opportunity to retrieve the situation. Whitlam asked Armstrong to give some thought 'about how to project an appropriate image of the new Australia in Britain' and to update British perceptions. This might be achieved, however, less by the actions of the high commissioner than by a film or play running in London— these, Whitlam said with some prescience, would leave 'deeper impressions'. Whitlam also wanted Armstrong to be 'more catholic' in his choice of speaking engagements, reflecting the view that Downer had perhaps restricted himself too much to the conservative side of politics.[61]

Finally, there were the administrative responsibilities which, Whitlam added, 'bulk large'. It was to be Armstrong's job to improve coordination of the various Australian government agencies working within the high commission. There was a blunt message in all of this—staffing numbers were to be cut. The 'empire' over which Armstrong presided was to be put under the microscope to see whether all officers in Australia House were 'involved in necessary work on the Government's behalf'. As Whitlam noted: 'While London is of course a very important post for us, it is difficult to believe that it is four times as important as Washington or ten times as important as Tokyo, which the present staffing levels would seem to imply'. In effect, it was a signal that the high commission's glory days were coming to a close.[62]

Whitlam concluded with some broad ranging reflections:

> Our relationship with Britain has changed. The British are less important to us than they were but there remains a number of very substantial elements in our relations—and some possible causes of friction or misunderstanding. The High Commission's contacts with the British, its methods of work and its organization need to be brought up to date so that they reflect the character of our relations with Britain … We certainly do not want any breach with Britain, but we do most certainly want to face up to realities and to stress our attitudes and qualities as Australians.[63]

It was, he added, to be 'exacting' work. Armstrong was aware of the daunting task ahead, and was keen to have the best minds of the Department of Foreign Affairs to help him.

He was therefore unnerved by the department's decision to replace senior diplomatic staff in Australia House so early in his appointment. As he complained in a somewhat plaintive cable to Canberra in early March 1973, he was 'anxious to avoid impairing the running of the High Commission owing to lack of continuity of senior experienced staff'. He noted that David McNicol, the replacement for Deputy High Commissioner Bill Pritchett, had not served previously in London. He needed 'every support possible' to do the job 'properly'. In short, he added, 'To … leave me surrounded by men with even less experience here than I have, would be most unfair to me, and make the job of High Commissioner so much more difficult and so much less effective'.[64] It was left to Waller to explain to Armstrong that the high turnover in senior positions in the high commission was 'consistent with the recent assumption of responsibility for its administration by Foreign Affairs'. In addition to emphasising McNicol's strong credentials, Waller also emphasised that the injection of new blood into the post was necessary since 'in the past, Australia House has not had the benefit of Foreign Affairs expertise on quite the same scale as has now become possible'. He reassured Armstrong that 'once the nucleus is established, you will have it for the remainder of your assignment'.[65] But it was a clear signal that while the prime minister maintained the power to appoint the high commissioner, the Department of Foreign Affairs was moving quickly to assert control over the mission. Evidently, Waller did enough to calm the nerves of the new and inexperienced high commissioner. Armstrong later confided to his successor, John Bunting, that while he had chaired the branch heads meetings in his first few months in the job, very quickly this task was 'handed over to David McNicol … a hard worker [who] has supported me very well indeed'.[66]

This left Armstrong free to concentrate on the more public and presentational aspects of the job. And it was in the field of Australian artistic endeavour that he chose to make the most of Whitlam's 'new nationalism'. It was not surprising that spruiking this element of the government's agenda came naturally to Armstrong—he and his wife had a substantial personal collection of Australian artworks, even loaning some of them for an exhibition at Australia House in 1973. Armstrong cherished his personal friendships with many high-profile Australian painters, among them William Dobell, Brett Whiteley and John Olsen, telling a London magazine that 'with no other men have I enjoyed the same careless hours, the same unhurried, simple savouring of the passing of time'.[67] During a speech in Bath in 1973 to honour the memory of Captain Arthur Phillip—whose remains are buried in St Nicholas' church in nearby Bathampton—Armstrong converted the 'founder of Australia' into a hero of national cultural sophistication. Noting that barely a year into the first settlement at Sydney Cove a play had been performed for Phillip and his officers, Armstrong went on to document the emergence of Australian film, theatre and the visual arts in a story that led directly to 'Australia's cultural revolution' under the Whitlam government. The high commissioner was speaking in the weeks following the opening of the Sydney Opera House, an event he saw as a 'turning of the tide' and a 'modern day symbol of all our art and cultural development'. No 'leading artist' in the world, he hoped, would 'be able to consider his or her life's work complete until they have performed in the Sydney Opera House'. And in his peroration he worked valiantly to extract a usable legacy from Phillip:

> For finding the site for this symbol of the Australian cultural revolution we have Captain Arthur Phillip to thank. Most certainly he must have walked on the site thousands of times. And for his encouragement of the arts way back in 1788 when 11 convicts acted out a play in a mud hut with his patronage, again we thank Captain Arthur Phillip.[68]

The lineage was awkward to say the least, but it showed the lengths to which some were prepared to go to give the Whitlam cultural renaissance a history of its own.

Yet Armstrong also found himself on the receiving end of British frustration with the Whitlam government's new style and approach to Anglo-Australian relations. In his consultations with Australian officials on a visit to Canberra in January 1974, Armstrong set out clearly the 'differences and irritants between the British and ourselves which have at times touched sensitive nerves in government circles, certainly in London and to some extent in Canberra'. What needled the British most were Whitlam's personal comments about Edward Heath at the Commonwealth Heads of Government Meeting in Ottawa the previous year, when Whitlam, frustrated by the United Kingdom's indifference to Australian concern over French nuclear testing in the Pacific, had labelled the British prime minister publicly as 'consistently and forthrightly negative'.[69] Other points of contention included British displeasure at Australian voting patterns in the United Nations, particularly on Rhodesia, Armstrong relating that 'they went so far as to call me in to transmit a written protest from the Secretary of State'. But he continued to dismiss any fallout from Whitlam's efforts on the new trappings of Australian nationhood, suggesting that 'many people here consider that some lessening of Australian interest in Britain is understandable since, in their view, Britain first turned its back on Australia and other members of the Commonwealth when it joined the EEC'. On the broader subject of trade relations, he reinforced the 'facts of life', which were that 'Britain is so preoccupied with attempting to preserve its own interests in the "hurly-burly" of the EEC that it is in no position to put forward other country's views unless they are likely to assist the British case'.[70]

At other times, Armstrong's correspondence with Whitlam bordered on outright frivolity. In April 1974, following the calling of a double dissolution election in Canberra, Armstrong cabled Whitlam a private message reporting on an Easter weekend visit to Ireland where he and his wife had 'many conferences with the Fairies, the little people and the leprechauns'. He had even 'talked to the ghost of Padraic Pearse'.[71] And he was happy to report to Whitlam that these interlocutors were 'all certain of your success and send their blessings on your endeavours'.[72] Whitlam clearly appreciated the joke, and wondered whether Armstrong's talents in garnering political support might be better exercised on Australian newspaper editors.[73] Armstrong relished this prime ministerial endorsement of his switch to vaudeville—and in advance of Whitlam's second visit to London in December 1974, he apparently cabled the prime minister suggestions for his speech to the Mansion House in London. After encouraging Whitlam to make 'warm reference to the Queen and the Royal Family' and extend a message to 'Australians living in Britain', Armstrong catalogued the achievements of Australian creative artists in Britain, confident that this proved the British were 'more dependent on us to sustain' their cultural life 'than vice-versa'. This was an extraordinary claim, and showed the extent to which Australian artistic endeavour abroad could be invested with a significance that it clearly could not bear. But what then followed was a series of jokes about after-dinner drinking, rowing, cricket and other sporting anecdotes which Armstrong felt would assist in giving Whitlam's speech some much-needed 'light touches'. He noted that 'cricketing will be right in the news when the prime minister comes to England' and further that 'the best stories I can suggest are both attributable to Don Bradman, who told them at the Lords Taverners dinner when he was over here this year':

> The story is about Bert Iremonger … a slow bowler whose average in test cricket was .0005. Bert's wife rang the pavilion to speak to Bert. She was told that he had just gone into bat. She said: 'I will hang on'. When Mrs Hutton rang the pavilion to speak to Len, and when she was told that Len had gone into bat, she said 'I will ring back tomorrow'.[74]

Whitlam seems to have ignored this injunction to draw on recycled Bradmania, instead giving a thoughtful exposition of the relationship of the 'new nationalism' to the Anglo-Australian connection. He continued in his emphatic denial of an anti-British content in the 'new nationalism':

> Those who see in some of our recent actions concerning Britain a manifestation of some strident new nationalism or anti-British feeling have completely misread our intentions and mistaken the mood of our people. What Australia is trying to do is establish an independent identity in the world and especially in our own region. We have grown up. Our actions are in no way anti-British. They are simply pro-Australian … there can never be any questions about the enduring strength of Australia's ties with the British people. The vast majority of our people are of British stock. We wish to build on British institutions. I believe that our understanding will deepen, rather than diminish, as Australia assumes her rightful place as a proud and independent nation.[75]

It has been suggested that Armstrong left the posting less of a republican than when he started. According to one report he had succumbed to the charms of London diplomacy and was 'not … as outspokenly republican as he was when he left Sydney'.[76] Nevertheless, in one of his final interviews before departure, he repeated that it was 'natural and inevitable' that Australia would become a republic. Armstrong, however, also seemed to have tired of trying to explain the changes to the relationship brought about by the 'new nationalism'. In early 1975 he was still arguing against the allegation that the post had been downgraded. His job had been difficult because of what he called 'misapprehensions' that he had discovered among the British people. Again, it was the issue of the new national anthem that was at fault:

> They think Australia is finished with Britain, that because we have adopted our own anthem we have ditched Britain. I have not found this attitude among British politicians. They understand exactly what Whitlam is doing. They accept that the child has grown up, and they love the man as much as they loved the baby. And the man still loves the parents, just as much as when it was a babe.[77]

While Whitehall, even if grudgingly, had accepted the essence of the 'new nationalism', Whitlam and Armstrong still seemingly struggled to have much influence on wider perceptions. Armstrong noted that 'people over here expect Australians to do certain things, expect them to take certain attitudes and to drink a lot of beer. I think the Australian visitor plays up to that'.[78] Although following his second visit to London, Whitlam told parliament that 'we are not a nation of philistines … there is more to the Australian image than Barry McKenzie',[79] he himself had recently appeared in the second of the Barry McKenzie films.[80]

Conclusion

Credited with opening up a 'traditionally stuffy Australia House', Armstrong finished his term, according to one newspaper, as 'the most popular High Commissioner Australia has had'.[81] He once said, 'My office is on the first floor of Australia House, and the door's open. So is the bar'.[82] It was this kind of openness that prompted some in the British press to depict him as the 'embodiment of the fresh, fiercely independent and slightly rough-diamond spirit of Australia'.[83] Or, as another Australian journalist put it, 'He mightn't look like a diplomat, but the cap seems to fit'. He had a 'certain presence, a self-confidence learned during 40 years of ups and downs in the hard world of Australian Labor politics. It never pays to underestimate a survivor'.[84]

Summing up his tenure at Australia House, Armstrong felt that he had done a competent job, and was at pains to stress that 'the Government has never been embarrassed by me. I have never done or said anything silly'.[85] This was perhaps partly because he had very quickly 'given up talking from the hip'.[86] Armstrong had stipulated to Whitlam that he only wanted a two-year term, and in his later reflections on the job he said that another year would have been 'repetitive'. He missed the sun and the surf of his native land. 'My main thoughts are to go back to Collaroy beach and lie on the warm sand … I have not been able to lead my natural way of life in Britain. Back home you can walk around in shorts and thongs and get the feeling of the sun. I dream about it'.[87] He died in 1977 only a day after receiving his Order of Australia.

12 A new pattern: officials, ministers and diplomats at Australia House, 1975–81

J.R. Nethercote

THE United Kingdom became a full member of the European Economic Community on 1 January 1973. This event epitomised a marked change in Australia's relations with Britain. As G.C. Bolton wrote in the quinquennial review of Australia's foreign relations, 'More than at any time in the past, the five years from 1971 to 1975 saw the erosion of formal and informal links between Australia and Britain'.[1] Even in trade, he noted, 'between 1970–71 and 1974–75 Britain's share of Australia's export market fell from 11.26 per cent to 5.47 per cent, and of imports from 21.36 per cent to 15.03 per cent'.[2] Such was the scale of change that in the succeeding volume on *Australia in World Affairs*, traversing the second half of the 1970s, Australia–UK relations were simply absorbed into a single chapter on Australia's relations with Western Europe.[3]

Just as the nature of Australia's relations with the United Kingdom was changing, so also was there change at Australia House, shaped by three particular factors. Terrorist activity, mainly from Irish sources, meant that access to the building, like many similar establishments in London, was increasingly restricted. The work of the high commission itself was the subject of long and searching review, led initially by J.E. Collings, a former commissioner of the Public Service Board. Consequential reductions in staffing and other rationalisations meant that many activities located in nearby Canberra House were progressively transferred back to Australia House itself. The high commission as a whole was a major target in successive campaigns of both the Whitlam and Fraser governments to reduce public expenditure. The quest for economies embraced staffing, overtime, travel, telephone usage, conference representation and transport.[4]

The official: Bunting

In such circumstances, the appointment of Sir John Bunting as high commissioner from 1 February 1975 was unusually appropriate. Regarded by Sir Robert Menzies as the 'prince of civil servants', Bunting was the first high commissioner not to come from the ranks of ministers. For two and half decades he had, however, been, in his own words, 'fairly close to the corridors of power in our national capital in Canberra'.[5] He was especially involved in the workings of the cabinet and from 1959 until 1975 served as its secretary. More than most ministers, he had a deep knowledge of Australian policy and practice, not least in the defence and security fields. He combined this experience of cabinet business with a long involvement in Anglo-Australian relations. Australia House fell within his jurisdiction as secretary of the Prime Minister's Department between 1959 and 1968. And he could draw on direct knowledge of the high commission from a fifteen-month assignment in the mid-1950s as official secretary.

This background, and his many visits to London—often in company with prime ministers and notably Menzies—meant that at the time of his appointment he was the best connected high commissioner to represent Australia in the United Kingdom since Bruce. As Gough Whitlam declared in announcing Bunting's arrival in London, 'his association and standing with the Queen's Household, the Commonwealth Secretariat and the British Civil Service [make] his appointment especially suitable and significant'.[6]

In a period when it seemed that the traditional relationship was undergoing so much change, Bunting's term was marked by reassuring signs of continuity. During his first summer in England the Australian cricket team retained the Ashes in a series of test matches that followed the inaugural one-day World Cup tournament, in the final of which Australia lost to the West Indies at Lord's. The final months were preoccupied with planning the Queen's visit to Australia in 1977 to mark the silver jubilee of her reign, a task complicated by increasing demonstrations against the governor-general, Sir John Kerr, arising from the dismissal of the Whitlam government on 11 November 1975.[7] In many respects, the role of the high commissioner seemed unaffected by the changing structure of relations between the two countries. It was as if there were a determination on both sides to minimise the effects of Britain's new position in Europe and the consequences for the Commonwealth. The Queen and Court continued to be attentive to those nations in the British Commonwealth which still recognised her as head of state. And for the high commissioner, there was still a steady round of dinner and other engagements, frequently including a speech. These embraced such occasions as the Lord and Lady Mayoress of London's Easter banquet, the Court and Livery Ladies Dinner of the Clothworkers Company, Shakespeare Birthday celebrations, Anzac Day commemorations, Trooping the Colour and numerous sporting occasions.[8]

Whatever the changes in trade and commerce, defence and migration, the high commissioner's representational role entailed a busy schedule. Bunting was naturally well fitted for these tasks, even if, as a traditional public servant, he sought neither the limelight nor the podium. He was, in the words of his close friend, Sir Frederick Wheeler (chairman, Public Service Board, 1960–71; secretary, Treasury, 1971–79), 'one of those rare men who can walk with prime ministers, and yet retain the common touch'. A newspaper profile at the time he became high commissioner observed: '[T]here is no questioning his ability to talk in a quiet, friendly fashion with almost anyone, even journalists'.[9]

A feature of Bunting's first year in London was a watching brief on the so-called loans affair, which was the centre of so much controversy in Canberra during 1975. A central figure, Tirath Khemlani, was a Pakistani broker based in London. Efforts to keep track of manoeuvres in Europe arising from Khemlani's activities, and those of other aspiring intermediaries, engaged both Bunting and other senior staff periodically.[10]

Bunting's high commissionership was, however, cut short. On leave in Scotland with members of his family in mid-February 1976, he was taken ill and admitted to a local hospital. A critical heart condition (dissecting aneurysm) was diagnosed, and he was promptly transferred to London for major surgery. Doctors considered the risk factor 'very high but that the risk of not operating … [was] even higher.' A cable on 19 February reported: 'Operation successfully concluded and Sir John is doing well'.[11]

While his recovery was impressive, Bunting's voice was for a time impaired. A statement from the prime minister, Malcolm Fraser, noted that '[a]fter medical advice, Sir John has told the Prime Minister that, given particularly the heavy representational role in London, he feels it best that arrangements for appointment of a successor as high commissioner now be set in train'.[12] Bunting, however, spent a further six months in London. Shortly before his retirement, and their departure for Australia for the silver jubilee tour, the Queen and Prince Philip dined as his guests at Stoke Lodge, where Her Majesty invested him as a Knight Commander of the Order of the British Empire. He thus became, after Sir Robert Garran and Sir Frederick Shedden, and with Sir Roland Wilson, the most honoured of Australia's public servants.

The minister: Freeth

Bunting's early return meant that a new high commissioner had to be found. Yet, so early in the life of a new government, there was no obvious appointee in either the ministerial or parliamentary ranks. The initial choice was K.C.O. (later Sir Keith) Shann. A former deputy secretary of the Department of Foreign Affairs, and previously ambassador to the Philippines and Indonesia, Shann was one of Australia's most distinguished diplomats. Since 1974 he had been ambassador in Tokyo where he wished to remain. Prime Minister Fraser, however, was keen to send to Tokyo John Menadue, Bunting's successor at the Department of the Prime Minister and Cabinet, having failed to persuade the foreign minister, Andrew Peacock, to take him as secretary of the Department of Foreign Affairs. Consequently, a suitably prestigious post was needed for Shann, and his appointment to London was announced. Had he gone, he would have been the first career diplomat to head the high commission in Australia House. Instead, he accepted an appointment as chairman of the Public Service Board and returned to Canberra.

The choice subsequently fell on Gordon Freeth, Shann's predecessor in Tokyo. Freeth was a comparative latecomer to international relations. The son of a bishop, he had been educated in Sydney and Perth before entering the law. He rowed for Australia at the Sydney Empire Games in 1938 and saw war service in the Royal Australian Air Force. In 1949 he won the Western Australian seat of Forrest for the Liberal Party and, following the 1958 elections, was elevated to the ministry. He held the portfolios of the interior, works, shipping and transport, and air before taking external affairs in 1969 following the appointment of his fellow Western Australian, Paul Hasluck, as governor-general.

Of distinguished presence and bearing, he would ordinarily have been thought of as a 'safe pair of hands'. But he had also been involved in two serious controversies in his eleven years as a minister. The first concerned an attempted redistribution of electorates in 1962–63 in which he, as minister for the interior with responsibility for electoral matters, incurred the considerable wrath of the Country Party leader and the deputy prime minister, John McEwen. This clash was resolved by his own replacement at the Department of the Interior by a Country Party minister and a further delay in effecting an already long-overdue redistribution after significant amendment of the electoral legislation. More seriously, in 1969, as minister for external affairs, he made a statement in the House of Representatives that was interpreted as displaying a relaxed attitude to Soviet naval activity in the Indian Ocean by the Democratic Labor Party, on whose support the Coalition government relied in the Senate and, in the form of preferences, in the House of Representatives.[13] Not only did controversy ensue but, at the 1969 general elections that followed shortly thereafter, he was defeated in his seat of Forrest. Freeth was appointed ambassador to Tokyo the following year and remained there until the end of 1973. After that, he returned to Perth and worked mainly in a law firm as a consultant.

The London appointment, as it happens, sparked some comment in the newspapers. It was partly based on the fact that he had been in private life for several years and therefore not particularly in touch with current government thinking; and partly a product of comment by the staff association in the Department of Foreign Affairs hostile to diplomatic appointments from outside the career stream. Fraser, in answering a question in the House of Representatives, especially took issue with the latter ground of complaint:

> There is a staff association which indicates that there should be a closed shop arrangement in relation to ambassadors and high commissioners, a contention which I will not accept for one moment, especially in relation to the United Kingdom and the United States, where there is particular advantage in having somebody with a political background and a close knowledge of the politics and politicians in his own country.[14]

Although a relative newcomer to London, Freeth found himself working in an office only a few hundred yards to the east of where his grandfather, Sir Evelyn Freeth, had worked most of his life, in Somerset House as secretary of the Estate Duty Office. His wife was a direct descendant of Lord Popham, one of the judges involved in the Guy Fawkes case.

As a former minister, Freeth was not used to attending to the details of management. He chaired weekly meetings of the most senior staff at the high commission, and monthly meetings of all branch heads. Otherwise, his disposition in overseeing the high commission, as the work of rationalisation and scaling down proceeded, was one of benign encouragement, leaving the task essentially in the hands of the deputy high commissioner and the official secretary. Moreover, with so many of the significant tasks in Anglo-Australian relations being handled directly from Canberra—particularly noteworthy were those matters in the hands of the minister for special trade negotiations—Freeth was relatively free to devote himself to the extensive representational responsibilities of an Australian high commissioner in London. Two of the more important events concerned former Australian prime ministers.

Following Menzies' death in 1978, there was a memorial service in Westminster Abbey in the presence of the Prince of Wales, addressed by the former British prime minister and foreign secretary, Lord Home, and attended by Dame Pattie Menzies. The Institute of Commonwealth Studies in the University of London organised a seminar to consider Menzies' contribution to the Commonwealth. British speakers followed the lead of Churchill in *The Second World War* in maintaining that the United Kingdom had had more agreeable relations with Australia when Menzies was the prime minister during the war than under his successors, Arthur Fadden and John Curtin.[15] Freeth, however, took up the cudgels for the nation he represented in reminding the audience that when Menzies was in office, the focal point of the war was Europe and the Middle East. Shortly after the Curtin government took office, the Japanese offensive in the Pacific began in earnest. When the attack on Pearl Harbor occurred, Curtin had been prime minister for only a little more than two months. The interpretation being offered was therefore false because it failed to take account of the dramatically different circumstances of the Menzies and Curtin governments.

In August of the following year, Freeth and his wife went to Crosshouse in Scotland for Andrew Fisher Festival Week. Fisher, born in Crosshouse in 1862, had a notable place in Australian history—he had been a minister in the first Labor government in the world, the one-week long Dawson government in Queensland; a minister in the first Labor government of the federation; and prime minister in three subsequent Labor governments, the second and third of which had majorities in both the House of Representatives and the Senate. From 1916 until 1921 he was Australian high commissioner in London. The district council of Kilmarnock and Loudoun had created a commemorative garden in his honour and invited Freeth to unveil a plaque.[16]

An unusual task calling for considerable tact and sensitivity on the high commissioner's part came in the form of supporting and attending to various needs of the former governor-general, Sir John Kerr, and Lady Kerr. They were living near London following Kerr's resignation the previous year, and his decision not to take up the ambassadorship to UNESCO to which he had been appointed by the Fraser government. Having completed his memoirs, *Matters for Judgment*, while residing in the Auvergne, Kerr welcomed (and sought) continuing involvement in public affairs. It fell to Freeth to meet these desires inasmuch as limited opportunities allowed.[17]

The diplomat: Plimsoll

Freeth, who had been knighted in 1978, returned to Australia early in 1980—no thought seems to have been given to an extension. The choice of successor was left to the foreign minister, Peacock, but with the proviso that after general elections due at the end of the year, the post might well be required by the prime minister for his own nominee. Peacock's choice was a great alumnus of the Australian diplomatic service, Sir James Plimsoll, at the time ambassador in Brussels.[18] He had been secretary to the Department of External Affairs from 1965 to 1970 and his head of mission posts had included the United Nations (New York), New Delhi, Washington and Moscow. It was the first time a foreign service officer had been appointed to head the London mission. There was, nevertheless, always a possibility that his tenure would be brief. One journalist noted at the time:

> Fraser will be free to appoint any of his senior Cabinet Ministers in the plum diplomatic post soon after the next election … Sir James will be 63 this coming Anzac Day. With holiday and long service leave entitlements he would be able to retire about a year after that, in other words about five months or so after the expected date of the next election in December.[19]

The journalist was prescient but not entirely accurate in his predictions for the London post. Following the general elections in October 1980, Plimsoll was replaced, not by a senior cabinet minister, but by Victor Garland who had held a variety of portfolios outside the cabinet only since the 1977 elections (although he had had a brief time as minister for posts and telecommunications in 1975–76, as well as having been minister for supply in the McMahon government).

Plimsoll, like Bunting before him, was well connected in London through extensive contacts with UK ministers and officials over many years. Like many of his contemporaries he was a frequent reader of British newspapers and periodicals, and he was well informed about British politics. Plimsoll's gifts as a public speaker meant that the extensive representational work would not be a burden. He also had a great curiosity about any place to which he was posted. One of his old friends, the former British high commissioner in Australia and now the foreign secretary, Lord Carrington, later recalled that Plimsoll 'appeared to be totally at ease in London and greatly respected not just as Australia's representative but as a considerable person in his own right. He had so many friends in this country that he was regarded in a rather special way'. It was Lord Carrington who led the criticism of his swift removal: 'I don't care who knows it, James, I think you have been treated very shabbily'. The remark found its way into the press but there was no retraction. [20] There was a 'feeling of shock' among members of the UK establishment.

Conclusion

The discreet role played by the three high commissioners surveyed in this chapter helped Anglo-Australian relations make the adjustment to the United Kingdom's new position both in Europe and in relation to the Commonwealth. Bunting, Freeth and Plimsoll also ensured a sense of continuity in the relationship in the aftermath of an era of rapid change. Social and cultural relations remained strong and Britain maintained its status as an important source for migrants, and skilled migrants at that. Trade had, at first, fallen away, not only proportionately but slightly even in absolute terms. But it revived swiftly and then prospered.

Australian governments of the 1970s had moved to establish a 'normal' diplomatic relationship, as if Australia and Britain were 'foreign' to one another; even the High Court of Australia would in 1999 find that the United Kingdom was a foreign power, so far as Australia was concerned. But for the purposes of Australian representation in London, and the role of the high commissioner to the United Kingdom, a sense of specialness and familiarity had survived the end of empire, British entry into the EEC, and military withdrawal east of Suez. Australia remained a settler society which, notwithstanding its nationalism and multiculturalism, was still deeply indebted to a British heritage in virtually every aspect of its national life. The high commissioners of the period after 1980 would be faced with both the complexities and opportunities presented by this persistent influence and the ambivalence that it produced.

Sir Alexander Downer with Lady Downer outside Stoke Lodge, the high commissioner's residence. [Australian High Commission, London, Department of Foreign Affairs and Trade]

Sir Alexander Downer (centre) laying a wreath at a cenotaph in London, 1971. [Australian High Commission, London, Department of Foreign Affairs and Trade]

Australian Prime Minister Sir Robert Menzies (left) with Sir Alexander Downer, c. 1966. [Australian High Commission, London, Department of Foreign Affairs and Trade]

Margaret Thatcher, then secretary of state for education and later prime minister of the United Kingdom (second from left), with J.I. Armstrong (second from right). [Australian High Commission, London, Department of Foreign Affairs and Trade]

Australian Prime Minister
E.G. Whitlam (left) with
J.I. Armstrong. [Australian
High Commission, London,
Department of Foreign
Affairs and Trade]

Sir John Bunting (left) with
Princess Anne (second from left),
Lady Bunting and Mark Phillips.
[Australian High Commission,
London, Department of Foreign
Affairs and Trade]

Sir John Bunting (centre front) and staff of Australia House at Christmas party, 23 December 1975. [Photograph courtesy of Lady Bunting]

Lord Carrington (left) with Sir John Bunting (second from left) and then Governor-General of Australia Sir John Kerr and Lady Kerr at the Australia Day reception, 26 January 1976. [Photograph courtesy of Lady Bunting]

Gordon Freeth
[Department of Foreign Affairs and Trade]

Sir James Plimsoll (left) [National Library of Australia]

13 The 'new equilibrium': the high commissioners after 1980

Jeremy Hearder

THIS chapter covers the work of no fewer than eight high commissioners over the course of almost three decades. They are the Hon. Sir Victor Garland KBE (1981–83), Alfred Parsons AO (1984–87), the Hon. Douglas McClelland AC (1987–90), Richard Smith AM (1991–94), the Hon. Neal Blewett AC (1994-98), Philip Flood AO (1998–2000), Michael L'Estrange AO (2000–05), and the Hon Richard Alston (2005–08). The present high commissioner is John Dauth LVO, who arrived in September 2008. Being the most recent years covered in this history, restrictions apply on the availability of official documents because of the thirty-year rule under the Archives Act. A full account, including access to the documents, will have to wait. But in pursuit of a first draft of history, what follows is a largely impressionistic survey. Over such a lengthy period priorities varied, and quiet times were interspersed with times of intensity and drama. This account owes much to the considerable cooperation and help received from those who held the distinguished office during these years.

A modern relationship

By the 1970s Australia's relationship with Britain had seemed of declining significance. There was the cumulative impact of the United Kingdom's having withdrawn its military presence 'east of Suez' in 1971, and its increasing preoccupation with Europe and the United States. Australia dealt with Britain both bilaterally and as part of the European Union, with which the British became increasingly, if not always comfortably, enmeshed. At UK ports of entry Australians no longer had any special privileges.

Yet under the new post-imperial conditions, the relationship between Australia and Britain blossomed. While nowhere near as critical to either country as in the period before the 1970s, the official relationship remained close and valuable to both nations while becoming a smaller part of the overall relationship between them. In relations between Australia and Britain generally, there continued to develop a level of activity and ease of connection in diplomacy, defence, business, culture and education that Australians, at least, enjoyed with no other country except possibly New Zealand. As the Hawke Labor government foreign minister, Gareth Evans, wrote in 1995: 'The ties of history, kinship and culture are so pervasive that the relationship seems to exist independently of governments and their policies'.[1] Indeed, for most of the period business was conducted between governments of opposite political persuasions without this distinction being of major significance. Parsons, for example, hosted dinners with an Australian Labor minister, a British Conservative minister and a Shadow Opposition Labour frontbencher, each talking frankly and rigorously about controversial issues but without animosity.[2] Since the 1970s, Australia and the United Kingdom have forged a modern bilateral relationship that remains powerfully influenced but no longer dominated by Australia's earlier history as a British settler society.

In 2004, Michael L'Estrange, then high commissioner, remarked in a London public lecture that there was discernible a 'new equilibrium' in the British–Australian relationship at government, business and community levels, including 'an unprecedented scale of interaction' between the people of both countries. In government, there were 'expanding areas of common policy interest and shared perspectives'. The most 'prominent example', he suggested, was the common response to the new realities created by the 'threat of fundamentalist global terrorism', but others included international trade liberalisation, border security, transnational crime, pensions policy, ageing, health, national resource utilisation, public sector management, higher education, and the commercial application of research and development. 'The intensity of two-way bilateral policy interest', L'Estrange explained, 'has developed because the policy challenges which both our countries face in many areas are so comparable, because the expectations and values of our respective communities are so similar, and because our systems of law and government share important similarities'.[3] As L'Estrange hinted, the modern relationship between the two countries was underpinned by both the common challenges they now faced, and the likenesses in their institutions and beliefs that owed much to a shared heritage.

The period covered by this chapter was one of major economic and policy change in both countries. The Australian economy, like Britain's, was deregulated, as the currency was floated, foreign banks allowed to open up for business, state enterprises sold off, industrial arbitration largely replaced by enterprise bargaining, and the old tariff walls dismantled.[4] Having even earlier discarded the 'White Australia' policy, Australian policy-makers now promoted their country as cosmopolitan, multicultural and 'open' to a globalising world. The populations of both Australia and Britain became increasingly diverse in ethnic composition, although their respective multiculturalisms arose out of different circumstances, and both were affected by movements of refugees. At one point in the 1980s pressure on Indo-Chinese refugee camps in Hong Kong led the United Kingdom to suggest that Australia consider taking more refugees from Vietnam and the Australian high commissioner, Doug McClelland, had to explain that on a pro rata basis Australia was already taking far more than the United Kingdom.[5]

With the end of empire, Australia also became more nationalistic, and especially in the 1990s there was intense debate about the possibility of Australia becoming a republic.

This growing sense of Australian nationalism, as L'Estrange put it, was 'partly the product of a search for a distinctive sense of Australian identity and purpose that was not seen as derivative from Britain, the United States or anywhere else'. Yet, in the 1980s and 1990s there were few Australians who imagined that a more highly developed sense of Australian national identity necessarily implied a downgrading of the bilateral relationship with the United Kingdom. There was rather 'recognition ... that a commitment to Australian distinctiveness, an appreciation of Britain's own special attributes and a recognition of the unique character of the Australia–Britain connection do not constitute some zero sum game'.[6]

In the more distant past, leading figures in each country had very different levels of personal knowledge of the other, and face-to-face contact was nearly always in London. It had been usual for the Australian prime minister and senior ministers to have considerable knowledge of the United Kingdom, while on the UK side first-hand knowledge of Australia was less common. This picture changed. Lord Carrington, defence secretary (1970–74) and foreign secretary (1979–82), had earlier in his career spent three years (1956–59) as UK high commissioner in Canberra. Official visits became increasingly common, facilitated by fast air travel. In 1979 Margaret Thatcher visited Australia as prime minister, while Bob Hawke had official talks with her in Britain in 1986. Thatcher again went to Australia in 1988, when her 'extremely friendly and useful' discussion with Hawke led her to invite him for further talks in London in 1989, at which he was accompanied by three ministers.[7]

Following his visit in 1989, Hawke instructed McClelland to identify two promising UK Labour Party Opposition frontbenchers to invite to visit Australia. With impeccable judgment, McClelland and his staff unanimously recommended that Tony Blair and Gordon Brown be invited, and both visited for two weeks in 1990.[8] A close Australian friend of Blair thought that the visit had confirmed Blair and Brown in the view

> that Labor could win elections on the basis of an economic reform and social justice agenda. Hawke and Keating showed how Labor could embrace economic reform as part of the programme for change whilst at the same time promoting the social wage for disadvantaged and working-class families. They saw Australian Labor as one of the inspirations for New Labour in the UK.[9]

In the years leading up to UK Labour's election victory in 1997, a stream of prominent Labour guests, including Blair and Prescott (shadow deputy leader), attended Blewett's dinners and receptions, all eager to learn of the Australian experiment.[10] Blair liked Australia, 'its irreverence and lateralism', and he formed close friendships with Australians at Oxford. Two of his ministers, Patricia Hewitt and Sir Ross Cranston, had Australian backgrounds, and Blair himself lived briefly in Adelaide as a very young child. Blair also thought it important that senior ministers, such as Straw (foreign secretary) and Hoon (defence secretary), as well as senior officials, should visit Australia to 'learn and apply',[11] which they did.

In sum, there was a transition from a 'post-colonial' to a more customary diplomatic relationship between Australia and Britain, and London became a more 'normal' part of Australia's overseas diplomatic network. Overall staffing numbers at Australia House reduced from around 600 at the beginning of the 1980s, to about 200 in 2005, a level more in keeping with Australia's other major missions; and the high commissioners came from a more varied background than in the earlier period covered by this volume. In 1980 a precedent had been created when Sir James Plimsoll became the first career appointee to the office of Australian high commissioner in London (see page 187). While four former government ministers would later assume the office, a further three career diplomats held the appointment, as did one who came from a background that was part public service, and part political.

Backgrounds

Of the three diplomats, Parsons, Smith and Flood, each had been very senior members of the service before assuming the role of high commissioner to the United Kingdom. Flood was a former secretary of the Department of Foreign Affairs and Trade (1996–98), while the other two had both been deputy secretaries. All had extensive overseas experience, including having been ambassador or high commissioner at a number of other important posts, although none had worked in Australia House before.

The appointments of these three career officers were interspersed with those of four former government ministers: Garland, McClelland, Blewett and Alston. Garland, a Western Australian Liberal member with a background as a chartered accountant, held a number of ministerial positions in the McMahon and Fraser governments. McClelland—the son of a New South Wales state parliamentarian and the father of the current (2009) federal attorney-general—was minister for the media and special minister of state in the Whitlam government, then president of the Senate (1983–87) before appointment to London. Blewett, a Tasmanian Rhodes Scholar, was a politics professor prior to his parliamentary career. Although he held a wide range of senior portfolios in the Hawke and Keating governments, he is best known as a reforming health minister (1983–90) who oversaw the setting up of a national health scheme (Medicare) and Australia's response to the AIDS crisis. Blewett's background in health policy led to his membership while in London of the executive board of the World Health Organization, and subcommittees, including a reform committee which he chaired. He attended meetings in Geneva for three to four weeks a year.[12] Alston, a barrister before becoming a Liberal senator for Victoria, was a long-serving minister for communications in the Howard government, but he also had a long-term interest in cultural matters and international affairs, particularly overseas aid.

L'Estrange's background included some parallels with the experiences of both the career officers and the politicians, but he fits neither category. A Rhodes Scholar from New South Wales, he had been a public servant in the Department of the Prime Minister and Cabinet and, in the four years before his appointment as high commissioner by the Howard government, served as secretary to the Cabinet and head of the Cabinet Policy Unit.[13] But L'Estrange also worked as a senior and later principal adviser in the Office of Leader of the Opposition (1988–95), and during 1995 as the director of the Liberal Party–aligned Menzies Research Centre.

Garland was the youngest ever appointee at forty-seven, and L'Estrange the second youngest at forty-eight. All the others were around sixty on taking up the post, continuing the traditional pattern of a final appointment before leaving public service. Smith, however, went on to become ambassador to the Philippines and then director-general of the Office of National Assessments, while L'Estrange became secretary of the Department of Foreign Affairs and Trade.

All appointees had had some earlier acquaintance with Britain. Blewett and L'Estrange had been Rhodes Scholars at Oxford. Smith and Alston had worked as schoolteachers in London after graduation. Flood was the son of an English migrant who had worked in Australia House. The present incumbent, Dauth, a career diplomat, earlier had been seconded to Buckingham Palace (1977–80), where he served as assistant press secretary to the Queen and press secretary to the Prince of Wales. All had had previous official working visits to the United Kingdom of one kind or another. For example Garland, in the two and a half years before his appointment, visited London frequently as minister for special trade negotiations.[14] For the career diplomats this degree of familiarity with the locale was in contrast to other postings, where it was usual for appointees to have had little or no previous exposure.

Apart from routine briefings by officials, most new appointees do not recall receiving any particular instructions from on high before leaving on posting. Flood, however, who was sent to London by a still fairly new government concerned to differentiate itself from its predecessor's stress on Asian engagement and republicanism, recalls specific instructions from Prime Minister Howard, and also from Alexander Downer, the foreign affairs minister, and Tim Fischer, the trade minister. In particular, they asked him to explain to the British the Howard government's, and Australia's, first white paper on Australian foreign policy (1997), which, as secretary, he had been closely involved in formulating.[15] While committed to its future in the East Asian region, the government emphasised that it attached great importance to strengthening links with the United Kingdom and Europe. Downer had remarked that one could be 'assertively, robustly and distinctively Australian' but at the same time 'have admiration and respect for the legacy of language, law, culture and institutions which have enriched Australia'.[16] On the economic side, Flood was asked to accord a high priority to pursuing Australia's commercial interests in the United Kingdom by developing strategies to attract British investment to Australia, expand bilateral trade and resolve outstanding market access issues. Howard, meanwhile, highlighted his interest in substantive celebrations in London in July 2000 to mark the centenary of the passage through the British parliament of the act providing for the creation of the Commonwealth of Australia. He wanted 'a great celebration in London' as a prelude to the events in Australia in 2001. He also wanted the high commission to raise the funds to cover expenses, and foreshadowed bringing over a large and high-level delegation from Australia (see pages 201–2).[17]

A special relationship

Despite the post-imperial evolution of the high commission into a 'normal' diplomatic post, in practice the high commissioners continued to have particular advantages in going about their work—advantages that derived from a residual sense of the specialness of the relationship. Among other things, there was unique access. Richard Smith, who had diplomatic experience in New Delhi, Washington, Geneva, Tel Aviv and Bangkok, recalled that it was possible to develop personal relationships in London that went beyond what could be expected elsewhere. This rapport promoted a unique level of frankness in discussion, if not always complete agreement.[18]

The high commissioners encountered a notable level of respect among the British élite for Australia as a very successful country that Britain had 'spawned'. In particular, Australia's modern record of economic management, including the currency and banking reforms of the early Hawke–Keating period, attracted considerable admiration in one of the world's main financial centres. It was expected that sensible policies would be maintained.[19] There was respect for the standing and achievements of numerous Australians based in Britain, most of whom were not household names, but who frequently occupied important posts. Some were not even widely known or identified as Australian, thereby underlining the ease with which Australians could move in Britain. Prowess and sportsmanship in games of British origin have also naturally gained esteem for Australia in Britain. For the UK government, there was an ease in relating to Australians, compared with others of very different cultures of governance, not least continental Europeans and Americans. 'We are in their world', commented Sir Victor Garland. By way of contrast, he added, Canadians suffered from being seen as 'pseudo-American' and unable to talk about cricket and rugby.[20]

Other advantages for the Australian high commissioner included the office and the residence. Australia House remains the oldest building continuously occupied by a 'foreign' mission in London, an Edwardian landmark on the Strand that is very central, facilitating excellent attendances at major exhibitions and other functions. The residence, Stoke Lodge, is also centrally located. Being only twenty minutes' drive from Westminster and Whitehall meant that even when parliament was sitting, it was fairly easy to arrange for appropriate members of the UK government and Opposition members to attend dinner parties for a visiting Australian minister and to debate issues around the dinner table.[21]

Being high commissioner meant holding positions ex officio in a number of important organisations of a bilateral or Commonwealth nature. Most high commissioners found that those involving significant time commitments were being a member of the Commonwealth War Graves Commission (see page 207), trustee of the Imperial War Museum, and vice-president of organisations that promoted friendly relations between the two countries, such as the Cook Society and the Britain–Australia Society.[22]

It is possible to identify two major themes over the period in which the high commissioners were centrally involved, and which stand out as having had the effect of making the relationship closer. One was the series of observances, mainly in the United Kingdom, of special anniversaries and dedications of memorials from 1987 to 2003, all of significance in the shared history between the two countries. The second was the impact of security and terrorism, especially in the years following the 11 September 2001 terrorist attacks.

Remembering: major anniversaries and memorials

The bicentenary of the arrival of the First Fleet was celebrated in Australia in 1988, but for many in the United Kingdom the more important anniversary was in 1987, with the departure from the Isle of Wight of the tall ships re-enactment. McClelland, who attended, had just arrived, and found himself much taken up with bicentennial matters. According to his own account, he visited 'every nook and cranny' of the United Kingdom, where many localities had their own committees working on what they could do to mark the occasion. He appeared on television and on radio in centres such as Edinburgh, Liverpool and Belfast. McClelland suggested, with Canberra's approval, that an Australian army detachment mount guard at Buckingham Palace to mark the occasion. The palace was persuaded to agree to this proposal 'as a very special exception to normal procedure'; a similar Dutch approach to mark the occasion of their tercentenary had been declined.[23]

McClelland, who got to know well the 'Anzac group' of members and peers (parliamentarians with a special interest in, and sympathy for, Australia), managed to persuade the UK parliament to conduct a short debate about Australia in January 1988.[24] In the House of Lords there were eight speakers in the course of nearly an hour.[25] In the Commons, during some twenty minutes of debate, the leader of the house and a further six members spoke to a motion about the presentation of a new vice-regal chair as a gift for the New Parliament House in Canberra. Some parliamentarians took the opportunity to refer to the plight of Aboriginal people, others to connections between their constituencies and Australia. One member expressed concern about 'the inhumane treatment of kangaroos and elephants in Australia'. Later, on a point of order, he corrected his reference to elephants.[26]

For some years Prime Minister Hawke had been keen to persuade the British government to release to Australia a vellum original of the British Constitution of Australia Act, 'our birth certificate'. The British initially were reluctant, but Sir Geoffrey Howe, the foreign secretary, who visited Australia in 1987, became convinced of the

Australian case. Another sympathiser was the British parliamentarian Alfred Morris, whom a number of Australian high commissioners had known well, and who was a long-standing member of the Anzac group. Morris, then in Opposition, decided to try to resolve the matter through legislation. In the House of Commons on 12 February 1990 he introduced a private member's bill. Eventually, on 23 August of that year, Howe and Morris together presented a vellum original at Parliament House, Canberra.[27]

The other notable Australian national anniversary to be celebrated in these years was the centenary of federation. As noted earlier in this chapter, the decision to mark this occasion with celebrations in London during 2000 arose from an instruction to Flood from Prime Minister John Howard. It was a major undertaking, involving numerous large-scale ceremonies and functions. It also became known as Australia Week, and a donation from the National Australia Bank covered much of the cost. Flood received 'excellent cooperation' from the Palace, Blair, the British parliament, Westminster Abbey, the City of London, business people and many others. Australia's Federation Guard, consisting of navy, army and air force components, took up duty at Buckingham Palace, St James's Palace and the Tower of London. One third of the guard were women, for the first time in British history; 'The Queen loved it'.[28] The presence of the Royal Australian Navy guarding the Tower of London was also notable. Traditionally, the monarch had not allowed the tower to be guarded by the navy, who were deemed to be untrustworthy because of the large number of sailors press-ganged into service.

For the British, the emphasis at many of the functions was 'respect and admiration for the kind of vibrant country Australia had become'.[29] In one speech, Blair spoke with such enthusiasm about Australia that one British newspaper was moved to comment that 'the more Blair went on painting this picture of utopia, the more one sensed that Mr Blair would actually prefer to be Prime Minister of Australia'.[30]

There was a full program of arts events sponsored by the Australia Council. Flood persuaded the National Gallery of Australia to lend forty paintings and drawings by Arthur Boyd from its collection for an exhibition at Australia House. That Carole Flood, the high commissioner's wife, had worked previously at the gallery was a major help. The exhibition was opened by Princess Anne. Flood, however, wanted to ensure that 'over and beyond the pageantry and symbolism there were substantive themes of benefit to Australia'.[31] Consequently, the celebrations promoted trade, two-way investment, British tourism to Australia, and images of Australia as a sophisticated and culturally diverse society. The British government responded positively to Australian efforts to deal with one particular legacy of colonialism, the issue of repatriation of Aboriginal human remains found in both British public and private collections. The two prime ministers issued a joint declaration during Howard's July 2000 visit vowing to accelerate the repatriation effort. Later amendments to British legislation resulted in the remains of many Indigenous people being returned to their country.[32]

Howard brought with him a major delegation of notables from both federal and state levels of government, probably the largest high-level group that had ever proceeded overseas, including the chief justice, five state premiers, the president of the Senate and the speaker of the House of Representatives, as well as four former prime ministers (all living former UK prime ministers were also involved). Among letters of appreciation which Flood received afterwards was one from Whitlam 'on behalf of the largest horde of admitted and aspiring Australian celebrities ever to descend on London'.[33]

Celebrations in 1993 of the seventy-fifth anniversary of Australia House, as a 'tangible symbol of the relationship' between the two countries, coincided with a visit to the United Kingdom by Prime Minister Paul Keating. Smith had got wind of a 'sly move' to be rid of the building. He had written to Canberra, but found on talking to Keating on arrival that he accepted the argument to retain it.[34] Indeed on an earlier visit, as treasurer, Keating had left no doubt of his deep appreciation of the building, its architecture and its history.[35]

The effort to remember and honour the cooperation and common sacrifice of Australia and Britain in war has involved the recent high commissioners. The commemoration of the final stages and the end of World War II in Europe helped strengthen relations by reminding the British public of the Australian contribution. Keating, who had recently given some public support to the idea that Britain had abandoned Australia over the fall of Singapore in 1942, attended the D-day commemoration in Portsmouth in June 1994, along with members of the royal family, President Clinton, and most of the monarchs whose countries had been allies.[36] In the following year Prince Charles, with Neal Blewett, unveiled a memorial in the village of Sutton Veny in Wiltshire where about 140 Australian soldiers and nurses died from the outbreak of influenza in 1918–19. Children from the local school tended their graves at the local church. L'Estrange later initiated an annual cricket game in Sutton Veny between the high commission and the village team.[37]

A much larger memorial was unveiled in London in 2003. It came about following a personal initiative of Flood. Although Anzac Day was traditionally well marked in London, he felt there should be an official monument to the cooperation between Australia and Britain in military campaigns, and was concerned that over time younger generations of Britons would become ever less aware of Australia's contribution in the two world wars. Noting the Canadian memorial located opposite the Canada Gate of Buckingham Palace, he recommended to Howard that it would be appropriate for an Australian memorial to be established, possibly near the Australia Gate. Flood received permission to raise the proposal with the British government. With scant regard for the new nationalist sensitivities in either country, its initial response was to suggest a joint memorial with New Zealand. But Flood felt the New Zealanders would prefer their own, and the government's view was strongly in favour of a dedicated Australian memorial. The high commissioner saw Tony Blair, who was 'positive', but he then had to secure the support of many London authorities with powers independent of the British government, including Royal Parks. An opportunity arose to speak to the Queen about the proposal, and she 'warmly welcomed it'. British agreement to the memorial became an outcome of Australia Week. On return to Australia, Flood was invited to be a member of the advisory committee in Australia that was charged with selecting a design for the memorial, and he later attended its opening.[38]

It was for his successor, L'Estrange, to gain support of interested groups for a suitable site at Hyde Park Corner, and to see through the long process of approvals, including from Westminster Council and Prince Charles. The memorial was opened by the Queen on Remembrance Day, 11 November 2003. The prime minister and armed services chiefs of each country attended, as did the Federation Guard. Air space over Heathrow airport was closed, and traffic around the site stopped during the ceremony. Taking place during the continuing challenge of terrorism and the Afghanistan and Iraq wars in which both countries were engaged, the event was 'a convergence of history and the contemporary'.[39]

Security and terrorism

London remained one of the most secure diplomatic capitals, yet the Irish Republican Army posed a threat throughout much of the period, until the Good Friday Agreement in Belfast in 1998. The situation in Northern Ireland, although a matter of some public interest in Australia, was not normally of direct concern to Australian governments. Most high commissioners visited there at least once, often in response to personal invitations from British ministers. Alston attended the reopening of the Stormont parliament on 8 May 2007.

In 1984, the Irish Republican Army made an attempt on the life of Margaret Thatcher during the Conservative Party annual conference at Brighton. Parsons, who was attending as an observer, was the only diplomat booked into the hotel in which Thatcher, her principal ministers, and senior party officials were staying. On 12 October at 2.54 a.m., an explosion in the hotel caused the death of five people and injuries to thirty, as well as doing considerable damage to the building. Parsons, who was on the sixth floor, recalls that in his room the whole of the wall, and the floor between him and the next room where the bomb was located, both disappeared, as did the block of rooms below him. Luckily, a partition panel had fallen on him first, shielding him from 'a great heap of bricks and other rubbish' that fell after the explosion. He was left 'totally unscathed' apart from the shock, but the wife of the chairman of the Scottish Conservative Party, who was next door, was blown into the high commissioner's room and later died. Parsons was spared worse as a result of a hotel booking error. A member of parliament, Sir Anthony Berry, who had been placed in the suite originally booked for Parsons, died from injuries sustained there.[40]

The 11 September 2001 terrorist attacks on New York and Washington DC brought in their wake heightened security measures in London, the need for which was underlined by the bombings in Bali in 2002, in London in 2005, and the attempts there and in Glasgow in 2007. Following the Bali bombings, the high commission arranged at short notice a memorial service at St Paul's Cathedral, which was attended by the Queen, Prince Philip, Prince Charles, Deputy Prime Minister John Prescott and other UK ministers, as well as the family and friends of the victims, both Australian and British. The cathedral was full, with huge numbers remaining outside in the rain. In 2007 the London memorial to the Bali bombings was unveiled in a ceremony in which Alston read out the name of each of the Australian victims.

The traditionally close strategic relationship between Australia and Britain developed an even greater intimacy in their common response to the dramatic changes following 11 September. After the attacks in New York and Washington, L'Estrange's immediate concerns turned to the security of his staff and of Australia House and its perimeter. Access to the building was tightened and contingency plans revisited. It was, says L'Estrange, 'a traumatic and destabilising period geostrategically', but professionally staff kept their heads. Policy staff 'fanned out and plugged into UK thinking', their work acquiring 'an added sense of urgency'.[41] London and Washington were the main centres of policy development in response to global terrorism, and L'Estrange recalled that professionally it was 'the best time to have been High Commissioner for 50 years'. Moreover, although terrorism was its focal point, this closeness spilled over helpfully into other fields.[42] L'Estrange's task was made easier by the 'very good rapport' between prime ministers Blair and Howard, although they led governments with different political labels and tendencies: 'They liked one another and had high regard for each other's opinions and abilities'.[43] But there were significant differences between the governments. For example, during 2006–07 Alston devoted much time to explaining the Howard government's policy on climate change.[44] Coincidentally, Howard served as chairperson-in-office of the Commonwealth early in the century, while Downer, his foreign minister, chaired the Commonwealth Ministerial Action Group. These responsibilities provided additional reasons to visit London, enabling further high-level contact in Whitehall. Over the two-year period (2002–04) in which he was Commonwealth chairperson-in-office, Howard made five short working visits.[45]

A key question, as decisions on the Iraq war loomed, was the outlook of allies. For Canberra, it was 'Would UK policy shift?' For the United Kingdom, it was 'Would Australian policy shift?' And the United States was asking similar questions. Would anyone shift ground? 'So getting the British bottom line was crucial', which meant keeping in close touch with Blair's thinking. L'Estrange recalled that in the end he had no doubt that, on Iraq, Blair would carry his party, despite some divisions and defections.[46] The United States, Australia and the United Kingdom formed a 'coalition of the willing' in the war against Iraq that began in 2003.

L'Estrange developed a close working relationship with Number 10, especially with Sir David Manning, who during 2001–03 was in a pivotal position as Blair's foreign policy adviser and head of the Defence and Overseas Secretariat in the Cabinet Office.[47] Manning, for his part, found L'Estrange 'extremely shrewd, experienced and well informed', and 'valued talking the issues through with him'. He considered that L'Estrange 'did an excellent job in projecting Australia to the whole of the British Government, and to the British media', and that 'his period as High Commissioner was almost certainly one of the high watermarks in recent years of the invaluable partnership between the UK and Australia'.[48] Besides 11 September, Al Qaida, Afghanistan and Iraq, other major subjects which they discussed included Iran and the confrontation between India and Pakistan, the latter precipitated by the terrorist attack on the Indian parliament in December 2001, followed by troop mobilisation and military exchanges across the line of control in Kashmir. British perspectives on a possible dangerous escalation in the situation were a source of significant interest, given their special insights on the subcontinent. The tension there did not subside until during the last quarter of 2002.[49]

Defence relations

There were a number of other issues on the high commissioners' agendas during the period that were also important in their own right, if less influential than the subjects already examined in setting the tone of the official relationship between the two countries. While the United States had in the 1950s gradually superseded Britain as Australia's primary security partner, there still remained some unfinished business from that twilight of British Australia. One was 1950s British atomic testing at Maralinga in the South Australian desert, and especially allegations of damage to the health of Aboriginal people living in the vicinity of the trials and contamination of their traditional lands. The 1984 Australian Royal Commission into British Nuclear Testing in Australia was presided over by Justice James McClelland, a flamboyant and outspoken former Whitlam government minister, and former chief justice of the NSW Land and Environment Court. On one occasion he took exception to public comments by the British high commissioner in Canberra, whom McClelland thought reluctant to cooperate with his inquiry: 'I suppose the British High Commissioner will be asking next that our history books omit all reference to the nasty way Henry VIII treated his wives'.[50]

When McClelland also said some 'rude things' about Margaret Thatcher, Parsons recalled that 'we had a bit of a problem, and I had to see Maggie once or twice'.[51] Nevertheless, in representations to Thatcher on Maralinga, Parsons 'found it difficult to keep the conversation on the subject'. Her technique was to 'divert the conversation by interrupting with say, a generalised comment about the unique colours of the Australian outback, or the stark beauty of the desert'. Given minimal chance of eliciting any substantive response, he endeavoured to reiterate his points, 'at least twice'. This was to ensure that 'at least the official note-taker did not miss it and in the belief that if it got into the official record, it would register somewhere in the system and have to be taken into account, even if not by the Prime Minister'.[52] When Douglas McClelland, on arrival in London in 1987, presented Thatcher with his letter of appointment, she was sufficiently well briefed to remark that he was not related to the judge of the same name.[53] It was not until 1993 that the United Kingdom agreed to pay £20 million to settle Australia's claims for the damage caused by the tests.[54]

Despite the decline in the defence relationship between Australia and Britain after the 'east of Suez' withdrawal, there was still a fairly constant flow of business in this field. McClelland was once called in by Thatcher, who told him that UK efforts to reconcile with Argentina after the Falklands war were being impeded by Australia's intention to sell second-hand Mirage planes to the Argentine air force. McClelland encountered reluctance in Canberra to stop a sale worth $180 million, but argued that it would not do Australia's name much good internationally if it went ahead. Kim Beazley, the defence minister, arranged for the Mirages to be sold elsewhere.[55]

In 1999 Howard wanted to secure a UK troop contribution to Interfet in East Timor under the leadership of General Peter Cosgrove. Early British reaction was that, with commitments in Bosnia, Kosovo and Northern Ireland, troops could not be spared for Timor. However, Flood's approaches to high-level figures in the Ministry of Defence, as well as to Blair, produced results. A Gurkha contingent, which had been based nearby in Brunei, arrived quickly.[56] The United Kingdom's assistance was welcomed by Howard, who had wanted the multinational force to include strong representation from the Asian region. Flood also played an important role in encouraging UK support in the UN Security Council in New York, which contributed to Australia achieving a UN 'blue helmet' operation in East Timor.

Pension rights

Pension rights for British migrants to Australia were the subject of a campaign by the Australian government over many years and, despite more general cooperation in social security issues, it largely fell on deaf ears. Britons in receipt of UK pensions attracted indexation if they went to the United States or the European Union, but not if they migrated to Australia, Canada, New Zealand or South Africa. When Alston once raised the matter with a British minister, the latter said he would 'put you down as having mentioned it'. On being further pressed, he agreed to change that to the high commissioner being 'outraged'.[57] Representations from visiting Australian ministers supplemented continuing efforts of high commissioners and their staff, but the British would not give ground because of the costs involved. Despite this 'miserly attitude', recalled Blewett, British ministers 'had no argument in principle'.[58]

The Commonwealth

Headquartered in London, the Commonwealth was an organisation in which Australia, as one of the oldest members and a major financial contributor, continued to have a significant role after 1980. Sometimes, there were strong policy divergences from the

United Kingdom, especially in relation to apartheid in South Africa during the 1980s. On the Commonwealth Committee on Southern Africa, which Parsons chaired for a time, Britain was in an isolated position, given Thatcher's hardline opposition to economic sanctions.[59] When the post of secretary-general of the Commonwealth later became vacant in 1989, the Hawke government nominated former prime minister Malcolm Fraser. But his own hard line against apartheid, and the differences between the British and Australian official perspectives on the issue, contributed to Thatcher's unwillingness to support the bid.[60]

Howard's time as chairperson-in-office of the Commonwealth led to Australia adopting a higher profile. Australia hosted the Commonwealth Heads of Government Meeting at Coolum in March 2002, and Commonwealth Ministerial Action Group meetings (at foreign minister level) two or three times a year, which Downer normally attended. L'Estrange was 'heavily involved', including once deputising for Downer at a Commonwealth Heads of Government Meeting in Abuja in September 2001, and accompanying Howard to the Commonwealth Ministerial Action Group meeting there in December 2003. In 2007 the group's meeting, at Kampala, Uganda, coincided with the Australian federal elections, so Alston attended as the prime minister's special representative and leader of the delegation.[61]

A continuing role, indeed 'a sacred duty' of the high commissioner, was involvement in the Commonwealth War Graves Commission. In 1990 McClelland represented the commission at Gallipoli on the seventy-fifth anniversary of the landing there. Afterwards, at the request of the Australian minister for veterans' affairs, Ben Humphreys, he visited Australian graves in Greece and Crete. Flood worked through the commission on a sensitive matter of Australian use of a new site at Gallipoli for Anzac Day observances. In return, Turkey insisted on support for a new Turkish monument for its war dead in the Palestine theatre of World War I, to be situated in Israel.[62]

An earlier matter involving the War Graves Commission concerned the Tomb of the Unknown Warrior in Westminster Abbey. The tomb was intended to represent all parts of the Commonwealth, and British authorities had resisted attempts of other countries to have similar memorials. In some ways, the proposal that Australia should have its own tomb 'struck at the heart of the relationship'. The proposal, supported by Prime Minister Keating, was a major undertaking. Richard Smith approached the War Graves Commission, but the reaction being not very positive, individual representations were made to each member of the commission. Smith later learned that the Queen had also been consulted.[63] Eventually there was agreement, clearing the way for the remains of an unknown Australian soldier, in a War Graves Commission cemetery in France, to be removed and interred in the Hall of Memory at the Australian War Memorial in Canberra.

Other aspects of the high commissioner role

Support and promotion of Australian business and investment were important parts of the high commissioner's role throughout the period covered in this chapter. So too was involvement in trade policy. Occasionally, Parsons found it necessary to register an Australian viewpoint at the highest level 'over some of the more outrageous excesses of the Common Agricultural Policy of the EU'.[64] Similarly, Garland and Flood, each of whom came into the job with comprehensive knowledge of the often complex trade policy issues, became involved in detailed discussions with British ministers. For the most part, Britain's own problems in Brussels precluded offering Australia much help, however willing the British were to listen. Indeed, Parsons was once invited by former prime minister Sir Edward Heath, whose own government negotiated UK accession to the Treaty of Rome, to put Australian views to a group in his own constituency.[65] Alston gave evidence before a committee of the House of Lords in 2005 about whether the European Union should cease subsidising beet sugar.[66]

The coexistence of two organisations, the Australian Business In Europe group and the Australia–New Zealand Chamber of Commerce, had for some time created unnecessary complications in the effective representation of Australian business in the United Kingdom. Eventually, the time seemed right for a merger into one organisation. The leader of the group trying to arrange the merger found L'Estrange 'very supportive' and helpful behind the scenes. The high commissioner strongly encouraged the two organisations to start talking with each other. There were sensitivities in relation to New Zealand, not least given the tendency of some involved in UK business to think of Australia and New Zealand as 'joined together'. It proved helpful to the credibility of the proposed new organisation, especially with UK business, that the concept had the endorsement of the high commissioner. Once the new organisation, Australian Business, was established, L'Estrange remained supportive, for example by hosting joint receptions at Australia House to which the 'heavy hitters' of UK business would come.[67]

Probably in no other Australian post was the head of mission in so much demand for public speaking. For instance, Flood encountered an interest in honouring the Nobel Prize–winning Australian scientist Lord Florey, in 1999, the centenary of his birth. The high commissioner was invited to speak at two Oxford Colleges and at the Royal Society.[68] Media briefings also formed a part of the high commissioner's work. Yet, despite a consciousness of Australia not found anywhere else except perhaps in New Zealand, the frequency of informative news about Australia in the 'ten ferociously competitive daily newspapers' of London[69] varied greatly. It was therefore important to make the most of suitable opportunities to correct public misconceptions about modern Australia. The high commissioner invariably played an important part in this mission throughout the period, through briefing the UK media, public speeches, and occasional appearances on British radio and television.[70] Flood recalled speaking about the Asian financial crisis, the Australian economy and the treatment of kangaroos and sheep.[71]

Garland was interviewed on British television after the devastating Ash Wednesday bushfires in Victoria in 1983. Occasionally there was a need to respond to requests to appear on Australian television. Following the London bombings in 2005, Alston was interviewed on the ABC *7.30 Report*. McClelland recalled having responded to charges of harsh treatment of animals in Australia, which arose periodically at the community rather than government level, notably about the culling of kangaroos. Earlier, Parsons witnessed the leader of one protest group scaling the front of Australia House onto the balcony outside his office, and being hustled away by security. The keeper of the Queen's horses twice raised concerns about the treatment of brumbies.[72]

In the period leading up to the referendum in November 1999 on the question of an Australian republic, Blewett, who had been appointed while Keating was prime minister, felt able to deliver pro-republican speeches, for example at a Menzies Memorial Lecture in 1995.[73] He continued when Howard took office. Prime Minister John Major was unconcerned about such debate on the republican question, but felt it could affect relations if the controversy became protracted. The palace also seemed relaxed; in Blewett's view, its main concern was that Australian republicanism did not influence British attitudes towards the monarchy.[74] Blewett's successor, Flood, felt in a different situation, since he was in office at the time of the referendum. Howard, in appointing him to London, had been aware of Flood's pro-republican sympathies, but trusted him to keep his views to himself. The high commissioner was involved in advising the palace throughout the period leading up to the referendum.[75]

Cultural activities were also important, and as discussed in chapter 14, the magnificent facilities of Australia House were used for special exhibitions and events. Blewett arranged for exhibitions of the art of Will Dyson and on the history of the Ashes test series, the latter opened by the cricket-loving John Howard. With Clive James, Alston opened an exhibition on the art of John Olsen. Modern high commissioners have been regularly called on to launch exhibitions of Aboriginal art, and in 2005 Alston launched an Indigenous cultural program.[76] In 1982, Lyn Garland, the wife of the high commissioner and a noted concert pianist, gave a recital at Australia House, which was attended by some 400 people, including half the UK cabinet.[77] Prime Minister Major did not visit Australia while in office but his wife, Dame Norma, wrote the authorised biography of Joan Sutherland.[78] In November 1996, Neal Blewett held a birthday banquet for Dame Joan at which the Majors were principal guests.[79]

High commissioners often drew on their high-level access to contribute to the post's reporting. As Foreign Minister Gareth Evans told McClelland in a letter congratulating him on his 'considerable success' in London, 'There is no adequate replacement for the considered comment of an experienced person on the spot, enjoying both wide access to the local leadership and an excellent understanding of our own national interests'.[80] Not least was this so at times of crisis, and to validate the authenticity of information and analysis. During the Falklands war a cable from Garland based on discussion with UK cabinet ministers drew the comment from Canberra that 'the source of such confirmatory comments is significant and was of more than passing interest to us. We continue to regard the wide range of high level contacts which you have developed as most valuable'.[81] The Australian government was evidently worried about some of the wider ramifications of the conflict, and especially those touching on the question of US policy.[82] Blewett, who often 'fed in' comments to reports by his staff, recalled two examples in particular. One concerned the 1997 UK general elections, where Blewett brought to bear his earlier experience as a political scientist with a specialist's knowledge of British political history.[83] He had consulted widely, including keeping in touch with David Butler, the Oxford psephologist, and predicted the 'landslide' win by the Labour Party that eventually occurred. Another report, he recalled, also in 1997, captured the 'febrile atmosphere' in London in the immediate aftermath of the death of Diana, Princess of Wales.[84]

Leadership forum 2003

In early 2003, L'Estrange conceived the idea of convening in London a select group of invitees from both countries, a leadership forum, to discuss the relationship and generally 'stir the pot'. The plan owed much to the precedent set by the Australian American Leadership Dialogue, founded in 1992 and conducted regularly since. To encourage as free a dialogue as possible at this inaugural gathering, it was to be a 'closed' discussion with no outcomes. L'Estrange was concerned about complacency, and the need to look for 'under-utilised opportunities' and discuss common challenges. He wanted a gathering of key leaders, small enough to allow all to speak and feel involved, yet broad enough to produce a wide range of views.

It was partly a matter of opportunity and timing. L'Estrange received the support of Downer and Howard, who would both be attending the opening of the Australian War Memorial at Hyde Park Corner on 11 November. The forum would be held soon after that. Achieving Blair's early agreement to attend was critical. L'Estrange then personally invited a select number of other key figures in the United Kingdom; and using links forged while he was cabinet secretary in Canberra, invited a select number of Australians.[85]

The forum of close to a hundred participants comprised Blair and Howard, their key ministers, leading Opposition parliamentarians from both countries, including Kevin Rudd, later Labor prime minister, and major figures in business, academia and community organisations. Bringing together such a group, reported one of the participants, was 'a big coup'.[86] They gathered over dinner at Australia House on the evening of Remembrance Day and discussions continued the next day. The UK government made available Lancaster House, and hosted a lunch. The forum, which, according to the London-based former Australian diplomat Michael Cook, was 'chaired brilliantly' by L'Estrange, turned out to be 'a huge success'.[87] Sir Roger Carrick, formerly a British high commissioner to Australia, recalled that it was doubtful whether the forum 'would have happened then, or included so many high level people on both sides without his standing, inspiration, leadership and intellect'.[88]

Mission management

High commissioners have ultimate responsibility for the welfare of staff, both Australia-based and locally engaged, and for effective use of official Australian resources. Overall staffing numbers continued to decline through this period, notably among the locally engaged staff. In early 1981 the total staff was 606, but by April 1983 a 38 per cent cut over two years had reduced London numbers to 'about 400', of whom seventy were Australia-based. Garland expressed the view to Bill Hayden, the new minister, that 'present operations are cut to the bone, and any further reductions would require discarding functions which up to now have been regarded as essential'.[89] But by 1993 Smith had to preside over another 'massive cut' of about 25 per cent, to about 250. Smith became closely involved, including in meetings with the Locally Engaged Staff Association.[90] By 2008 there were just over 200 personnel, of whom forty were Australia-based.[91]

This gradual reduction seems not to have been driven by any long-term plan to achieve a particular level of operation. Rather, it was due to a general desire to modernise, to the exploitation of new technologies, and to reactions to periodic pressure on Canberra agencies represented in Australia House, especially the Department of Foreign Affairs and Trade, to stay within tight budgets and achieve 'efficiency dividends'. Some agencies withdrew completely, while others reduced the scale of their operations. In 2002–03, L'Estrange introduced the locally engaged staff to a new arrangement for a more modern employment system, for which an overwhelming majority voted in favour.

In the mid-1990s, Blewett presided over 'an imaginative refurbishment' of Australia House, which had been initiated and developed by Smith.[92] Most of the state agents-general relocated into the new Australia Centre area of the building, opened in 1996 (see page 233). This provided centralised access to information on trade and investment from Austrade and state government offices, while the agents-general retained their separate identity and profile.

Stoke Lodge remained the high commissioner's residence, despite some attempts to sell it. It was well liked by the Queen and many British visitors.[93] In 1988, when McClelland learned that there was a move afoot in Canberra to sell it, he was about to accompany Thatcher on an Australian visit. She asked him not only about what matters Australian ministers were likely to raise with her, but also if there was anything he would like her to bring up. He told her of the proposal to put Stoke Lodge up for sale. She was shocked: 'The best bungalow in London?' It was said that Thatcher told Hawke that a proposal to sell would be up to him, but 'don't expect me to visit you in the suburbs'.[94] McClelland, however, ascertained that neither Hawke nor Keating, the treasurer, had realised that Stoke Lodge had been included in a long list of overseas properties that the Department of Finance had drawn up for proposed sale. Neither favoured discarding it.

Hawke suggested McClelland talk to Keating about renovations. As for a cost estimate, McClelland 'plucked a figure out of the sky' to which Keating agreed.[95]

Conclusion

This chapter has attempted to describe the breadth of activity and responsibility that engaged the high commissioners in the most recent period. Traditional tasks continued; crises, pressures and opportunities arose; and there was a constantly changing managerial role for the high commissioner as head of mission. The position remained demanding. London was at the heart of a unique bilateral relationship but one, in the words of one former incumbent, that 'should not be taken for granted', needing to be constantly 'worked at'.[96] The high commissioner had a primary role here, staying abreast of developments, judging where to be personally involved, and carrying out the wide responsibilities of a demanding position. McClelland felt that he treated the role 'as if occupying a marginal seat'.[97] It was the high commissioner on the spot who was usually in the best position to identify opportunities to advance national interests, and to pursue them.

Sir Victor Garland (third from right) arranging for the Australian government to borrow 15,000 million Japanese yen, 15 July 1981. [Photograph courtesy of Sir Victor Garland]

Alfred Parsons at Stoke Lodge. [Photograph courtesy of Alfred Parsons]

Alfred Parsons (right) with former UK Prime Minister Sir Edward Heath. [Photograph courtesy of Alfred Parsons]

Douglas McClelland (left) accompanying Australian Prime Minister Bob Hawke (third from right) on a visit to the Australian test cricket team captained by Allan Border (second from right) at Lords in 1989. Dean Jones is in the foreground. [Photograph courtesy of Douglas McClelland]

Douglas McClelland inside Australia House.
[Photograph courtesy of Douglas McClelland]

Meeting of Australian and UK ministers in the cabinet room at Number 10 Downing Street,
London, 1989. Douglas McClelland is seated second from right. Facing each other are
UK Prime Minister Margaret Thatcher (third from left) and Australian Prime Minister
Bob Hawke (fourth from right). [Photograph courtesy of Douglas McClelland]

Richard Smith (left), accompanying Australian Prime Minister Paul Keating to Australia House in 1993. [Photograph courtesy of Richard Smith]

Australian Prime Minister Paul Keating (left) speaking at the 75th anniversary of Australia House as Richard Smith looks on. [Photograph courtesy of Richard Smith]

Neal Blewett (second from left) with Prince Charles (second from right) at the unveiling of a memorial at Sutton Veny in Wiltshire, which honours about 140 Australian soldiers and nurses who died in the influenza outbreak in 1918–19. [Photograph courtesy of Neal Blewett]

Philip Flood (left) and Carole Flood (second from right) with the Queen (second from left) and the Duke of Edinburgh at Stoke Lodge, London, 8 March 2000. [Photograph courtesy of Philip Flood]

Michael L'Estrange (left) welcoming UK Prime Minister Tony Blair to Australia House, November 2002. [Department of Foreign Affairs and Trade]

Michael L'Estrange (centre) opening an exhibition of paintings by Indigenous artist Rosella Namok (right) at the October Gallery in central London, October 2004. [Department of Foreign Affairs and Trade]

Richard Alston (left) at Stratford-on-Avon on Shakespeare's birthday.
[Photograph courtesy of Richard Alston]

Former Australian high commissioners to the United Kingdom at a colloquium at University
House, Australian National University, Canberra, April 2009. From left: Victor Garland, Alfred
Parsons, Douglas McClelland, Richard Smith, Neal Blewett, Philip Flood and Richard Alston.
[Photograph courtesy of Jeremy Hearder]

14 Australia's house

Simon Sleight

FOOTSORE and weary, the Cathcarts seek the familiar. Arriving from Kenya on their once-in-a-lifetime tour—'the Big-Un'—in Murray Bail's *Homesickness* (1980), Doug Cathcart and his wife make haste for Australia House. Here, in contrast to their trying encounters with Africa's food and museums and their instant aversion to London's cloying history and dismal bathrooms, the couple find to their relief that 'it was easy'. 'They could sit down beneath the chandeliers ... and leaf through their own newspapers, amid the sounds and brown appearances of their own people'.[1] The Cathcarts, in short, have come home. Could he have witnessed the scene, Sir George Reid would doubtless have expressed delight. Not for nothing did he suggest in 1914 that the Australian High Commission be named 'Australia House', believing 'that the word "House" carries with it the idea of a "home" for Australia in London, and would mark out this particular part of London as Australian'.[2] Across almost a century this simple proposal has shaped public perceptions of, and expectations for, this iconic national building. Preceding and following the Cathcarts, tens of thousands of visitors have brought their own aspirations to Australia House, made use if its facilities and taken away a range of impressions about its utility. This chapter charts their stories, shifting attention away from high politics and focusing upon the everyday activities and evolving group dynamics of those stepping off the Strand and across a national threshold.

Place, scholars now generally acknowledge, is space made meaningful.[3] The study of place—or what Henri Lefebvre refers to as 'social space'—promises to enhance historical understanding of the ways in which people and settings interact. For Lefebvre and others inspired by his writings, space and spatial practice are interdependent: spaces and spatial convention anticipate behaviour, while the users of space mould its form and manipulate its meanings.[4] This two-way process can be seen by looking within the walls of London's Australia House. As a national building conceived for an imperial capital, Australia House is at least doubly situated. Like an airport transit lounge or border crossing point, the high commission embodies a peculiar sovereignty, its usage revealing much about the contingent place where identity is fostered and modified beyond the usual boundaries of state. Promoted by Reid as far more than merely a bureaucratic hub for Australian diplomats, Australia House has long played host to activities beyond the remit of other foreign missions. Unsurprisingly, this ambitious course has resulted over time in a confusion of roles—as Olwen Pryke illustrates in her doctoral study of the building's representative meaning, the issue of the high commission's primary purpose was 'never conclusively resolved', with compromise a keynote and a 'tense interplay between symbolic and more practical functions' characterising its history.[5]

An instructive way to think about these functions is to ponder Isabel Edgar's 1930 description of Australia House as 'a national "foyer"';[6] regarded in this light the high commission serves to facilitate personal interaction and represents an anteroom for the nation-space of Australia. Keeping in mind Edgar's image of the building, what can be discovered about its social role? How, we might ask, did Australia House cater to the needs of successive generations of Australian and British visitors? What expectations did they attach to the building and how did these shift over time? And, over the course of nearly a century, to what extent has Australia House lived up to its name?

The national foyer: its early years

In advance of its opening in August 1918, the London *Times* described for readers the layout of Australia House. Its catalogue provides a useful orientation:

> The building has 10 floors, allocated as follows:– Lower basement: stores, treasury, cinematograph and lecture hall … Upper basement: strong room and other accommodation for Commonwealth Bank and photographic department. Ground floor: entrance hall, exhibition hall, Strand branch of the Commonwealth Bank, and offices of the Orient Royal Mail Steamship Line to Australia. Entresol floor: telephone exchange, claims branch, and Inland Revenue. First floor: rooms of the High Commissioner, official secretary, assistant secretary, suite of rooms for the Prime Minister of Australia, and intelligence and registration branches. Second and third floors: claims branch and Inland Revenue. Fourth floor: accounts, customs, shipping, priority, pensions, and supply departments. Fifth floor: offices of H.M. Australian Navy, and the Commonwealth Line of steamers. Sixth floor: military adviser, arsenal, munition workers and publicity departments.[7]

Photographs included in the subsequent commemorative program depict a rather cheerless interior, tastefully furnished with Australian materials but devoid of social activity.[8] Indeed, with the building accommodating wounded Australian soldiers for presentation to the King, the high commission more resembled a convalescent home than the thriving social centre it was to become. The presence of a visitors' book (signed by the royal couple after the investiture) indicates an intention for house guests to inspect the premises, but the book's initial location in the high commissioner's office suggests that callers were envisaged to be few in number and select in status.[9] Nonetheless, provision in the lower basement and on the ground floor for a lecture theatre, exhibition space, banks and ticketing facilities all hint at more public uses, and indeed throughout the 1920s the range of services on offer at Australia House expanded considerably in line with increasing numbers of visitors entering the building.[10] In the entrance foyer, the British Australasian bookstall soon commenced trading in Australian periodicals, leaflets and assorted souvenirs; in 1925, staff from the locally produced *British Australian and*

New Zealander newspaper moved in (also opening an inquiry bureau close to their already established bookshop); in 1926, the high commissioner's room received a Marconi wireless set—henceforth allowing news bulletins to be circulated among visitors and staff—and at around the same time the Australian Travel Service opened offices to serve the needs of tourists.[11]

Allied to these services, and the various government departments already detailed, two other facilities at the high commission also merit discussion. In 1919, the Australia House Cinema commenced free screenings for filmgoers attracted by a large sign on the Strand. The cinema operated between 10 a.m. and 5 p.m. on weekdays and 10 a.m. and midday on Saturdays, with early features including a film showing the work of returned servicemen cultivating oranges at Kerang in Victoria, and scenes of the Australian bush that were said to have elicited 'cries of pleasure' from a homesick audience.[12] Later the Duke and Duchess of York attended a private viewing of a film recording the 1927 royal tour of Australia and opening of the federal parliament, and in 1936 a Gordon Donkin presented footage from his own trip around Australia.[13] The cinema's more regular fare— government-sponsored films promoting Australia to British audiences—proved immensely popular, with staff reporting annual attendances of 400,000 by the end of the 1920s.[14] High Commissioner Ryrie and newspaper editor Charles Chomley expressed concern, however, about the type of people attending the free daytime screenings, observing that audiences were composed in large measure of 'the idle and the curious', a group with ample time to spare yet precious little cash for investment.[15] Could 'a different class' of spectator be attracted, Chomley asked, by opening the cinema on Sundays and in the evenings when potential settlers and businessmen could attend?[16]

The Australia House Library formed the second noteworthy attraction. Located in its initial inception in what is now the Downer Room on the first floor, the library operated during the 1920s as a limited reference collection, with Australian newspapers and a selection of periodicals including the *Bulletin* on hand, as well as guidebooks and timetables to serve the needs of tourists and statistical, legislative and reference material for those readers interested in the business affairs of individual states.[17] Clearly the facility was well used: in 1926, the *British Australian and New Zealander* noted that 'for some months past, visitors to the library have averaged about 400 a day' and further commended H.N. Southwell, the 'indefatigable' librarian, for his diligence.[18] Southwell's duties far exceeded the standard tasks of colleagues in other establishments. As well as cataloguing and maintaining the reading collection, Southwell answered 'innumerable questions' about attractions in Britain and life in Australia and hosted regular meetings in the library for organisations including the Australian Women's Welfare Committee.[19] He also sold tickets for evening balls in Australia House, collected names of volunteers for events such as the annual Armistice Day poppy appeal and compiled the *Australian Guide Book to London*, already in its fifth edition by 1925.[20] Supplementing this workload, Southwell became involved in other aspects of Australia House life, chairing meetings of the Australia House Junior Cricket Club, arranging bowls matches and a tour to Warwickshire for Australia House bowls players, and even dressing up as Father Christmas in 1927 for a high commission treat for 200 of London's impoverished children.[21]

Southwell's activities indicate a lively staff culture at Australia House in the 1920s. Sports teams flourished, with at least four men's cricket sides competing in and around London while their female colleagues formed a Physical Exercises Section and took to Northampton the 'Australia House March', a routine climaxing in the formation of a circle of twenty-four gymnasts, the display in the centre of an Australian flag, and a 'really good Australian coo-ee'.[22] Back at base, the Australia House Social Club hosted evening balls as well as whist drives, fancy dress parties and comic plays. In March 1927, the Musical and Dramatic Section put on 'Lord Richard in the Pantry', following up this well-reviewed entertainment with 'A Little Bit of Fluff' in 1928.[23] Evening social occasions such as these allowed the various branches of Australia House to mix and for the staff—around 340-strong in 1928—to bring their British friends and partners or else make further Australian acquaintances if they were British themselves.[24] It was here, too, that modern international dance routines like the Charleston and Yale Blues were practised alongside others more specifically national in content like the 'Boomerang' and the 'Kangaroo hop'.[25] Underscoring the sense of community at this time, several members of the Australia House staff travelled to Tooting Cemetery in January 1925 to lay two permanent wreaths on the grave of former colleague and ex–Australian Imperial Force soldier Robert Rae, a man who had lost an arm fighting in France before finding work operating the lifts at Australia House for some five years.[26] Ex-soldiers like Rae, it transpired, could be useful men to have around, for when a large and boisterous group of King's College undergraduate 'raggers' invaded the Australia House Cinema after the Lord Mayor's Show that year, it was another former military man who defended the building, throwing numerous assailants to the ground and putting in 'a lively ten minutes' on the stage to disperse the remainder.[27] 'Some of the students got souvenirs', gloated Charles Chomley, 'and none of them is likely to forget Australia in a hurry'.[28] A similar sense of duty was mirrored the following year, in 1926, when during the crippling transport strike all but a handful of staff turned up to work, with one person walking sixteen miles to do so.[29] Clearly many employees were highly committed, regarding their duties at Australia House as something of a national cause.

As suggested by the number of facilities on offer for tourists, the high commission geared up in this period to welcome that section of the public aptly identified by Richard White and Ros Pesman as 'the travelling class'.[30] In an era before cheap airfares, this was the privileged portion of society in possession of the material wherewithal and time to make the long voyage from Australia, and who closely associated first-hand experience of Britain with social prestige.[31] Whether gathering for business or pleasure, such people composed the predominant Australian clientele of the building in the 1920s and 1930s. For them, Australia House had become part of the London circuit, a place to make acquaintances and broker deals. Many also expressed interest in the possibility of receiving invitations to royal garden parties or formal presentations at Court, and in the 1920s the unenviable task of selecting which names to put forward fell to the hospitality officer at Australia House, Mr H.K. Ellison.[32] With not nearly enough invitations to go around, disappointment inevitably followed, and the federal Labor parliamentarian, Albert Green, vented a frustration probably felt by many when he accused Ellison of favouring only the 'upper strata' and not speaking with 'an Australian twang'.[33] For its part the *British Australian and New Zealander* defended Ellison's efforts to make the lists representative and conveyed a deep unease about the Australian High Commission getting involved in such a delicate social dance.[34] Delivering a comment encapsulating that 'tense interplay' alluded to earlier, Chomley wrote decisively that 'Australians at home should realise that the biggest function of Australia House is not to entertain them but to represent Australia here'.[35] The criticism from disillusioned visitors, though, proved hard to transcend.[36]

Not all interactions between Australia House and the public were quite so contentious. Indeed, many public events passed off with little or no criticism, even if some observers baulked at the costs intermittently charged by the high commission for hire of its premises.[37] So it was that Australia House hosted numerous successful lectures, receptions, recitals and fundraising meetings for causes including the Dominion War Nurses' Memorial and the Australian Bush Fire Fund.[38] Keen to increase access to Australia House for groups of Australians, in 1925 High Commissioner Cook told an assembly of 140 boys visiting under the auspices of the Young Australia League to regard the building as their home in London and to come and go as they pleased.[39] They were all part-owners of Australia House, Cook continued, each laying claim to 'one sixth millionth' of its fabric. That said, he cautioned, 'he would repeat the warning he had given to a former contingent of boys not to take their fraction of the house away with them'.[40] Such wariness was not misplaced, with two urns, a porcelain kangaroo and lion, a cricket bat, some stumps and a pair of batsman's pads removed from the building by evening revellers at a later function laid on for the touring Australian cricket team.[41] 'Borrowing' items from one's own home was one thing; helping oneself to the fixtures and fittings of Australia House quite another.

Such anecdotes highlight what any domestic host knows only too well: some of the rooms in one's house are readily available to visitors while others are best kept hidden. Callers at Australia House have never enjoyed a free run of the building, with government departments including defence strictly off limits. Instead, public activity has been concentrated in specific areas (now much reduced in scope). At the height of its accessibility from the 1920s to 1970s, Australia House accommodated visitors in four principal locations: the basement, the ground floor and portions of the first and fourth floors. In the basement callers attended film screenings (most especially in the

1920s and early 1930s), lectures and—from the late 1940s—dined in a popular canteen beloved by hard-up young Australians.[42] On its ground floor the building featured a much-used newspaper reading room as well as travel agencies, banking facilities, visa and migration services, the bookstall, public toilets, a telephone and notice boards where job advertisements and travel messages could be scanned by interested parties.[43] Market stalls and an art gallery (discussed below) also shared this space for a time, and for special occasions ballroom dancers twirled around the elaborate marble floor or else over a specially laid surface. Climbing the stairs or taking the lift to the first floor, social activity centred upon what became the Downer Room, the setting for many years of the reference library and currently the venue for intermittent public lectures and seminars. Three floors further up, visitors to the building in the 1920s and 1930s patronised the bookshop and travel centre operated by the *British Australian and New Zealander* and called in to see the newspaper's editorial staff nearby. A select few might also have gained access to the high commissioner on the first floor, while elsewhere in the building other visitors collected war pensions, picked up mail, dropped off charity donations or (in the early years) enjoyed a tour of Australia House led by William Finnegan, the building's long-serving caretaker.[44] For reasons discussed below, visitors to the building now find the social aspect of the high commission greatly altered, although the ground floor and Downer Room in particular retain a sense of glamour befitting a prestigious members' club.

As well as catering to the demands of antipodean visitors, Australia House, in its role as a 'national foyer', has also served as a staging post for British migrants heading the other way. It was here, on many occasions from the 1920s to 1950s, that groups of Barnardo's boys, girls recruited at British labour exchanges, and child migrants travelling under Richard Linton's 'Big Brother' scheme were farewelled.[45] In April 1929, a body of Barnardo's boys visited Australia House before setting sail for Sydney following a fundraising drive by the *Daily Mirror*.[46] The Prince of Wales assured them from personal experience how lucky they were to be going to New South Wales, and promised rich opportunities for those prepared to work hard.[47] In 1921, by way of contrast, the *British Australasian* reported that the Migration Branch at Australia House was 'crowded all day' with adults seeking information on a new life in Australia, and in June 1939, Mr T.H. Garrett arrived from Canberra to supervise applications from a new group anxiously seeking escape: Jewish refugees from Hitler's Germany.[48] Between these two dates migration to Australia ebbed and flowed considerably, but processing migrants and hosting farewell events remained throughout an important part of the high commission's work and a function that would expand dramatically after 1945.

To the outside world, milling around the Strand and the Aldwych in the period before World War II, Australia House presented an evolving—if not always dynamic—picture of Australian resources and products. Within the building, Australia was advertised mainly in two sets of publicly orientated spaces: the alcoves of the large Exhibition Hall on the ground floor and the numerous office windows facing the streets. In 1918, the first presentation hosted by the building in its exhibition space featured an Albatross aircraft and other equipment from the Great War, a reminder to visitors of the sacrifices Australia had made for the imperial cause.[49] By the mid-1920s Australian produce rather than military hardware took pride of place in Exhibition Hall, with the annual apple exhibit and displays of Australian wine and timber among the attractions drawing the attention of visitors.[50] Gradually, Australia House officials also grasped the potential for promoting cultural endeavour, and after witnessing the crowds flocking in to see Will Longstaff's celebrated painting, *Menin Gate at Midnight*, in 1928, plans were made for an ambitious gallery of Australian art in the Exhibition Hall.[51] Despite a successful opening in May 1929, with several paintings sold, it appears that the impetus for the Australian art gallery soon dissipated, although the organisers behind another cultural endeavour—Australian Authors' Week—were not discouraged from holding their event in the autumn of 1931.[52]

In the times in between the various displays, Exhibition Hall was used for social functions and also to host a modest kind of Australian marketplace, where customers could purchase Australian preserves, soups and fruit.[53] In its role as a point of sale for Australian goods, the space attracted much condemnation by the 1930s, with the *British Australian and New Zealander* not alone in noting the disjuncture between the fine marble setting and the rather poor selection of wares and, by 1935 at least, observing the apparent lack of public interest in the available items.[54]

Displays in the Australia House windows were also largely a hit-and-miss affair and a constant source of discussion. Sometimes individual states—particularly South Australia—produced enticing arrangements, but at other times the window displays provoked censure. In 1925, 'Live Wire Aussie' made an appeal for modernity, arguing the case for electric signs and slogans such as 'Australia, the land of prosperity calls you' and 'Australia is 98 per cent British, help to keep it so'.[55] But three years later a correspondent in the *British Australian and New Zealander*, J.B. Downing, condemned the windows of the Migration Department as offering no strong inducement to would-be migrants used to the innovative displays of shops in nearby Kingsway.[56] By 1930 it seems the department's windows were at last in order, at least for the time being. How ironic then, that the newly installed selection of Australian photographs, noted as 'far more attractive … than ever were there before', appeared just as the Migration Department had closed its doors in the wake of the Great Depression and passers-by, no longer able to obtain free passages, could only gaze upon what they had missed.[57] Five years hence and the ground floor windows were again underused; with banks, shipping companies and government offices hogging much of the available frontage, South Australia indicated its displeasure by relocating for a time from Australia House to Oxford Street in an effort to make more of an impression upon the passing British public.[58]

Criticism of the Australia House windows encapsulates the increasingly negative sentiment about the high commission building in the 1930s, which had much to do with that seismic event already mentioned: the Wall Street crash. When the Australian government found itself in severely straitened circumstances, the distant citadel on the Strand proved an easy target, with heavy staff cutbacks further reducing the satisfaction visitors felt upon entering the building.[59] So it was that the 1930s bore witness to a marked reduction in the number and diversity of events held at Australia House, a diminution of the lively staff culture of the 1920s, and a decline in available funds to present an appealing image of Australia. Emblematic of the reduced circumstances were two changes: the cessation of screenings at the Australia House Cinema and the apparent curtailment of funding for the library, which left it in a parlous state by 1939.[60] In 1940, criticism came to a head following two disastrous decisions on the part of Australia House. The first related to the cancellation of all official aspects of the annual Australia Day festivities for the first time in as long as most of the Australian community in London could remember.[61] The second concerned a new wave of visitors striding down the Strand towards the building: Australian diggers.

Open house: 1940–72

When Australian soldiers began arriving en masse in England in June 1940,[62] officials at Australia House were unprepared. With the building shut to their needs, troops on furlough instead sought hospitality at the offices of individual agents-general, in the auditorium of the Strand Theatre and later at the rooms of the Royal Empire Society.[63] 'Some desperate effort must be made to wake up Australia House', chided a correspondent from Sydney in July 1940; 'It is an outrage that this million pound building, so admirably fitted for the purpose of entertaining our troops, should be closed up like a dismal, dark, unhealthy morgue'.[64] In the face of such censure, only belatedly did Australia House soften its stance, at once opening its doors to a very different group of visitors from the members of the travelling class.

Initially known as the Australian Forces Centre, the rooms set aside for Australian servicemen in the high commission were soon extended in scale, and advertised by March 1942 as the Boomerang Club.[65] Open for business between 9 a.m. and 9 p.m. throughout the week and presided over by Mrs Ethel Bruce, the wife of the high commissioner, the club offered a wide-ranging suite of facilities from its headquarters in the basement of Australia House.[66] Here the Australian soldier on leave could eat a three-course lunch for a shilling, socialise with fellow servicemen, visit the in-house barber's, get his uniform pressed and shoes shined, enjoy a hot shower, play billiards and table tennis, make use of the club's writing and reading rooms, acquire new kit, place phone calls, seek advice from Mrs Duncan on accommodation options in the capital, or simply catch up on rest.[67] Personnel could also consult Mrs Troy about entertainment tickets for London shows or visit the bookstall, still in operation on the ground floor. Indeed, following the influx of servicemen, the *Evening Standard* described Mrs Fraser Smith as one of the busiest bookstall keepers in London.[68] 'Throughout the day she is besieged with inquiries', noted the newspaper; 'There is a demand for postcards of London, particularly since the City fires,[69] but by far the greatest demand is for pictures and postcards of Australia'.[70] Downstairs in the basement, romance blossomed over the club's service counters. Despite stern warnings not to 'mess up with my boys' from supervisor Mrs Delmar-Morgan, British volunteer Doris Brooks and Australian airman Alfred Whealing started dating and married six weeks later in September 1945.[71] Not all encounters yielded such dramatic results, but the words of another visitor are characteristic of a shared response to the high commission's wartime amenities. The Boomerang Club and its associated facilities had become 'a Mecca for Australians—a little bit of Aussie where one could always find a pal'.[72] No longer the preserve of the well-heeled traveller, Australia House now formed part of the soldier's domain.

As well as facilitating access to London's entertainment districts, the Boomerang Club also hosted events of its own. Alongside a boxing contest in July 1942, the club held regular tea dances for servicemen and their partners and staged concerts by well-known entertainers including Gracie Fields.[73] Cabaret evenings and impersonations also became features of important anniversaries like Australia Day or the Club's birthday, granting visiting Australian comedians and servicemen the opportunity to let off steam and poke fun at the military hierarchy.[74] By late April 1942, moreover, members of the Boomerang Club were broadcasting to a far wider audience than that physically present within Australia House. The BBC's 'Anzac Hour' and 'Anzacs Calling Home' radio shows had taken to the airwaves, with several episodes recorded in the high commission.[75] Jack Payne's band provided musical entertainment in the first broadcast before Sergeant Douglas Power recited verses of his own poetry for his parents in Toowoomba and Wing Commander Anderson spoke to his wife in Orange, New South Wales.[76] In a period well before cheap international telephone calls, this personal communication must have been treasured, boosting morale and bringing Australia House into the homes of listeners half a world away.

When he visited the Boomerang Club in May 1944, shortly before Australia House suffered minor bomb damage, Australian Prime Minister John Curtin commended the staff there for their 'sense of national duty'.[77] Over the course of the war years they had welcomed thousands of servicemen and transformed Australia House into a social hub and base for exploring London. It was here that soldiers on leave came for rest and recuperation, with the wounded receiving extra helpings of dinner and repatriated servicemen especially warm welcomes.[78] Though it did not provide sleeping accommodation for Australian troops—by April 1944 that role had fallen to Harrington Hall in South Kensington[79]—the high commission helped ensure that Anzacs were fed, watered, entertained and oriented towards the attractions of the capital. In the eyes of its military guests, Australia House had become a home away from home.

With the return of troops to Australia at the war's conclusion, the Boomerang Club lapsed for a time before being revived as a ladies' social and charitable endeavour. In its new guise club members visited sick Australians in London hospitals, greeted new arrivals from Australia and helped 'business girls' find work.[80] From its basement and ground-floor home, the club also organised annual gala balls and ran the Australia House canteen.[81] Its culinary services must have been in demand, for in the postwar years Australia House would host more visitors than ever. In the quarter century following World War II, more than 1,500,000 Britons set out for a new life in Australia, the majority travelling under the 'ten pound Pom' scheme.[82] The high commission handled most of the applications, overseeing the process from initial inquiry to formal interview and medical examination.[83] With the announcement of assisted passages 'A new kind of queue' had formed outside Australia House and staff numbers swelled to meet the challenges of the building's new primary function. By October 1949, between seventy and one hundred single men and women were being processed every day at Australia House for migration purposes, and in January 1955 the building advertised extended opening hours—until 8 p.m. three nights a week—to cater to demand.[84] Later that year Australia House featured as a location for the Ealing Studios comedy *Touch and Go*. Starring Jack Hawkins and Margaret Johnston, the film was about a British family weighing up the prospects for a better life in Australia.[85] Its title captured the flavour of the contemporary scramble for passages and the part, albeit fleeting, played by Australia House in facilitating the journeys of those wishing to leave.

Cultural expansion followed hard on the heels of administrative growth, with Sir Thomas White's arrival as high commissioner in 1951 signalling renewed artistic endeavour. Shortly after the war, Australian Prime Minister Ben Chifley had ordered a thorough 'sprucing up' of Australia House,[86] a directive met with gusto by the wife of White's predecessor. Replete with pink carpets and blue, red and pink furnishings, Mrs Beasley's reception room on the first floor became a space to welcome important guests and drink evening cocktails.[87] White perceived supplementary uses, turning the room and accessible parts of the surrounding building into a centre for literary, musical and artistic patronage. With his backing the Australian Musical Association, Australian Artists' Association and Society of Australian Writers were each initiated in 1952, the latter growing out of a circle of Australian writers including Peter Porter which had held meetings in the Australia House basement.[88] Lectures, lunchtime recitals and vocal competitions took place in the building over the following years.[89] The Australian Musical Association proved an especially successful venture, maintaining a membership of more than 200 for the next two decades while also arranging master classes for young talent and building a substantial collection of musical scores in the Australia House Library.[90] A book profiling Australia, *The Sunburnt Country* (1953), marked an early success for the Society of Australian Writers, selling over 23,000 copies in the first year of its release and featuring contributions from authors such as Martin Boyd and George Johnston.[91] Under

White's successor, Sir Eric Harrison, the artistic momentum generated in this period culminated in the commissioning of large murals for the first floor rotunda at Australia House. Begun in 1958 and unveiled in 1960, Tom Thompson's paintings present Australia as a land rich in resources and open to industrious workers.[92] In their own celebratory style, the murals signal art and inward migration as twin concerns of Australia House in its immediate postwar guise.

Revealing as they are, however, the triumphant presence of the paintings in the heart of the building also masks the emergence in this period of alternative meeting points for the Australian community in London. During the late 1940s and 1950s, those Australian states operating premises outside Australia House established their own rival reception centres in an attempt to draw visitors and promote their individual business agendas. Victoria opened a reading room in April 1947, for example; Queensland followed suit with a reception room in Queensland House (409–10 Strand) in April 1955.[93] From its centre in the Earl's Court area—'Kangaroo Valley' as it became known—an increasingly young Australian community could now also turn to venues like the Overseas Visitors' Club (instigated in 1955) for accommodation, food and guidance, to evening clubs such as the Kangaroo Paddock and the Down Under Club for entertainment (the latter featuring Rolf Harris), and to pubs including the Surrey for Australian beer on tap.[94]

Such ventures indicate a surge in visitor numbers, a trend facilitated by cheap fares on migrant ships returning from Australia and the advent of mass transit air travel.[95] Australian officials in London viewed this influx with a mixture of pride and alarm. While White was happy to sponsor ventures—including a memorial exhibition of paintings by Dora Meeson—taking place beyond the walls of Australia House,[96] others sensed a loss of control. In October 1955, Sir John Lienhop, the Victorian agent-general in London, appealed to young Australian visitors, for the sake of national prestige, not to hitchhike or travel around Britain in dilapidated vehicles. Appreciating the 'adventuring spirit' behind such adventures, Lienhop nonetheless noted pointedly that:

> Young men and girls—especially girls—from Australia are getting a reputation here as unashamed beggars of lifts from motorists … [A] cult has grown up of calculated riding on the cheap which is giving people a strange idea of the morals of young Australians.

> I would also like to appeal to the rowdy Australian exhibitionists who are touring the country in ever-increasing numbers in battered old cars and taxis covered in vulgar signs and, unfortunately, Australian flags … [T]hey bring discredit and disrepute to their home country when they turn their cars into disgraceful circus carriages covered with signs and drawings which scandalise and annoy many good residents of this country. I am not being a Puritan when I ask that these young people show a little quiet pride in themselves … and travel about in a demeanour and in dress that does Australia credit. I am sure parents in Australia can do a lot to discourage this increasing practice.[97]

Gazing down from their offices on the lively trade in camper vans which had sprung up around the high commission,[98] one wonders how many other Australian officials shared these sentiments in the years that followed. During the mid-1960s related fears emerged that there might be as many as 50,000 Australians living 'underground' in Britain by ignoring immigration rules.[99] Sir Alexander Downer, the high commissioner, refuted the claims, noting that the best estimate of Australians in Britain at any one time was around 30,000.[100] Whatever the truth of the matter, the new wave of visitors, like the soldiers who had come before, presented a challenge to a longer-established Australian community in Britain still clinging to its 'travelling class' credentials.

Amid these shifting currents and despite the emergence of rival venues, a journalist entering Australia House in 1965 found that the building still retained its relevance as a social centre. Walking in, he reported:

> The cockney porter points the way through the revolving doors—'in there, guv'—and you pad silently down a rich red carpet into the visitors' lounge. Around long tables expatriates scan their hometown newspapers; others in comfortable green leather chairs pore over letters collected from the mail desk; the Qantas reception girl smiles expectantly; the woman at the inquiries counter sends visitors off in 10 different directions; a Victorian buys a Russian phrase book; the young sit pen in mouth at neat writing desks struggling for words to reassure parents at home.

> This is Australia House, London ... Most of the 12,500 Australians who pass through [the building] every year appear to like it. There have been only three letters and one verbal complaint this year ... Apparently Australia House succeeds. In a spot check of Australians and Britons around the building I could not find one willing to say a bad word about it or the staff.[101]

This historical moment, it seems, represented an Indian summer for Australia House in its role as 'national foyer'. Expecting record numbers of emigrants to Australia, the high commission maintained its high staffing levels (peaking in 1971 at 1,138),[102] while elsewhere in the building a newly appointed librarian, Athalie Colquhoun, encountered a still vigorous social scene incorporating club meetings and regular visits by genealogists, business people and well-known writers.[103] One of those writers, a young Peter Conrad, recalls that his first walk upon arrival in London in 1968 commenced at the high commission: 'You started at Australia House with its piles of hometown newspapers and ended up at the gates of Buckingham Palace, where you looked up to see if the flag was flying'.[104] A sense of self-declared 'deference' drew Conrad towards the high commission, he later noted, looking back from 2004 with a hint of embarrassment.[105] Conrad need not have felt self-conscious: the symbolic pilgrimage was doubtless made often at this time, although as the 1960s advanced shadows were beginning to darken the path. Britain's overtures towards Europe appeared to threaten the historically special relationship with Australia, however much high commissioners Harrison and Downer might hope otherwise.[106] The status of Australia House and those using it stood to be directly affected by these developments.

From foyer to embassy

As explained in chapter 10, on 1 November 1972 responsibility for running Australia House transferred from the Prime Minister's Department to the Department of Foreign Affairs.[107] Soon afterwards the axe began to swing. The newly incumbent Gough Whitlam had demanded that Australia House be run not as a special case but rather as a normal foreign embassy like those in Washington or Tokyo, and the cutbacks commenced in earnest.[108] Some 200 staff found themselves out of work initially, with others employed in departments including public service, information, education and overseas telecommunications following suit under Whitlam's successor, Malcolm Fraser.[109] *Poste restante* services ('a big up-front public relations gesture to tens of thousands of voters who travel to the UK every year') and banking facilities went as well in sweeping changes that also affected the holdings of the library and marked the rise to ascendancy of career diplomats over earlier appointees such as Bill Cumming with interests in cultural affairs.[110] An article in the *Sydney Morning Herald* in November 1978 captured the new attitude. Noting that service reductions to visitors by this stage also entailed the closure of the bookshop, travel facilities and canteen (in addition to the requirement for visitors to enter by a side door), the *Herald*'s journalist termed the high commission 'A House, yes, but a home no more'.[111]

While there is a danger of overstating the impact of the 1972 shift in the short term— each day in 1978 around 800 people continued to frequent the newspaper reading room and another eighty made inquiries about social security payments—the Indian summer had given way to autumn and indeed early winter.[112] Under the guidance of Sir Phillip Lynch's 'razor gang' (described as 'the beginning of the end' by Athalie Colquhoun) six more departments were axed and a further thirty-five per cent of the staff dismissed by November 1981.[113] The visitors' book had been put away by this time too, and the message exchange board taken down.[114] 'Heartbreak House'—the moniker first bestowed on the high commission in 1974 in light of the sheer number of British nationals seeking a new life overseas—became, in the next decade, even more apt a term, now that the generous migration scheme to Australia had ended.[115] The huge popularity as cultural exports of Paul Hogan, Kylie Minogue and 'Dame Edna' certainly stoked demand for tourist visas, but prospective migrants faced diminished chances of making a visit to Australia permanent.[116] With a reduced capacity to handle general inquiries from the British public and fewer facilities for Australian arrivals, Australia House appeared less able, or likely, to maintain a social function. No doubt fed up with the level of services now on offer, one visitor expressed his displeasure in antagonistic fashion, serially blocking the high commission's public toilets throughout the year of 1984.[117] Though hardly the most imaginative method of civic disobedience, the activities of this unknown individual expressed, in crude terms, how the public mood was becoming sour.

This state of affairs scarcely improved in the early 1990s. In 1994 the Australia House Library was closed under yet another cutback and after years of funding reductions.

Access to the facility had become discretionary in November 1993 and eleven months later formal closure followed.[118] In its report on the options for the refurbishment of Australia House in 1995, the Parliamentary Committee on Public Works stated that the building was Australia's 'showcase' in London and 'a focus to present Australia in all its facets'.[119] Yet by this stage the high commission had already lost its varied and substantial reference collection,[120] surely an integral part in any presentation of Australian culture to interested parties. The reorientation instigated in the early 1970s towards bureaucratic and commercial activities had reached fruition and at the behest of the deputy high commissioner, David Goss, the library made way for expanded consular and migration services.[121] Continuing a trend, another service had been abolished and a further area of Australia House closed to outside users. As outlined earlier, in the decades either side of World War II members of the public had gained easy access to the basement cinema and lecture theatre, the ground floor and portions of the first and fourth floors. Now visitors found that only the ground-floor reading room remained open to all on a regular basis, even if, as the floor plans accompanying the Public Works report attest, access was possible on a controlled basis to the theatre and Downer Room for specific events.[122]

Newspaper correspondents and staff lamented these changes.[123] Perhaps sensing the need to fill a cultural void, Australia House responded decisively in the aftermath of the library closure. In separate initiatives the high commission established the Australia Centre in the mid-1990s and appointed notable Australian art dealer Rebecca Hossack as cultural attaché in December 1994.[124] The creation of an Australia Centre—with a separate entrance on the Strand—had been suggested as part of the 'rationalisation' of high commission space under the Public Works investigation and was intended as an umbrella body under which the various agents-general, Australian business organisations, prospective migrants and tourists might gather.[125] Although initially lacking much at all in the way of a cultural aspect (a commemorative leaflet notes the facility's financial imperatives), the creation of the Australia Centre ultimately paved the way for a merger of premises with the academically focused Menzies Centre for Australian Studies, King's College London[126]—the centre bringing its regular public seminars, conferences, book launches and teaching expertise down from Russell Square when it relocated in 2005.[127] Even by the mid-90s, Australia House and the Menzies Centre had established strong connections, not least in the form of the popular literary readings that Professor Brian Matthews arranged first at Russell Square and then—as 'Literary Links' events from 1995—at Australia House.[128] Backed by High Commissioner Neal Blewett, invited speakers included Thomas Keneally, Clive James, Kathy Lette and John Mulvaney, the success of the endeavour also marking an early accomplishment for Rebecca Hossack in her new role as the high commission's first cultural development officer.[129]

When the vacancy filled by Hossack had been advertised, the British press responded with glee. 'So they do give a XXXX for culture', quipped the *Daily Telegraph*, with the *Daily Mail* purporting to quote, with similar pith, Barry Humphries' well-known caricature 'Sir Les Patterson'.[130] Hossack's appointment, under Blewett's stewardship, represented a bold move for the high commission and a resolute return to the cultural arena. After suggesting that the monthly 'Literary Links' events move to Australia House and promoting the complementary poster exhibition in the building (a venture that later evolved into a book), Hossack concentrated her energies on organising a major undertaking, the *new*IMAGES program, for 1997.[131] Funded jointly by the Australia Council and British Council, this year-long series of events had the remit of enhancing the popular image of Australia in Britain and vice versa.[132] Australia House played host to several *new*IMAGES events—including a 'Night Skies' exhibition of astrological images—and provided a British base for the several hundred visitors ranging from members of youth orchestras to writers, film school students and biodiversity experts who travelled from Australia to participate.[133] An 'Ashes' exhibition of cricketing memorabilia, Australian opera at Spitalfields market, waratahs at the Chelsea Flower Show and a Geelong–Essendon exhibition football match comprised further highlights in a veritable smorgasbord of events.[134]

All of which makes the high commission's decision not to offer a renewal to Hossack's contract in 1997 highly surprising. In correspondence to the *Age*, Blewett stated tersely: 'I do not share the view of some that Hossack is indispensable for a successful London cultural program'.[135] Blewett was responding to a furore in the newspaper letters pages over Hossack's position, a public tussle in which big-hitters like Barry Humphries, Clive James, Kathy Lette and Geoffrey Robertson—many of whom had experienced first-hand the value of the Australia House initiative—expressed their outrage.[136] Given the lack of a comparable follow-up to *new*IMAGES in later years, there was some justification for the expatriates' concerns. Blewett, however, was also right. Australian cultural enterprise in London would continue apace without an attaché, even if, as discussed in my concluding remarks, most such enterprise was increasingly unlikely to have any formal ties to Australia House.

In 2000, the high commission advertised the arrival of a new century with a highly apt exhibition. 'Arthur Boyd and the Exile of the Imagination' encapsulated a state of mind that many British and Australian visitors to Australia House would have shared throughout the building's history—namely the experience, however momentary, of being caught between cultures.[137] Polly Borland's adjacent photographs of fifty living Australians considered to have made a significant contribution to Britain underscored the point: however transient it might be, the Australian community in the United Kingdom has cultivated deep roots.[138] Later in the year, Phillip Knightley and a group of fellow expatriates gathered at the high commission to watch television coverage of the Sydney Olympics opening ceremony.[139] For events of overriding significance, Australia House is still to the fore among Australian venues in London. In the aftermath of the 2002 Bali bombing, it was here that concerned visitors (including Princess Anne) signed a book of condolence; after terror attacks on British soil in 2005 and again following the 2009

Victorian bushfires, the building similarly acted as a focal point by establishing telephone hotlines to dispense information and reassurance.[140] And for elections or referenda, the high commission building becomes Australia's single most popular voting booth, handling between 14,000 and 30,000 votes during recent counts.[141]

Australia House retains its public profile via such activities as well as through media-friendly enterprises including use of its premises for the filming of the BBC television series *Wanted Down Under* and the first Harry Potter film, and to launch the British broadcast of the popular Australian comedy series *Kath & Kim*.[142] These events, however, are exceptional. With staffing levels hovering at around 200 in 2006,[143] the building is no longer geared up to handle a large daily influx of visitors. One of the last vestiges of the club-like atmosphere so characteristic of the building's history finally went in 2004 with the closure of the newspaper reading room on the ground floor. In this case the rise of the internet as much as the high commission's changed status accounted for the development; as Jeremy Mitchell, the public affairs manager, put it, why would anyone want to read old news when they could get the latest headlines at home on their laptops?[144] As such services to casual callers have dwindled, security has increased. Irish Republican Army bombing campaigns in the 1970s and 1980s prompted the installation of a Plexiglas screen in the entrance foyer; by 2004 it was no longer possible to lodge visa applications in person (they had to be posted); and in 2006 the *Age* commented negatively on the installation outside the building of a ring of toughened bollards to deter would-be car bombers.[145]

Approaching Australia House today, it would be tempting to conclude that the arrival of a tight security regime (particularly since the events of September 2001) lies at the root of the building's altered outlook towards its users. Yet as this analysis has illustrated, the decline of the high commission's public facilities predates such concerns. Australia House now presents itself as a government office on a par with dozens of other diplomatic missions across the globe: a place to promote investment, handle visa applications and replace lost passports, but not a location to pause or meet up with old friends. 'See you at Oz House' is no longer a common utterance among new arrivals into Britain; expectant visitors no longer turn up at the reception desk saying simply 'I'm an Australian'.[146] Buried deep within the high commission's website, however, reference is made to a continuing function many officials would probably rather abandon. In the absence of almost all other social facilities that visitors once enjoyed, Australians in Britain can still apply to Australia House for tickets to Royal Ascot and the Queen's summer garden parties.[147] A spirit of conviviality lingers on.

Conclusion

If Australia House is now less central to the Australian community in London, it is a sign of that community's strength rather than its weakness. Instead of relying on the national government to provide, Australians in the British capital have established their own institutions, cultural events and commercial ventures.[148] Australia House is now more an embassy than a home-from-home for Australians.[149]

Yet, one also senses that the building itself resists its current incarnation. Exhibition Hall on the ground floor retains its grandeur and elegance, and continues to inspire awe in visitors to the building. In the basement the auditorium remains, but the screen flickers to life more irregularly than in the building's early years. Up and along the marble staircase on the first floor the Downer Room is still resplendent and used for a range of events—but less heavily than during its career as a library—while in the adjacent rotunda, Thompson's murals continue to present a historically valuable view that too few Australians can enjoy. With the building approaching its hundredth year, its rich and varied history as Australia's house should be celebrated.

World War I equipment on display in Exhibition Hall at Australia House, December 1918. [Australian War Memorial]

Dancers at a high commission ball organised by Australia House staff, 1929. [*BANZ*, 25 April 1929, p. 14, State Library of Victoria, courtesy Newspapers Collection]

Mrs Barnardo and the Prince of Wales farewell fifty Barnardo's boys—bound for Australia —in the Australia House Library. [*BANZ*, 25 April 1929, p. 6, State Library of Victoria, courtesy of Newspapers Collection]

London calling: BBC *Anzac Hour* interviewees speak to Australia from the Boomerang Club, 1943. [Australian War Memorial]

Gracie Fields entertains guests at the Boomerang Club, July 1943 (left); Royal Australian Air Force 'Glee Party' on stage in Australia House on Australia Day, 1943 (right). [Australian War Memorial]

Public inquiries (1946) and a medical examination (1962) for an intending migrant at Australia House. [National Archives of Australia Image Numbers A12111, 1/1956/14/19 (left); A12111, 1/1962/14/16]

Australia House, London, 1960. [National Archives of Australia Image Number A12111:1/1960/14/5]

Appendix 1
High commissioners to the United Kingdom, 1910–2010

Date of arrival in London

22 January	1910	Rt Hon. Sir George Reid
22 January	1916	Rt Hon. Andrew Fisher
11 November	1921	Rt Hon. Sir Joseph Cook, GCMG
11 May	1927	Hon. Sir Granville Ryrie, KCMG, CB
7 October	1933	Rt Hon. Stanley M. Bruce, CH, MC*
15 August	1946	Hon. John A. Beasley (deceased 2 September 1949)†
21 June	1951	Hon. (later Sir) Thomas W. White (KBE 1952), DFC
November	1956	Rt Hon. Sir Eric J. Harrison, KCVO ‡
May	1964	Hon. (later Sir) Alexander Downer (KBE 1965)
29 January	1973	Hon. John I. Armstrong
1 February	1975	Sir John Bunting (AC 1982, KBE 1976), CBE
13 April	1977	Hon. (later Sir) Gordon Freeth (KBE 1978)
17 March	1980	Sir James Plimsoll, AC, CBE
24 April	1981	Hon. (later Sir) Victor Garland (KBE 1982)
19 January	1984	Alfred R. Parsons (AO 1986)
20 March	1987	Hon. Douglas McClelland, AC
8 March	1991	Richard J. Smith (AM 1997)
21 April	1994	Hon. Neal Blewett (AC 1995)
24 May	1998	Philip J. Flood, AO
31 July	2000	Michael G. L'Estrange (AO 2007)
25 February	2005	Hon. Richard Alston
3 September	2008	John Dauth, LVO

* Bruce was resident minister from September 1932 to 6 October 1933.

† Beasley was resident minister from January to 15 August 1946.

‡ Harrison was resident minister from 19 April 1950 to March 1951.

Appendix 2
Senior representatives of the Department of External Affairs, 1924–72

Date of arrival in London

1 October	1924	Richard (later Rt Hon. the Lord 1960) Casey, CH (KG 1969, GCMG 1965), DSO, MC, Liaison Officer
August	1933	F. Keith (later Sir 1950) Officer, OBE, MC, External Affairs Officer
30 April	1937	Alfred T. Stirling (CBE 1953), External Affairs Officer
12 July	1945	John E. Oldham, External Affairs Officer
30 October	1945	Alan S. (later Sir 1954) Watt (CBE 1952), External Affairs Officer
1 July	1946	John D.L. Hood (CBE 1954), External Affairs Officer
2 July	1947	Peter R. (later Sir 1970) Heydon (CBE 1959), External Affairs Officer
7 May	1950	John P. Quinn (OBE 1957), External Affairs Officer
29 January	1951	J. Keith (later Sir 1968) Waller (CBE 1961), External Affairs Officer
5 January	1953	Colin T. Moodie, External Affairs Officer
21 March	1954	Laurence R. (later Sir 1963) McIntyre, OBE (CBE 1960), Senior External Affairs Representative
28 December	1956	Owen L. Davis (OBE 1967), Senior External Affairs Representative
26 May	1959	Keith C.O. (later Sir 1980) Shann (CBE 1964), Senior External Affairs Representative
17 January	1966	Thomas K. Critchley, CBE (AO 1976), Senior External Affairs Representative
4 September	1969	William B. Pritchett (AO 1984), Deputy High Commissioner

Appendix 3
Who were the early agents-general?

Frank Bongiorno

A round fifty men served as agents-general for the six colonies, and later states, in the years before 1910. The 'typical' colonial agent-general had been a member of parliament (43), and usually a minister or speaker (39). Very few politicians were able to secure the agent-generalship without having tasted ministerial office—a notable exception was the 'cultivated' businessman and Victorian parliamentarian, Robert Murray Smith, agent-general from 1882 to 1886. His conservatism and attachment to free trade in a protectionist colony had largely forestalled domestic political advancement, but he was a highly successful agent-general.

An appointment to an agent-generalship typically came towards the end of a political career, although some (12) did return to parliament afterwards and a small number, such as the Tasmanians Edward Braddon and Philip Fysh, achieved subsequent political distinction. More common, though, were ex-Victorian premiers such as Duncan Gillies and Graham Berry who were well past their prime when they re-entered parliament after service in London.

Sixteen of the agents-general, or just under a third, had been premiers before assuming the office but a further three—John Douglas (Queensland), Edward Braddon (Tasmania) and Henry Lefroy (Western Australia)—became premiers afterwards. Not all ex-premiers led the colony or state they would later represent in London. Robert Herbert, Tasmanian agent-general from 1893 until 1896, had been private secretary to Queensland's first governor, George Bowen, before becoming that colony's first premier in 1859. Herbert returned to England in 1866 and was enlisted as the island colony's agent-general soon after his retirement from a long and distinguished career in the Colonial Office that culminated in his appointment as permanent under-secretary (1871–92). In the depressed 1890s, Tasmania also drew on the services of Westby Perceval, a former New Zealand parliamentarian, who became Tasmanian agent-general after being replaced in 1896 as New Zealand's representative by William Pember Reeves. Perceval was Tasmanian-born.

The former premiers assumed the agent-generalship in quite a wide variety of circumstances. Few were quite as bold as Tasmania's Adye Douglas, who as premier in 1885 piloted through parliament the legislation creating the position before appointing himself the inaugural agent-general. Ex-premiers who became agents-general included major figures such as Charles Cowper, five-time premier of New South Wales, Berry, thrice Victorian premier, and Gillies, who led that colony for almost five years. But there were also less distinguished former premiers such as the Western Australian, Sir Cornthwaite Rason (1907–11), described by his biographer as '[o]ne of Australia's most lightweight premiers', and James Munro, briefly Gillies' successor as Victorian premier, who combined leadership of the temperance cause with massive financial speculation. His vast business empire was in the process of liquidation when he arranged to have himself appointed agent-general in 1892. Public protests ensued at such an obvious attempt to avoid his creditors and Sir Archibald Michie, himself a previous Victorian agent-general (1873–79), described Munro as 'merely bolting'.[1] When the vast scale of the losses became clear, Munro's successor as premier, William Shiels, recalled him from London. Munro was eventually revealed as having lost hundreds of thousands of pounds and early in 1893 became a bankrupt.

He was not, however, the only politician whose appointment as agent-general was closely connected with financial embarrassment. A posting to London was not only useful in avoiding creditors—it would temporarily yield a substantial and secure income. Cowper had experienced chronic financial problems in the period leading up to his appointment as agent-general for New South Wales in 1870. Alexander Stuart, a businessman and politician who held the office of treasurer in New South Wales in 1876–77, was nearly bankrupt when Henry Parkes appointed him agent-general of that colony in 1879, probably to get rid of a staunch government opponent. So large were Stuart's debts and so hopeless his financial position that he resigned even before leaving Sydney. John Douglas, Queensland's agent-general in 1869–70, also seems to have been insolvent at the time he occupied his post. Both Stuart and Douglas, despite these setbacks, later went on to serve as premier of their respective colonies. Arthur Macalister, a Queensland premier on three occasions, died broke in Scotland a couple of years after he ceased to be his colony's agent-general, while Rason was declared bankrupt soon after leaving the Western Australian position.

A small number of those categorised above as parliamentarians are perhaps better seen as civil servants, for they were official members of legislative councils before responsible government rather than elected politicians. An example is William Colburn Mayne (New South Wales, 1864–71), who had been inspector-general of police and a member of the legislative council before self-government and briefly after it. He also served as auditor-general. Similarly Charles Pasley, colonial engineer of Victoria and one of the officers who commanded the attack on the Eureka Stockade, was a nominee member of the colony's legislative council before self-government. He did, however, fight and win an election after self-government. Malcolm Fraser, Western Australia's first agent-general, held various significant administrative posts and was a member of that colony's legislative council before self-government.

Few public servants, however, made it to London after the advent of responsible government. A distinguished exception, and a man whose influence was such that he seems really almost to deserve the title 'politician', was Timothy Coghlan, the New South Wales statistician and later that colony's long-serving agent-general. (He was either agent-general or acting in the position for much of the period between 1905 and his death in London in 1926.) Earlier, Richard Daintree, a photographer and Queensland government geologist, had been appointed agent-general in 1872 when the office suddenly and unexpectedly fell vacant. He happened to be in London, where he had organised his colony's display in the Exhibition of Art and Industry.

Virtually all of the agents-general had some prior experience in Britain. The overwhelming majority—about two-thirds—originally came from England or Scotland; only twelve were Australian-born. New South Wales did not produce a native-born agent-general until Coghlan, while Victoria's first was J.W. Taverner as late as 1904. Just one of South Australia's nine agents-general between 1858 and 1909, John Cox Bray (1892–94), was born in Australia, while Queensland had only two native-born out of its eight. On the other hand, Tasmania had four and Western Australia three (out of just five) Australian-born agents-general before 1910.

The remainder were born elsewhere but to British parents. There was one American, John Jenkins, a former premier of South Australia who represented that state in London between 1905 and 1908. His parents, however, were Welsh. Only one out of the fifty, the early agent-general for New South Wales, W.C. Mayne (1864–71), was Irish-born and he was Protestant, presumably Church of Ireland. Catholics were almost unknown among early agents-general, with Coghlan and Perceval, the latter a convert, being unusual in this respect. Yet, among the early New South Wales agents-general were two Jews, the long-serving Saul Samuel (1880–97) and his relative by marriage, Julian Salomons (1899–1900).

Even among the dozen native-born, half had either been educated in Britain or spent part of their early professional lives there. On the other hand, there were a few British-born agents-general, such as Thomas Playford of South Australia, who came to the colonies as children. While in London Playford, an orchardist, 'pined to return to his beloved property in the Adelaide Hills', but he was nevertheless successful in the post. It was a common pattern for an agent-general to have had fairly recent experience of travel to the United Kingdom, on official duties, business, or to visit family; a 'taster', perhaps, before accepting office. Berry, for instance, as Victorian premier, had travelled to England in 1879 in an 'embassy' whose objective was to persuade the Colonial Office to intervene in the colony's long-running constitutional crisis.

About half the agents-general had a background in business, finance or pastoralism, which is not surprising considering the important place of commercial activities among the duties of the position, as well as that colonial parliamentarians typically had business experience. Yet a large number of the agents-general also had what might be broadly called 'literary interests', and not a few were published authors, which might have reflected an expectation that an appointee would be able to mix socially and intellectually with the British élite. About a fifth were lawyers, and there was a sprinkling of professional military men, as well as a couple of doctors. Very few came from truly humble backgrounds. Coghlan's father was a plasterer and he was a scholarship boy, while Taverner began working life 'cutting thistles for five shillings a day'. Only one agent-general had obvious trade union credentials: the South Australian Labor politician, A.A. Kirkpatrick, who was a compositor. Yet even he had his own printing firm.

About sixty per cent of the agents-general died outside Australia and, for several of them, assuming the office was a step towards permanent residence in Britain. Many occupants of the office were able to set up the next stage of their careers while serving their colony in the imperial capital. Coghlan, for instance, combined official duties with private ventures that resulted in some conflicts of interest, while his Victorian contemporary, Taverner, stayed in London for almost a decade after he ceased to be agent-general in 1913. Agents-general commonly received imperial honours, including knighthoods, as well as honorary doctorates, both of which would only have enhanced their standing in British society. An example is John Cockburn, Scottish-born, English-educated—he trained as a doctor at King's College London—and a former South Australian politician and premier notable for his advanced liberalism. He served as agent-general from 1898 until 1901, was appointed Knight Commander of the Order of St Michael and St George in 1900, and spent the rest of his life—which ended almost three decades later—living in England. Cockburn was involved in a bewildering variety of business, educational, intellectual and philanthropic activities, but also acted 'as a sort of unofficial ambassador for South Australia'. Another South Australian, Jenkins, having failed to gain a federal government subsidy to establish a telegraphic link between Papua and Australia, set himself up as a London-based steel importer.

Among those who died 'overseas' were several men who had effectively been appointed by the colonies while already living in England. In some cases, they had spent a phase of their lives in the relevant colony before returning to the United Kingdom; in others—although the distinction is necessarily tenuous—they were colonial expatriates of long standing, now living in London, who retained links with their former home. An example of the latter is Daniel Cooper. He was born in England, went out to New South Wales with his parents, was educated and spent his early career in England, returned to Sydney where he made his fortune, and finally left for England in 1861 where he lived for the rest of his life. Yet he also served as agent-general for New South Wales in the 1880s. Similarly, Parramatta-born, but English-educated James Youl lived the last fifty years of his life in Britain as a wealthy gentleman. (He was responsible for introducing trout and salmon to Australia and New Zealand, having earlier been a Tasmanian pastoralist.) He frequently represented Tasmania in London, including as agent-general in 1888.

In a few instances, men who had pursued imperial careers that included one or more Australasian colonies were enlisted as agents-general. Queensland briefly appointed a former governor, Sir Henry Wylie Norman. The English-born Charles Pasley was living in London when he became Victoria's agent-general for a couple of years in the early 1880s. A military engineer, he had earlier served in Britain, Canada, Bermuda, Victoria and New Zealand. Andrew Clarke, another soldier, served in various administrative roles during the 1840s and 1850s in both Tasmania and Victoria, colonies he would later represent—sometimes simultaneously—in London. Even Edward Braddon might be considered under this heading of 'imperial careering'.[2] Although mainly remembered in Australia as a leading Tasmanian politician, this phase of his career occurred late, and he had spent the bulk of his working life as an Anglo-Indian civil servant.

In sum, the predominance of politicians, ministers and ex-premiers that has been noticed among Australian high commissioners since the appointment of George Reid in 1910 was foreshadowed in the earlier history of the agents-general. Yet, at the same time, the strength of a belief in a wider Britishness that transcended distinctions between centre and periphery, colony and metropole, allowed for considerable flexibility and variety in appointments. Moreover, the relatively free movement of colonists themselves between Britain and the antipodes, evident in the lives of so many of the agents-general, both reflected Australia's colonial status and helped shape the character of the office. In this way, the work of the agents-general might be seen as contributing texture to the imperial webs of meaning, activity and influence that helped constitute the Victorian empire. The emergence of stronger dominion nationalisms in the twentieth century would gradually undermine this fluidity, though a little of it remains even today.

About the authors

Bernard Attard

Bernard Attard is a lecturer in economic history in the School of Historical Studies at the University of Leicester. He is the co-editor with Carl Bridge of *Between Empire and Nation: Australia's External Relations 1901–39* (2000), and has written widely about Australian economic diplomacy, the London Stock Exchange, and Australasia's external debts before World War II.

Frank Bongiorno

Frank Bongiorno is senior lecturer in Australian history in the Menzies Centre for Australian Studies and the Department of History, King's College London. He has previously held lectureships at the Australian National University, Griffith University and the University of New England, and has had visiting appointments at the University of Cambridge and University of Texas at Austin. He is the author of *The People's Party: Victorian Labor and the Radical Tradition 1875–1914* (1996) and has published about forty scholarly articles and book chapters on various aspects of Australian political, cultural, labour and social history, ranging from the diplomatic activities of Herbert Vere Evatt to the arrival of the contraceptive pill in Australia.

Carl Bridge

Carl Bridge is professor and head of the Menzies Centre for Australian Studies at King's College London. He taught previously in the history departments at Flinders University and the University of New England. His publications include *Munich to Vietnam* (1991), *Between Empire and Nation* (2000), *A Delicate Mission: R.G. Casey's Washington Diaries* (2008) and *Australians in Britain: The Twentieth-Century Experience* (2009). He is currently writing a short biography of William Morris Hughes.

James Curran

James Curran is a senior lecturer in history at the University of Sydney. He is the author of *The Power of Speech: Australian Prime Ministers Defining the National Image* (2004). His next book, co-authored with Stuart Ward, is *The Unknown Nation: Remaking Australia in the Wake of Empire* (Melbourne University Press, forthcoming 2010). Before joining academia, Dr Curran served as a policy officer in the International Division of the Prime Minister's Department and as an analyst at the Office of National Assessments. He is currently working on a history of the Australia–US alliance from the Guam doctrine to the early Hawke period.

Kent Fedorowich

Kent Fedorowich is reader in British imperial and Commonwealth history at the University of the West of England, Bristol. He is the author of *Unfit for Heroes: Reconstruction and Soldier Settlement between the Wars* (1995) and co-editor, with Martin Thomas, of *International Diplomacy and Colonial Retreat* (2001) and, with Carl Bridge, *The British World: Diaspora, Culture and Identity* (2003). He has also co-authored, with Bob Moore, *The British Empire and its Italian Prisoners of War, 1940–1947* (2002).

Jeremy Hearder

Jeremy Hearder is a graduate of the University of Melbourne and Stanford University. He spent thirty-eight years in the Department of Foreign Affairs and Trade, which included serving overseas in Vientiane, Dar es Salaam, Bangkok, Nairobi, Brussels, Harare (as high commissioner), Suva (as high commissioner), Chicago (as consul-general) and Wellington. Afterwards he became a part-time consultant in the department, and is currently writing a biography of Sir James Plimsoll.

David Lee

David Lee has been the director of the Historical Publications and Information Section of the Department of Foreign Affairs and Trade since 1997. He is the general editor of the *Documents on Australian Foreign Policy* series. His most recent publication, co-authored with Jane Doulman, is *Every Assistance and Protection: A History of the Australian Passport* (2008). In 2010, he expects to publish a biography of Stanley Melbourne Bruce, Australian prime minister from 1923 to 1929 and high commissioner in London from 1933 to 1945.

David Lowe

David Lowe is director of the new Alfred Deakin Research Institute at Deakin University. He has published on Australia's involvement in wars, including the cold war, and on aspects of Australia's overseas policies in the 1940s and 1950s. He is the author of *Menzies and the Great World Struggle: Australia's Cold War 1948–1954* (1999) and co-author, with Joan Beaumont, Chris Waters and Garry Woodard, of *Ministers, Mandarins and Diplomats: Australian Foreign Policy Making 1941–1969* (2003). His biography of Percy Spender is due to be published by Chatto and Pickering in 2010.

Neville Meaney

Neville Meaney is an honorary associate professor of history at the University of Sydney. He has a longstanding research interest in international history, especially concerning the way in which ideology, culture and geopolitics have interacted to shape the changing character of Australia's relations with the world. He has published widely in the field and his most recent works are *Towards a New Vision: Australia and Japan Across Time* (2007), '"In History's Page": Identity and Myth', in Deryck M. Schreuder and Stuart Ward (eds), *Australia's Empire* (2008), and *Australia and World Crisis, 1914–23* (2009).

J.R. Nethercote

J.R. Nethercote is based at the Public Policy Institute, Australian Catholic University, Canberra. As well as writing extensively on parliamentary and public service matters, he was editor of the *Canberra Bulletin of Public Administration* for twenty years and subsequently of the *Australasian Parliamentary Review*. Among the many books he has edited or jointly edited are *The Menzies Era* (1995), *The House on Capital Hill* (1996), *Liberalism and the Australian Federation* (2001) and *Restraining Elective Dictatorship* (2009).

Olwen Pryke

Olwen Pryke has worked for the History Council of New South Wales, taught history at the University of Sydney and the University of New South Wales, and undertaken a number of historical consultancies. She is now employed at the State Library of New South Wales. Her doctoral research was a cultural history of Australia House, Australia's High Commission in London. She remains interested in representations of Australia in Britain and the intersections between travel and identity.

Simon Sleight

Simon Sleight is a graduate of Warwick University, University College London and Monash University. He is an adjunct research associate at the School of Historical Studies, Monash University, where he completed his doctoral thesis in 2008, and a research assistant at the Menzies Centre for Australian Studies, King's College London. His work explores the processes of 'making place', the evolution of youth cultures, and the Australian presence in Britain. Recent publications include 'Interstitial Acts: Urban Space and the Larrikin Repertoire in late-Victorian Melbourne' in *Australian Historical Studies* (June 2009) and 'Reading the *British Australasian* community in London, 1884–1924', in *Australians in Britain: The Twentieth-Century Experience*, edited by Carl Bridge et al. (2009).

Stuart Ward

Stuart Ward teaches British and Australian history in the School of English, German and Romance Studies at the University of Copenhagen. He recently completed a term (2008–09) as Keith Cameron Chair of Australian History at University College Dublin. His research has covered the political, diplomatic, economic and cultural repercussions of the decline of the British Empire since World War II. His major publications include *Australia and the British Embrace* (2001), *British Culture and the End of Empire* (ed., 2001) and *Australia's Empire* (ed., with D.M. Schreuder, 2008). He will shortly publish a book co-authored with James Curran: *The Unknown Nation: Remaking Australia in the Wake of Empire*.

Notes

List of abbreviations used in the notes and bibliography

ADB	*Australian Dictionary of Biography*	CPP	*Commonwealth Parliamentary Papers*
ANZW	*Australian and New Zealand Weekly*	NAA	National Archives of Australia
BA	*British Australasian*	NLA	National Library of Australia
BANZ	*British Australian and New Zealander*	PP	*Parliamentary Papers (UK)*
CPD	*Commonwealth Parliamentary Papers*	TNA	The National Archives (UK)

Introduction

1   See, for instance, 'Career Envoy John Dauth Wins Plum London Post, *Australian*, 7 August 2008.

2   More than 800,000 Australians visit the United Kingdom each year and a similar number of Britons visit Australia. See Michael L'Estrange, *The Australia–Britain Relationship Today: Patterns of History, Dynamics of Change*, Menzies Lecture, Menzies Centre for Australian Studies, King's College London, 27 October 2004, p. 25.

3   See Carl Bridge and Kent Fedorowich (eds), *The British World: Diaspora, Culture and Identity*, Frank Cass, London, 2003; Carl Bridge and Bernard Attard (eds), *Between Empire and Nation: Australia's External Relations from Federation to the Second World War*, Australian Scholarly Publishing, Melbourne, 2000; Stuart Ward, *Australia and the British Embrace: The Demise of the Imperial Ideal*, Melbourne University Press, 2001.

4   Adapted from Lord Paul Gore-Booth (ed.), *Satow's Guide to Diplomatic Practice*, 5th edn, Longman, London, 1979, p. 388.

5   Lorna Lloyd, *Diplomacy with a Difference: The Commonwealth Office of High Commissioner, 1880–2006*, Martinus Nijhoff, Leiden, 2007.

6   *Commonwealth Parliamentary Debates (CPD)*, House of Representatives (H. of R.), vol. 51, 7 September 1909, p. 3057.

7   For a useful overview of many of these developments, see W.J. Hudson and M.P. Sharp, *Australian Independence: Colony to Reluctant Kingdom*, Melbourne University Press, 1988. For the Australian Navy, see Nicholas Lambert, 'Sir John Fisher, the Fleet Unit Concept, and the Creation of the Royal Australian Navy', in David Stevens and John Reeve (eds), *Southern Trident: Strategy, History and the Rise of Australian Naval Power*, Allen & Unwin, Crows Nest, New South Wales, 2001, pp. 214–24.

8   Missions were also opened in China (1941), New Zealand (1943) and India (1944).

9   David Lee, *Search for Security: The Political Economy of Australia's Postwar Foreign and Defence Policy*, Allen & Unwin in association with the Department of International Relations, Research School of Pacific and Asian Studies, Australian National University, Canberra, 1995; David Lee, *Australia and the World in the Twentieth Century*, Circa, Beaconsfield, Victoria, 2006, pp. 92–149.

10   Ann Twomey, *The Chameleon Crown: The Queen and Her Australian Governors*, Federation Press, Sydney, 2006; Deborah Gare, 'Dating Australia's Independence: National Sovereignty and the 1986 Australia Acts', *Australian Historical Studies*, vol. 30, no. 113, October 1999, pp. 251–66. The parliament of the United Kingdom possessed the legal right to make constitutional legislation

for the Commonwealth of Australia. From the adoption of the 1931 Statute of Westminster, this could only happen if specifically requested by the government of the Commonwealth of Australia. This power was only removed by the enactment in 1986 by both Australia and the United Kingdom of the Australia Act, which 'repatriated' the Australian Constitution and gave Australia absolute ownership of its lawmaking, to the complete and final exclusion of Britain.

11 Two women have served in an acting capacity. In 2008, Frances Adamson was acting high commissioner for six months from March to September, while Rosaleen McGovern, deputy high commissioner during 1996–8, was also acting high commissioner for shorter periods.

12 Jon Cleary's novel *The High Commissioner* (1966), made into a movie in 1968 starring Rod Taylor and Christopher Plummer, was about a former New South Wales premier as high commissioner.

13 The classic study of prime ministerial power in Australia foreign policy formulation is P.G. Edwards, *Prime Ministers and Diplomats. The Making of Australian Foreign Policy 1901–1949*, Oxford University Press in association with the Australian Institute of International Affairs, Melbourne, 1983.

14 Reid later was elected to the House of Commons, Bruce an international civil servant, Bunting chairman of the Official Establishments Trust, Plimsoll ambassador in Tokyo then governor of Tasmania, Smith went on to be ambassador in Manila and then director-general of the Office of National Assessments, and L'Estrange became secretary of the Department of Foreign Affairs and Trade.

15 Zoë Laidlaw, *Colonial Connections 1815–45: Patronage, the Information Revolution and Colonial Government*, Manchester University Press, 2005, pp. 67–80; Zoë Laidlaw, 'Closing the Gap: Colonial Governors and Unofficial Communications in the 1830s', in Simon J. Potter (ed.), *Imperial Communication: Australia, Britain, and the British Empire c. 1830–50*, Menzies Centre for Australian Studies, King's College London, 2005, pp. 64–87.

16 A. Martin, 'Immigration Policy before Federation', in James Jupp (ed.), *The Australian People: An Encyclopedia of the Nation, Its People and Their Origins*, Cambridge University Press, Cambridge, 2001, pp. 42–4; Robin F. Haines, *Emigration and the Labouring Poor: Australian Recruitment in Britain and Ireland, 1831–60*, Macmillan Press, London, 1997, p. 1.

17 Olwen Pryke, 'Australia House: Representing Australia in London, 1901–1939', PhD thesis, University of Sydney, 2006, pp. 87, 91–3, 282–3.

18 *Canberra Times*, 14 December 1972.

19 David Malouf, 'Made in England: Australia's British Inheritance', *Quarterly Essay*, no. 12, 2003, especially pp. 64–5.

20 Pryke, 'Australia House'.

21 Ibid., pp. 260, 326–7.

1 When is a diplomat not a diplomat? The office of high commissioner

1 Letter, Campbell to Sir Edward Harding, Permanent Under-Secretary of State for the Dominions, 25 August 1939, TNA: DO 35/541/3, C 97/46.

2 Memorandum by Floud, September 1937, TNA: DO 35/548/23, E 31/35.

3 Whiskard's obituary, *Times*, 21 May 1957; letter, Whiskard to Sir Eric Machtig, Permanent Under-Secretary of State for the Dominions, 6 April 1941, TNA: DO 121/111.

4 For Cross's controversial role in wartime Australia, see Kent Fedorowich, '"At War with Canberra": Sir Ronald Cross and the British High Commission, 1941–42', *London Papers in*

Australian Studies, no. 16, Menzies Centre for Australian Studies, King's College London, 2008, pp. 1–49.

5   Lorna Lloyd, '"What's in a Name?" The Curious Tale of the Office of High Commissioner', *Diplomacy and Statecraft*, vol. 11, 2000, pp. 47–78.

6   For the various derivations and the evolution of the post of high commissioner in South Africa prior to union, see John Benyon, *Proconsul and Paramountcy in South Africa: The High Commission, British Supremacy and the Subcontinent 1806–1910*, University of Natal Press, Pietermaritzburg, 1980.

7   Ronald Hyam and Peter Henshaw, *The Lion and the Springbok: Britain and South Africa since the Boer War*, Cambridge University Press, Cambridge, 2003, pp. 102–17, examines South Africa's attempts to incorporate these colonial territories into a 'Greater South Africa' and the struggle which ensued with the British between 1910 and 1961.

8   Chris Cook and John Paxton, *Commonwealth Political Facts*, Macmillan, London, 1979, pp. 12–78.

9   Two excellent studies are Norman Hillmer, 'A British High Commissioner for Canada 1927–28', *Journal of Imperial and Commonwealth History*, vol. 1, 1973, pp. 339–56; P.G. Edwards, 'The Rise and Fall of the High Commissioner: S.M. Bruce in London 1933–1945', in A.F. Madden and W.H. Morris-Jones (eds), *Australia and Britain: Studies in a Changing Relationship*, Sydney University Press, 1980, pp. 39–56.

10   Lloyd, *Diplomacy with a Difference*.

11   John Hilliker, *Canada's Department of External Affairs*, vol. 1, *The Early Years, 1909–1946*, Institute of Public Administration of Canada/McGill–Queen's University Press, Montreal, 1990, p. 15. The migration portfolio was transferred to the Department of the Interior until 1917, when it was moved to the Department of Immigration and Colonization.

12   Kent Fedorowich, 'Anglicisation and the Politicisation of British Immigration to South Africa, 1899–1929', *Journal of Imperial and Commonwealth History*, vol. 19, 1991, pp. 222–46.

13   Lloyd, *Diplomacy with a Difference*, p. 2.

14   This 'right' had been conceded to the dominion leaders during the proceedings of the Imperial War Conference of 1918. Great Britain, *Parliamentary Papers* (*PP*), Cmd 9177, 'Imperial War Conference, 1918. Extracts from Minutes of Proceedings and Papers laid before the Committee', pp. 155–65.

15   Quotation cited in Claude Bissell, *The Imperial Canadian: Vincent Massey in Office*, University of Toronto Press, 1986, p. 75.

16   Lloyd, *Diplomacy with a Difference*, pp. 3–4; W.D. McIntyre, *Dominion of New Zealand: Statesmen and Status 1907–1945*, New Zealand Institute of International Affairs, Wellington, 2007, pp. 180–91.

17   Three useful studies are Stephen Chan, *The Commonwealth in World Politics. A Study of International Action 1965 to 1985*, Lester Crook Academic, London, 1988; W.D. McIntyre, *The Significance of the Commonwealth, 1965–1990*, Macmillan Academic and Professional, Basingstoke, 1991; Krishnan Srinivasan, *The Rise, Decline and Future of the British Commonwealth*, Palgrave Macmillan, Basingstoke, 2005.

18   Lloyd, *Diplomacy with a Difference*, pp. 4–6. Also see the work of Joe Garner, a former British high commissioner and Whitehall insider who began his career in the Dominions Office in 1930. He was head of Her Majesty's Diplomatic Service (1965–68) and the last permanent under-secretary of state in the Commonwealth Office (1962–68) before its merger with the Foreign Office. *The Commonwealth Office, 1925–68*, Heinemann, London, 1978.

19   Hilliker, *Canada's Department of External Affairs*, vol. 1, pp. 11–14.

20 Essential reading on these developments is Edwards, *Prime Ministers and Diplomats*; Ian McGibbon (ed.), *Undiplomatic Dialogue: Letters between Carl Berendsen and Alister McIntosh 1943–1952*, Auckland University Press in association with the Ministry of Foreign Affairs and Trade and the Historical Branch, Department of Internal Affairs, Auckland, 1993, pp. 1–13.

21 A.J. van Wyck, 'The High Commissioner in Great Britain', in Tom Wheeler (ed.), *History of the South African Department of Foreign Affairs 1927–1993*, South African Institute of International Affairs, Johannesburg, 2005, p. 36.

22 Nicholas Mansergh, *The Commonwealth Experience*, Weidenfeld & Nicolson, London, 1969, still remains the best overview despite its age. Also see Philip Wigley, *Canada and the Transition to Commonwealth: British–Canadian Relations, 1917–26*, Cambridge University Press, Cambridge, 1977; Edwards, *Prime Ministers and Diplomats*; D.W. Harkness, *The Restless Dominion: The Irish Free State and the British Commonwealth of Nations, 1921–31*, Macmillan, London, 1969; R.F. Holland, *Britain and the Commonwealth Alliance 1918–1939*, Macmillan, London, 1981. Essential is John Darwin, 'A Third British Empire? The Dominion Idea in Imperial Politics', in Judith M. Brown and Wm. Roger Louis (eds), *The Oxford History of the British Empire*, vol. 4, *The Twentieth Century*, Oxford University Press, Oxford, 1999, pp. 64–87.

23 H. Blair Neatby, *William Lyon Mackenzie King*, vol. 2, *1924–1932 The Lonely Heights*, University of Toronto Press, 1963; Roger Graham, *Arthur Meighen*, vol. 2, *And Fortune Fled*, Clarke, Irwin & Co., Toronto, 1963; C.P. Stacey, *Canada and the Age of Conflict*, vol. 2, *1921–1948 The Mackenzie King Era*, University of Toronto Press, 1981.

24 For Ireland, see Deirdre McMahon, 'Ireland and the Empire-Commonwealth, 1900–1948', in Brown and Louis (eds), *The Oxford History of the British Empire*, vol. 4, pp. 138–62; Deirdre McMahon *Republicans and Imperialists: Anglo-Irish Relations in the 1930s*, Yale University Press, New Haven, 1984; Donal Lowry, 'New Ireland, Old Empire and the Outside World, 1922–49: The Strange Evolution of a "Dictionary Republic"', in Mike Cronin and John M. Regan (eds), *Ireland: The Politics of Independence, 1922–49*, Macmillan, London, 2000, pp. 164–216; Donal Lowry 'The Captive Dominion: Imperial Realities behind Irish Diplomacy 1922–49', *Irish Historical Studies*, vol. 36, 2008, pp. 202–26.

25 Letter, Austen to his sister Ida, 7 November 1926, in Austen Chamberlain, *The Austen Chamberlain Diary Letters*, Robert C. Self (ed.), Cambridge University Press, Cambridge, 1995, p. 295; memorandum, Amery, 9 March 1925, 'The Dominions and the Colonial Office. Proposals for Reorganisation', TNA: DO 121/1. Also see J.A. Cross, *Whitehall and the Commonwealth: British Departmental Organisation for Commonwealth Relations, 1900–1966*, Routledge & Kegan Paul, London, 1967.

26 Philip Williamson and Edward Baldwin (eds), *Baldwin Papers. A Conservative Statesman, 1908–1947*, Cambridge University Press, Cambridge, 2004, p. 199.

27 L.S. Amery, *My Political Life*, vol. 2, *War and Peace 1914–1929*, Hutchinson, London, 1953, pp. 387–8.

28 Letter, Lord Passfield (Sidney Webb), Secretary of State for Dominion Affairs, to MacDonald, 30 May 1930, TNA: DO 121/102; letter, J.H. Thomas, Passfield's successor, to Hertzog, 2 October 1930; Christopher Cunneen, *King's Men: Australia's Governors-General from Hopetoun to Isaacs*, Allen & Unwin, Sydney, 1983, pp. 173–93.

29 W.J. Hudson, 'The Yo-yo Variations: A Comment', *Historical Studies*, vol. 14, no. 55, 1970, p. 425. This article was a response to J.R. Poynter, 'The Yo-yo Variations: Initiative and Dependence in Australia's External Relations, 1918–1923', *Historical Studies*, vol. 14, no. 54, 1970, pp. 231–49. See also the excellent biography by W.J. Hudson, *Casey*, Oxford University Press, Melbourne, 1986.

30   Edwards, *Prime Ministers and Diplomats*, pp. 66–97, 113; W.J. Hudson and Jane North (eds), *'My Dear PM': R.G. Casey's Letters to S.M. Bruce, 1924–29*, Australian Government Publishing Service, Canberra, 1980. The other example of an Australian insider was F.L. McDougall, who after the 1923 Imperial Economic Conference remained as an 'economic advisor' (and much more) at the Australian High Commission. Wendy Way, 'F.L. McDougall and Commodity Diplomacy', in Bridge and Attard (eds), *Between Empire and Nation*, pp. 93–110; W.J. Hudson and Wendy Way (eds), *Letters from a 'Secret Service Agent': F.L. McDougall to S.M. Bruce, 1924–29*, Australian Government Publishing Service, Canberra, 1986.

31   New Zealand followed Australia's example in 1926. Although it took a back seat throughout most of the 1926 Imperial Conference, behind the scenes, Prime Minister J.G. Coates was instrumental in providing crucial liaison arrangements with the Foreign Office, a situation which mirrored Australian practices pioneered by Bruce. McIntyre, *Dominion of New Zealand*, p. 125.

32   Letter, Stephenson to Machtig, 25 November 1942, TNA: DO 35/548/47, E 192/2.

33   Letter, Cross to Batterbee, 10 June 1942, Rhodes House Library, Oxford: Sir H.F. Batterbee Papers, MSS NZ s13, 6/3, folio 15.

34   Roy MacLaren, *Commissions High: Canada in London, 1870–1971*, McGill–Queen's University Press, Montreal, 2006, contains substantive chapters on these men's careers. Also see J.L. Granatstein, *A Man of Influence: Norman A. Robertson and Canadian Statecraft 1929–68*, Deneau Publishers, Ottawa, 1981, pp. 205–45, 283–321.

35   Ibid. Ritchie has written three works about his diplomatic career, the best of which is about his experiences while at Canada House just before and during World War II. See *The Siren Years: A Canadian Diplomat Abroad 1937–1945*, Macmillan, London, 1974.

36   Letter, Amery to Sir Austen Chamberlain, Secretary of State for Foreign Affairs, 15 August 1927, TNA: PREM 1/65. Sir Gerald Campbell was the exception here, but his choice as UK high commissioner in Canada was made predominantly because he had served for many years as a senior consular officer in the United States. His insights into the psyche of Americans were invaluable for the Dominions Office, which wanted a skilled observer with extensive North American experience to monitor closely Canada's relations with its southern neighbour. Sir William Clark, the first appointee to Ottawa, was a long-standing Board of Trade official who had served many years in the Department of Overseas Trade and the Indian Civil Service. See the obituaries of both men in the *Times*, 6 July 1964 (Campbell) and 24 November 1952 (Clark).

37   Letter, Liesching to Batterbee, 28 July 1938, Rhodes House Library, Oxford: Batterbee Papers, MSS NZ s13, 9/1, folios 6–7. Liesching was appointed as British high commissioner in South Africa (1955–58).

38   Harding's obituary, *Times*, 5 October 1954.

39   Kent Fedorowich, 'Lord Harlech in South Africa, 1941–44', in Christopher Baxter and Andrew Stewart (eds), *Diplomats at War: British and Commonwealth Diplomacy in Wartime*, Martinus Nijhoff, Leiden, 2008, pp. 195–225.

40   Letter, Harlech to Violet Milner, 8 March 1941, Bodleian Library, Oxford: Violet Milner Papers, VM 25, C83/6.

41   Joe Garner, *The Commonwealth Office 1925–68*, Heinemann, London, 1978, p. 181.

42   Letter, MacDonald to Addison, 5 November 1945, Durham University Library, Special Collections: Malcolm MacDonald Papers, 12/7, folios 7–8. It was MacDonald, in October 1945, who recommended a full review of conditions of service, which Clark eventually undertook two years later. Letter, MacDonald to Addison, 19 October 1945, TNA: DO 35/4228.

43 Diary entries, 3 and 4 February 1941, in John Colville, *The Fringes of Power: Downing Street Diaries 1939–1955*, rev. edn, Weidenfeld & Nicolson, London, 2004, pp. 301–2, 375; diary entries, 8 and 25 March and 2 May 1941, in John Reith, *The Reith Diaries*, Charles Stuart (ed.), Collins, London, 1975, pp. 275–7.

44 Memorandum by A.R. Cutler, Australian High Commissioner in New Zealand, 3 January 1951, NAA: A461/8, item A348/1/20. Polson, who was seventy-four years of age, not surprisingly turned down the nomination. Jordan was succeeded by Doidge.

45 J.F. Hilliker, 'Distant Ally: Canadian Relations with Australia during the Second World War', *Journal of Imperial and Commonwealth History*, vol. 13, 1984, pp. 46–67; Ronald G. Haycock, 'The "Myth" of Imperial Defence: Australian–Canadian Bilateral Military Cooperation, 1942', *War & Society*, vol. 2, 1984, pp. 65–84.

46 G. Heaton Nicholls, *South Africa in My Time*, George Allen & Unwin, London, 1961, p. 383.

47 Paul Hasluck, *Diplomatic Witness: Australian Foreign Affairs 1941–1947*, Melbourne University Press, 1980, p. 117.

48 War journal, 19 November 1942, Churchill Archive Centre, Cambridge: Colonel Gerald Wilkinson Papers, WILK 1/1.

49 Vincent Massey, *What's Past Is Prologue: The Memoirs of the Right Honourable Vincent Massey*, Macmillan, Toronto, 1963, p. 306.

50 Letter, MacDonald to Viscount Cranborne, Secretary of State for the Dominions, 30 April 1941, TNA: PREM 4/44/10.

51 Memoirs of M.L. Shepherd (1911–36), NAA: A1632, item 1, part 2, folio 391.

52 'Report of the High Commissioner for 1935', 31 July 1936, NAA: A461/9, item G348/1/6, folios 37–8.

53 'Report of the High Commissioner for 1934', 31 July 1935, ibid., item F348/1/6, folio 47.

54 Joy Damousi, 'War and Commemoration: "The Responsibility of Empire"', in Deryck M. Schreuder and Stuart Ward (eds), *Australia's Empire*, companion series, *Oxford History of the British Empire*, Oxford University Press, Oxford, 2008, pp. 288–311. Also see Julie Summers, *Remembered: The History of the Commonwealth War Graves Commission*, Merrell in association with the Commonwealth War Graves Commission, London, 2007; David Lloyd, *Battlefield Tourism: Pilgrimage and the Commemoration of the Great War in Britain, Australia and Canada, 1919–1939*, Berg, Oxford, 1998.

55 'Memorandum on the Functions of the High Commissioner in Canada for His Majesty's Government in Great Britain', 21 May 1928, TNA: PREM 1/65.

56 For the breakdown see Lloyd, *Diplomacy with a Difference*, pp. 67–9. In 1920, India established its first high commission in London. With support from Amery, its high commission network was controversially extended into some but not all of the dominions during World War II.

57 Memorandum, Dominions Office, 25 November 1944, TNA: DO 35/4228.

58 Lloyd, *Diplomacy with a Difference*, p. 43.

59 'Relations with Australia', 22 January 1942, TNA: CAB 66/21, WP(42)33; letter, Cross to Attlee, 22 September 1942, TNA: DO 35/548/47, E 192/2; letter, Stephenson to Machtig, 25 November 1942, ibid.

60 Lord Hankey, *Diplomacy by Conference: Studies in Public Affairs 1920–1946*, Ernest Benn, London, 1946, p. 14.

61 Alfred Stirling, *Lord Bruce: The London Years*, Hawthorne Press, Melbourne, 1974, p. 242.

62 Lloyd, *Diplomacy with a Difference*.

63   See the forthcoming special section in the *Journal of Imperial and Commonwealth History*, edited by Kent Fedorowich and Carl Bridge and due for publication in 2010, which looks at the dominions' high commissioners in London during the first three years of World War II.

2 Foundations: Australia's early representation in Great Britain

1   Barbara Atkins, 'The Problem of the Representation of Australia in England: The Origins and Development of the Australian Agencies-General During the Nineteenth Century', MA thesis, University of Melbourne, 1959; Bernard Attard, 'The Australian High Commissioner's Office: Politics and Anglo-Australian Relations, 1901–1939', DPhil thesis, Oxford University, 1991; John Robert Thompson, 'The Australian High Commission in London: Its Origins and Early History 1901–1916', MA thesis, Australian National University, 1972.

2   Atkins, 'Problem of the Representation', p. 40.

3   *European Mail: A Summary of News for Australia and New Zealand*, 24 November 1875, p. 12.

4   There is some disagreement over the dates when the various colonies transferred their business to an agent-general. See Atkins, 'Problem of the Representation', pp. 143–4; Attard, 'Australian High Commissioner's Office', p. 13; State Records New South Wales, 'Agency Detail: Agent General for New South Wales in London', agency no. 1913.

5   State Records New South Wales, 'Agency Detail: Agent General for New South Wales', agency no. 1913.

6   *Colonial Representation in London: Our Self Governing Colonies: How Their Interests Are Promoted in the United Kingdom*, reproduced in Henry Sell (comp.), *Sell's Dictionary of the World's Press*, King, Sell & Railton, London, 1899, p. 2 (italics in original).

7   'Australia in London: Past and Future', *Argus*, 4 September 1909.

8   Atkins, 'Problem of the Representation', pp. 70, 118, 263.

9   Bruce Smith, 'Australian Loyalty to the British Empire', *Sydney Quarterly Magazine*, December 1888, p. 373, cited in Atkins, 'Problem of the Representation', p. 259.

10   The office remained a commercial agency, its functions almost entirely confined to purchasing and shipping material required by the government. However, from 1870 these duties were significantly increased and 'a new class of business, understood to be of a semi-diplomatic nature, though never expressly defined, was by general consent assigned to the office'. See Barbara Penny, 'Establishing a Nineteenth Century Government Office—The Australian Agencies-General', *Australian Journal of Public Administration*, vol. 22, June 1963, p. 178.

11   'Agents-General and General Agents', *British Australasian*, 3 December 1896, p. 2032.

12   *Age*, 16 April 1895, cited in Thompson, 'Australian High Commission', pp. 16–17.

13   Arthur Beavan, *Imperial London*, J.M. Dent & Co., London, 1901, pp. 101–2.

14   *Age*, 16 April 1895, cited in Thompson, 'Australian High Commission', p. 17.

15   *Official Record of the Proceedings and Debates of the Australasian Federal Conference, 1890*, Government Printer, Melbourne, 1890, pp. 84–5, cited in Thompson, 'Australian High Commission', p. 14. Alfred Deakin was a member of the Victorian Legislative Assembly and the colony's delegate to the Australasian Federal Conference.

16   Atkins, 'Problem of the Representation', p. 266.

17   Sir Alexander Galt was appointed in November 1879. See David Farr, *The Colonial Office and Canada, 1867–1887*, University of Toronto Press, 1955, pp. 260–1.

18   Atkins, 'Problem of the Representation', p. 266.

19   William Morris Hughes, *CPD*, H. of R., 7 September 1909, p. 3059.

20 Henry Hodges to Edmund Barton, 11 October 1901, cited in Thompson, 'Australian High Commission', pp. 56–62.

21 New South Wales Legislative Assembly, 'Commercial Agents, Report by Mr Joseph Barling', *Votes and Proceedings*, vol. 2, 1902, pp. 9–10.

22 Sir John Quick and Sir Robert Garran, *The Annotated Constitution of the Australian Commonwealth*, Angus & Robertson, Sydney, 1901, pp. 632–3.

23 *Advertiser*, 30 May 1901, cited in Thompson, 'Australian High Commission', p. 19.

24 *Australasian* (Melbourne), 20 February 1904, ibid., p. 20.

25 *Australasian*, 30 January 1904, ibid.

26 James excused his assessment: 'This picture may perhaps be overdrawn but it represents what I have heard from many sources but can only accept to the extent of 50 per cent'. Walter James to Alfred Deakin, 26 May 1905, Deakin Papers, NLA: MS 1540, items 1/1155–1161.

27 'The High Commissionership', *Sydney Morning Herald*, 23 July 1901, p. 4.

28 'Australia Still Slumbers', *British Australasian*, 13 July 1905, p. 3.

29 For accusations of disunity, see George Fairbairn, *CPD*, H. of R., 7 September 1909, pp. 3074–5; Foster, ibid., p. 3083.

30 Timothy Coghlan to George Reid, 23 June 1905, Deakin Papers, NLA: MS 1540, item 16/408.

31 Alfred Deakin to Timothy Coghlan, 26 July 1905, Deakin Papers, ibid., item 15/2427.

32 'Unrepresented', *British Australasian*, 16 November 1905, p. 3.

33 'Commonwealth in London: Captain Collins's Appointment', *Argus*, 17 February 1906, p. 14; 'The Commonwealth, The London Office, Reasons for the Establishment', *Sydney Morning Herald*, 17 February 1906, p. 14.

34 Walter James to Alfred Deakin, 31 March 1905, Deakin Papers, NLA: MS 1540, item 1/1128.

35 'Unrepresented', *British Australasian*, 16 November 1905, p. 3.

36 NAA: 'Agency Notes for CA 241: Australian High Commission, United Kingdom (London)'.

37 *Australasian*, 3 March 1906, cited in Thompson, 'Australian High Commission', p. 47. See also 'Commonwealth in London, Office to Be Opened', *Argus*, 16 February 1906, p. 5; 'Commonwealth in London, Captain Collins's Appointment', *Argus*, 17 February 1906, p. 14.

38 NAA: 'Agency Notes for CA 241: Australian High Commission, United Kingdom (London)'.

39 *Australasian*, 3 March 1906, cited in Thompson, 'Australian High Commission', p. 47. Chris Cunneen and Ann Smith conclude: 'Although his influence on government policy was minimal, and his social pretensions made him slightly ridiculous, Collins was a capable administrator in both the Colonial and Commonwealth service'. Chris Cunneen and Ann Smith, 'Collins, Sir Robert Henry Muirhead, 1852–1927', *Australian Dictionary of Biography* (*ADB*), vol. 8, Melbourne University Press, 1981, pp. 79–80.

40 'Commonwealth London Office, Reasons for the Establishment', *Sydney Morning Herald*, 17 February 1906, p. 14; 'Commonwealth London Office, Details of Its Establishment', *Sydney Morning Herald*, 9 March 1906, p. 7.

41 NAA: 'Agency Notes for Agency CA 976, Commonwealth Offices, London (United Kingdom)'.

42 Colonial Office minute no. 10242, 27 March 1906, cited in Thompson, 'Australian High Commission', p. 48.

43 Joseph Cook, *CPD*, H. of R., 1 December 1908, pp. 2443–5. See the discussion of Captain Collins in ibid., pp. 2435–52.

44 Littleton Groom, *CPD*, H. of R., 11 August 1909, p. 2304. In Sir John Forrest's opinion: 'It certainly was not intended when [Collins] was first sent to London that he should remain as long as he has done; but he has saved the Commonwealth a good deal more than his office has cost us, and all he has been instructed to do he has done well'. *CPD*, H. of R., 1 December 1908, p. 2451.

45 William (Billy) Hughes, *CPD*, H. of R., 7 September 1909, p. 3059.

46 See, for example, Senator Higgs, *CPD*, Senate, 16 November 1905, p. 5254, and William (Billy) Hughes, *CPD*, H. of R., 7 September 1909, p. 3059. The *British Australasian* exclaimed: 'The failure to appoint a High Commissioner now amounts to a scandal … We want a High Commissioner at once'. 'Australia Still Slumbers', *British Australasian*, 13 July 1905, p. 3.

47 Senator George Henderson, *CPD*, Senate, 7 October 1909, p. 4216.

48 Attard, 'Australian High Commissioner's Office', pp. 60–7; Thompson, 'Australian High Commission', pp. 52–122.

49 J.A. La Nauze, *Alfred Deakin: A Biography*, Melbourne University Press, 1965, p. 594. On the competition with New Zealand and South Africa, see Attard, 'Australian High Commissioner's Office', p. 26.

50 Littleton Groom, *CPD*, H. of R., 11 August 1909, p. 2301.

51 The bill produced no fewer than fourteen divisions in its course through parliament. See Henry Gyles Turner, *The First Decade of the Australian Commonwealth 1901–1910*, Mason, Firth & McCutcheon, Melbourne, 1911 (facsimile edition, Heritage Publications, Melbourne, 1975), p. 248.

52 Labor Party member Egerton Lee Batchelor feared that 'the measure has been introduced at this stage in the session with a view of making no appointment until recess'. See *CPD*, H. of R., 7 September 1909, p. 3066.

53 Andrew Fisher, *CPD*, H. of R., 26 November 1909, cited in Attard, 'Australian High Commissioner's Office', p. 62.

54 *Commonwealth of Australia Gazette*, no. 65, 18 December 1909, p. 1833.

55 Senator Edward Needham, *CPD*, Senate, 7 October 1909, p. 4214.

56 Parliament of the Commonwealth of Australia, Commonwealth Acts, vol. 8, no. 22, 1909.

57 For example, see the discussion in *CPD*, Senate, 17 August 1905, pp. 1055–71.

58 Senator James Charles Stewart, ibid., p. 1068.

59 Senator William Guy Higgs, ibid., p. 1058.

60 Ibid., p. 1057.

61 Bruce Smith, *CPD*, H. of R., 7 September 1909, p. 3088.

62 James Catts, ibid., p. 3550.

63 Labor Party member, William Robert Nuttal Maloney, ibid., p. 3077.

64 William Wilks, ibid., p. 3546. See also Attard, 'Australian High Commissioner's Office', pp. 65–6.

65 William Wilks, *CPD*, H. of R., 7 September 1909, p. 3063.

66 See, for example, 'The High Commissionership', *Sydney Morning Herald*, 23 July 1901, p. 4; 'Australian High Commissioner, Report from Agents-General', *Standard*, 13 November 1905, in Deakin Papers, NLA: MS 1540, item 15/2455; 'Unrepresented', *British Australasian*, 16 November 1905, p. 3.

67 See the discussion in Thompson, 'Australian High Commission', pp. 64–86. See also 'Wanted, a High Commissioner', *British Australasian*, 27 June 1907, p. 3.

68 Turner, *First Decade of the Australian Commonwealth*, p. 10.

69 Senator Millen, Address in Reply to the Governor-General's Speech, *CPD*, Senate, 17 September 1908, p. 52.

70 *Bulletin*, 11 November 1909, reproduced in Thompson, 'Australian High Commission', p. 111.

71 Forrest was considered a likely candidate from as early as 1904—see David John O'Keefe, *CPD*, H. of R., 20 October 1904, pp. 5794–5.

72 Deakin was employed as an anonymous political correspondent by the English *Morning Post* between 1900 and 1910. See Alfred Deakin, *Alfred Deakin, Federated Australia: Selections from Letters to the Morning Post 1900–1910*, J.A. La Nauze (ed.), Melbourne University Press, 1968, p. 214.

73 *Commonwealth of Australia Gazette*, no. 5, 22 January 1910, p. 48. For Captain Collins's appointment as official secretary, see *Commonwealth of Australia Gazette*, no 23, 16 April 1910, p. 877. Collins continued to serve in this subordinate post until his retirement in 1917.

74 Editorial, *Argus*, 12 January 1910, p. 6.

75 'Australia in London', *Sydney Morning Herald*, 15 January 1910, p. 12.

76 'Australia in London: Past and Future', *Argus*, 4 September 1909, press clipping in NAA: A59, whole series, 'High Commissioner, Press Cuttings'.

77 'Australia in London', *Sydney Morning Herald*, 15 January 1910, p. 12.

3 The first high commissioners: George Reid and Andrew Fisher

1   Lloyd, *Diplomacy with a Difference*. Lloyd is primarily interested in the post–World War II phenomenon where the 'difference' between the status and role of the office of a high commissioner and that of an ambassador narrowed to be almost one of form. In the early period when Australia was establishing its high commission in London, the Australian identification with Britishness was central and pervasive and the formal constitutional structures still treated the dominions as subordinate parts of Britain's empire.

2   *CPD*, H. of R., vol. 51, 7 September 1909, p. 3057.

3   Joy Melleuish, 'Australia and British Policy: Colonial Autonomy and the Imperial Idea, 1885–1902', PhD thesis, University of Sydney, 1965, pp. 183–5.

4   *Sydney Morning Herald*, 2 October 1886.

5   Roger Thompson, *Australian Imperialism in the Pacific*, Melbourne University Press, 1980, pp. 108–10.

6   *Official Record of the Proceedings and Debates of the Australasian Federation Conference, 1890*, Robert S. Brain, Melbourne, 1890, pp. 84–5.

7   John Quick and R.R. Garran, *The Annotated Constitution of the Australian Commonwealth*, Angus & Robertson, Sydney, 1901, pp. 631–40.

8   This appeal caused a political controversy in Australia, known as the 'dreadnought affair', in which Prime Minister Andrew Fisher resisted conservative demands that Australia should respond positively to Britain's request. See Neville Meaney, *A History of Australian Foreign and Defence Policy, 1901–23*, vol. 1, *The Search for Security in the Pacific, 1901–14*, Sydney University Press, 1976, pp. 175, 177–81.

9   Meaney, *Search for Security*, ch. 6.

10   *CPD*, H. of R., vol. 51, 3 September 1909, pp. 3021–2.

11   *CPD*, H. of R., vol. 50, 11 August 1909, p. 2301 and vol. 51, 3 and 7 September 1909, pp. 3022, 3057–8.

12   Thompson, 'Australian High Commission', pp. 142–88.

13   W.J. Ashley (ed.), *British Dominions: Their Present Commercial and Industrial Condition*, Longmans, Green & Co., London, 1911, p. 36.

14   *Times*, 16 May 1912.

15   George Reid, *My Reminiscences*, Cassell & Co., London, 1917, p. 274.

16   Bernard Attard, 'Australian High Commissioner's Office', p. 93.

17   *CPD*, H. of R., vol. 59, 25 November 1910, pp. 6859–60.

18   *Morning Post*, 31 May 1911.

19   Meaney, *Search for Security*, pp. 217–21.

20   Ibid., chs 8 and 9.

21   George Reid, 'The Australian Premiers in England', *Review of Reviews*, Australian edition, September 1897, pp. 297–9; *Sydney Morning Herald*, 25 May 1905; George Reid, *Some Aspects of the Evolution of the British Empire: An Address Delivered before the Royal Colonial Institute on March 11, 1913 by the Right Hon. Sir George Reid*, n.p., London, 1913, pp. 4–5.

22   Reid, *Some Aspects*, pp. 8–9.

23   Letter, Reid to Lewis Harcourt, Colonial Secretary, 25 March 1914, Harcourt Papers, Bodleian Library: MSS 452/345-6.

24   Reid, *My Reminiscences*, p. 266; *CPP*, session 1914-15-16-17, vol. 5, no. 298, 'Sixth Annual Report of the High Commission of the Commonwealth to the United Kingdom'.

25   Eric Wren, *Randwick to Hargicourt: History of the 3rd Battalion, A.I.F.*, Ronald G. McDonald, Sydney, 1935, p. 32, cited in Thompson, 'Australian High Commission', p. 277.

26   Reid, *My Reminiscences*, pp. 352–4.

27   Ibid., pp. 356–7.

28   *CPP*, session 1914-15-16-17, vol. 5, no. 229, 'Correspondence Respecting Extension of Term of Appointment of the Right Honourable Sir George Reid'.

29   Cited in Thompson, 'Australian High Commission', p. 281.

30   *Official Report of the Sixth Commonwealth Conference of the A.L.P. held in Adelaide, May 31 – June 7, 1915*, Worker Trade Union Printery, Sydney, 1915.

31   *Argus*, 3 and 5 August 1914.

32   Neville Meaney, *A History of Australian Foreign and Defence Policy, 1901–23*, vol. 2, *Australia and World Crisis, 1914–23*, Sydney University Press, 2009, pp. 78–81, 97–8, 109.

33   Letter, Fisher to Munro Ferguson, 11 November 1915, Novar Papers, NLA: MS 696/3845.

34   Letter, Munro Ferguson to Bonar Law, 8 November 1915, Novar Papers, NLA: MS 696/691.

35   *Daily Telegraph*, 29 January 1916.

36   *Times*, 31 January 1916. See for press cuttings from a wide range of interviews and speeches, NAA: A1 1916/17188. Strangely, this collection of press cuttings does not include extracts from the *Times*.

37   *Sydney Morning Herald*, 3 March 1916.

38   Letter, Fisher to Pearce, 24 February, Pearce Papers, AWM: 3 DRL 2222 7/43.

39   *Daily Telegraph*, 29 January 1916.

40   Meaney, *Australia and World Crisis*, pp. 17, 136–7.

41   Despatch, British Colonial Secretary, Sir Walter Long to Australian Governor-General, Sir Ronald Munro Ferguson, 8 March 1917, enclosing the First Report of the Dardanelles Commission, NAA: A11804 1920/21. See also David Day, *Andrew Fisher: Prime Minister of Australia*, Fourth Estate, London, 2008, pp. 370–3.

42   See letters in Fisher Papers, NLA: MS 2919/1/124-375; Bernard Attard, 'Andrew Fisher, the High Commissionership and the Collapse of Labor', *Labour History*, no. 68, May 1995, pp. 121–5.

43   'Annual Report of the High Commissioner, 1916', NAA: A458 F108/8; Peter Bastian, *Andrew Fisher: An Underestimated Man*, University of New South Wales Press, Sydney, 2009, pp. 298–304.

44   D.J. Murphy, 'Andrew Fisher', *ADB*, vol. 8, 1981, p. 507.

45   Letter, Fisher to Higgs, 5 September 1919, cited in Day, *Andrew Fisher*, pp. 395–6.

4 Diplomacy by default: empire foreign policy and the high commissioners during the 1920s

This essay is based on the research for my unpublished doctoral thesis, 'The Australian High Commissioner's Office: Politics and Anglo-Australian Relations, 1901–1939', DPhil, Oxford University, 1991, a copy of which has been deposited with the National Library of Australia. Greater detail about particular points can be found there. For encouragement, assistance and generosity in allowing me access to research material, I thank Geoffrey Bolton, Carl Bridge, Peter Edwards and the late Bill Hudson. I also thank the editors of this volume for providing the best possible opportunity to publish more of this research. I hope some of the judgments have matured, even though they remain my own.

1   Good accounts of these developments can be found in Mansergh, *Commonwealth Experience*, and R.F. Holland, *Britain and the Commonwealth Alliance 1918–1939*, Macmillan, Basingstoke, 1981.

2   There is an excellent treatment of these issues in Hudson and Sharp, *Australian Independence*.

3   *PP*, Cmd 2768, 1926, 'Imperial Conference, 1926. Summary of Proceedings', p. 14.

4   For a cogent overview of Australia's defence and foreign policies between the two world wars that remains informative, Paul Hasluck, *The Government and the People 1939–1941*, Australian War Memorial, Canberra, 1952, chs 1 and 2.

5   *CPD*, vol. 114, 3 August 1926, in Neville Meaney (ed.), *Australia and the World: A Documentary History from the 1870s to the 1970s*, Longman Cheshire, Melbourne, 1985, no. 187, p. 359.

6   The major statement of Australian defence policy was made by Bruce after the 1923 Imperial Conference: *CPD*, vol. 106, 27 March 1924, Meaney, *Australia and the World*, no. 181, pp. 343–6; for the quotes: *CPD*, vol. 107, 27 June 1924, Meaney, *Australia and the World*, no. 182, pp. 346–8.

7   Mansergh, *Commonwealth Experience*, vol. 2, p. 12.

8   *PP*, Cmd 2301, 1924–25, no. 5, telegram, Governor-General to Secretary of State, 16 July 1924, p. 9.

9   *CPD*, vol. 114, 3 August 1926, Meaney, *Australia and the World*, no. 187, p. 360.

10   *CPD*, vol. 107, 27 June 1924, Meaney, *Australia and the World*, no. 182, pp. 346–48.

11   *CPD*, vol. 115, p. 71, quoted in Hasluck, *Government and the People*, p. 19.

12   *CPD*, vol. 114, 3 August 1926, Meaney, *Australia and the World*, no. 187, p. 360.

13 Edwards, *Prime Ministers and Diplomats*, pp. 27–8, 189–92.

14 L.F. Fitzhardinge, *The Little Digger, 1914–52: William Morris Hughes, A Political Biography*, Angus & Robertson, Sydney, 1978, pp. 326–8; telegram, Stonehaven to Dominions Secretary, 21 December 1927, TNA: DO 35/22/12270; J.A. Cross, *Whitehall and the Commonwealth*, Routledge & Kegan Paul, London, 1967, pp. 46–8.

15 *Age*, 26 July 1923 (reporting a discussion of Nationalist party members of parliament); Attard, 'Australian High Commissioner's Office', pp. 240–1, 263.

16 *CPD*, vol. 114, 3 August 1926, Meaney, *Australia and the World*, no. 187, p. 361.

17 Letter, Alan McDougall to Fisher, 30 June 1920, Fisher Papers, NLA: MS 2919, 1/523.

18 *Age*, 28 January 1921; Attard, 'Australian High Commissioner's Office', pp. 168–9; Fitzhardinge, *Little Digger*, pp. 497–8.

19 *Daily Telegraph*, 12 November 1921.

20 For biographical detail, J.R.M. Murdoch, 'Joseph Cook: A Political Biography', PhD thesis, University of New South Wales, 1969, and F.K. Crowley, 'Cook, Sir Joseph', *ADB*, vol. 8, 1981, pp. 96–9.

21 Quoted in Murdoch, 'Cook', pp. 374–5.

22 Ernest Scott, *Australia during the War* 6th edn, Angus & Robertson, Sydney, 1940, p. 39.

23 Murdoch, 'Cook', p. 353.

24 Ibid., pp. 355–6, 378.

25 Cook to Latham, 15 November 1921, Latham Papers, NLA: MS 1009, 1/948.

26 *Brisbane Courier*, 15 November 1921; *Daily Telegraph*, 12 November 1921. For the office's low reputation at the end of Fisher's term, Attard, 'Andrew Fisher', pp. 126–7.

27 Letter, Munro Ferguson to Stamfordham, 11 March 1918, Novar Papers, NLA: MS 696, folios 305–8.

28 Latham diary quoted in Edwards, *Prime Ministers and Diplomats*, p. 44.

29 Letter, Long to Munro Ferguson, 13 December 1918, Wiltshire and Swindon Archives: 947/625.

30 Letter, Hughes to Shepherd, 3 September 1923, NAA: A1632, p. 357; 'the gentleman' is not named, but the context suggests it is Cook.

31 Cablegram, Governor-General to Secretary of State, 13 January 1922, NAA: CP268/1, 1/331; Attard, 'Australian High Commissioner's Office', pp. 176–8.

32 *CPD*, vol. 98, 24 November 1921, p. 13246.

33 Letter, Bruce to Amery, 6 May 1925, NAA: AA1970/555.

34 For an introduction, W.J. Hudson, *Australia and the League of Nations*, Sydney University Press in association with the Australian Institute for International Affairs, Sydney, 1980.

35 'Functions and duties of the High Commissioner', supplied by Secretary of the Prime Minister's Department, 9 October 1919, NAA: A461, N348/1/2.

36 The Manchurian crisis of 1932 was the other major episode involving an Australian high commissioner at the League before Bruce's appointment, Attard, 'Australian High Commissioner's Office', pp. 235–6.

37 Quoted in W.K. Hancock, *Survey of British Commonwealth Affairs*, vol. 1, *Problems of Nationality 1918–1936*, Oxford University Press, London, 1937, p. 87.

38 P.M. Sales, 'W.M. Hughes and the Chanak Crisis of 1922', *Australian Journal of Politics and History*, vol. 17, December 1971, pp. 392–405; Fitzhardinge, *Little Digger*, pp. 485–96; Mansergh, *Commonwealth Experience*, vol. 2, pp. 9–12.

39   Cablegram, Hughes to Lloyd George, 20 September 1922, Meaney, *Australia and the World*, no. 177, p. 335.

40   Cablegram no. 40, H.M. Consul in Geneva, 20 September 1922, TNA: CO 532/213/47041.

41   Fisher, Notes on the Work of the Sixth (Political) Commission at the Third Assembly of the League of Nations, 1922, TNA: FO 371/8335, W 8634/8634/98. Cecil was the chairman of the League of Nations Union and representative of South Africa.

42   Cablegrams [two], Cook to Hughes, 21 September 1921, Hughes Papers, NLA: MS 1538, 16/2391-2.

43   Cablegram, Secretary of State to Governor-General, 3 October 1922, Hughes Papers, NLA: MS 1538, 16/2466; Fitzhardinge, *Little Digger*, pp. 492–6.

44   Deborah Lavin, 'Amery, Leopold Charles Maurice Stennett (1873–1955)', *Oxford Dictionary of National Biography*, Oxford University Press, Oxford, September 2004; online edition, January 2008, www.oxforddnb.com/view/article/30401, accessed 22 April 2009; John F. Naylor, 'Hankey, Maurice Pascal Alers, first Baron Hankey (1877–1963)', *Oxford Dictionary of National Biography*, www.oxforddnb.com/view/article/33683, accessed 22 April 2009.

45   Edwards, *Prime Ministers and Diplomats*, pp. 69–70; *Times*, 26 January 1935; although christened Alexander, he was known by his third name.

46   Memorandum, A.W.A. Leeper to Prime Minister, 2 June 1924, NAA: M1135.

47   Leeper, Report on My Service with the Commonwealth Government, [November 1924], NAA: M1135.

48   Memorandum, A.W.A. Leeper to Prime Minister, 2 June 1924, NAA: M1135 (emphasis in original).

49   *PP*, Cmd, 2301, 1924-25, no. 5, telegram, Governor-General to Secretary of State, 16 July 1924, p. 9.

50   W.J. Hudson, 'Casey, Richard Gavin Gardiner', *ADB*, vol. 13, 1993, pp. 381–5; Hudson and North (eds), *'My Dear P.M.'*, p. vii; letter, Amery to Chamberlain, 24 November 1924, TNA: FO 371/10563, W 10461/4972/50.

51   Hudson, *Casey*, p. 59.

52   Letters, Bruce to Cook, 14 October 1924, NAA: M1135; Casey to Cook, 14 November 1924, ibid.; Cook to Bruce, 29 November 1924, ibid..

53   Letter, Bruce to Cook, 14 October 1924, ibid.

54   Letter, Casey to Bruce, 27 November 1924, *'My Dear P.M.'*, no. 1, p. 1.

55   Leeper, Report on My Service with the Commonwealth Government, [November 1924], NAA: M1135.

56   Hudson, *Casey*, pp. 61–2.

57   Letter, Bruce to Casey, 16 January 1926, NAA: A1420/3.

58   Letter, Amery to Bruce, 16 March 1925, NAA: AA1970/555.

59   Letter, Amery to Chamberlain, 24 November 1924, TNA: FO 371/10565, W 10461/4972/50; L.S. Amery, *The Leo Amery Diaries*, vol. 1, *1896–1929*, John Barnes and David Nicholson (eds), Hutchinson, London, 1980, p. 392, 18 November 1924.

60   Letter, Cook to Bruce, 29 November 1924, NAA: M1135.

61   *Amery Diaries*, p. 392, 18 November 1924.

62   *Amery Diaries*, pp. 400, 401, 12 and 18 March 1925; letter, W.S. Hankinson to Lt Col. Sir Ronald Waterhouse, 8 April 1925, TNA: CO 532/317/15593; Keith Middlemas and John Barnes, *Baldwin*, Weidenfeld & Nicolson, London, 1970, pp. 356–7.

63 High Commissioner's Engagements, quarter ended 30 September 1925, NAA: A458, E108/8; *Amery Diaries*, p. 423, 20 October 1925.

64 *Commonwealth Parliamentary Papers* (*CPP*), 1926–28, vol. 5, 'Report of the High Commissioner … for the Year 1925', p. 921.

65 Letter, Casey to Bruce, 23 February 1928, *'My Dear P.M.'*, no. 105, p. 299. The last recorded meeting with the other high commissioners took place on 3 May 1927: High Commissioner's Engagements during the quarter 1 April 1927 – 30 June 1927, NAA: A461, A348/1/6.

66 For the cables between Bruce and Cook between 16 February and 17 March 1926 regarding the special assembly, NAA: CP317/8, bundle 2; cablegram, Cook to Bruce, 2 June 1927, NAA: CP268/1.

67 Hudson, *Australia and the League of Nations*, pp. 157–65.

68 Cablegram, Cook to Bruce, 3 June 1926, NAA: CP317/8, bundle 2.

69 Cablegram, Cook to Bruce, 8 August 1926, NAA: AA1970/559, bundle 1; statement for press, S.M. B[ruce], 30 August 1926, NAA: CP268/1.

70 Letter, Bruce to Casey, 16 January 1926, NAA: Bruce Papers, A1420/3.

71 Imperial Conference 1926 – Inter-Imperial Relations Committee; 8th meeting … 8 November 1926, TNA: CAB 32/56, p. 3; *PP*, Cmd 2768, p. 156.

72 Letter, Amery to Bruce, 14 March 1927, TNA: DO 35/34/1865.

73 Cablegram, Dominions Secretary to Prime Minister, 24 April 1928, NAA: A981 Defence 289.

74 Letter, Casey to Bruce, 20 September 1928, *'My Dear P.M.'*, no. 153, p. 409; letter, Glasgow to Bruce, 7 January 1928; cablegram, Prime Minister to Dominions Secretary, 28 April 1928, NAA: A981 Defence 289.

75 Cablegram, Page to Bruce, 15 December 1926, NAA: AA1970/559, bundle 1; *Argus*, 2 and 3 February 1927.

76 Cablegram, Page to Bruce, 15 December 1926, NAA: AA1970/559, bundle 1.

77 Cabinet minutes, 21 March 1927, NAA: A2718/XM, vol. 2; South Australian *Register*, 24 March 1927.

78 *Sydney Morning Herald*, 31 March 1927; Attard, 'Australian High Commissioner's Office', pp. 200–1.

79 P. Serle, *Dictionary of Australian Biography*, Angus & Robertson, Sydney, 1949, pp. 301–2; A.J. Hill, 'Ryrie, Sir Granville de Laune', *ADB*, vol. 11, 1988, pp. 502–4; George Pearce, *Carpenter to Cabinet*, Hutchinson, London, 1951, p. 181; *Daily Telegraph*, 23 March 1927.

80 Letter, Hughes to Shepherd, 24 September 1927, NAA: A1632, p. 377.

81 Letter, Stonehaven to Salisbury, 30 May 1927, Hatfield House Library: MSS 4M/121/95; quoted by permission of the Marquess of Salisbury.

82 *Brisbane Courier*, 24 March 1927; South Australian *Register*, 24 March 1927.

83 Letter, Bruce to Ryrie, 13 June 1927, NAA: A3299; Edwards, *Prime Ministers and Diplomats*, p. 76; W.J. Hudson, 'Fuhrman, Osmond Charles William', *ADB*, vol. 8, 1981, pp. 592–3.

84 Robert Hyslop, 'Trumble, Thomas (1872–1954)', *ADB*, vol. 12, 1990, p. 269.

85 Letter, Bruce to Ryrie, 13 June 1927, NAA: A3299; minute, Relations between Australian Liaison Officer and High Commissioner, 15 June 1927, TNA: FO 372/2322, T 7554/213/814.

86 Letter, Casey to Bruce, 14 December 1927, *'My Dear P.M.'*, no. 76, p. 213.

87 Letter, Casey to Bruce, 1 March 1928, *'My Dear P.M.'*, no. 109, p. 306.

88 Letter, Casey to Bruce, 30 August 1928, *'My Dear P.M.'*, no. 150, p. 399.

89 Minutes, 5 July 1928, TNA: CAB 2/5.

90 *Amery Diaries*, 5 July 1928, p. 554; letter, Casey to Bruce, 20 September 1928, *'My Dear P.M.'*, no. 153, pp. 409–10.

91 Letter, Casey to Bruce, 18 July 1929, *'My Dear P.M.'*, no. 207, p. 540; Hudson, *Australia and the League of Nations*, p. 155.

92 Letter, Bruce to Casey, 20 March 1928, NAA: A1420/5.

93 Letter, Casey to Bruce, 28 November 1929, NAA: A1420/8.

94 'Report of the High Commissioner for 1929', pp. 64–7, NAA: A458, F108/8[15]; *Times*, 14 February 1929.

95 Draft cablegram, Prime Minister to Secretary of State, 14 July 1929, NAA: A1420/8. The minutes of these meetings are in TNA: CAB 2/5.

96 The 'Casey experiment' is Hankey's phrase in letter, Hankey to Bruce, 26 January 1925, NAA: M1135.

97 Attard, 'Australian High Commissioner's Office', pp. 259–61.

98 *Amery Diaries*, 11 November 1928, p. 571.

99 Telegram, Under-Secretary of State to Imperial Secretary, 12 November 1928, TNA: DO 114/22, no. 383.

5 The high commissioners, empire development and economic diplomacy between the wars

Like the previous chapter, this essay is based on the research for my unpublished doctoral thesis, 'The Australian High Commissioner's Office: Politics and Anglo-Australian Relations, 1901–1939', DPhil, Oxford University, 1991. The same acknowledgments apply, but I would also like to thank the then deputy high commissioner, Mr A.L. Vincent, and official secretary, Mr D.C. Rutter, who encouraged this project; Sir Victor Garland, who provided insights into the role of a modern high commissioner; and Mr J. Stratton, who gave me a tour of Australia House.

1 For accounts of key aspects on which this and the following paragraph are based: Barrie Dyster and David Meredith, *Australia and the International Economy in the Twentieth Century*, Cambridge University Press, Cambridge, 1990, ch. 5 and p. 132; Stuart Macintyre, *The Oxford History of Australia*, vol. 4, *The Succeeding Age*, Oxford University Press, Melbourne, 1986, ch. 9; W.H. Richmond, 'S.M. Bruce and Australian Economic Policy, 1923–29', *Australian Economic History Review*, vol. 23, September 1983, pp. 238–57; Michael Roe, *Australia, Britain and Migration, 1915–1940*, Cambridge University Press, Cambridge, 1995, chs 1–4.

2 *PP*, Cmd 2009, 'Imperial Economic Conference. Record of Proceedings', p. 58.

3 Large numbers had been employed during the war and in the immediate postwar period in connection with the administrative work related to the Australian Imperial Force, Australian munitions workers, repatriation and war graves.

4 *Times*, 1 March 1921; *CPP*, 1922, vol. 2, 'Report of the Acting High Commissioner for the Year 1921', p. 1606; Memorandum … to Prime Minister's Department, 4 June 1925, NAA: A461, N348/1/8, part 1.

5 Schedule of Information for Secretary of the High Commissioner of South Africa, NAA: A2911, 2441/11.

6 Figures are summarised from *CPP*, 1929–31, vol. 2, 'Report upon the Organization of the High Commissioner's Office'; for the different departments 'represented', see Coleman Report, Appendix F, NAA: A6252, item 7, part 2.

7   *CPP*, 1926–28, vol. 5, 'Report of the High Commissioner for 1927', p. 1009.

8   Ibid.

9   Memorandum by the Prime Minister, 25 January 1924, NAA: A461, J334/1/1, part 1.

10 Ibid.

11 *CPP*, 1920–21, vol. 4, Final Report of the Royal Commission upon Public Expenditure. Appendix C, p. 1409.

12 W.J. Hudson and Christine Steele, 'Shepherd, Malcolm Lindsay (1873–1960)', *ADB*, vol. 11, 1988, p. 592; Robert Hyslop, 'Trumble, Thomas (1872–1954)', *ADB*, vol. 12, 1990, p. 269.

13 Bruce to Cook, 9 April 1926, NAA: A1606, C17/1, part 4; *Argus*, 10 April 1926; K.R. Page, 'Collins, James Richard (1869–1934)', *ADB*, vol. 8, 1981, pp. 77–8.

14 Bernard Attard, 'Financial Diplomacy', in Bridge and Attard (eds), *Between Empire and Nation*, p. 112.

15 Letter, Collins to Lyons, 30 January 1934, NAA: CP268/3, I/280.

16 Casey's activities are discussed in chapter 4.

17 Letter, Hughes to Hunter, 30 September 1920, NAA: A461, N348/1/8, part 1; memorandum by the Prime Minister, 25 January 1924, NAA: A461, J334/1/1, part 1.

18 Roe, *Australia, Britain and Migration*, pp. 22, 65, 66.

19 *Times*, 29 December 1927; Roe, *Australia, Britain and Migration*, pp. 100, 102. Unfortunately, I have been unable to discover Mrs Manning's given name.

20 Alfred Stirling, 'McDougall, Frank Lidgett (1884–1958)', *ADB*, vol. 10, 1986, pp. 258–9; Wendy Way, 'The Ideas of F.L. McDougall: A Biographical Approach', PhD thesis, Australian National University, 2008.

21 Letter, McDougall to Bruce, 29 November 1928, in Hudson and Way (eds), *Letters from a 'Secret Service Agent'*, no. 196, p. 682–3; also letters, McDougall to Bruce, 9 March 1927, no. 97, pp. 322–3; McDougall to Bruce, 16 June 1927, no. 113, pp. 378–9; McDougall to Bruce, 20 July 1927, no. 118, p. 399; McDougall to Bruce, 9 May 1928, no. 163, pp. 570–1.

22 Stirling, 'McDougall', p. 258. Wendy Way deals specifically with this theme in 'F.M.L. McDougall and Commodity Diplomacy', in Bridge and Attard (eds) *Between Empire and Nation*, pp. 93–110.

23 Attard, 'Financial Diplomacy'.

24 Attard, 'Australian High Commissioner's Office', pp. 192–6; letter, Collins to Lyons, 30 January 1934, NAA: CP268/3, I/280.

25 David Cannadine, *Ornamentalism: How the British Saw Their Empire*, Oxford University Press, New York, 2001, especially p. 122.

26 Cablegram, High Commissioner to Prime Minister, 27 September 1919, NAA: CP268/3, 20/194; Attard, 'Australian High Commissioner's Office', pp. 159–64, 257–8; Attard, 'Andrew Fisher', pp. 126–7.

27 *CPP*, 1922, vol. 2, 'Report of the Acting High Commissioner for 1921', p. 1601.

28 Memoirs of M.L. Shepherd (hereafter, Shepherd Memoir), pp. 387, 401, NAA: A1632.

29 J.R.M. Murdoch, 'Joseph Cook: A Political Biography', PhD thesis, University of New South Wales, 1969, p. 96; Shepherd to Hughes, 22 January 1925, in Shepherd Memoir, p. 370, NAA: A1632.

30 Letter, Cook to Hughes, 9 March 1922, Hughes Papers, NLA: MS 1538, 16/2286 (emphasis in original).

31 *Times*, 14 January 1922.

32 Melbourne *Herald*, 24 July 1922.

33 *CPP*, 1925, vol. 2, 'Report of the High Commissioner for 1924', pp. 935, 958; John M. MacKenzie, *Propaganda and Empire: The Manipulation of British Public Opinion, 1880–1960*, Manchester University Press, 1984, pp. 107–12.

34 *CPP*, 1923–24, vol. 2, 'Report of the High Commissioner for 1922', p. 580; 'Report of the High Commissioner for 1923', p. 619.

35 *CPP*, 1926–28, vol. 5, 'Report of the High Commissioner for 1926', p. 983.

36 Ibid., p. 921.

37 High Commissioner's Engagements, January 1st to March 31st 1925, NAA: A458, E108/8.

38 *Times*, 20 August 1927.

39 Shepherd Memoir, pp. 412, 413, NAA: A1632.

40 *Times*, 20 August 1927.

41 *Times*, 14 July 1927.

42 *Bulletin*, 27 March 1929. For this article and the complaints about Ryrie's speeches, see NAA: A461, D348/1/5.

43 Letter, Casey to Bruce, 21 November 1929, NAA: A1420/8.

44 Minute, R.V.N. H[opkins] to Grigg, 3 February 1930, TNA: T 160/807/F11935/1.

45 Cablegram, Prime Minister's Department to High Commissioner's Office, 4 August 1928, NAA: A461, N348/1/8, part 1; cablegrams, Prime Minister to High Commissioner, 20 January and 1 March 1930, ibid., part 2; 'Report of the High Commissioner for 1930', p. 71, NAA: A461, B348/1/6; Roe, *Australia, Britain and Migration*, p. 151.

46 For the rest of this paragraph: letter, Scullin to Ryrie, 18 November 1930; memorandum [Farrands], n.d. but December 1930 (begins: 'For some years …'), NAA: A461, L348/1/2; minute paper, Executive Council, 12 March 1931; memorandum, 4 March 1931, NAA: M348/1/2; Hyslop, 'Trumble', p. 269.

47 Letter, Trumble to Scullin, 12 November 1930, NAA: A461, L348/1/2.

48 The best account of the crisis remains C.B. Schedvin, *Australia and the Great Depression*, Sydney University Press, 1970.

49 Attard, 'Financial Diplomacy', p. 127.

50 Schedvin, *Australia and the Great Depression*, p. 232; for the rest of this paragraph unless otherwise indicated, Attard, 'Australian High Commissioner's Office', pp. 219–33.

51 *Times*, 4 October 1937.

52 Cablegram, Coleman to Prime Minister, 5 August 1930, NAA: A461, L348/1/2; *CPD*, vol. 135, 14 September 1932, p. 450.

53 Casey resigned at the end of 1930 to enter conservative politics in Australia.

54 Unless indicated otherwise, the rest of this paragraph is based on, Attard, 'Australian High Commissioner's Office', pp. 219–32.

55 'Report of the High Commissioner for 1931', p. 1, NAA: A461: C348/1/10.

56 This information is in a letter from Ryrie's son to the author dated 3 February 1986.

57 *Times*, 15 March and 21 June 1932.

58 *Times*, 4 October 1937.

59 *Times*, 11 February 1932.

60 *Sydney Morning Herald*, 3 December 1931.

61 Schedvin, *Australia and the Great Depression*, pp. 262–6, 351–2.

62 *Times*, 11 February 1932.

63 *Times*, 6 and 7 January 1932; letter, Hankinson to Batterbee, 21 June 1932, TNA: DO 35/410 11648/27; Heather Radi, 'Bruce, Stanley Melbourne (1883–1967)', *ADB*, vol. 7, 1979, p. 458.

64 Letters, Bruce to Latham, 22 March 1932, NAA: M104/1; Bruce to Casey, 19 January 1933, NAA: A1421/1; leader, *Daily Telegraph*, 12 September 1933.

65 Letter, Bruce to Lyons, 11 April 1933, Lyons Papers, NLA: MS 4581, 2/11. Page tried to dissuade Bruce from leaving politics in 1933; a year later, he offered to make way for him in his own seat, undated memorandum by the Member for Cowper, Page Papers, NLA: MS 1633, 2577; Earle Page, *Truant Surgeon*, Angus & Robertson, Sydney, 1963, p. 227.

66 Cablegram, from Gullett, 7 April 1933, NAA: AA1970/559, 1/1; leader, *Sydney Morning Herald*, 25 September 1933; also see Radi, 'Bruce', p. 458.

67 Letter, Bruce to Latham, 11 May 1933, NLA: MS 1009, folder 1, folios 3377–80.

68 Letter, Bruce to Casey, 13 September 1933, NAA: A1421/1.

69 Bernard Attard, 'Moral Suasion, Empire Borrowers and the New Issue Market during the 1920s', in R.C. Michie and Philip Williamson (eds), *The British Government and the City of London in the Twentieth Century*, Cambridge University Press, Cambridge, 2004, pp. 195–214.

70 The classic account is Ian M. Drummond, *Imperial Economic Policy, 1917–1939*, University of Toronto Press, 1974, pp. 300–39; also see Attard, 'Financial Diplomacy' and Tim Rooth, 'Ottawa and After', in Bridge and Attard (eds), *Between Empire and Nation*, pp. 133–57.

71 Letter, Casey to Batterbee, 10 June 1932, Churchill College, Cambridge: HNKY 5/7.

72 *Official Year Book of the Commonwealth of Australia*, Commonwealth Bureau of Census and Statistics, Canberra, no. 26, 1933, pp. 234, 431. The trade surplus refers to merchandise and gold production; that is, the commodity balance of trade.

73 For alternative accounts of the conversions: Neville Cain and Sean Glynn, 'Imperial Relations Under Strain: The British–Australian Debt Contretemps of 1933', *Australian Economic History Review*, vol. 25, March 1985, pp. 39–58, and Kosmas Tsokhas, 'Coldly Received: Australia and the London Capital Market in the 1930s', *Australian Journal of International Affairs*, vol. 46, May 1992, pp. 61–80.

74 E.g., cablegram [in two parts], Lyons to Bruce, 9 and 10 February 1932, NAA: M110/2; cablegram, Lyons to Bruce, 18 May 1933, ibid.

75 Interview with the Chancellor of the Exchequer, 31 March 1933, NAA: M110/1; telephone conversation with Mr Latham, 5 April 1933, ibid.

76 Interview with the Governor and the Deputy Governor of the Bank of England, 11 May 1933, ibid.; interview with the Chancellor of the Exchequer, 12 May 1933, ibid.

77 Interview with the Governor and the Deputy Governor of the Bank of England, 11 May 1933, ibid.

78 Cablegram sent to the Prime Minister, 13 May 1933, NAA: M110/2; cablegram, Lyons to Bruce, 18 May 1933, ibid.

79 Letter, Bruce to Casey, 13 September 1933, NAA: A1421/1.

80 Drummond, *Imperial Economic Policy*, pp. 300–39.

81 Ibid., pp. 264, 271; Ian M. Drummond, *British Economic Policy and the Empire 1919–1939*, George Allen & Unwin, London, 1972, pp. 211–22.

82 Economic Commission, 20 June 1933, League of Nations, *Journal of the World Monetary and Economic Conference. Corrigenda*, 22 December 1933, p. 3.

83 *CPD*, vol. 152, 26 November 1936, p. 236; for an account of the visit and its aftermath, Bernard Attard, 'The Limits of Influence: The Political Economy of Australian Commercial Policy after the Ottawa Conference', *Australian Historical Studies*, vol. 29, no. 111, October 1998, pp. 325–43.

84 Letter, Bruce to Casey, 9 November 1935, NAA: M1129/4. The Country Party joined the United Australia Party in government after the federal election in September 1934.

85 Cablegram, Bruce to Lyons, 16/17 October 1934, NAA: A1606, AY17/1. Further material about the conversions can be found in NAA: A1606, AY17/1 and A461, F344/1/7; for a summary of the results: *Official Year Book of the Commonwealth of Australia*, no. 33, 1939, p. 860.

86 Drummond, *Imperial Economic Policy*, pp. 339–54, 404–7.

87 Letter, Bruce to Menzies, 7 March 1935, Menzies Papers, NLA: MS 4936, series 1. In 1934, Bruce had also failed to persuade the government to accept an interpretation of article 10 of the Ottawa agreement even though he had been the principal architect of the treaty. See Attard, 'Limits of Influence'.

88 Sean Turnell, 'F.L. McDougall: Éminence Grise of Australian Economic Policy', *Australian Economic History Review*, vol. 40, no. 1, March 2000, pp. 51–70.

89 Hudson, *Australia and the League of Nations*, pp. 169–80; Turnell, 'McDougall', pp. 60–4; Way, 'Ideas of F.L. McDougall', ch. 7.

90 The trade diversion episode continues to invite contrasting responses—see Drummond, *Imperial Economic Policy*, pp. 398–403; D.C.S. Sissons, 'Manchester v. Japan: The Imperial Background of the Australian Trade Diversion Dispute with Japan, 1936', *Australian Outlook*, vol. 30, no. 3, 1976, pp. 480–502; Kosmas Tsokhas, 'The Wool Industry and the 1936 Trade Diversion Dispute Between Australia and Japan', *Australian Historical Studies*, vol. 23, no. 93, October 1989, pp. 442–61; A.T. Ross, 'Australian Overseas Trade and National Development Policy 1932–39: A Story of Colonial Larrikins or Australian Statesmen?', *Australian Journal of Politics and History*, vol. 36, no. 2, 1990, pp. 184–204.

91 Letter, Bruce to Giblin, 11 July 1936, NAA: M104/4. For some evidence of Bruce's influence on the government, W.K. Hancock, *Survey of British Commonwealth Affairs*, vol. 2, *Problems of Economic Policy 1918–1939, Part 1*, Oxford University Press, London, 1940, p. 249.

92 R.G. Menzies, *Afternoon Light*, Cassell Australia, Melbourne, 1967, p. 117.

93 Cablegram, Bruce to Lyons, 21 November 1932, NAA: CP268/3, I/280.

94 D.I. McDonald, 'McLaren, Sir John Gilbert (1871–1958)', *ADB*, vol. 10, 1986, pp. 324–5; *Times*, 3 June 1935.

95 Selwyn Cornish, 'McFarlane, Stuart Gordon (1885–1970)', *ADB*, vol. 15, 2000, pp 210–11.

96 Kathleen Dermody, 'Duncan, John Shiels (1886–1949)', *ADB*, vol. 14, 1996, p. 52.

97 Letter, Bruce to Lyons, 25 January 1934, NAA: A461: I348/1/2, part 1.

98 *CPD*, vol. 158, 29 November 1938, p. 2177.

99 Letter, McLaren to Latham, 26 July 1935, NLA: MS 1009, folder 1, folios 4210–11.

100 *CPP*, 1937–40, vol. 3, 'Report of the High Commissioner for 1938', pp. 1723–24; cablegram, Prime Minister's Office to High Commissioner's Office, 21 May 1938, NAA: A461: N348/1/8, part 2.

101 Bruce had recommended twice this intake. Cablegrams, Bruce to Lyons, 21 November 1938, in R.G. Neale (ed.), *Documents on Australian Foreign Policy 1937–49*, vol. I, *1937–38*, Australian Government Publishing Service, Canberra, 1975, nos 318–19, pp. 516–18; *Times*, 2 December 1938; cablegram, High Commissioner's Office to Prime Minister's Department, 7 December 1938, NAA: A461: N348/1/8, part 2.

6 'Ambassador-at-large par excellence': S.M. Bruce and the League of Nations

1   Quoted in Stirling, *Lord Bruce*, p. 61.

2   For the evolution of the office of high commissioner in the British Commonwealth, see Lloyd, *Diplomacy with a Difference*.

3   K.C. Wheare, *The Statute of Westminster and Dominion Status*, Clarendon Press, Oxford, 1938.

4   Letter, Bruce to Lyons, 11 April 1933, Lyons Papers, NLA: MS 4851, box 2, folder 11.

5   Letter, Casey to Bruce, 5 March 1933, NAA: A1420/1, item 1.

6   Letter, Bruce to Lyons, 23 August 1932, NLA: MS 4851, box 2, folder 11.

7   Letter, Bruce to Page, 25 January 1934, NAA: M104/1, 2; telegram, Bruce to Latham, 11 September 1933, Latham Papers, NLA: MS 1009/52/729; see also letter from Norman to Bruce, 19 September 1933, Bank of England Papers, NLA Australian Joint Copying Project: M 2491.

8   Hudson, *Australia and the League of Nations*, pp. 193–6.

9   Ibid.

10   Bruce attended his first meeting of the Council on 4 October 1933, minute by Keith Officer, 5 October 1933, NAA: A10356, 6.

11   Letter, Bruce to Lyons, 20 March 1933, NAA: A981, EUR6/1.

12   By 1935 there were ten non-permanent members. China, Germany and Panama were no longer represented on the League, while Chile, Ecuador, Romania and Turkey had been elected. Minute by Keith Officer, 'China's Claim for Seat on Council of League of Nations', 5 July 1935, NAA: A981 League Cou 3.

13   Provisional Minutes of 77th Session of the Council, 4 October 1933, NAA: A10356, 6.

14   Memorandum, Keith Officer to the Secretary, Department of External Affairs, 25 September 1934, NAA: A981 League 15th Ass 4; Report by Bruce on the 15th Assembly of the League of Nations, September 1934, ibid.

15   Dispatch, Sir Samuel Hoare to Sir E. Drummond, 6 July 1935, NAA: A981, ABY 24, part 1.

16   Frank Hardie, *The Abyssinian Crisis*, Batsford, London, 1974, pp. 8–64.

17   Mark Thompson, *The White War: Life and Death on the Italian Front 1915–1919*, Faber and Faber, London, 2008.

18   Letter, Bruce to Lyons, 21 October 1935, Report to the Council of the League of Nations by the Council Committee on 'Dispute Between Ethiopia and Italy', 5 April 1935, NAA: ABY 24, part 1.

19   Lloyd, *Diplomacy with a Difference*, p. 39.

20   David Carlton, 'The Dominions and British Policy in the Abyssinian Crisis', *Journal of Imperial and Commonwealth History*, vol. 1, no. 1, 1972, pp. 59–77; Carl Bridge, 'Australia and the Italo-Abyssinian Crisis of 1935–6', *Journal of the Royal Australian Historical Society*, vol. 92, no. 1, June 2006, pp. 1–14.

21   Cablegram, Bruce to Lyons, 19 October 1935, NAA: A981, ABY 35, part 1.

22   Cablegram, Bruce to Lyons, 22 August 1935, NAA: A981, ABY 24, part 1.

23   Ibid.

24   Robert Self, *Neville Chamberlain: A Biography*, Ashgate, Aldershot, 2006, p. 246.

25   Memorandum for Cabinet, G.F. Pearce, Minister for External Affairs, 'Italo-Abyssinian Dispute', 22 October 1935, NAA: A981, ABY 35, part 1.

26 Sir Samuel Hoare, *House of Commons*, 22 October 1935, cols 17–33.

27 Supplementary note by W.R. Hodgson on the Italo-Abyssinian Dispute, 10 February 1936, NAA: A981, ABY 36; Hardie, *Abyssinian Crisis*, pp. 164–203.

28 Record of conversation of British ministers with Bruce, 25 May 1936, TNA, DO 121/2.

29 Stirling, *Lord Bruce*, p. 28. 'I wish to be a Dominion.'

30 Susan Williams, *The People's King: The True Story of the Abdication*, Penguin Books, London, 2003.

31 Letter, Bruce to Baldwin, 16 November 1936, NAA: M104/1, 4.

32 W.K. Hancock, *Smuts*, vol. 2, *The Fields of Force 1919–1950*, Cambridge University Press, Cambridge, 1962, pp. 274–5.

33 Hudson, *Australia and the League of Nations*, pp. 169–73.

34 Ibid., pp. 172–3.

35 F.L. McDougall, 'The Origins of FAO', n.d. 1951, FAO Archives, Rome.

36 Speech, S.M. Bruce to the Second Committee of the League of Nations, 19 September 1935, NAA: M104, 3.

37 Report on nutrition submitted by the second committee to the Assembly, 5 October 1936, NAA: A981, League 17th Ass 5, part 2.

38 Margaret E. Burton, *The Assembly of the League of Nations*, University of Chicago Press, 1941, p. 228.

39 Hudson, *Australia and the League of Nations*, pp. 179–80; report on Bruce 'Kandidater tel Nobels fredspris 1937', the Norwegian Nobel Institute; Lord Boyd Orr, *As I Recall*, MacGibbin and Kee, London, 1966, p. 219.

40 David Bird, *J.A. Lyons, the Tame Tasmanian: Appeasement and Rearmament in Australia, 1932–39*, Australian Scholarly Publishing, Melbourne, 2008, pp. 142–3.

41 F.P. Walters, *A History of the League of Nations*, Oxford University Press, London, 1952, p. 695.

42 Stirling, *Lord Bruce*, p. 29.

43 Ibid., p. 27.

44 League of Nations, 91st Extraordinary Session of the Council, Third Meeting, 17 March 1936, NAA: A981, League Cou 11.

45 See, particularly, cablegram, South African Prime Minister to Charles te Water, High Commissioner in London, 12 March 1936, and letter, Bruce to Malcolm MacDonald, 17 March 1936, conveying cablegram from Lyons, TNA: DO 35/185/68882A/31.

46 Meeting of High Commissioners at the Dominions Office, 9 March 1936, TNA: DO 35/185/6882A/8.

47 Cablegram, Bruce to Lyons, received 12 September 1936, NAA: A981 League Refo 5.

48 Anthony R. Deluca, *Great Power Rivalry at the Turkish Straits: The Montreux Conference and Convention of 1936*, Columbia University Press, New York, 1981, p. 10.

49 Dispatch, P. Loraine, British Ambassador to Turkey to Anthony Eden, 16 April 1936, NAA: A981, TUR 9, part 2; Deluca, *Great Power Rivalry*, p. 28.

50 Cablegram, Secretary of State for Dominion Affairs to Dominion Governments, 29 May 1936, NAA: A981, TRE 556.

51 Handwritten minute, Pearce to Hodgson, 29 May 1936, NAA: A981, TRE 556.

52 Cablegram, Bruce to Pearce, 3 June 1936, ibid.

53 Cecil Edwards, *Bruce of Melbourne: Man of Two Worlds*, Heinemann, London, 1965, p. 239.

54 Bruce would later describe Aras as sharing 'the specially friendly feeling for Australia held by all Turkish political leaders'. Note by Bruce on Turkey, 11 February 1942, NAA: M100.

55 Deluca, *Great Power Rivalry*, p. 58.

56 Ibid., p. 91.

57 Letter, R. Bellairs to Duke of Portland, 17 July 1936, TNA: ADM 116/3656A 261028.

58 *Actes de la Conference de Montreux, 22 Juin–20 Juillet. Compte Rendu des Séances Plenières et Procès-Verbal de Comité Technique*, Paris, 1936, p. 185.

59 'Australia's Debt to Mr Bruce', Melbourne *Herald*, 17 October 1936.

60 Sir George Rendel, *The Sword and the Olive*, J. Murray, London, 1957, pp. 92–3.

61 Undated notes by S.M. Bruce, c. 1936, NAA: AA1910, 33.

62 Letter, Aras to Bruce, dated 22 September 1936, enclosing letter, Atatürk to Bruce; and reply, Bruce to Atatürk, 22 September 1936: 'May I assure your Excellency that the personal nature of those gifts has touched me very deeply and that I regard myself as singularly fortunate in being the possessor of such an excellent and artistically executed portrait of the distinguished founder of the new Turkish Republic. May I add that I shall treasure most highly the very valuable and beautiful cigarette case which accompanied the portrait of Your Excellency.' NAA: M104, 4; Edwards, *Bruce of Melbourne*, pp. 239–40.

63 Letter, Bruce to Casey, 22 October 1936, NAA: A1421, 3.

64 Handwritten letter, Hughes to Bruce, 5 November 1936, NAA: M104, 4.

65 McDougall's circle included the British diplomats Gladwyn Jebb and Rex Leeper; R.M. Barrington-Ward, the assistant editor of the *Times*; Noel Hall, professor of political economy, University of London; Mike 'Lester' Pearson, a Canadian diplomat in London; Sir George Schuster, company director and expert on colonial development; and Sir Alfred Zimmern, professor of international relations at Oxford University.

66 Hancock, *Smuts*, pp. 271–2.

67 Letter, Bruce to J. Avenol, 1 March 1937, NAA: M104, 5/2; minute by Gladwyn Jebb, UK Foreign Office, 9 January 1937, TNA: FO 371/21215, W373/5/50.

68 Martin C. Dubin, 'Toward the Bruce Report: The Economic and Social Programs of the League of Nations in the Avenol Era', in United Nations Library, *The League of Nations in Retrospect: Proceedings of the Symposium Organised by the United Nations Library and the Graduate Institute of International Studies*, Geneva, 6–9 March 1980, W. De Gruyter, New York, 1983, p. 52.

69 League of Nations Sixteenth Ordinary Session, 13 September – 6 October 1937, p. 35, Sp.S. 169.

70 Letter, Bruce to Avenol, 1 March 1937, League of Nations Archives, Geneva.

71 Inis L. Claude, *Swords into Plowshares: The Problems and Progress of International Organization*, University of London Press, 1965, p. 357.

72 Letter, Avenol to Bruce, 27 May 1939, League of Nations Archives 1933–1946/50/38247/38247 (R.5805).

73 'The Development of International Co-operation in Economic and Social Affairs', Report of the Special Committee, 22 August 1939, League of Nations Archives, Geneva.

74 Victor-Yves Ghebali, *La Société des Nations et la Réforme Bruce 1939–1940*, Centre Européen de la Dotation Carenegie Pour la Paix Internationale, Geneva, 1970.

75 David Mitrany, *The Progress of International Government*, Allen & Unwin, London, 1933; I. Claude, *Swords into Plowshares*, pp. 344–67; Ernest Haas, *Beyond the Nation State: Functionalism and International Organisation*, Stanford University Press, 1964; Walter Schiffer, *The Legal Community*

of Mankind: A Critical Analysis of the Modern Concept of World Organization, Columbia University Press, New York, 1954.

76 Hudson, *Australia and the League of Nations*, pp. 178–9; note by Bruce of conversation with R.A. Butler, UK Foreign Office, 2 February 1940, NAA: M100, February 1940.

7 *'Undependable busybody'? S.M. Bruce and World War II*

1   Diary entry for 13 September 1939, in Cadogan, *The Diaries of Sir Alexander Cadogan*, David Dilks (ed.), Cassell, London, 1971, p. 216.

2   Massey, *What's Past Is Prologue*, p. 298.

3   Hasluck, *Government and the People*, p. 227; Edwards, 'Rise and Fall'; I.M. Cumpston, *Lord Bruce of Melbourne*, Longman Cheshire, Melbourne, 1989, p. 175; an 'English gentleman': Frank Anstey cited in Edwards, *Bruce of Melbourne*, p. 191.

4   Cited in Edwards, *Bruce of Melbourne*, p. 56.

5   On British rearmament: letter, Bruce to R.G. Casey (Australian Treasurer), 1 December 1937, NAA: A1421, item 3, and letter, Bruce to Lyons, 16 December 1937, NAA: M104, item 5(i); on a new battleship for the Far East: Bruce's record of conversation with Lord Stanhope (First Lord of the Admiralty), 24 November 1938, NAA: M104, item 6(i); on the Empire Air Training Scheme: Edwards, *Bruce of Melbourne*, pp. 278–80.

6   Bridge, 'Australia and the Italo-Abyssinian Crisis', pp. 1–14.

7   Cumpston, *Lord Bruce of Melbourne*, pp. 162–7. See also Bird, *J.A. Lyons*, ch. 6.

8   Edwards, *Bruce of Melbourne*, p. 259.

9   Cablegram, Bruce to Menzies, 16 August 1939, in R.G. Neale (ed.), *Documents on Australian Foreign Policy, 1937–49*, vol. II, *1939*, Australian Government Publishing Service, Canberra, 1975, p. 172; cablegram, Menzies to Neville Chamberlain, 18 August 1939, ibid., p. 173.

10 Cablegram, Bruce to Menzies, 30 August 1939, ibid., p. 208.

11 Record of High Commissioners' Meeting, 30 August 1939, TNA: DO 121/5.

12 'He [Neville Chamberlain] told me very confidentially that Bruce had been to see him the previous evening and had expressed doubts about the message being sent out after the Cabinet reaffirming our policy of support to Poland, notwithstanding the Russo-German Pact of non-aggression. This had much reduced his confidence in Bruce—never, I gather, very high.' Hankey diary, 23 August 1939, cited in Stephen Roskill, *Hankey: Man of Secrets*, Collins, London, 1970, p. 414.

13 Roskill, *Hankey*, p. 414.

14 P.G. Edwards, 'S.M. Bruce, R.G. Menzies and Australia's War Aims and Peace Aims, 1939–1940', *Historical Studies*, vol. 17, no. 66, 1976, pp. 11–14.

15 The episode is analysed in Edwards, *Bruce of Melbourne*, pp. 286–8.

16 Cablegram, Menzies to Casey (for Roosevelt), 26 May 1940, in H. Kenway, H.J.W. Stokes and P.G. Edwards (eds), *Documents on Australian Foreign Policy, 1937–49*, vol. III, *January–June 1940*, Australian Government Publishing Service, Canberra, 1979, pp. 332–3.

17 Bruce's comment on Churchill's memorandum, 20 November 1939, cited in Edwards, *Bruce of Melbourne*, p. 284.

18 Cablegram, Bruce to Menzies, 6 July 1940, NAA: M100; letter, Bruce to Halifax, 1 August 1940, ibid.

19 Cablegram, Churchill to Menzies, 11 August 1940, in W.J. Hudson and H.J.W. Stokes (eds), *Documents on Australian Foreign Policy, 1937–49*, vol. IV, *July 1940 – June 1941*, Australian Government Publishing Service, Canberra, 1980, p. 85.

NOTES TO PAGES 106–112

20 Cablegram, Bruce to Menzies, 26 September 1940, ibid., pp. 183; cablegram, Menzies to Bruce (for Churchill), 29 September 1940, ibid., p. 186.

21 Entry for 26 February 1941, *Diaries of Sir Alexander Cadogan*, pp. 258–9.

22 Cablegram, Bruce to Menzies, 13 August 1941, W.J. Hudson and H.J.W. Stokes (eds), *Documents on Australian Foreign Policy, 1937–49*, vol. V, *July 1941 – June 1942*, Australian Government Publishing Service, Canberra, 1982, p. 74.

23 Cablegrams, Fadden to Bruce, Bruce to Fadden, 29 August 1941, NAA: M100.

24 Cablegram, Bruce to Curtin, 22 October 1941, NAA: A5954, 7/559; cablegram, Churchill to Curtin, 2 November 1941, NAA: A5954, 7/589.

25 Edwards, *Bruce of Melbourne*, p. 321.

26 For Casey, see Carl Bridge (ed.), *A Delicate Mission: The Washington Diaries of R.G. Casey, 1940–42*, National Library of Australia, Canberra, 2008, pp. 11–13.

27 Bruce cited in Edwards, *Bruce of Melbourne*, p. 324; cablegram, Bruce to Curtin, 23 February 1942, NAA: M100.

28 Bruce's notes, quoted in Edwards, *Bruce of Melbourne*, pp. 344–5.

29 Cablegram, Bruce to Curtin, 6 August 1942, NAA: M100; Stirling, *Lord Bruce*, p. 251.

30 See, for example, 'Conversation with Attlee', 28 June 1942, NAA: M100; 'Conversation with Sir E. Bridges' (UK Cabinet Secretary), 9 April 1943, ibid.; cablegram, Curtin to Bruce, 7 August 1942, ibid.; letter, Curtin to Bruce, 1 June 1943, ibid.

31 Bruce's notes, cited in Edwards, *Bruce of Melbourne*, p. 341.

32 The story can be followed in Bruce's confidential notes for May–June 1942 and June–July 1943, NAA: M100.

33 Cablegram, Bruce to Curtin, 4 June 1942, cited in Edwards, *Bruce of Melbourne*, p. 348.

34 Bruce, Note on Functioning of War Cabinet, n.d. [September 1942], NAA: M100; Churchill's unsent reply, TNA: PREM 4/50/11.

35 Edwards, 'Rise and Fall', p. 53.

36 Conversation with Attlee, 30 October 1942, NAA: M100.

37 Note, Churchill to Dominions Secretary, 3 February 1944, TNA: PREM 4/43A/14.

38 Cumpston, *Lord Bruce of Melbourne*, pp. 102, 176.

39 Stirling, *Lord Bruce*, p. 221.

40 Letter, Bruce to Officer, 6 August 1943, Officer Papers, NLA: MS 2629/1.

41 Cumpston, *Lord Bruce of Melbourne*, p. 177.

8 John Beasley and the postwar world

1 Letter, Fowler to Chifley, 9 July 1948, NAA: A2908/V37; letter, J.H. Garrett to Fowler, 12 July 1948, ibid.

2 Bede Nairn, 'Beasley, John Albert', *ADB*, vol. 13, 1993, pp. 140–3.

3 Cabinet decision, 1135A, 'Overseas Appointments', Cabinet, 30 July 1946, NAA: A2908, B32, part 1; minute paper for the Executive Council, 7 August 1946, Department of Prime Minister, Departmental no. 49, Executive Council no. 36, ibid.

4 Letter, Chifley to Beasley, 23 November 1945, NAA: A2908, B32, part 1.

5 Christopher Waters, *The Empire Fractures: Anglo-Australian Conflict in the 1940s*, Australian Scholarly Publishing, Melbourne, 1995.

6   See, for instance, 'Mr Beasley's Mission', *Sydney Morning Herald*, 21 December 1945, NAA: A5954, 2211/3.

7   Ken Buckley, Barbara Dale and Wayne Reynolds, *Doc Evatt: Patriot, Internationalist, Fighter, Scholar*, Longman Cheshire, Melbourne, 1994, part 4.

8   Nairn, 'Beasley', p. 142.

9   'Mr. Beasley's Mission', *Sydney Morning Herald*, 21 December 1945, NAA: A5954, 2211/3.

10 'The Honourable J.A. Beasley', typescript, n.d. [c. August–September 1945], TNA: DO 35/1116, G554/5.

11 Nairn, 'Beasley', pp. 141–2; 'Mr Beasley Ill: Collapses in His Office', *Age*, 20 January 1944, Australian Dictionary of Biography File for John Albert Beasley, ADB Office, Research School of Social Sciences, Australian National University, Canberra.

12 Letter, Ben Cockram to Sir John Stephenson, 30 August 1945, TNA: DO 35/1116, G554/5.

13 W.G. Spence, *Australia's Awakening: Thirty Years in the Life of an Australian Agitator*, Worker Trustees, Sydney, n.d. [first published 1909], p. 53.

14 Letter, Cockram to Stephenson, 30 August 1945, TNA: DO 35/1116, G554/5. See also 'Appointment of Resident Ministers in London and Washington', 25 January 1945, NAA: A2908, B32, part 2.

15 See, for instance, 'Mr Beasley to Retain Defence Portfolio', *Argus* (Melbourne), 19 December 1945; 'Beasley to Retain Defence Post', *Daily Telegraph* (Sydney), 19 December 1945, NAA: A5954, 2211/3.

16 Letter, Beasley to Shedden, 30 December 1946, 10 April 1947, NAA: A5954, 43/1.

17 'Demand for Berths to Australia', *Argus*, 7 February 1946, NAA: A5954, 2211/3; 'Australia Can Support 12 Million', *Argus*, 12 February 1946, ibid.; '5,500 Await Berths to Australia', *Argus*, 21 February 1946, ibid.; 'No Ships for Brides', *Sydney Morning Herald*, 25 February 1946, ibid.; 'Transfer of War Brides Slowed by Lack of Ships', *Argus*, 25 February 1946, ibid.; 'Beasley Seeing British Minister Today', *Herald* (Melbourne), 1 March 1946, ibid.; 'Mr. Beasley "Let Down" Over Bride Ship', *Argus*, 18 April 1946, ibid.; 'Beasley and Forde May Return to Contest Next Elections', *Sun*, 16 September 1948, Beasley ADB File; informal record, High Commissioners' Meeting, 14 November 1947, TNA: DO 35/2792.

18 Letter, Beasley to Chifley, 16 March 1948, Personal Papers of Prime Minister Chifley, NAA: M1455/1, 291.

19 'The Honourable J.A. Beasley', typescript, n.d. [c. August–September 1945], TNA: DO 35/1116, G554/5.

20 Letter, Cockram to Stephenson, 30 August 1945, TNA: DO 35/1116, G554/5.

21 Memorandum, JCS [Sir John Stephenson] to Secretary of State [for Dominions Affairs], 26 September 1945, TNA: DO 35/1116, G554/5.

22 'Beasley's Stormy Political Career', *Sydney Morning Herald*, 13 September 1949, NAA: A5954, 2211/3.

23 *Sun*, 30 January 1946, Beasley ADB File.

24 *CPD*, H. of R., 21 March 1946, extract in NAA: A2908, B32, part 1; 'Beasley Took Food as Duty', *Daily Telegraph*, 23 February 1946, NAA: A5954/2211/3; letter, Beasley to Frank Strahan, 10 October 1946, NAA: A2908, B32, part 1; letter, Strahan to Beasley, 14 August [sic—November] 1946, ibid; *CPD*, Senate, 14 November 1946, ibid.

25 'Mr Beasley's Cheery Greeting to London—"Topper" and All', *Herald* (Melbourne), 24 January 1946, NAA: A5954, 2211/3.

26 'Life with the Beasleys', *Smiths Weekly*, 15 May 1948, NAA: A5954, 43/1.

27 Letter, Robinson to Beasley, 13 September 1945, NAA: A2908, B32, part 2.

28 'Life with the Beasleys', *Smiths Weekly*, 15 May 1948, NAA: A5954, 43/1.

29 'She Now Sells Golden Slippers', *People*, 31 January 1951, pp. 18–20, Beasley ADB File.

30 Letter, Beasley to Shedden, 23 March 1948, NAA: A5954, 43/1.

31 'Beasley's Stormy Political Career', *Sydney Morning Herald*, 13 September 1949, NAA: A5954, 2211/3; 'Australia House Renovations', *Argus*, 20 February 1946, ibid.

32 Letter, Beasley to Chifley, 30 April 1948, NAA: A2908, B32, part 1; letter, Chifley to Beasley, 14 May 1948, ibid.; 'Life with the Beasleys', *Smiths Weekly*, 15 May 1948, NAA: A5954, 43/1.

33 'Life with the Beasleys', *Smiths Weekly*, 15 May 1948, NAA: A5954, 43/1.

34 'Canteen', NAA: A2908, B32, part 1.

35 'Australia House Renovations', *Argus*, 20 February 1946, NAA: A5954, 2211/3.

36 Letter, Officer to Peter Heydon, 15 October 1946, Sir Keith Officer Papers, NLA: MS 2629/1/1043, box 2, mainly quoted in Alan Fewster, *Trusty and Well Beloved: A Life of Keith Officer, Australia's First Diplomat*, Miegunyah Press, Melbourne, 2009, p. 303.

37 Details are in NAA: A461, B348/1/5, part 2.

38 Letter, Joe Hewitt to Beasley, 3 October 1945, NAA: A2908, B32, part 2; letter, Beasley to Shedden, 12 February 1946, NAA: A5954, 43/1; Richard Kingsland, 'Mighell, Sir Norman Rupert (1894–1955)', *ADB*, vol. 15, 2000, pp. 366–7.

39 Letter, Officer to William Dunk, 3 June 1946, Officer Papers, NLA: MS 2629/1/1013, box 2; letter, Dunk to Officer, 20 June 1946, Officer Papers, NLA: MS 2629/1/1018, box 2; Fewster, *Trusty and Well Beloved*, p. 299. See also Beasley's complaint to the prime minister regarding the failure of the Department of External Affairs to communicate vital information to the high commission about an aviation agreement with Canada: letter, Beasley to Chifley, 18 June 1946, Chifley Papers, NAA: M1455/1, 121.

40 Paul McGuire, 'Efforts to Get War Brides Home', *Argus*, 1 March 1946, NAA: A5954, 2211/3.

41 Letter, Officer to Dunk, 7 October 1946, Officer Papers, NLA: MS 2629/1/1043, box 2; Fewster, *Trusty and Well Beloved*, p. 303.

42 'Beasley Makes Heated Attack on Soviet', *Sydney Morning Herald*, 28 August 1946, NAA: A5954, 2211/3; 'Angry Session at Conference: Australia and Soviet Again; "Decisions of Big Four"', *Age*, 28 August 1946, NAA: A5954, 2097/2; 'Australia Must Keep Her Temper Better', *Age*, 29 August 1946, ibid.; 'Praise for Mr Beasley's Tactics', *Argus*, 29 August 1946, ibid.; 'Soviet Hits at "Naive" Australians', *Daily Telegraph*, 29 August 1946, ibid.; Paul McGuire, 'Blunt Words at Paris Conference', *Argus*, 29 August 1946, ibid.

43 Letter, Beasley to Chifley, 16 March 1948, Chifley Papers, NAA: M1455/1, 291.

44 David Lee, 'Britain and Australia's Defence Policy, 1945–1949', *War & Society*, vol. 13, no. 1, 1995, pp. 61–80.

45 Letter, Beasley to Chifley, 23 January 1948, Chifley Papers, NAA: M1455/1, 241. For Bevin's speech and its context, see Alan Bullock, *Ernest Bevin, Foreign Secretary: 1945–1951*, Heinemann, London, 1983, pp. 513–25.

46 F.K. Roberts, 'Report of Conversation between Secretary of State and Beasley', 6 April 1948, TNA: FO 800/444, p. 96; Waters, *Empire Fractures*, p. 121.

47 'Record of a Conversation between the Secretary of State and the Australian High Commissioner', 20 April 1948, TNA: FO 800/444, p. 101.

48 Letter, Beasley to Shedden, 19 May 1948, NAA: A5954, 43/1.

49 Nairn, 'Beasley', p. 142.

50 'Must Fight for Freedom', *Herald* (Melbourne), 27 November 1946, NAA: A5954, 2211/3.

51 'Beasley Warns on Red "Menace" to Empire', *Herald*, 13 November 1946, NAA: A5954, 2211/3.

52 Letter, Beasley to Shedden, 10 April 1947, NAA: A5954, 43/1.

53 Informal note, High Commissioners' Meeting, 12 December, 1947, TNA: DO 35/2792, pp. 22–3.

54 For the Australian official reaction to Western Union, see letter, Chifley to Attlee, 22 January 1948, doc. 313 and letter, Chifley to Attlee, 10 February 1948, doc. 318, in Pamela Andre (ed.), *Documents on Australian Foreign Policy 1937–49*, vol. XVI, *Beyond the Region 1948–49*, Department of Foreign Affairs and Trade, Canberra, 2001, pp. 373–6, 381–2.

55 Minute, Burton to Evatt, 3 May 1948, doc. 324, in ibid., pp. 390–1.

56 Informal note, High Commissioners' Meeting, 19 December 1947, TNA: DO 35/2792, p. 16.

57 Informal note, High Commissioners' Meeting, 16 April 1948, TNA: DO 35/2794, p. 411.

58 Informal note, High Commissioners' Meeting, 14 May 1948, ibid., pp. 401–2.

59 Informal note, High Commissioners' Meeting, 16 July 1948, ibid., pp. 370–1.

60 Memorandum, L. Ridsdale to G. Jebb, 6 July 1948, TNA: FO 371/73060, Z 5667/273/72; Waters, *Empire Fractures*, p. 140.

61 P.G. Edwards, 'The Origins of the Cold War, 1947–1949', in Carl Bridge (ed.), *Munich to Vietnam: Australia's Relations with Britain and the United States since the 1930s*, Melbourne University Press, 1991, pp. 70–86.

62 Informal note, High Commissioners' Meeting, 18 March 1949, TNA: DO 35/2794.

63 *Argus*, 13 June 1949, NAA: A5954, 2211/3.

64 Note, High Commissioners' Meeting, 9 June 1947, TNA: DO 35/2792, p. 100. See also, in the same file, notes, High Commissioners' Meetings, 3 April 1947 (p. 114), 18 April 1947 (p. 109) and 20 June 1947 (pp. 56–7).

65 Cablegram, Watt to Beasley, 12 September 1946, NAA: A11549/1, 7; cablegram, Beasley to Prime Minister and Evatt, 13 September 1946, ibid.; cablegram, Evatt to Beasley, 16 September 1946 [received], ibid.; cablegram, Beasley to Evatt, 17 September 1946, ibid.

66 Note, High Commissioners' Meeting, 18 April 1947, TNA: DO 35/2792, p. 110. See also note, High Commissioners' Meeting, 7 March [1947], ibid., p. 119, for Canada's position and Beasley's response.

67 Informal note, High Commissioners' Meeting, 20 June 1947, TNA: DO 35/2792, pp. 61–2.

68 Informal note, High Commissioners' Meeting, 13 February 1948, TNA: DO 35/2794, p. 423.

69 See, for instance, informal notes, High Commissioners' Meetings, 4, 23 February, 4 March 1949, TNA: DO 35/2794.

70 Informal note, High Commissioners' Meeting, 2 April 1948, TNA: DO 35/2794, p. 405. See also Beasley to Chifley, 28 February 1948, Chifley Papers, NAA: M1455/1, 291.

71 Informal note, High Commissioners' Meeting, 17 December 1948, TNA: DO 35/2794, p. 310.

72 Informal note, High Commissioners' Meeting, 23 February 1949, ibid., p. 258; informal note, Meeting with Commonwealth Delegations held at the Offices of the United Kingdom Delegation, Paris, 30 November 1948, TNA: DO 121/55.

73 Garner, *Commonwealth Office*, p. 299.

74 Informal notes, High Commissioners' Meetings, 7 and 8 January 1949, TNA: DO 35/2857; R.J. Moore, *Making the New Commonwealth*, Clarendon Press, Oxford, 1987, p. 167.

75 Memorandum, Ian Maclennan to Gilbert Laithwaite, 6 January 1949, TNA: DO 35/2857.

76 Informal note, High Commissioners' Meeting, 8 February 1949, TNA: DO 35/2794.

77 '"Brains Trust" Episode', *Age*, 14 December 1946, NAA: A5954, 2211/3; 'Mr Beasley Resents Dr Joad's References to Australia, *Argus*, 13 December 1946, ibid.; 'Joad Unabashed by Beasley Protest' and 'Mr Beasley, Our Stout Defender', *Herald* (Melbourne), 13 December 1946, ibid.

78 Memorandum, 11 November 1947, TNA: DO 35/2792; memorandum, 13 November 1947, ibid.; 'Informal Record of a Meeting held in the Foreign Secretary's Room', 14 November 1947, ibid.

79 Memorandum, Francis Cumming-Bruce to the Secretary of State for Commonwealth Relations, Philip Noel-Baker, 24 November 1948, TNA: DO 121/55.

80 Diary entry, Patrick Gordon Walker, 24 October 1948, Churchill College Archives: Gordon Walker Papers, GNWR 1/7; Moore, *Making the New Commonwealth*, pp. 167–8.

81 Memorandum, Cumming-Bruce to Noel-Baker, 24 November 1948, TNA: DO 121/55.

82 F.K. Roberts, report, 'Conversation between Bevin and Beasley', 6 April 1948, TNA: FO 800/444, p. 96; Waters, *Empire Fractures*, p. 121.

83 F.K. Roberts, report, 'Conversation between Bevin and Chifley', 10 July 1948, TNA: FO 800/444, p. 113; Waters, *Empire Fractures*, p. 139–40.

84 Memorandum, L. Ridsdale to G. Jebb, 6 July 1948, TNA: FO 371/73060, Z 5667/273/72; Waters, *Empire Fractures*, p. 229n23.

85 'Beasley Dead', *Sydney Morning Herald*, 13 September 1949, NAA: A5954, 2211/3; 'Denies Link with Shipping Line', *Argus*, 13 June 1949, ibid.; 'Mr. Beasley Left £33,000', *Sun*, 4 May 1950, Beasley ADB File.

86 See, for instance, Beasley's complaint that he learned of the decision to send emissaries to the various Commonwealth countries in 1949 (they were to discuss the issue of keeping a republican India in the Commonwealth) from a press statement. He had not been informed of the prime minister–to–prime minister communication on the matter. Informal note, High Commissioners' Meeting, 1 April 1949, Annex A, TNA: DO 35/2794.

87 Letters, Beasley to Shedden, 12 February 1946 and 10 April, 23 September 1947, NAA: A5954, 43/1; letter, Beasley to Chifley, 29 July 1947, Chifley Papers, NAA: M1455/1, 177; letter, Beasley to Chifley, 30 July 1948, Chifley Papers, NAA: M1455/1, 291.

9 Cold war London: Harrison and White

1 Record of Harrison's speech, 'Partnership in Empire', Royal Empire Society, London, 16 November 1950, Harrison Papers, NLA: MS 5548, box 1, folder 5.

2 Record of Harrison's speech, accepting toast, 16 December 1957, NLA: MS 5548, box 1, folder 5.

3 Letter, Menzies to Harrison, 4 February 1957, Menzies Papers, NLA: MS 4936, series 1, box 14; letter, Harrison to Menzies, 12 February 1957, ibid.

4 Quoted in Robert O'Neill, *Australia in the Korean War 1950–53*, vol. 1, *Strategy and Diplomacy*, Australian War Memorial and Australian Government Publishing Service, Canberra, 1981, p. 28.

5   Australia Day Broadcast, 26 January 1955, White Papers, NLA: MS 9148, series 10, box 22, folder 10.

6   Edwards, *Prime Ministers and Diplomats*.

7   Waters, *Empire Fractures*.

8   David Lowe, 'Percy Spender, Minister and Ambassador', in Joan Beaumont, Christopher Waters, David Lowe, with Garry Woodard, *Ministers, Mandarins and Diplomats: Australian Foreign Policy Making, 1941–1969*, Melbourne University Press, 2003, pp. 62–87.

9   On Australian anticipation of, and preparations for, a third world war, see David Lowe, *Menzies and 'the Great World Struggle': Australia's Cold War 1948–54*, University of New South Wales Press, Sydney, 1999.

10 As, for example, World War II did for Bruce. See David Lee, 'Stanley Bruce at the Wartime Australian High Commission in London', in Christopher Baxter and Andrew Stewart (eds), *Diplomats at War: British and Commonwealth Diplomacy in Wartime*, Martinus Nijhoff, Leiden, 2008, pp. 157–8.

11 Paul Hasluck, *The Chance of Politics*, Text Publishing, Melbourne, 1997, p. 62.

12 Ibid.; Stuart Macintyre, 'Sir Eric John Harrison', *ADB*, vol. 14, 1996, p. 398; A.W. Martin, *Robert Menzies: A Life*, vol. 1, *1894–1943*, Melbourne University Press, 1993, p. 381.

13 Commonwealth Relations Office Memorandum, 28 April 1950, TNA: DO 35/2281; Attlee to Shinwell, 3 May 1950, ibid.; James (Defence) to Syers (CRO), 21 April 1950, ibid.

14 Encompassing Australia, New Zealand and the United Kingdom, ANZAM was an arrangement for regional defence planning. Although it had evolved under the Chifley Labor government in the late 1940s, the actual boundaries of the ANZAM area were agreed in 1950.

15 Minutes of meeting at 10 Downing St, 'Higher Direction in War', 8 January 1951, TNA: PREM 8/1352.

16 Dening's handwritten note, on note by R.H. Scott of his visit with Lord MacDonald to Bevin in hospital, 27 April 1950, TNA: FO 371/84544.

17 W. Garnett (UK High Commission, Canberra) to Secretary of State, Commonwealth Relations, 3 August 1951, TNA: FO 371/93017.

18 Memorandum, Lord Ogmore to Prime Minister, memo A, 1 September 1950, TNA: DO 35/2775; memorandum, Ogmore to Garner, Sedgewick, Ross, 30 August, ibid.

19 Record of conversation between Secretary of State for Commonwealth Relations and Harrison, 22 March 1951, TNA: FO 371/92073.

20 Record of Gordon-Walker's conversation with Harrison, 8 March 1951, TNA: DO 35/2928.

21 These episodes are described in O'Neill, *Australia in the Korean War*, vol. 1, pp. 139, 146–8.

22 John Rickard, 'White, Sir Thomas Walter', *ADB*, vol. 16, 2002, p. 534.

23 Martin, *Robert Menzies*, pp. 123–4, 232, 237, 245–6, 248, 422.

24 Colin Troupe Moodie, 'Memoir', unpublished, p. 30.

25 Ibid., p. 31.

26 Press release, 21 October 1952, White Papers, NLA: MS 9148, series 10, box 24, folder 23.

27 Newsclippings, multiple references from British publications, March 1953, White Papers, NLA: MS 9148, folio box 2.

28 Newsclippings, *Sydney Morning Herald*, 11 August 1956, White Papers, NLA: MS 9148, series 18, box 27, folder 42.

29 The majority of diplomatic cables relating to these episodes, and in which White does not feature, are in the British files TNA: FO 371/111871, FO 371/112047; and the Australian files NAA: A1838 T184 3004/11/8 part 6, A462 (TS) 439/1/39 part 1, and A1838 383/4/1 all parts.

30 Lowe, 'Percy Spender', pp. 80–7.

31 For example, Macintyre handed key telegrams to Foreign Office officials, e.g. Copy of External to Crotonate, no. 1493, 13 August 1954, TNA: FO 371/11873; memorandum left by Jockel, 26 August 1954, ibid.

32 Note, Lord Reading to Eden, 7 April 1954, DF 1071/164G, TNA: FO 371/110251.

33 See, for example, the British file on the visit, TNA: PREM 11/404.

34 Notes in preparation for interview, 9 September 1956, White Papers, NLA: MS 9148, series 3, box 5, folder 14.

35 Extract from *Yorkshire Post*, 2 January 1952, White Papers, NLA: MS 9148, series 18, box 35, folder 5; transcript, 'Guest of Honour', ABC, 1 July 1956, White Papers, NLA: MS 9148, folder 33.

36 Dispatch, Paul McGuire (Rome) to Casey, 14 June 1954, dispatch no. 8, NAA: A1838 145/10/6; David Goldsworthy, *Losing the Blanket: Australia and the End of Britain's Empire*, Melbourne University Press, 2002, pp. 73–7.

37 Lowe, 'Percy Spender', pp. 62–87.

38 Ibid., p. 86.

39 Transcript of oral history, Sir Keith Waller, 1977, NLA: TRC 314, tape 2; 2/5, 2/6.

40 *West Australian*, 22 May 1956.

41 Harrison, 'Political Appreciation', August 1960, NAA: A2908/15 H36.

42 Harrison, 'Political Appreciation at 28 September 1960', ibid.

43 Harrison, 'Political Appreciation at 6 January 1961', ibid.

44 Goldsworthy, *Losing the Blanket*, p. 96.

45 Letter, Harrison to Menzies, 20 November 1957, Menzies Papers, NLA: MS 4936, series 1, box 14, folder 119.

46 Letter, Harrison to Menzies, 16 May 1961, Menzies Papers, ibid., series 1, box 14.

47 Memorandum, J. Chadwick to R. Clutterbuck, 24 May 1961, TNA: DO 161/161.

48 Letter, Harrison to Menzies, 30 January 1962, Menzies Papers, NLA: MS 4936, series 1, box 14, folder 122; letter, Harrison to Menzies, 30 April 1962, ibid.; letter, Menzies to Harrison, 14 May 1962, ibid.

49 See, especially, Stuart Ward, *Australia and the British Embrace: The Demise of the Imperial Ideal*, Melbourne University Press, 2001; Goldsworthy, *Losing the Blanket*, p. 120–38.

50 Letter, Menzies to Harrison, 30 May 1961, Menzies Papers, NLA: MS 4936, series 1, box 14.

51 Letter, Menzies to Harrison, 15 January 1962, Menzies Papers, ibid., series 40, box 574, folder 25.

52 Letter, Menzies to Harrison, 13 December 1963, Menzies Papers, ibid., series 1, box 14; letter, Harrison to Menzies, 14 December 1963, ibid.

53 William Strang's minute of his conversation with Casey, 22 November 1951, TNA: FO 371/91162.

10 Sir Alexander Downer and the embers of British Australia

I would like to thank Mads Clausen for his assistance in locating sources.

1   'Our Anglophile in London', *Australian*, 3 November 1967.

2   The phrase 'violently Anglophile', was borrowed from one of Downer's closest associates in the Macmillan government, Lord Carrington (first lord of the Admiralty and former UK high commissioner in Canberra, 1956–59). 'Note on Mr A.R. Downer', undated, early 1960s, TNA: DO 175/52. This assessment was designed as preparation for a visit to London by Downer in his capacity as minister for immigration in the Menzies government, 1958–63.

3   Letter, Downer to Bunting, 5 November 1964, NAA: M1003, 'Sir John Bunting'.

4   'Little Chap', *Nation*, 2 April 1966. Downer considered a defamation action against the publisher, but Bunting advised caution.

5   This gradual change of heart is documented in Ward, *Australia and the British Embrace*.

6   Address to the Royal Commonwealth Society, March 1965, NAA: A463 1965/2040.

7   He replied to Calwell that 'I never comment on a brief report of what somebody has said. I will obtain the full text of the speech and, if it becomes necessary to comment on it, I will do so'. The matter did not arise again. NAA: A463 1965/2040.

8   Letter, Downer to Bunting, 1 April 1965, ibid.

9   Minute, Munro to Bunting, 13 April 1965, ibid.

10 Letter, Bunting to Downer, undated 1965, ibid.

11 *Age*, 14 May 1966; see also *Sydney Morning Herald*, 14 May 1967, which claimed that 'senior Ministers' were 'known to be furious' at Downer's remarks.

12 *Times*, 7 November 1966.

13 All three quoted in despatch, Sir Charles Johnston to Commonwealth Office, 15 November 1966, TNA: DO 175/163.

14 Minute, Garner to Sir Neil Pritchard, Deputy Under-Secretary of State, Commonwealth Office, 16 November 1966, TNA: DO 175/163.

15 Letter, Johnston to Garner, 30 November 1966, TNA: DO 175/164.

16 *Times*, 12 November 1966.

17 Garner to Pritchard, 21 November 1966, TNA: DO 175/163.

18 Downer's conversation with Jim Callaghan was conveyed in a despatch to Holt, 3 May 1967, NAA: M1003, 'Defence East of Suez'.

19 Record of conversation, Healey and Downer, 12 January 1967, NAA: M1003, 'Sir Harold Wilson'.

20 Cabinet submission no. 283 (Fairhall), May 1967, NAA: A5842/2, vol. 10; Cabinet minute (Foreign Affairs and Defence Committee), decision no. 357, 25 May 1967, NAA: A5842/2, vol. 10.

21 Cabinet minute, Foreign Affairs and Defence Committee, 30 January 1966, cited in Jeppe Kristensen, '"In Essence Still a British Country": Britain's Withdrawal from East of Suez', *Australian Journal of Politics and History*, vol. 41, no. 1, March 2005, p. 44.

22 McEwen, interviewed by Peter Grose, *Australian*, 18 June 1966.

23 Cabinet submission no. 504, 'UK/Australia Trade Discussions' (McEwen), 12 October 1967, NAA: A5842/2, vol. 16. See also McEwen's comments in Cabinet submission no. 466, 'United Kingdom/Australia Trade Discussions', 14 September 1967, ibid., vol. 15.

24 Cablegram, McEwen to Holt, 8 June 1967, NAA: A1838 727/4/2, part 7.

25 Record of discussion, Holt and Wilson, 15 June 1967, ibid., part 7.

26 Wilson's EEC application was yet again rejected out of hand by President de Gaulle at a press conference on 27 November 1967. De Gaulle reiterated his view that 'a very vast and deep transition is still needed' before the British would be ready to join the EEC. And, on this occasion, he brought down his verdict even before negotiations began, saving considerable time and bother for all concerned. The east of Suez decision, by contrast, was 'accelerated' in January 1968 in the wake of a crippling sterling crisis, bringing forward the timetable for British withdrawal.

27 Letter, Hall to Shears, Canberra, 8 November 1967, TNA: FCO 20/50.

28 Downer, Address to the Royal Commonwealth Society Luncheon, Bath, 11 October 1967, TNA: FCO 20/50.

29 *Times*, 12 October 1967.

30 Letter, Snelling to Johnston, 16 November 1967, NAA: FCO20/54.

31 Letter, Downer to Menzies, 19 April 1968, NAA: M1003.

32 Record of conversation, Downer and Callaghan, 16 January 1967, NAA: M1003.

33 These reports were quoted in a despatch from the British High Commission on 8 November 1967. The reports themselves are undated, but they are clearly from the immediate context of Downer's anti–Common Market activities in late 1967. Letter, Hall to Shears, 8 November 1967, TNA: FCO 20/50.

34 *Australian*, 3 November 1967.

35 Letter, Downer to Casey, 23 January 1968, NAA: M1003.

36 Letter, Downer to McMahon, 13 April 1966, NAA: M1003.

37 This episode from 1966 is recounted in Goldsworthy, *Losing the Blanket*, p. 168.

38 Alexander Downer, *Six Prime Ministers*, Hill of Content, Melbourne, 1982, p. 115.

39 Conservative member for Huntingdonshire.

40 Letter, Sir David Renton to Downer, 19 January 1968, NAA: M1002/96.

41 Telegram, Pritchett to Waller, Secretary of the Australian Department of Foreign Affairs (marked 'personal for Waller only'), 26 November 1972, NAA: A1838 67/1/3, part 6. The context of Pritchett's telegram is discussed later in this chapter.

42 Letter, Downer to Bunting, 9 February 1968, ibid., part 3.

43 Letter, Downer to Bunting, 20 July 1967, NAA: A3211 1969/2294, part 1. In a letter to Gorton the following April he reiterated that Adeane 'disagrees with many of [the Wilson government's] decisions, particularly over defence and the handling of Rhodesia. On east of Suez he seems completely on our side'. Letter, Downer to Gorton, 19 April 1968, ibid.

44 Cablegram, Downer to Bunting, 9 February 1968, NAA: A1838 67/1/3, part 3.

45 Letter, Downer to Oliphant, 3 October 1972, NAA: M1002/200.

46 Letter, Downer to James Orr (Private Secretary to the Duke of Edinburgh), 28 November 1968; letter, Downer to Gorton, 4 December 1968, NAA: M1003.

47 Letter, Downer to Bunting, 28 April 1970, NAA: M1003.

48 Letter, Downer to Heath, 19 May 1970, NAA: M1002/96.

49 Heath had initially appointed Anthony Barber to this role, but an early cabinet reshuffle brought on by the death of the chancellor, Iain Macleod, saw Barber moved to the chancellorship and Rippon to the task of negotiating entry to the EEC.

50 Cabinet submission no. 258 (McEwen), May 1970, NAA: A5619 C743, part 2.

51 Cabinet submission no. 257, 'International Trade Relations', 5 May 1970, NAA: A5619 C742.

52 Record of conversation, McEwen, Barber, O'Neill, 8 July 1970, TNA: FCO 30/802.

53 Telegram, Johnston to Foreign and Commonwealth Office, 17 September 1970, TNA: FCO 30/804.

54 Press statement, Anthony, 'EEC Discussions', 4 June 1971, NAA: A1838 727/4/2, part 12.

55 Anthony, 'Comments to Press', 27 June 1971, ibid.

56 Letter, Downer to McMahon, 10 June 1971, NAA: M1003.

57 Letter, McMahon to Heath, 15 June 1971, NAA: A1838 727/4/2, part 14; letter, Heath to McMahon, 2 July 1971, TNA: PREM 15/367.

58 Letter, Waller to Bunting, Canberra, 20 August 1971, NAA: A1209 1971/9449, part 1. The Foreign Office and Commonwealth Office were merged in October 1968 as part of a broad-ranging review of Britain's diplomatic representation abroad.

59 Letter, Waller to Bunting, 7 October 1971, ibid.

60 Letter, Bowen to McMahon, 22 August 1972, ibid., part 2.

61 Memorandum, Bailey to Bunting, 24 August 1972, ibid.

62 Cablegram, Downer to Bunting, 9 May 1972, NAA: M1003, 'Sir John Bunting'.

63 Letter, Boswell to Bailey, 9 May 1972, NAA: A1209 1971/9449, part 5.

64 Memorandum by Boswell, 'Points—Australia House: Arguments for Continuing Present Arrangements', undated [October 1971], ibid., part 1.

65 Note for file, Bunting, 4 August 1972, ibid., part 2.

66 Letter, McMahon to Bowen, 15 August 1972, ibid.

67 Letter, Downer to Bunting, 1 September 1972, ibid.

68 On Waller's reaction, see note for file, Bunting, 8 August 1972, ibid; for Bowen's reaction to McMahon's letter, see note for file, Bunting, 17 August 1972, ibid.

69 Letter, Bowen to McMahon, 22 August 1972, ibid.

70 See exchange of letters between McMahon and Bowen on 21 and 22 September 1972 respectively in ibid.

71 According to his obituary in the *Times*, Downer originally intended to spend half of his retirement years at Oare House in Wiltshire, and the other half at his country house Martinsell in the Adelaide Hills. 'But the onus of maintaining two estates in England and Australia proved too great, and Oare had to his great regret to be sacrificed.' *Times*, 6 April 1981.

72 *Sydney Morning Herald*, 8 November 1972.

73 Cablegram, Downer to McMahon, 19 October 1972, NAA: M1003, 'Downer to McMahon'.

74 Letter, Downer to Aitken, 22 November 1972, NAA: M1002, 284.

75 Cablegram, Pritchett to Waller, 21 November 1972, NAA: A1838 67/1/3, part 6. It was in this context that Pritchett dissected the main characteristics of the 'expatriate establishment'.

76 Telegram, Pritchett to Waller, 26 November 1972, ibid. The Heath government regrouped in January 1973 and managed to pass the required legislation with only minor changes.

11 The 'new line in the Strand': John Armstrong and the 'new nationalism'

I would like to thank Philippa Macaskill for her invaluable assistance in locating newspaper and oral history sources for this chapter. I also thank the Armstrong family for the generous access they provided to the personal papers of J.I. Armstrong.

1   John Armstrong, quoted in *Daily Mail* (UK), 1 February 1973.

2   'Our Man in London', *Australasian Express*, 9 August 1973.

3   Record of conversation, Harold Wilson and Gorton, London, 7 January 1969, TNA: FCO 24/384/1.

4   Outward cablegram, 'Relations with the United Kingdom', Canberra, 18 December 1972, NAA: A1838 67/1/3, part 7.

5   Correspondence, John Armstrong to Greenhill, 7 March 1973, TNA: FCO 68/516, cited in Lloyd, *Diplomacy with a Difference*, pp. 257–63. See also NAA: A1209, 1973/6398.

6   Lloyd, *Diplomacy with a Difference*, p. 262.

7   Robert O'Neill, 'Defence Policy', in W.J. Hudson (ed.), *Australia in World Affairs 1971–75*, George Allen & Unwin for the Australian Institute of International Affairs, Sydney, 1980, pp. 14, 23. The British themselves decided to withdraw in 1974 and by early 1975 the force had been disbanded.

8   Diplomatic reports, no. 268/73 of 3 April 1973 and no. 269/73 of 3 April 1973, TNA: FCO 32/948.

9   Note on British/Australian Relations, 6 August 1973, TNA: FCO 24/1610.

10 Recorded interview with John Armstrong, 11 and 12 November 1975, Mel Pratt Collection, NLA: TRC 121/68.

11 *Sydney Morning Herald*, 22 February 1975.

12 Correspondence, Bill Peters, British High Commission, Canberra, to John K Hickman, South West Pacific Department, Foreign and Commonwealth Office, 15 December 1972, TNA: FCO 24/1369.

13 Curtin had used the phrase in both Australia and Britain. See James Curran, *The Power of Speech: Australian Prime Ministers Defining the National Image*, Melbourne University Press, 2004, pp. 22–4; See also Neville Meaney, 'Britishness and Australia: Some Reflections', *Journal of Imperial and Commonwealth History*, vol. 31, no. 2, May 2003, pp. 121–35.

14 *CPD*, Senate, 25 February 1953, p. 235.

15 *CPD*, Senate, 30 November 1938, pp. 2319–25; 17 October 1951, pp. 767–8; 2 December 1948, p. 4000.

16 *Advertiser* (Adelaide), 13 December 1972.

17 *CPD*, Senate, 3 July 1946, p. 2081.

18 Ken Turner, 'Armstrong, John Ignatius (1908–1977)', in Ann Millar (ed.), *The Biographical Dictionary of the Australian Senate*, vol. 2, *1929–1962*, Melbourne University Press, 2004, p. 440.

19 Nevertheless, the Armstrong plans provided a basis for a subsequent visit by Queen Elizabeth II and the Duke of Edinburgh in 1954. See NAA: A3211, 1974/7499.

20 *CPD*, H. of R., 26 October 1948, pp. 2067–8.

21 The story was told by Senator Doug McClelland during a condolence motion following Armstrong's death; *CPD*, Senate, 15 March 1976, p. 112.

22 *CPD*, Senate, 11 August 1954, p. 160.

23 *CPD*, Senate, 5 March 1952, pp. 838–9; 5 August 1954, pp. 75–6.

24 *CPD*, Senate, 10 November 1954, p. 1309.

25 Ken Turner, 'Armstrong', p. 442.

26 *Age*, 24 March 1973.

27 Record of conversation, Prime Minister and Minister for Foreign Affairs with the Right Honourable Sir Morrice James, Canberra, 20 December 1972, NAA: A1838 67/1/3, part 7.

28 New Australian High Commissioner: Notes on Anglo-Australian Relations, 7 February 1973, TNA: FCO 24/1669.

29 Policy planning paper, *Anglo-Australian Relations: Prospects and Initiatives*, 1 December 1971, Department of Foreign Affairs, NAA: A1838, 67/1/3, part 4.

30 Ibid.

31 *Sydney Morning Herald*, 24 March 1973.

32 Pritchett to Waller, 11 December 1972, NAA: A1838 67/1/3, part 7.

33 *Canberra Times*, 14 December 1972.

34 *Sydney Morning Herald*, 22 February 1975.

35 Outward cablegram, 12 December 1972, 0.112142, NAA: A1838, 67/1/3, part 7.

36 Telegram, James to Foreign and Commonwealth Office, British High Commission, Canberra, 11 December 1972, TNA: FCO 24/1369.

37 The government-funded feature film *The Adventures of Barry McKenzie* (1972), based on a comic strip produced by Barry Humphries and Nicholas Garland for the British satirical magazine *Private Eye*, had been a popular hit during 1972. Directed by Bruce Beresford and produced by Phillip Adams, 'Bazza' was the classic 'ocker' played by Barry Crocker. His Fosters-driven 'adventures' were mainly in London, where he was on holiday with his Aunt Edna (played by Humphries). The sequel, *Barry McKenzie Holds His Own* (1974), included a scene in Australia House with a high commissioner, Sir Alec Ferguson, played by Ed Devereaux. See Anne Pender, 'The Mythical Australian: Barry Humphries, Gough Whitlam and "New Nationalism"', *Australian Journal of Politics and History*, vol. 51, no. 1, March 2005, pp 67–79; also Tony Moore, *The Barry McKenzie Movies*, Currency Press and the Australian Film Commission, Strawberry Hills, New South Wales, 2005.

38 *Sydney Morning Herald*, 22 February 1975.

39 *Advertiser* (Adelaide), 13 December 1972.

40 *Times*, 14 December 1972.

41 Correspondence, Charles Johnston to Denis Greenhill (Foreign and Commonwealth Office), 9 March 1973, TNA: FCO 24/1669.

42 Correspondence, Morrice James to Sir Eric Norris, 30 January 1973, TNA: FCO 24/669.

43 John Menadue, *Things You Learn Along the Way*, David Lovell Publishing, Melbourne, 1999, pp. 113–14. Menadue was head of the Prime Minister's Department from 1974 to 1976.

44 Mel Pratt, interview with Armstrong, NLA: TRC 121/68.

45 *National Times*, 18–23 December 1972.

46 *Sydney Morning Herald*, 28 March 1973.

47 *Canberra News*, 28 September 1973.

48 Press conference, 31 January 1973, transcript, NAA: A1838, 67/1/3, part 7 (emphasis added).

49 'National Anthem', Australia Day broadcast by the Prime Minister, 26 January 1973, NAA: A3211 1973/128, part 1.

50 *Sun News-Pictorial* (Melbourne), 7 March 1974.

51 Press conference, 31 January 1973, transcript, NAA: A1838, 67/1/3, part 7.

52 Speech notes, Address to Victoria League, 16 July 1974, Armstrong private papers.

53 Inward cablegram, Armstrong to Whitlam, 5 March 1973, NAA: A1838, 67/1/3, part 7.

54 *Daily Express* (London), 23 February 1973, in NAA: A3211, 1974/7499.

55 Correspondence, Willesee to Armstrong, Canberra, 5 April 1973, Armstrong private papers.

56 Inward cablegram, Armstrong to Whitlam, 5 March 1973, NAA: A1838, 67/1/3, part 7.

57 *Daily Telegraph*, 1 February 1973.

58 Correspondence, Whitlam to Armstrong, 6 April 1973, NAA: A1838, 67/1/3, part 13.

59 Ibid.

60 Ibid.

61 Ibid.

62 Ibid.

63 Ibid.

64 Outward cablegram, Armstrong to Prime Minister, Special Minister of State, Secretary of Foreign Affairs, 9 March 1973, Armstrong private papers.

65 Inward cablegram, Personal for Armstrong from Waller, 'Staffing at Australia House', 12 March 1973, Armstrong private papers.

66 Notes for John Bunting, undated, but likely early 1975, as Armstrong was preparing to hand over to Bunting, Armstrong private papers.

67 *The Diplomatist*, July 1973.

68 John Armstrong, Speech in Honour of Captain Arthur Phillip, undated but likely November 1973, NAA: A3211, 1973/8139.

69 Television interview, Gough Whitlam and David Frost, August 1973, in Oakes, Laurie, Farmer, Richard, and MacCallum, Mungo (eds), *Whitlam and Frost: The Full Text of Their TV Conversations Plus Exclusive New Interviews*, Sundial, London, 1974.

70 'Consultations in Canberra: High Commissioner's Notes', 10 January 1974, NAA: A3211, 1974/7499.

71 The Irish poet and revolutionary, executed for his leadership of the Easter Uprising in Dublin in 1916.

72 Post Office telegram, Armstrong to Whitlam, 17 April 1974, Armstrong private papers.

73 Correspondence, Whitlam to Armstrong, 19 April 1974, Armstrong private papers.

74 'Secret Pre-tour Jokes Cable: Gough Gets Advice on How to Behave', *Nation Review*, 13–19 December 1974.

75 Whitlam, Mansion House, London, 19 December 1974, in *Australia and Europe: Principal Speeches during the Visit of the Prime Minister of Australia to Europe, 14 December 1974 to 21 January 1975*, Australian Government Publishing Service, Canberra, 1975, p. 25.

76 *Daily Telegraph*, 1 March 1975.

77 *Sydney Morning Herald*, 22 February 1975.

78 *Canberra News*, 28 September 1973.

79 *CPD*, H. of R., 11 February 1975, p. 61.

80 Moore, *Barry McKenzie Movies*, pp. 48–52.

81 *Daily Telegraph*, 1 March 1975.

82   *Bulletin*, date unclear, Biographical Cuttings, NLA.

83   According to the *Northern Territory News*, 11 September 1974, this was how the British press saw Armstrong.

84   *Age*, 24 March 1973.

85   *Sydney Morning Herald*, 22 February 1975.

86   *Age*, 24 March 1973.

87   *Sydney Morning Herald*, 22 February 1975.

12 A new pattern: officials, ministers and diplomats at Australia House, 1975–81

1   G.C. Bolton, 'The United Kingdom', in Hudson (ed.), *Australia in World Affairs*, p. 209.

2   Ibid., p. 215.

3   J.D.B. Miller, 'Australia and Western Europe', in P.J. Boyce and J.R. Angel (eds), *Independence and Alliance—Australia in World Affairs 1976–80*, George Allen & Unwin for the Australian Institute of International Affairs, Sydney, 1983.

4   See, for example, Australian High Commission, London, Office Notice no. 1975/39, 24 September 1975, NAA: A3211, 1977/7499, part 2.

5   Sir John Bunting, Address on 'Government and the Press—a View from the Pacific', Wilton Park, n.d., p. 1, NAA: M4541 2005, item 3.

6   Media release, Australian High Commission in the United Kingdom, 13 February 1975, NAA: A3211, item 1974/7499, part 2.

7   Sir John Kerr to Sir John Bunting, 6 May 1976, NAA: M4541 2005, item 3.

8   For an example of the range of functions to which a high commissioner is invited, see Bunting to Freeth, 22 March 1977, NAA: A3211 2003, 1977/625.

9   Bruce Juddery, 'Those Bygone Days of Golf and Government', *Canberra Times*, 8 February 1975.

10   Paul Kelly, *The Unmaking of Gough*, Angus & Robertson, Sydney, 1976, chs 12 and 13.

11   See cables, London to Canberra, 16, 18 and 19 February 1976, NAA: A3211, 1975/119.

12   Prime Minister's Statement, 16 September 1976, ibid.

13   For the Freeth speech, see *CPD*, H. of R., vol. 64, 14 August 1969, pp. 310–17. See also Andrew Farran, 'The Freeth Experiment', *Australian Outlook*, vol. 26, no. 1, April 1972, pp. 46–58; Ian Hancock, *John Gorton: He Did It His Way*, Hodder, Sydney, 2002, pp. 233–5; Peter Golding, *Black Jack McEwen: Political Gladiator*, Melbourne University Press, 1996, pp. 309–12.

14   *CPD*, H. of R., vol. 103, 22 February 1977, p. 259.

15   Winston S. Churchill, *The Second World War*, vol. 3, Cassell, London, 1950, p. 367.

16   Press release, 14 August 1979, NAA: A3211, 1977/7212, part 2.

17   Sir John Kerr, *Matters for Judgment*, Macmillan, Melbourne, 1978.

18   I am grateful to Jeremy Hearder for providing generous access to his extensive research on the career of Sir James Plimsoll.

19   Peter Costigan, *Herald* (Melbourne), 4 February 1980.

20   Lord Carrington, letter to Jeremy Hearder, 26 June 1996; *Age*, 12 December 1980; Sir William Heseltine, letter to Jeremy Hearder, 12 May 1997.

13 The 'new equilibrium': the high commissioners after 1980

1 Gareth Evans and Bruce Grant, *Australia's Foreign Relations in the World of the 1990s*, Melbourne University Press, 1995, p. 306.

2 Conversation with author, Alfred Parsons, 9 September 2008 (hereafter Parsons).

3 L'Estrange, *The Australia–Britain Relationship Today*, pp. 4, 10, 21, 23–4.

4 Paul Kelly, *The End of Certainty. The Story of the 1980s*, Allen & Unwin, Sydney, 1992.

5 Conversation with author, Douglas McClelland, 2 October 2008 (hereafter McClelland).

6 L'Estrange, *Australia–Britain Relationship*, pp. 18, 20.

7 Letter, Margaret Thatcher to McClelland, 6 August 1988, courtesy of McClelland.

8 McClelland.

9 Letter to author, Professor Geoffrey Gallop AC, former premier of Western Australia, 6 May 2009.

10 Conversation with author, Neal Blewett, 18 September 2008 (hereafter Blewett).

11 Conversation with author, Michael L'Estrange, 14 November 2008 (hereafter L'Estrange).

12 Blewett.

13 In 1984, L'Estrange served with Mr Justice Hope's Royal Commission into Australia's Security and Intelligence Agencies. In 1986 he was awarded a Harkness Fellowship and spent two years studying at the School of Foreign Service at Georgetown University in Washington DC and at the Institute of International Studies at the University of California at Berkeley.

14 Conversation with author, Sir Victor Garland, 12 December 2008 (hereafter Garland).

15 Department of Foreign Affairs and Trade, *In the National Interest: Australia's Foreign and Trade Policy White Paper*, Commonwealth of Australia, Canberra, 1997, available at: http://australianpolitics.com/foreign/elements/whitepaper.pdf, accessed 10 September 2009.

16 Conversation with author, Philip Flood, 27 November 2008 (hereafter Flood).

17 Flood.

18 Conversation with author, Richard Smith, 12 September 2008 (hereafter Smith).

19 Flood; conversation with author, Richard Alston, 19 October 2008 (hereafter Alston); Parsons.

20 Garland.

21 Unpublished memoirs, Alfred Parsons, courtesy of Parsons.

22 From a list supplied by Flood, as at May 2000. Other positions were vice-president of the Australia/ New Zealand Chamber of Commerce, governor of the Commonwealth Foundation, patron of the Australian Music Foundation, and member of the boards of the Royal Humane Society and the Royal Life Saving Society. A further four were honorary, with optional commitments: vice-president of the Royal Overseas League, patron of London Legacy, honorary freeman of the Worshipful Company of Butchers, and honorary freeman of the Tallow Chandlers Company.

23 McClelland.

24 McClelland.

25 *CPD*, vol. 492, no. 64, 25 January 1988, pp. 466–80.

26 Ibid., 18 January 1988, pp. 674–8.

27 McClelland; also see Derek Kinrade, *Alf Morris People's Parliamentarian: Scenes from the Life of Lord Morris of Manchester*, National Information Forum, London , 2007, pp. 302–5.

28 Unpublished notes, Philip Flood, courtesy of Flood.

29 Ibid.

30 *Daily Telegraph*, London, 7 July 2000.

31 Unpublished notes, Flood.

32 James Button, 'Aboriginal Remains Will Be Returned', *Sydney Morning Herald*, 7 October 2005; 'Britain to Return Aboriginal Bones', *Sydney Morning Herald*, 13 September 2009.

33 Unpublished notes, Flood.

34 Smith.

35 Parsons.

36 Blewett.

37 L'Estrange.

38 Flood.

39 L'Estrange.

40 Unpublished memoirs, Parsons.

41 L'Estrange.

42 L'Estrange.

43 Letter to author, Sir David Manning, 26 May 2009.

44 Alston.

45 In March and September 2002, May and November 2003, and June 2004. Courtesy of the office of the Hon. John Howard AC.

46 L'Estrange.

47 *New Statesman*, 23 September 2002, which described Manning as 'one of the most important people in the country' at the time.

48 Letter to author, Sir David Manning, 26 May 2009.

49 L'Estrange.

50 James McClelland, *Stirring the Possum: A Political Autobiography*, Penguin, Ringwood, Victoria, 1989, p. 210.

51 Interview with Alfred Parsons, 23 May 1995, NLA: TRC 2981/22.

52 Unpublished memoirs, Parsons.

53 McClelland.

54 Evans and Grant, *Australia's Foreign Relations*, p. 308.

55 McClelland.

56 Flood.

57 Alston.

58 Neal Blewett, 'Four Years in Another Country', *Federal Gallery*, March 2001, p. 35.

59 Unpublished memoirs, Parsons.

60 Ibid.; McClelland.

61 L'Estrange; Alston.

62 Alston; Flood.

63 Smith.

64 Unpublished memoirs, Parsons.

65 Parsons.

66 Alston.

67 Conversation with author, Rohan Courtney, former president, Britain–Australia Society, 24 March 2009. Conversation with John Martin, inaugural chairman, Australian Business, 25 June 2009.

68 Flood. In 1981 Garland had participated in the unveiling of a commemorative stone for Florey in Westminster Abbey.

69 Richard Alston, *The Australia–UK Relationship: Menzies' Modern Legacy*, Sir Robert Menzies Lecture Trust, Melbourne, 2007.

70 Blewett; Flood; Alston.

71 Flood.

72 McClelland; Parsons.

73 Neal Blewett, 'The Politics of the Republic', in *Public Lectures in Australian Studies 1995–6*, Menzies Centre for Australian Studies, Institute of Commonwealth Studies, University of London, 1996.

74 Blewett.

75 Flood.

76 Blewett; Alston.

77 Garland.

78 Norma Major, *Joan Sutherland*, Macdonald/Queen Anne, London, 1987.

79 Blewett. In 1982, Sir Victor Garland also had held a large reception for Dame Joan Sutherland.

80 Letter, Gareth Evans to McClelland, 10 December 1990, courtesy of McClelland.

81 Letter, Peter Henderson AC, Secretary, Department of Foreign Affairs to Garland, 17 January 1983, courtesy of Garland.

82 Garland.

83 In 1972 he published *The Peers, the Parties and the People: The British General Elections of 1910*, Macmillan, London.

84 Blewett.

85 L'Estrange.

86 Conversation with Professor Carl Bridge, head, Menzies Centre for Australian Studies, King's College London, 25 March 2009.

87 Letter to author, M.J. Cook AO, 18 March 2009. Distinguished visiting fellow, 1997– , Menzies Centre for Australian Studies, King's College London; ambassador to the United States, 1989–93; director-general, Office of National Assessments, 1981–89.

88 Letter to author, Sir Roger Carrick, 25 March 2009. UK high commissioner in Canberra, 1994–97; former president, Britain–Australia Society.

89 Letter, Garland to Hayden, 18 April 1983, courtesy of Garland.

90 Smith; Jan Payne (consultant ed.), *Australia House: 75 Years of Service*, Public Affairs Branch, Australian High Commission, London, 1993, p. 13.

91 Department of Foreign Affairs and Trade, Management Information Systems Section, Overseas Staff Profile for London 01/02/08.

92 Blewett, 'Four Years in Another Country', p. 33.

93 Garland.

94   Blewett, 'Four Years in Another Country', p. 36.

95   McClelland.

96   L'Estrange, *Australia–Britain Relationship*, p. 12.

97   McClelland.

14 Australia's house

1   Murray Bail, *Homesickness*, Farrar, Straus and Giroux, New York, 1999 (originally 1980), p. 68. Also see pp. 12, 14, 19, 25, 28, 30, 37–8, 59, 66.

2   Pryke, 'Australia House', p. 1.

3   See, for instance, Yi-Fu Tuan, *Space and Place: The Perspective of Experience*, University of Minnesota Press, Minneapolis, 1977, pp. 6, 136; Tim Cresswell, *Place: A Short Introduction*, Blackwell, Malden, 2004, p. 7.

4   Henri Lefebvre, *The Production of Space*, trans. Donald Nicholson-Smith, Blackwell, Oxford, 1991 (originally 1974), p. 35.

5   Pryke, 'Australia House', pp. 16, 213–14.

6   Edgar quoted in Angela Woollacott, *To Try Her Fortune in London: Australian Women, Colonialism, and Modernity*, Oxford University Press, New York, 2001, p. 76.

7   *Times*, 20 July 1918, p. 3.

8   *Australia House, London: The Offices in Great Britain of the Government of the Commonwealth of Australia Opened by His Majesty the King, August 3 1918*, Printing-Craft, London, 1918.

9   Signing noted in the *Times*, 5 August 1918, p. 4.

10 Between 1921 and 1925 High Commissioner Cook estimated that visitor numbers increased from 3,000 to 10,000 per annum, with return calls entailing that total visits amounted to 60,000 a year (May to September being particularly busy). In the late 1920s, over 5,000 people a year paused to sign the visitors' book. In 1933, during the Great Depression, only 2,459 signed; by 1937 numbers had risen to 6,897. Figures from Pryke, 'Australia House', pp. 228–9.

11 See Woollacott, *To Try Her Fortune*, p. 77; *British Australian and New Zealander* (hereafter *BANZ*), 24 April 1924, p. 19; ibid., 6 May 1926, p. 1. For a history of the newspaper, which changed its name in 1924, refer to Simon Sleight, 'Reading the *British Australasian* Community in London, 1884–1924', in Carl Bridge, Robert Crawford and David Dunstan (eds), *Australians in Britain: The Twentieth-Century Experience*, Monash University ePress, Melbourne, 2009, pp. 7.1–7.14. See *BANZ*, 30 May 1929, p. 11 for photographs of the bookstall and tourist office.

12 See *British Australasian* (hereafter *BA*), 20 October 1921, p. 4; 27 October 1921, p. 4.

13 *BANZ*, 1 December 1927, p. 11; 2 January 1936, p. 9.

14 Noted in Pryke, 'Australia House', p. 187.

15 See *BANZ*, 18 August 1927, p. 5; 12 June 1930, p. 7.

16 Ibid., 12 June 1930, p. 7.

17 Refer to *BA*, 17 May 1923, p. 18; *BANZ*, 26 August 1926, p. 3; R.A. Rye, *The Students' Guide to the Libraries of London*, University of London Press, 1927, p. 288; Simon Sleight, '*Ex Libris* Australia House: Paper Trails to and from a Unique London Institution', *Australian Studies*, vol. 17, no. 2, 2002, pp. 117–50.

18 See *BANZ*, 29 May 1924, p. 3; 26 August 1926, p. 3.

19 Ibid., see 26 February 1925, p. 21; 19 March 1925, p. 12. An earlier article in the same newspaper noted that questions to the librarian 'ranged from best hotels and places to visit to winners of races and fights' (see 3 January 1924, p. 14).

20 Ibid., see for instance 26 March 1925, p. 12; 29 March 1928, p. 18. Refer to ibid., 17 December 1925, p. 16 for a reference to the guidebook.

21 Ibid., see 7 April 1927, p. 28; 9 June 1927, p. 10; 10 May 1928, p. 15; 6 January 1927, p. 5.

22 Ibid., see 31 May 1928, p. 22; 4 June 1936, p. 10; 9 May 1929, p. 24.

23 Refer to ibid., 24 March 1927, p. 21; ibid., 31 March 1927, p. 2; ibid., 23 February 1928, p. 11.

24 Staff figures from Pryke, 'Australia House', p. 260. By 1933, 156 staff worked at Australia House.

25 See *BANZ*, 30 October 1930, p. 13; 27 November 1941, p. 7.

26 Ibid., see 15 January 1925, p. 12.

27 Refer to 'Australia House Battle: King's College Raggers Routed', ibid., 12 November 1925, p. 13.

28 Ibid.

29 Ibid., see 6 May 1926, p. 1.

30 See Ros Pesman, *Duty Free: Australian Women Abroad*, Oxford University Press, Melbourne, 1996, p. 22; Richard White, 'Bluebells and Fogtown: Australians' First Impressions of England, 1860–1940', *Australian Cultural History*, no. 5, 1986, p. 44.

31 Pesman, *Duty Free*.

32 Noted in *BANZ*, 26 August 1926, p. 3.

33 Ibid., see 15 November 1928, pp. 5–6. Refer to Pryke, 'Australia House', pp. 260–1 for percentages of Australian employees at work in the building between 1921 and 1935, and pp. 261–3 for further analysis of the Green comments.

34 *BANZ*, 15 November 1928, p. 5.

35 Ibid., 26 August 1926, p. 3.

36 In July 1929, for example, a Melbourne *Herald* correspondent charged that Australia House was 'flooded out with women, social climbers who are breaking their hearts to get invitations to this, that or the other social function'. Delia Russell, quoted in Pryke, 'Australia House', p. 231.

37 See, for example, *BA*, 15 December 1921, p. 3.

38 Refer to *BANZ*, 15 August 1929, p. 15 (visit by Melbourne child rescuer Edith Onians); ibid., 1 May 1930, p. 16 (gathering of the Anzac Fellowship of Women); ibid., 11 December 1930, p. 11 (assembly in library to bestow award upon Henry Handel Richardson); ibid., 29 June 1932, p. 10 (musical recital by Miss Greta Callow); ibid., 29 March 1928, p. 18 (tickets on sale for Overseas Nurses Memorial Ball); ibid., 2 March 1939, p. 11 (report on fundraiser for Australian Bush Fire Fund).

39 Ibid., 5 February 1925, p. 5.

40 Ibid.

41 Ibid., 11 September 1930, p. 8.

42 Canteen noted in *Australian and New Zealand Weekly* (hereafter *ANZW*, formerly the *British Australian and New Zealander*), 29 October 1949, p. 14, and *Sydney Morning Herald*, 21 November 1978, p. 7.

43 On the travellers' exchange board—identified as 'one of the most-used services' in the late 1960s and 1970s—see John Dyson, 'Australia's Bustling Home from Home', *Reader's Digest*, November 1980, p. 168. An example is included: 'Brisbane electrician, age 24, wants three others to join in two-month trip round Europe. Share expenses. Stay at youth hostels and camps'.

44 On Finnegan (who served for thirty-six years), see *BANZ*, 19 May 1932, p. 10 and ibid., 15 April 1944, p. 6.

45 Refer, for instance, to ibid., 29 January 1925, p. 5; ibid., 5 April 1928, p. 7; ibid., 3 May 1928, p. 12; ibid., 6 July 1939, p. 13; *ANZW*, 16 May 1953, p. 11. An article in *BANZ*, 17 September 1925, p. 4, further notes an allocation of office space in Australia House for the Big Brother organisation.

46 Ibid., see 25 April 1929, p. 6 for further details.

47 Ibid.

48 *BA*, 20 October 1921, p. 4; *BANZ*, 1 June 1939, p. 7. On the controversial role played by Australia House and the Australian government with regard to Jewish refugees, see *Age*, 5 September 2001, p. 15.

49 Reported in *BA*, 29 August 1918, p. 4.

50 See *BANZ*, 2 April 1925, p. 4; ibid., 9 October 1930, p. 8.

51 The display of *Menin Gate at Midnight* is noted in *BANZ*, 9 February 1928, p. 6 and 1 March 1928, p. 7 ('hundreds of people came to see it'). The gallery's opening is reported in ibid., 23 May 1929, p. 7 and included works by E. Philips Fox and George Coates. Australia House also hosted meetings of the Dominions' Artists' Club after its establishment in 1925 (ibid., 5 February 1925, p. 10).

52 See *BANZ*, 25 February 1932, p. 9. The event was held from 29 September to 5 October 1931.

53 Ibid., 18 September 1930, p. 14.

54 Ibid., see 12 June 1930, p. 7; 18 April 1935, p. 5.

55 Ibid., see 26 February 1925, p. 21.

56 Ibid., see 8 November 1928, p. 7.

57 Ibid., 7 August 1930, p. 8.

58 Ibid., see 1 August 1935, pp. 5, 12. With the South Australian offices relocated for the time being, the list of Australian states—always prodigal children when it came to Australia House—not incorporated within the high commission building was extensive. Queensland and Western Australia had resisted incorporation from the outset, and only New South Wales (which had pressed to be moved from its second-floor offices) and Victoria (operating from an adjacent building but technically incorporated) remained. On its Strand flank, Australia House features six colonnades, designed to represent national unity, but practice has not always mirrored intention.

59 For figures, see Pryke, 'Australia House', pp. 247, 260.

60 Referred to in ibid., p. 255 and Sleight, '*Ex Libris* Australia House', p. 117.

61 For reaction, see *BANZ*, 25 January 1940, p. 2; ibid., 1 February 1940, p. 4; ibid., 1 February 1940, p. 15.

62 Arrival noted in ibid., 27 June 1940, p. 8.

63 See ibid., 4 July 1930, p. 8; ibid., 8 August 1940, supplement p. iii.

64 Quoted in ibid., 11 July 1940, p. 8.

65 Amenities described in ibid., 23 October 1941, p. 6; ibid., 26 March 1942, p. 12.

66 Ibid., 26 March 1942, p. 12.

67 See ibid., 16 April 1942, p. 6.

68 *Evening Standard* excerpt reproduced in *BANZ*, 20 February 1941, supplement p. iii.

69 Caused during 'the Blitz', Germany's aerial bombing of London.

70 *BANZ*, 20 February 1941, supplement p. iii.

71 'For Doris, the eyes had it', *Manly Daily* (Sydney), 12 October 2005, p. 15.

72 See *BANZ*, 31 December 1942, supplement p. iii.

73 See ibid., 18 June 1942, supplement p. iii; ibid., 19 November 1942, supplement p. iii; ibid., 25 September 1943, p. 9; ibid., 28 January 1943, p. 6.

74 For example, ibid., 8 April 1944, p. 6.

75 Advertised for late April in ibid., 26 March 1942, p. 12.

76 See 'Boomerang Club—Broadcasts to Australia', ibid., 30 April 1942.

77 See ibid., 13 May 1944, p. 6 and ibid., 22 July 1944, p. 10 (the latter for a report noting broken windows and minor injuries resulting from the explosion of a flying bomb).

78 See ibid., 19 May 1945, p. 11; ibid., 6 November 1943, p. 11; ibid., 23 September 1944, p. 16.

79 Noted in ibid., 25 March 1944, p. 15 and ibid., 1 April 1944, p. 3.

80 See *BA*, 14 September 1946, p. 7; ibid., 3 July 1947; *ANZW*, 29 October 1949, p. 14; H.C. Mills, 'The Story of the Boomerang Club', transcript of lecture held at Australia House, 28 July 1971, pp. 4–13.

81 *ANZW*, 29 October 1949, p. 14.

82 A. James Hammerton and Alistair Thomson, *Ten Pound Poms: Australia's Invisible Migrants*, Manchester University Press, 2005, p. 9.

83 On the medical examinations and migration interviews, see ibid., p. 89.

84 *ANZW*, 15 October 1949, p. 7; ibid., 1 January 1955, p. 7. A decade later, in 1965, more than 500 applications a day were being processed in the building (*ANZW*, 6 March 1965, p. 8).

85 *ANZW*, 7 May 1955, p. 16; *Touch and Go* (dir. Michael Truman, 1955).

86 *BANZ*, 27 April 1946, p. 3.

87 *BA*, 7 June 1947, p. 13; *ANZW*, 17 June 1949.

88 Information from manuscript version of *Lusting for London: Australian Writers at the Hub of Empire, 1870–1950* by Peter Morton. My thanks to the author.

89 See *ANZW*, 6 June 1953, p. 11; ibid., 7 November 1953, p. 8; 'Records of the Australian Musical Association', NLA: MS 7996, boxes 3, 5, 6, 7; *ANZW*, 25 June 1955, p. 14.

90 Noted in Stephen Alomes, *When London Calls: The Expatriation of Australian Creative Artists to Britain*, Cambridge University Press, Cambridge, 1999, p. 145. Also see the *Times*, 3 December 1975, p. 11.

91 *ANZW*, 6 June 1953, p. 11; Alomes, *When London Calls*, pp. 97–8.

92 For an analysis, see Sarah Scott, 'Imaging the Nation: The Australia House Murals', *Australian Studies*, vol. 17, no. 2, 2002, pp. 151–77.

93 *BA*, 5 April 1947, p. 5; *ANZW*, 30 April 1955, p. 48.

94 See *ANZW*, 4 June 1960, pp. 1, 10; ibid., 31 March 1962, p. 6; ibid., 29 September 1962, p. 6; Stephen Alomes, 'Beyond "Kangaroo Valley": The Rituals of Australian London', *Australian Studies*, vol. 17, no. 1, 2002, pp. 8, 11–12. Attesting to the youthfulness of visitors, in 1960 a newspaper article noted that 'Each year about 35,000 Australians come to Britain … and it seems to be the girls, the never ending stream of Australian girls, who dominate the scene' (*ANZW*, 28 April 1962, p. 6).

95 In June 1960, for example, the Overseas Visitors Club advertised berths from Australia to Britain for £A80 (including in the price two days of accommodation in Athens, a rail ticket

to London, sightseeing and a week's lodgings at the club). Six years later Qantas promoted 'under 26' airfares starting at £144 one way. See *ANZW* 4 June 1960, p. 10; ibid., 19 November 1966, p. 5.

96 Ibid., 25 June 1955, p. 12.

97 Ibid., 8 October 1955, p. 14.

98 Noted in Alomes, 'Beyond "Kangaroo Valley"', p. 8.

99 *ANZW*, 19 November 1966, p. 12. The allegation was first expressed in the Sydney *Sun-Herald*.

100 Ibid.

101 John Newnham, 'Our House in London', *Sydney Morning Herald*, 31 December 1965, p. 2.

102 *ANZW*, 6 March 1965, p. 8; Payne (consultant ed.), *Australia House: 75 Years of Service*, p. 25.

103 Information from Sleight, '*Ex Libris* Australia House', pp. 120–1 and interview with Athalie Colquhoun, 18 March 2003. Visiting writers included Sir John Betjeman and Barry Oakley. A photograph of the ground-floor bookshop—at this time operated by Angus and Robertson—features in *ANZW*, 10 September 1966, p. 10.

104 Peter Conrad, 'Abroad Minded', *Weekend Australian*, 4–5 December 2004, p. 31.

105 Ibid.

106 *ANZW*, 20 January 1962, p. 3; ibid., 9 June 1962, p. 1; ibid., 7 July 1962, p. 10.

107 Ashley McKeon, 'Australia House Staff Look for Legislative Morale Boost', *Australian Financial Review*, 13 July 1973.

108 Ibid.

109 See Tony Maiden, 'Australia House Swallows Its Fraserism Dose', *Australian Financial Review*, 17 February 1976, p. 12. Pryke notes that by 1976 staff numbers had been almost halved in five years, with Australia House now employing 670 people (see Pryke, 'Australia House', p. 327).

110 See Maiden, 'Australia House'; McKeon, 'Australia House Staff'; Sleight, '*Ex Libris* Australia House', pp. 124–5.

111 Philip Derriman, 'A House, Yes, but a Home No More', *Sydney Morning Herald*, 21 November 1978, p. 7.

112 Paul Byrne, 'He's Costing Us $12m [a] Year', *Daily Telegraph* (Sydney), probably June 1978, n.p. (Item located in 'Australia House', Australia House filing cabinets (uncatalogued), University of London Senate House Library.)

113 Axed departments included Public Service, Health and the CSIRO, leaving a total of 334 locally engaged staff. See 'Australia House Finds Where the Razor Cuts', *Sydney Morning Herald*, 13 October 1981, p. 1; ibid., 12 November 1983, p. 34 (*Good Weekend* section); interview with Athalie Colquhoun, 18 March 2003.

114 See Dyson, 'Australia's Bustling Home from Home', p. 168.

115 Noted in Pryke, 'Australia House', pp. 327–8.

116 See Richard Conrad Glover, 'In 1988, Poms should be so lucky to get Australian neighbours', *Sydney Morning Herald*, 29 August, 1988, p. 4; Richard Conrad Glover, 'What's New? Australia Always Drew a Big Queue', *Sydney Morning Herald*, 1 February 1989, p. 3.

117 Noted in Valerie Lawson, 'Grand Old Dame of Diplomacy Seeks a New Role for Today's World', *Sydney Morning Herald*, 14 March 2005, p. 11.

118 Sleight, '*Ex Libris* Australia House', pp. 127–8.

119 Parliamentary Committee on Public Works, *Report Relating to the Refurbishment of Australia House, London*, Commonwealth Parliament Printer, Canberra, 1995, pp. 4, 8.

120 The collection contains approximately 17,500 book titles and over 300 journal series. It is now housed in the University of London Library at Senate House.

121 Recollections of Athalie Colquhoun, 18 March 2003. To his credit, however, Goss argued that access to the Australian collection should remain free of charge in its new home.

122 See *Report Relating to the Refurbishment of Australia House*, appendix ('Public Access Areas' plan).

123 See, for example, the letter by H.E. Hayward in *Sydney Morning Herald*, 23 November 1990, p. 10; Evan Whitton, 'The Men on a Mission with the London High Commission', *Sydney Morning Herald*, p. 34 (*Good Weekend* section); comment by Bernard Lyman (1989), cited in Pryke, 'Australia House', p. 331.

124 The centre opened officially in 1997. Of lesser, though still noteworthy, importance, in 1994 the high commission also employed an epicurean envoy, Lew Kathreptis, to promote Australian produce and cooking at Australia House functions. See 'Our Chef in London', *Age*, 3 May 1994, p. 2 (*Epicure* section).

125 Refer to *Report Relating to the Refurbishment of Australia House*, pp. 6, 8, 10; Pryke, 'Australia House', p. 332; *The Australia Centre*, Australia House, London, c. 1997, pp. 1, 7.

126 Founded in 1982 as part of the Institute of Commonwealth Studies, University of London.

127 Refer to *The Australia Centre*, pp. 2–3. Current occupants include Austrade, government offices for three states (Victoria, South Australia and Western Australia), Tourism Australia, Certified Practising Accountants (CPA) Australia, Australian Business and Wine Australia. For a list of forthcoming conferences and seminars scheduled to take place at the Menzies Centre, visit its website: www.klc.ac.uk/schools/humanities/depts/menzies.

128 Noted in Roslyn Russell, 'Literary Links: A Continuing British–Australian Saga', *National Library of Australia News*, March 1998, p. 8; Alomes, *When London Calls*, p. 270.

129 Russell, 'Literary Links', p. 8. A report in the *Independent* on the appearance of Clive James (James Rampton, 'An Hour with Clive James, Australia House, London', 7 July 1995, available for upload at www.independent.co.uk) called the building 'an unusual venue' for such an event. Rampton also noted that 'it was standing-room only' to see James in Exhibition Hall, an observation endorsed in the *Australian* by Jill Neville: '[The] Literary Links evenings … have certainly hotted up dear old Australia House'. (Neville quoted by Russell in 'Literary Links', p. 8.)

130 See Jane Cornwell, 'Dream Time', *Age*, 12 November 1994, p. 12 (*Saturday Extra* section).

131 The book appeared as Roslyn Russell, *Literary Links: Celebrating the Literary Relationship between Australia and Britain*, Allen & Unwin, Sydney, 1997. A short catalogue of the exhibition was also published: *Literary Links: a British Council / National Library of Australia exhibition*, National Library of Australia, Monash University and the British Council, Canberra, Melbourne and London, 1995.

132 Stephanie Bunbury, 'New Images for the Old Country', *Age*, 4 February 1997, p. 5 (*Metropolitan* section).

133 Ibid.

134 See ibid.; Susan Owens, 'Art of Diplomacy', *Sun-Herald*, 14 December 1997, p. 11 (*Tempo* magazine section).

135 Blewett quoted in *Age*, 17 November 1997, p. 8.

136 Discussed in Paula McGinley, 'Rebecca's Empire', *theage(melbourne)magazine*, 29 September 2006, p. 58.

137 A review of the exhibition by Grazia Gunn features in the *Times Literary Supplement*, 14 July 2000, p. 17. The exhibition ran from 26 June to 30 July.

138 Helen McCabe, 'Boyd's Spirit to Charm Britain', *Herald Sun*, 5 April 2000, p. 53.

139 Matt Condon, 'No Place Like Home', *Sun Herald*, 4 March 2001, p. 26 (*Sunday Life* section).

140 Noted in *MX* (Melbourne), 17 October 2002, p. 8; *Southern Star* (Brisbane), 13 July 2005, p. 4.

141 Noted in 'UK Votes', *Herald Sun*, 7 November 2001, p. 12; 'Election 2004: Expats Vote in London', *Advertiser* (Adelaide) 28 September 2004, p. 6; Charles Miranda, 'Australia Decides: Rush on at UK Booths', *Sunday Mail* (Adelaide), 25 November 2007, p. 23. Dylan Nicholls includes a photo of a voting queue outside the high commission in *What Are You Doing Here? The Question of Australians in London*, Pen Press, Brighton, facing p. 98.

142 See Nick Butterly, 'Wizard's Latest Includes Chunk of Oz', *Courier Mail*, 19 January 2006, p. 3; Felicity Collins and Sue Turnbull, 'The Global Adventures of Kath and Kim', *Age*, 26 July 2004, p. 4 (*A3* section).

143 Noted in Pryke, 'Australia House', p. 328.

144 See Valerie Lawson, 'Grand Old Dame of Diplomatic Outposts Seeks a New Role for Today's World', *Sydney Morning Herald*, 14 March 2005, p. 11.

145 Annabel Crabb and Mark Forbes, 'Australia's London Face Forced to Hide', *Age*, 12 August 2006, p. 6. The article also includes a photograph of associated building work.

146 Noted in Dyson, 'Australia's Bustling Home from Home', p. 168.

147 Visit www.uk.embassy.gov.au/lhlh/EventsRoyal.html for details.

148 The British Australian Rules Football League; an annual Australian film festival at the Barbican; Walkabout pubs; the 'Toast Australia' event on Clapham Common; Sunday afternoons at 'The Church' in Kentish Town: these are just some of the well-established attractions on offer to today's antipodeans in the United Kingdom.

149 See, for example, Philip Derriman, 'A House, Yes, but a Home No More', *Sydney Morning Herald*, 21 November 1978, p. 7; Evan Whitton, 'Australia's House Away from Home', *Sydney Morning Herald*, 12 November 1983, p. 34 (*Good Weekend* section).

Appendix 3

Unless otherwise stated, the source of biographical information and quotation was Australian Dictionary of Biography, *online edition, http://adbonline.anu.edu.au/adbonline.htm;* Dictionary of New Zealand Biography, *http://www.dnzb.govt.nz/dnzb/; and* European Mail: A Summary of News for Australia and New Zealand, *24 November 1876.*

1 Quoted in Michael Cannon, *The Land Boomers*, Melbourne University Press, 1966, p. 122.

2 David Lambert and Alan Lester (eds), *Colonial Lives Across the British Empire: Imperial Careering in the Long Nineteenth Century*, Cambridge University Press, Cambridge, 2006.

Bibliography

Unpublished government sources

Australia

National Archives of Australia, Canberra

Prime Minister's Department/Department of the Prime Minister and Cabinet
CP268/1, Non-current personal files, 1916–53
CP268/3, Non-current, personal files, 1920–54
A2718, Bruce-Page ministry—volumes of minutes and minutes and submissions (incomplete), with partial indexes, 1923–29
A461, Correspondence files, multiple number series, 1934–50
A462, Correspondence files, multiple number series, fourth system, 1951–55
A463, Correspondence files, annual single number series with occasional 'G' [General Representations] infix, 1956–
A1209, Correspondence files, annual single number series (classified), 1957–
A5842, Second Holt ministry—copies of cabinet submissions and associated decisions, 1966–67
A5619, Cabinet files, single number series with 'C' [Cabinet] prefix, 1968–72

Department of External Affairs/Foreign Affairs
A1, Correspondence files, annual single number series, 1903–38
A10356, Records from the League of Nations and records relating to Australia's representation at the League of Nations, 1920–46
A458, Correspondence files, multiple number series, second system, 1923–34
A1606, Correspondence files, two-number system with letter prefix, secret and confidential series (third system), 1926–39
A981, Correspondence files, alphabetical series, 1927–42
A11549, Records of the Australian delegation to the Paris Peace Conference, 1946
A1838, Correspondence files, multiple number series, 1948–89
A3299, Dr J.S. Cumpston's collection of material about the history of the Department of External Affairs and its antecedents, 1901–60

Australian High Commission, London
A59, Hansard and press cuttings relating to the High Commissioner London, 1909–10
A2911, General correspondence files, two- and three-number system with year suffix, 1909–16
A6252, Unregistered papers relating to the High Commissioner's Office, London, 1915–33
CP317/8, Inward and outward cablegrams to High Commissioner and Miscellaneous, 1919–26
A2908, Correspondence files, classified single number series with alphabetical prefix, 1920–68
A3211, Correspondence files, annual single number series, 1960–

Department of Defence
A5954, 'The Shedden Collection' [records collected by Sir Frederick Shedden during his career with the Department of Defence and in researching the history of Australian defence policy], two-number series, 1901–71

Other series

A1632, Memoirs of Malcolm Lindsay Shepherd, 1901–60

A11804, General correspondence of Governor-General (excluding war files), 1912–27

AA1970/555, Papers accumulated as a Member of Parliament and Prime Minister [S.M. Bruce], 1918–29

AA1970/559, Papers accumulated as Prime Minister, Australian Minister in London and Australian High Commissioner to Britain [S.M. Bruce], 1923–56

M1135, Papers relating to Lord Casey's time as Liaison Officer between the Australian Government and the Foreign Office, 1924–35

A1420, Folders of correspondence between Prime Minister Stanley Melbourne Bruce and External Affairs Liaison Officer (London), Major R.G. Casey, 1924–30

M104, Folders of annual correspondence [S.M. Bruce], 1926–64

M110, Binders of debt conversion conversation notes, cables and correspondence [S. M. Bruce], 1932–33

M1002, Downer family papers, 1932–81

A1421, Correspondence with (Assistant) Federal Treasurer R.G. Casey [S.M. Bruce], 1933–38

M100, Monthly war files [S. M. Bruce], 1939–45

M1129, Correspondence files, alphabetical series [R.G. Casey], 1939–75

M1455, Correspondence of Joseph Benedict Chifley as Prime Minister, 1945–49

M348, 'Sequence files' (box copies of outward correspondence) of J.F. Richardson, annual single number series, 1960–82

M1003, High Commissioner files [A.R. Downer], 1964–72

M4541, Personal correspondence of Sir John Kerr when Governor-General and later, alphabetical series, 1972–91

United Kingdom

The National Archives

Prime Minister's Office

CAB 2, Committee of Imperial Defence and Standing Defence Sub-committee: Minutes, 1902–39

CAB 32, Cabinet Office: Imperial and Imperial War Conferences: Minutes and Memoranda, 1917–37

CAB 66, War Cabinet and Cabinet: Memoranda (WP and CP series), 1939–45

PREM 1, Prime Minister's Office: Correspondence and Papers, 1916–1940

PREM 4, Prime Minister's Office: Confidential Correspondence and Papers, 1934–46

PREM 8, Prime Minister's Office: Correspondence and Papers, 1945–51

PREM 11, Prime Minister's Office: Correspondence and Papers, 1951–64

PREM 15, Prime Minister's Office: Correspondence and Papers, 1970–74

Foreign Office/Foreign and Commonwealth Office

FO 800, Foreign Office, Private Offices: Various Ministers' and Officials' Papers, 1824–1968

FO 371, Foreign Office: Political Departments: General Correspondence, 1906–66

FO 372, Foreign Office: Treaty Department and Successors: General Correspondence from 1906, 1906–57

FCO 20, Commonwealth Office: Common Market Department: Registered Files (EC series), 1967–68

FCO 24, Commonwealth Office, Far East and Pacific Department and Foreign and Commonwealth Office, South West Pacific Department: Registered Files (H and FW series), 1967–78

FCO 30, Foreign Office and Foreign and Commonwealth Office: European Economic Organisations Department and Successors: Registered Files (ME and MW series), 1967–78

FCO 32, Commonwealth Office and Foreign and Commonwealth Office: Pacific and Indian Ocean Department and Pacific Dependent Territories Department: Registered Files (Q and HP series), 1967–78

FCO 68, Foreign and Commonwealth Office: Commonwealth Co-ordination Department: Registered Files (HC series), 1968–78

Colonial Office/Dominions Office

CO 532, Colonial Office: Dominions Original Correspondence, 1907–25

DO 35, Dominions Office and Commonwealth Relations Office: Original Correspondence, 1915–71

DO 114, Confidential Print Dominions, 1924–51

DO 121, Dominions Office and Commonwealth Relations Office: Private Office Papers, 1911–64

DO 161, Commonwealth Relations Office and Commonwealth Office: Constitutional Department and Successors: Registered Files (CON series), 1953–67

DO 175, Commonwealth Relations Office and Commonwealth Office: General Department and Successors: Registered Files, Migration (MIG series), 1954–67

Other series

ADM 116, Admiralty: Record Office: Cases, 1852–1965

T 160, Treasury: Registered Files: Finance Files (F series), 1887–1948

Published government sources

Australia

Andre, Pamela (ed.), *Documents on Australian Foreign Policy 1937–49*, vol. XVI, *Beyond the Region, 1948–49*, Department of Foreign Affairs and Trade, Canberra, 2001.

Colonial Representation in London: Our Self Governing Colonies: How Their Interests Are Promoted in the United Kingdom, reproduced in Sell, Henry (comp.), *Sell's Dictionary of the World's Press*, King, Sell & Railton, London, 1899.

Commonwealth Parliamentary Debates, 1901– .

Commonwealth Parliamentary Papers, 1901– .

Department of Foreign Affairs and Trade, *In the National Interest: Australia's Foreign and Trade Policy White Paper*, Commonwealth of Australia, Canberra, 1997.

Hudson, W.J., and North, Jane (eds), *'My Dear PM': R.G. Casey's Letters to S.M. Bruce, 1924–29*, Australian Government Publishing Service, Canberra, 1980.

Hudson, W.J., and Stokes, H.J.W. (eds), *Documents on Australian Foreign Policy, 1937–49*, vol. IV, *July 1940 – June 1941*, Australian Government Publishing Service, Canberra, 1980.

——(eds), *Documents on Australian Foreign Policy, 1937–49*, vol. V, *July 1941 – June 1942*, Australian Government Publishing Service, Canberra, 1982.

Hudson, W.J., and Way, Wendy (eds), *Letters from a 'Secret Service Agent': F.L. McDougall to S.M. Bruce*, Australian Government Publishing Service, Canberra, 1986.

Kenway, H., Stokes, H.J.W., and Edwards, P.G. (eds), *Documents on Australian Foreign Policy, 1937–49*, vol. III, *January–June 1940*, Australian Government Publishing Service, Canberra, 1979.

Neale, R.G. (ed.), *Documents on Australian Foreign Policy 1937–49*. vol. I, *1937–38*, Australian Government Publishing Service, Canberra, 1975.

——, *Documents on Australian Foreign Policy, 1937–49*, vol. II, *1939*, Australian Government Publishing Service, Canberra, 1975.

New South Wales Legislative Assembly, *Votes and Proceedings*, vol. 2, 1902.

Official Records of the Proceedings and Debates of the Australasian Federal Conference, 1890, Government Printer, Melbourne, 1890.

Official Year Book of the Commonwealth of Australia, Commonwealth Bureau of Census and Statistics, Canberra, no. 26, 1933.

Parliamentary Committee on Public Works, *Report Relating to the Refurbishment of Australia House, London*, Commonwealth Parliament Printer, Canberra, 1995.

Payne, Jan (consultant ed.), *Australia House: 75 Years of Service*, Public Affairs Branch, Australian High Commission, London, 1993.

United Kingdom

Parliamentary Papers

Personal papers and memoirs

Australia

Armstrong, John Ignatius, held by family

Deakin, Alfred, MS 1540, NLA

Fisher, Andrew, MS 2919, NLA

Flood, Philip, unpublished notes

Harrison, Sir Eric John, MS 5548, NLA

Hughes, William Morris, MS 1538, NLA

Latham, Sir John, MS 1009, NLA

Lyons, J.A. (Joseph Aloysius), MS 4851, NLA

Menzies, Sir Robert, MS 4936, NLA

Munro Ferguson, Ronald Craufurd (Lord Novar), MS 696, NLA

Officer, Sir Keith, MS 2629, NLA

Page, Sir Earle, MS 1633, NLA

Parsons, Alfred, unpublished memoirs

Pearce, Sir George Foster, 3 DRL 2222, Australian War Memorial (Canberra)

White, Sir T.W. (Thomas Walter), MS 9148, NLA

United Kingdom

Batterbee, Sir Harry Fagg, MSS NZ s13, Rhodes House Library (Oxford)

Hankey, Maurice (Lord Hankey of the Chart), HNKY, Churchill Archives Centre (Cambridge)

Harcourt, Lewis, MSS 452, Bodleian Library (Oxford)

MacDonald, Malcolm, GB 033 MAC, Special Collections (Durham University Library)

Milner, Violet, VM25, Bodleian Library (Oxford)

Walker, Baron Gordon, GNWR, Churchill Archives Centre (Cambridge)

Wilkinson, Colonel Gerald, WILK, Churchill Archives Centre (Cambridge)

Oral histories

Interview with Keith Waller, 1974–77, TRC 314, NLA [by Professor J. D. B. Miller]

Interview with John Armstrong, 11 and 12 November 1975, TRC 121/68, NLA [by Mel Pratt]

Interview with Alfred Parsons, 23 May 1995, TRC 2981/22, NLA [by Michael Wilson]

Interview with Athalie Colquhoun, 18 March 2003 [by Simon Sleight]

Interview with Alfred Parsons, 9 September 2008, DFAT [by Jeremy Hearder]

Interview with Richard Smith, 12 September 2008, DFAT [by Jeremy Hearder]

Interview with Neal Blewett, 18 September 2008, DFAT [by Jeremy Hearder]

Interview with Douglas McClelland, 2 October 2008, DFAT [by Jeremy Hearder]

Interview with Richard Alston, 19 October 2008, DFAT [by Jeremy Hearder]

Interview with Michael L'Estrange, 14 November 2008, DFAT [by Jeremy Hearder]

Interview with Philip Flood, 27 November 2008, DFAT [by Jeremy Hearder]

Interview with Sir Victor Garland, 12 December 2008, DFAT [by Jeremy Hearder]

Published diaries, memoirs, autobiographies and papers

Amery, L.S, *The Leo Amery Diaries*, vol. 1, *1896–1929*, John Barnes and David Nicholson (eds), Hutchinson, London, 1980.

——*My Political Life*, vol. 2, *War and Peace 1914–1929*, Hutchinson, London, 1953.

Bridge, Carl (ed.), *A Delicate Mission: The Washington Diaries of R.G. Casey, 1940–42*, National Library of Australia, Canberra, 2008.

Cadogan, Alexander, *The Diaries of Sir Alexander Cadogan*, David Dilks (ed.), Cassell, London, 1971.

Chamberlain, Austen, *The Austen Chamberlain Diary Letters*, Robert C. Self (ed.), Cambridge University Press, Cambridge, 1995.

Colville, John, *The Fringes of Power: Downing Street Diaries 1939–1955*, rev. edn, Weidenfeld & Nicolson, London, 2004.

Deakin, Alfred, *Federated Australia: Selections from Letters to the Morning Post 1900–1910*, J.A. La Nauze (ed.), Melbourne University Press, 1968.

Downer, Alexander, *Six Prime Ministers*, Hill of Content, Melbourne, 1982.

Garner, Joe, *The Commonwealth Office, 1925–68*, Heinemann, London, 1978.

Hasluck, Paul, *Diplomatic Witness: Australian Foreign Affairs 1941–1947*, Melbourne University Press, 1980.

——*The Chance of Politics*, Text Publishing, Melbourne, 1997.

Kerr, Sir John, *Matters for Judgment*, Macmillan, Melbourne, 1978.

McClelland, James, *Stirring the Possum: A Political Autobiography*, Penguin, Ringwood, Victoria, 1989.

McGibbon, Ian (ed.), *Undiplomatic Dialogue: Letters between Carl Berendsen and Alister McIntosh 1943–1952*, Auckland University Press in association with the Ministry of Foreign Affairs and Trade and the Historical Branch, Department of Internal Affairs, Auckland, 1993.

Massey, Vincent, *What's Past Is Prologue: The Memoirs of the Right Honourable Vincent Massey*, Macmillan, Toronto, 1963.

Menadue, John, *Things You Learn Along the Way*, David Lovell Publishing, Melbourne, 1999.

Menzies, R.G., *Afternoon Light*, Cassell Australia, Melbourne, 1967.

Nicholls, G. Heaton, *South Africa in My Time*, George Allen & Unwin, London, 1961.

Orr, Lord Boyd, *As I Recall*, MacGibbin and Kee, London, 1966.

Page, Earle, *Truant Surgeon*, Angus & Robertson, Sydney, 1963.

Pearce, George, *Carpenter to Cabinet*, Hutchinson, London, 1951.

Reid, George, *My Reminiscences*, Cassell & Co., London, 1917.

Reith, John, *The Reith Diaries*, Charles Stuart (ed.), Collins, London, 1975.

Ritchie, Charles, *The Siren Years: A Canadian Diplomat Abroad 1937–1945*, Macmillan, London, 1974.

Spence, W.G., *Australia's Awakening: Thirty Years in the Life of an Australian Agitator*, Worker Trustees, Sydney, n.d. [first published 1909].

Williamson, Philip, and Baldwin, Edward (eds), *Baldwin Papers. A Conservative Statesman, 1908–1947*, Cambridge University Press, Cambridge, 2004.

Published lectures, speeches and interviews

Alston, Richard, *The Australia–UK Relationship: Menzies' Modern Legacy*, Sir Robert Menzies Lecture Trust, Melbourne, 2007.

Blewett, Neal, 'The Politics of the Republic', in *Public Lectures in Australian Studies, 1995–6*, Menzies Centre for Australian Studies, Institute of Commonwealth Studies, University of London, 1996.

L'Estrange, Michael, *The Australia–Britain Relationship Today: Patterns of History, Dynamics of Change*, Menzies Lecture, Menzies Centre for Australian Studies, King's College London, 27 October 2004.

Oakes, Laurie, Farmer, Richard, and MacCallum, Mungo (eds), *Whitlam and Frost: The Full Text of Their TV Conversations Plus Exclusive New Interviews*, Sundial, London, 1974.

Reid, George, *Some Aspects of the Evolution of the British Empire: An Address Delivered before the Royal Colonial Institute on March 11, 1913 by the Right Hon. Sir George Reid*, n.p., London, 1913.

Whitlam, Gough, *Australia and Europe: Principal Speeches during the Visit of the Prime Minister of Australia to Europe, 14 December 1974 to 21 January 1975*, Australian Government Publishing Service, Canberra, 1974.

Newspapers and periodicals

Australia

Advertiser

Age

Argus

Australasian

Australasian Express

Australian

Australian and New Zealand Weekly

Australian Financial Review

Brisbane Courier

British Australasian

British Australian and New Zealander

Bulletin

Canberra News

Canberra Times

Commonwealth of Australia Gazette

Courier Mail

Daily Telegraph
The Diplomatist
European Mail: A Summary of News for Australia and New Zealand
Federal Gallery
Herald
Herald Sun
Manly Daily
Nation
Nation Review
National Library of Australia News
National Times
Northern Territory News
People
Register
Southern Star
Sun-Herald
Sun-News Pictorial
Sunday Mail
Sydney Morning Herald
Sydney Quarterly Magazine
West Australian

United Kingdom

Daily Express
Daily Mail
Independent
Morning Post
New Statesman
Standard
Times

Reference sources

Australian Dictionary of Biography.
Dictionary of New Zealand Biography.
Meaney, Neville (ed.), *Australia and the World: A Documentary History from the 1870s to the 1970s*, Longman Cheshire, Melbourne, 1985.
Millar, Ann (ed.), *The Biographical Dictionary of the Australian Senate*, vol.2, *1929–1962*, Melbourne University Press, 2004.
Oxford Dictionary of National Biography.
Serle, P., *Dictionary of Australian Biography*, vol.1, Angus & Robertson, Sydney, 1949.

Secondary sources

Alomes, Stephen, *When London Calls: The Expatriation of Australian Creative Artists to Britain*, Cambridge University Press, Cambridge, 1999.

——'Beyond "Kangaroo Valley": The Rituals of Australian London', *Australian Studies*, vol. 17, no. 1, 2002, pp. 3–24.

Ashley, W.J. (ed.), *British Dominions: Their Present Commercial and Industrial Condition*, Longmans, Green & Co., London, 1911.

Attard, Bernard, 'Andrew Fisher, the High Commissionership and the Collapse of Labor', *Labour History*, no. 68, May 1995, pp. 115–31.

——'The Limits of Influence: The Political Economy of Australian Commercial Policy after the Ottawa Conference', *Australian Historical Studies*, vol. 29, no. 111, October 1998, pp. 325–43.

——'Financial Diplomacy', in Carl Bridge and Bernard Attard, (eds), *Between Empire and Nation: Australia's External Relations from Federation to the Second World War*, Australian Scholarly Publishing, Melbourne, 2000, pp. 111–32.

——'Moral Suasion, Empire Borrowers and the New Issue Market during the 1920s', in R.C. Michie and Philip Williamson (eds), *The British Government and the City of London in the Twentieth Century*, Cambridge University Press, Cambridge, 2004, pp. 195–214.

Australia House, London: The Offices in Great Britain of the Government of the Commonwealth of Australia Opened by His Majesty the King, August 3 1918, Printing-Craft, London and Mansfield, 1918.

Bail, Murray, *Homesickness*, Farrar, Straus and Giroux, New York, 1999.

Bastian, Peter, *Andrew Fisher: An Underestimated Man*, University of New South Wales Press, Sydney, 2009.

Beavan, Arthur, *Imperial London*, J.M. Dent & Co., London, 1901.

Benyon, John, *Proconsul and Paramountcy in South Africa: The High Commission, British Supremacy and the Subcontinent 1806–1910*, University of Natal Press, Pietermaritzburg, 1980.

Bird, David S., *J.A. Lyons, the Tame Tasmanian: Appeasement and Rearmament in Australia, 1932–39*, Australian Scholarly Publishing, Melbourne, 2008.

Bissell, Claude, *The Imperial Canadian: Vincent Massey in Office*, University of Toronto Press, 1986.

Bolton, G.C., 'The United Kingdom', in Hudson, W.J. (ed.), *Australia in World Affairs 1971–75*, George Allen & Unwin for the Australian Institute of International Affairs, Sydney, 1980, pp. 209–30.

Bridge, Carl, 'Australia and the Italo-Abyssinian Crisis, 1935-6', *Journal of the Royal Australian Historical Society*, vol. 92, no. 1, 2006, pp. 1–14.

——and Attard, Bernard (eds), *Between Empire and Nation: Australia's External Relations from Federation to the Second World War*, Australian Scholarly Publishing, Melbourne, 2000.

——and Fedorowich, Kent (eds), *The British World: Diaspora, Culture and Identity*, Frank Cass, London, 2003.

Buckley, Ken, Dale, Barbara, and Reynolds, Wayne, *Doc Evatt: Patriot, Internationalist, Fighter, Scholar*, Longman Cheshire, Melbourne, 1994.

Bullock, Alan, *Ernest Bevin, Foreign Secretary: 1945–1951*, Heinemann, London, 1983.

Burton, Margaret E., *The Assembly of the League of Nations*, University of Chicago Press, 1941.

Cain, Neville, and Glynn, Sean, 'Imperial Relations Under Strain: The British–Australian Debt Contretemps of 1933', *Australian Economic History Review*, vol. 25, March 1985, pp. 39–58.

Cannadine, David, *Ornamentalism: How the British Saw Their Empire*, Oxford University Press, New York, 2001.

Michael Cannon, *The Land Boomers*, Melbourne University Press, 1966.

Carlton, David, 'The Dominions and British Policy in the Abyssinian Crisis', *Journal of Imperial and Commonwealth History*, vol. 1, no. 1, 1972, pp. 59–77.

Chan, Stephen, *The Commonwealth in World Politics. A Study of International Action 1965 to 1985*, Lester Crook Academic, London, 1988.

Churchill, Winston S., *The Second World War*, vol. 3, Cassell, London, 1950.

Claude, Inis L., *Swords into Plowshares: The Problems and Progress of International Organization*, University of London Press, 1965.

Cleary, Jon, *The High Commissioner*, Collins, London, 1966.

Cook, Chris and Paxton, John, *Commonwealth Political Facts*, Macmillan, London, 1979.

Cresswell, Tim, *Place: A Short Introduction*, Blackwell, Malden, 2004.

Cross, J.A., *Whitehall and the Commonwealth: British Departmental Organisation for Commonwealth Relations, 1900–1966*, Routledge & Kegan Paul, London, 1967.

Cumpston, I. M., *Lord Bruce of Melbourne*, Longman Cheshire, Melbourne, 1989.

Cunneen, Christopher, *King's Men: Australia's Governors-General from Hopetoun to Isaacs*, Allen & Unwin, Sydney, 1983.

Curran, James, *The Power of Speech: Prime Ministers Defining the National Image*, Melbourne University Press, 2004.

Damousi, Joy, 'War and Commemoration: "The Responsibility of Empire"', in Deryck M. Schreuder and Stuart Ward (eds), *Australia's Empire*, companion series, *Oxford History of the British Empire*, Oxford University Press, Oxford, 2008, pp. 288–311.

Darwin, John, 'A Third British Empire? The Dominion Idea in Imperial Politics', in Judith M. Brown and Wm. Roger Louis (eds), *The Oxford History of the British Empire*, vol. 4, *The Twentieth Century*, Oxford University Press, Oxford, 1999, pp. 64–87.

Day, David, *Andrew Fisher: Prime Minister of Australia*, Fourth Estate, London, 2008.

Deluca, Anthony R., *Great Power Rivalry at the Turkish Straits: The Montreux Conference and Convention of 1936*, Columbia University Press, New York, 1981.

Drummond, Ian M., *British Economic Policy and the Empire 1919–1939*, George Allen & Unwin, London, 1972.

——*Imperial Economic Policy, 1917–1939*, University of Toronto Press, 1974.

Dubin, Martin C., 'Toward the Bruce Report: The Economic and Social Programs of the League of Nations in the Avenol Era', in United Nations Library, *The League of Nations in Retrospect: Proceedings of the Symposium Organised by the United Nations Library and the Graduate Institute of International Studies*, Geneva, 6–9 March 1980, W. De Gruyter, New York, 1983.

Dyson, John, 'Australia's Bustling Home from Home', *Reader's Digest*, November 1980.

Dyster, Barrie, and Meredith, David, *Australia and the International Economy in the Twentieth Century*, Cambridge University Press, Cambridge, 1990.

Edwards, Cecil, *Bruce of Melbourne: Man of Two Worlds*, Heinemann, London, 1965.

Edwards, P.G., 'S.M. Bruce, R.G. Menzies and Australia's War Aims and Peace Aims, 1939–1940', *Historical Studies*, vol. 17, no. 66, 1976, pp. 1–14.

——'The Rise and Fall of the High Commissioner: S.M. Bruce in London, 1933–1945', in A.F. Madden and W.H. Morris Jones (eds), *Australia and Britain: Studies in a Changing Relationship*, Sydney University Press, 1980, pp. 39–56.

——*Prime Ministers and Diplomats. The Making of Australian Foreign Policy 1901–1949*, Oxford University Press in association with the Australian Institute of International Affairs, Melbourne, 1983.

——'The Origins of the Cold War, 1947–1949', in Bridge, Carl (ed.), *Munich to Vietnam: Australia's Relations with Britain and the United States since the 1930s*, Melbourne University Press, 1991, pp. 70–86.

Evans, Gareth, and Grant, Bruce, *Australia's Foreign Relations in the World of the 1990s*, Melbourne University Press, 1995.

Farr, David, *The Colonial Office and Canada, 1867–1887*, University of Toronto Press, 1955.

Farran, Andrew, 'The Freeth Experiment', *Australian Outlook*, vol. 26, no. 1, April 1972, pp. 46–58.

Fedorowich, Kent, 'Anglicisation and the Politicisation of British Immigration to South Africa, 1899–1929', *Journal of Imperial and Commonwealth History*, vol. 19, 1991, pp. 222–46.

——' "At War with Canberra": Sir Ronald Cross and the British High Commission, 1941–42', *London Papers in Australian Studies*, no. 16, Menzies Centre for Australian Studies, King's College London, 2008, pp. 1–49.

——'Lord Harlech in South Africa, 1941–44', in Christopher Baxter and Andrew Stewart (eds), *Diplomats at War: British and Commonwealth Diplomacy in Wartime*, Martinus Nijhoff, Leiden, 2008, pp. 195–225.

Fewster, Alan, *Trusty and Well Beloved: A Life of Keith Officer Australia's First Diplomat*, Miegunyah Press, Melbourne, 2009.

Fitzhardinge, L.F., *The Little Digger, 1914–52: William Morris Hughes, A Political Biography*, Angus & Robertson, Sydney, 1978.

Gare, Deborah, 'Dating Australia's Independence: National Sovereignty and the 1986 Australia Acts', *Australian Historical Studies*, vol. 30, no. 113, October 1999, pp. 251–66.

Ghebali, Victor-Yves, *La Société des Nations et la Réforme Bruce 1939–1940*, Centre Européen de la Dotation Carenegie Pour la Paix Internationale, Geneva, 1970.

Golding, Peter, *Black Jack McEwen: Political Gladiator*, Melbourne University Press, 1996.

Goldsworthy, David, *Losing the Blanket: Australia and the End of Britain's Empire*, Melbourne University Press, 2002.

Gore-Booth, Lord Paul (ed.), *Satow's Guide to Diplomatic Practice*, 5th edn, Longman, London, 1979.

Graham, Roger, *Arthur Meighen*, vol. 2, *And Fortune Fled*, Clarke, Irwin & Co., Toronto, 1963.

Granatstein, J.L., *A Man of Influence: Norman A. Robertson and Canadian Statecraft 1929–68*, Deneau Publishers, Ottawa, 1981.

Haas, Ernest, *Beyond the Nation State: Functionalism and International Organisation*, Stanford University Press, 1964.

Haines, Robin F., *Emigration and the Labouring Poor: Australian Recruitment in Britain and Ireland, 1831–60*, Macmillan Press, London, 1997.

Hammerton, A. James and Thomson, Alistair, *Ten Pound Poms: Australia's Invisible Migrants*, Manchester University Press, 2005.

Hancock, Ian, *John Gorton: He Did It His Way*, Hodder, Sydney, 2002.

Hancock, W.K., *Survey of British Commonwealth Affairs*, vol. 1, *Problems of Nationality, 1918–1936*, Oxford University Press, London, 1937.

——*Survey of British Commonwealth Affairs*, vol. 2, *Problems of Economic Policy 1918–1939, Part 1*, Oxford University Press, London, 1940.

——*Smuts*, vol.2, *The Fields of Force, 1919–1950*, Cambridge University Press, Cambridge, 1962.

Hankey, Lord Maurice, *Diplomacy by Conference: Studies in Public Affairs 1920–1946*, Ernest Benn, London, 1946.

Hardie, Frank, *The Abyssinian Crisis*, Batsford, London, 1974.

Harkness, D.W., *The Restless Dominion: The Irish Free State and the British Commonwealth of Nations, 1921–31*, Macmillan, London, 1969.

Hasluck, Paul, *The Government and the People, 1939–1941*, Australian War Memorial, Canberra, 1952.

——*The Government and the People, 1942–1945*, Australian War Memorial, Canberra, 1970.

Haycock, Ronald G., 'The "Myth" of Imperial Defence: Australian–Canadian Bilateral Military Cooperation, 1942', *War & Society*, vol. 2, 1984, pp. 65–84.

Hilliker, John, 'Distant Ally: Canadian Relations with Australia during the Second World War', *Journal of Imperial and Commonwealth History*, vol. 13, 1984, pp. 46–67.

——*Canada's Department of External Affairs*, vol. 1, *The Early Years, 1909–1946*, Institute of Public Administration of Canada/McGill–Queen's University Press, Montreal, 1990.

Hillmer, Norman, 'A British High Commissioner for Canada 1927–28', *Journal of Imperial and Commonwealth History*, vol. 1, 1973, pp. 339–56.

Holland, R.F., *Britain and the Commonwealth Alliance 1918–1939*, Macmillan, London, 1981.

Hudson, W.J., 'The Yo-yo Variations: A Comment', *Historical Studies*, vol. 14, no. 55, 1970, pp. 424–29.

——*Australia and the League of Nations*, Sydney University Press, 1980.

——*Casey*, Oxford University Press, Melbourne, 1986.

——and Sharp, M.P., *Australian Independence: Colony to Reluctant Kingdom*, Melbourne University Press, 1988.

Hyam, Ronald and Henshaw, Peter, *The Lion and the Springbok: Britain and South Africa since the Boer War*, Cambridge University Press, Cambridge, 2003.

Kelly, Paul, *The Unmaking of Gough*, Angus & Robertson, Sydney, 1976.

——*The End of Certainty. The Story of the 1980s*, Allen & Unwin, Sydney, 1992.

Kinrade, Derek, *Alf Morris People's Parliamentarian: Scenes from the Life of Lord Morris of Manchester*, National Information Forum, London , 2007.

Kristensen, Jeppe, '"In Essence Still a British Country": Britain's Withdrawal from East of Suez', *Australian Journal of Politics and History*, vol. 41, no. 1, March 2005, pp. 40–52.

Laidlaw, Zoë, 'Closing the Gap: Colonial Governors and Unofficial Communications in the 1830s', in Simon J. Potter (ed.), *Imperial Communication: Australia, Britain, and the British Empire c. 1830-50*, Menzies Centre for Australian Studies, King's College London, 2005, pp. 64–87.

——*Colonial Connections 1815-45: Patronage, the Information Revolution and Colonial Government*, Manchester University Press, 2005.

Lambert, David, and Lester, Alan (eds), *Colonial Lives Across the British Empire: Imperial Careering in the Long Nineteenth Century*, Cambridge University Press, Cambridge, 2006.

Lambert, Nicholas, 'Sir John Fisher, the Fleet Unit Concept, and the Creation of the Royal Australian Navy', in David Stevens and John Reeve (eds), *Southern Trident: Strategy, History and the Rise of Australian Naval Power*, Crows Nest, New South Wales, 2001, pp. 214–24.

La Nauze, J.A., *Alfred Deakin: A Biography*, Melbourne University Press, 1965.

Lee, David, 'Britain and Australia's Defence Policy, 1945–1949', *War & Society*, vol. 13, no. 1, 1995, pp. 61–80.

——*Search for Security: The Political Economy of Australia's Postwar Foreign and Defence Policy*, Allen & Unwin in association with the Department of International Relations, Research School of Pacific and Asian Studies, Australian National University, Canberra, 1995.

——*Australia and the World in the Twentieth Century*, Circa, Beaconsfield, Victoria, 2006.

——'Stanley Bruce at the Wartime Australian High Commission in London', in Christopher Baxter and Andrew Stewart (eds), *Diplomats at War: British and Commonwealth Diplomacy in Wartime*, Martinus Nijhoff, Leiden, 2008, pp. 149–71.

Lefebvre, Henri, *The Production of Space*, trans. Donald Nicholson-Smith, Blackwell, Oxford, 1991.

Lloyd, David, *Battlefield Tourism: Pilgrimage and the Commemoration of the Great War in Britain, Australia and Canada, 1919–1939*, Berg, Oxford, 1998.

Lloyd, Lorna, '"What's in a Name?" The Curious Tale of the Office of High Commissioner', *Diplomacy and Statecraft*, vol. 11, 2000, pp. 47–78.

——*Diplomacy with a Difference: The Commonwealth Office of High Commissioner, 1880–2006*, Martinus Nijhoff, Leiden, 2007.

Lowe, David, *Menzies and 'the Great World Struggle': Australia's Cold War 1948–54*, University of New South Wales Press, Sydney, 1999.

——'Percy Spender, Minister and Ambassador', in Joan Beaumont, Christopher Waters, David Lowe, with Garry Woodard, *Ministers, Mandarins and Diplomats: Australian Foreign Policy Making, 1941–1969*, Melbourne University Press, 2003, pp. 62–87.

Lowry, Donal, 'New Ireland, Old Empire and the Outside World, 1922–49: The Strange Evolution of a "Dictionary Republic"', in Mike Cronin and John M. Regan (eds), *Ireland: The Politics of Independence, 1922–49*, Macmillan, London, 2000, pp.164–216

——'The Captive Dominion: Imperial Realities behind Irish Diplomacy, 1922–49', *Irish Historical Studies*, vol. 36, 2008, pp. 202–26.

Macintyre, Stuart, *The Oxford History of Australia*, vol. 4, *The Succeeding Age*, Oxford University Press, Melbourne, 1986.

McIntyre, W.D., *The Significance of the Commonwealth, 1965–1990*, Macmillan Academic and Professional, Basingstoke, 1991.

——*Dominion of New Zealand: Statesmen and Status 1907–1945*, New Zealand Institute of International Affairs, Wellington, 2007.

MacKenzie, John M., *Propaganda and Empire: The Manipulation of British Public Opinion, 1880–1960*, Manchester University Press, 1984.

MacLaren, Roy, *Commissions High: Canada in London, 1870–1971*, McGill–Queen's University Press, Montreal, 2006.

McMahon, Deirdre, *Republicans and Imperialists: Anglo-Irish Relations in the 1930s*, Yale University Press, New Haven, 1984.

——'Ireland and the Empire-Commonwealth, 1900–1948', in Judith M. Brown and Wm. Roger Louis (eds), *The Oxford History of the British Empire*, vol. 4, *The Twentieth Century*, Oxford University Press, Oxford, 1999, pp. 138–62.

Major, Norma, *Joan Sutherland*, Macdonald/Queen Anne, London, 1987.

Malouf, David, 'Made in England: Australia's British Inheritance', *Quarterly Essay*, no. 12, 2003, pp. 1–66.

Mansergh, Nicholas, *The Commonwealth Experience*, Weidenfeld & Nicolson, London, 1969.

Martin, A.W., 'Immigration Policy before Federation', in James Jupp (ed.), *The Australian People: An Encyclopedia of the Nation, Its People and Their Origins*, Cambridge University Press, Cambridge, 2001, pp. 39–44.

——*Robert Menzies: A Life*, vol. 1, *1894–1943*, Melbourne University Press, 1993.

Meaney, Neville, *A History of Australian Foreign and Defence Policy, 1901–23*, vol. 1, *The Search for Security in the Pacific, 1901–14*, Sydney University Press, 1976.

——'Britishness and Australia: Some Reflections', *Journal of Imperial and Commonwealth History*, vol. 31, no. 2, May 2003, pp. 121–35.

——*A History of Australian Foreign and Defence Policy, 1901–23*, vol. 2, *Australia and World Crisis, 1914–23*, Sydney University Press, 2009.

Middlemas, Keith, and Barnes, John, *Baldwin*, Weidenfeld & Nicolson, London, 1970.

Miller, J.D.B., 'Australia and Western Europe', in P.J. Boyce and J.R. Angel (eds), *Independence and Alliance—Australia in World Affairs 1976–80*, George Allen & Unwin for the Australian Institute of International Affairs, Sydney, 1983, pp. 157–68.

Mitrany, David, *The Progress of International Government*, Allen & Unwin, London, 1933.

Moore, R.J., *Making the New Commonwealth*, Clarendon Press, Oxford, 1987.

Moore, Tony, *The Barry McKenzie Movies*, Currency Press and the Australian Film Commission, Strawberry Hills, New South Wales, 2005.

Neatby, H. Blair, *William Lyon Mackenzie King*, vol. 2, *1924–1932 The Lonely Heights*, University of Toronto Press, 1963.

Official Report of the Sixth Commonwealth Conference of the A. L. P. held in Adelaide, May 31–June 7, 1915, Worker Trade Union Printery, Sydney, 1915

O'Neill, Robert, 'Defence Policy', in W.J. Hudson (ed.), *Australia in World Affairs, 1971–75*, Allen & Unwin, Sydney, 1980, pp. 11–36.

——*Australia in the Korean War 1950–53*, vol. 1, *Strategy and Diplomacy*, Australian War Memorial and Australian Government Publishing Service, Canberra, 1981.

Pender, Anne, 'The Mythical Australian: Barry Humphries, Gough Whitlam and "New Nationalism"', *Australian Journal of Politics and History*, vol.51, no.1, March 2005, pp. 67–79.

Penny, Barbara, 'Establishing a Nineteenth Century Government Office—The Australian Agencies-General', *Australian Journal of Public Administration*, vol. 22, June 1963, pp. 178–98.

Pesman, Ros, *Duty Free: Australian Women Abroad*, Oxford University Press, Melbourne, 1996.

Poynter, J.R., 'The Yo-yo Variations: Initiative and Dependence in Australia's External Relations, 1918–1923', *Historical Studies*, vol. 14, no. 54, 1970, pp. 231–49.

Quick, John, and Garran, R.R., *The Annotated Constitution of the Australian Commonwealth*, Angus & Robertson, Sydney, 1901.

Reid, George, 'The Australian Premiers in England', *Review of Reviews*, Australian edition, September 1897.

Rendel, Sir George, *The Sword and the Olive*, J. Murray, London, 1957.

Richmond, W.H., 'S.M. Bruce and Australian Economic Policy, 1923–29', *Australian Economic History Review*, vol. 23, September 1983, pp. 238–57.

Roe, Michael, *Australia, Britain and Migration, 1915–1940*, Cambridge University Press, Cambridge, 1995.

Rooth, Tim, 'Ottawa and After', in Carl Bridge and Bernard Attard (eds), *Between Empire and Nation: Australia's External Relations from Federation to the Second World War*, Australian Scholarly Publishing, Melbourne, 2000, pp. 133–57.

Roskill, Stephen, *Hankey: Man of Secrets*, Collins, London, 1970.

Ross, A.T., 'Australian Overseas Trade and National Development Policy 1932–39: A Story of Colonial Larrikins or Australian Statesmen?', *Australian Journal of Politics and History*, vol. 36, no. 2, 1990, pp. 184–204.

Russell, Roslyn, *Literary Links: Celebrating the Literary Relationship between Australia and Britain*, Allen & Unwin, Sydney, 1997.

Rye, R.A., *The Students' Guide to the Libraries of London*, University of London Press, 1927.

Sales, P.M., 'W.M. Hughes and the Chanak Crisis of 1922', *Australian Journal of Politics and History*, vol. 17, December 1971, pp. 392–405.

Schedvin, C.B., *Australia and the Great Depression*, Sydney University Press, 1970.

Schiffer, Walter, *The Legal Community of Mankind: A Critical Analysis of the Modern Concept of World Organization*, Columbia University Press, New York, 1954.

Scott, Ernest, *Australia during the War*, 6th ed., Angus & Robertson, Sydney, 1940.

Scott, Sarah, 'Imaging the Nation: The Australia House Murals', *Australian Studies*, vol.17, no. 2, 2002, pp. 151–77.

——*Neville Chamberlain: A Biography*, Ashgate, Aldershot, 2006.

Sissons, D.C.S., 'Manchester v. Japan: The Imperial Background of the Australian Trade Diversion Dispute with Japan, 1936', *Australian Outlook*, vol. 30, no. 3, 1976, pp. 480–502.

Sleight, Simon, '*Ex Libris* Australia House: Paper Trails to and from a Unique London Institution', *Australian Studies*, vol. 17, no. 2, 2002, pp. 117–50.

——'Reading the *British Australasian* Community in London, 1884–1924', in Carl Bridge, Robert Crawford and David Dunstan (eds), *Australians in Britain: The Twentieth-Century Experience*, Monash University ePress, Melbourne, 2009.

Srinivasan, Krishnan, *The Rise, Decline and Future of the British Commonwealth*, Palgrave Macmillan, Basingstoke, 2005.

Stacey, C.P., *Canada and the Age of Conflict*, vol.2, *1921–1948 The Mackenzie King Era*, University of Toronto Press, 1981.

Stirling, Alfred, *Lord Bruce: The London Years*, Hawthorn Press, Melbourne, 1974.

Summers, Julie, *Remembered: The History of the Commonwealth War Graves Commission*, Merrell in association with the Commonwealth War Graves Commission, London, 2007.

Thompson, Mark, *The White War: Life and Death on the Italian Front 1915–1919*, Faber and Faber, London, 2008

Thompson, Roger, *Australian Imperialism in the Pacific*, Melbourne University Press, 1980.

Tsokhas, Kosmas, 'The Wool Industry and the 1936 Trade Diversion Dispute Between Australia and Japan', *Australian Historical Studies*, vol. 23, no. 93, October 1989, 442–61.

——'Coldly Received: Australia and the London Capital Market in the 1930s', *Australian Journal of International Affairs*, vol. 46, May 1992, pp. 61–80.

Tuan, Yi-Fu, *Space and Place: The Perspective of Experience*, University of Minnesota Press, Minneapolis, 1977.

Turnell, Sean, 'F.L. McDougall: Éminence Grise of Australian Economic Policy', *Australian Economic History Review*, vol. 40, no. 1, March 2000, pp. 51–70.

Turner, Henry Gyles, *The First Decade of the Australian Commonwealth 1901–1910*, Mason, Firth & McCutcheon, Melbourne, 1911 (facsimile edition, Heritage Publications, Melbourne, 1975).

Twomey, Ann, *The Chameleon Crown: The Queen and Her Australian Governors*, Federation Press, Sydney, 2006.

van Wyck, A.J., 'The High Commissioner in Great Britain', in Tom Wheeler (ed.), *History of the South African Department of Foreign Affairs 1927–1993*, South African Institute of International Affairs, Johannesburg, 2005.

Walters, F.P., *A History of the League of Nations*, Oxford University Press, London, 1952.

Ward, Stuart, *Australia and the British Embrace: The Demise of the Imperial Ideal*, Melbourne University Press, 2001.

Waters, Christopher, *The Empire Fractures: Anglo-Australian Conflict in the 1940s*, Australian Scholarly Publishing, Melbourne, 1995.

Way, Wendy, 'F.L. McDougall and Commodity Diplomacy', in Carl Bridge and Bernard Attard (eds), *Between Empire and Nation: Australia's External Relations from Federation to the Second World War*, Australian Scholarly Publishing, Melbourne, 2000.

Wheare, K.C., *The Statute of Westminster and Dominion Status*, Clarendon Press, Oxford, 1938.

White, Richard, 'Bluebells and Fogtown: Australians' First Impressions of England, 1860–1940', *Australian Cultural History*, no. 5, 1986, pp. 44–59.

Wigley, Philip, *Canada and the Transition to Commonwealth: British–Canadian Relations, 1917–26*, Cambridge University Press, Cambridge, 1977.

Williams, Susan, *The People's King: The True Story of the Abdication*, Penguin Books, London, 2003.

Woollacott, Angela, *To Try Her Fortune in London: Australian Women, Colonialism, and Modernity*, Oxford University Press, New York, 2001.

Wren, Eric, *Randwick to Hargicourt: History of the 3rd Battalion, A.I.F.*, Ronald G. McDonald, Sydney, 1935.

Theses

Atkins, Barbara, 'The Problem of the Representation of Australia in England: The Origins and Development of the Australian Agencies-General During the Nineteenth Century', MA thesis, University of Melbourne, 1959.

Attard, Bernard, 'The Australian High Commissioner's Office: Politics and Anglo-Australian Relations, 1901–39', DPhil thesis, University of Oxford, 1991.

Melleuish, Joy, 'Australia and British Policy: Colonial Autonomy and the Imperial Idea, 1885–1902', PhD thesis, University of Sydney, 1965.

Murdoch, J.R.M., 'Joseph Cook: A Political Biography', PhD thesis, University of New South Wales, 1969.

Pryke, Olwen, 'Australia House: Representing Australia in London, 1901–1939', PhD thesis, University of Sydney, 2006.

Thompson, John Robert, 'The Australian High Commission in London: Its Origin and Early History, 1901–1916', MA thesis, Australian National University, 1972.

Way, Wendy, 'The Ideas of F.L. McDougall: A Biographical Approach', PhD thesis, Australian National University, 2008.

Index

Page locators printed in italics refer to photographs and their captions.